Y0-ALK-758

Louis Pasteur in his laboratory
By permission, from the painting by Albert Edelfelt

THE HARVARD CLASSICS
EDITED BY CHARLES W ELIOT LL D

SCIENTIFIC PAPERS

PHYSIOLOGY · MEDICINE · SURGERY
GEOLOGY

WITH INTRODUCTIONS, NOTES
AND ILLUSTRATIONS

"DR ELIOT'S FIVE-FOOT SHELF OF BOOKS"

P F COLLIER & SON
NEW YORK

Copyright 1897
BY G. P. PUTNAM'S SONS
Entered at Stationers' Hall, London

Copyright 1861, 1862, 1883, 1889, 1890, 1891
BY OLIVER WENDELL HOLMES

Copyright 1892
BY HOUGHTON, MIFFLIN & COMPANY
All Rights Reserved

Copyright 1910
BY P. F. COLLIER & SON

CONTENTS

	PAGE
THE OATH OF HIPPOCRATES	3
THE LAW OF HIPPOCRATES	4
JOURNEYS IN DIVERSE PLACES . . . . AMBROISE PARÉ	9
TRANSLATED BY STEPHEN PAGET	
ON THE MOTION OF THE HEART AND BLOOD IN ANIMALS .	65
WILLIAM HARVEY . . . TRANSLATED BY ROBERT WILLIS	
THE THREE ORIGINAL PUBLICATIONS ON VACCINATION AGAINST SMALLPOX . . . . . . EDWARD JENNER	153
THE CONTAGIOUSNESS OF PUERPERAL FEVER	235
O. W. HOLMES	
ON THE ANTISEPTIC PRINCIPLE OF THE PRACTICE OF SURGERY	271
LORD LISTER	
THE PHYSIOLOGICAL THEORY OF FERMENTATION	289
LOUIS PASTEUR	
TRANSLATED BY F. FAULKNER AND D. C. ROBB (Revised)	
THE GERM THEORY AND ITS APPLICATIONS TO MEDICINE AND SURGERY (Revised) . . . . . . LOUIS PASTEUR	382
TRANSLATED BY H. C. ERNST	
ON THE EXTENSION OF THE GERM THEORY TO THE ETIOLOGY OF CERTAIN COMMON DISEASES (Revised) LOUIS PASTEUR	391
TRANSLATED BY H. C. ERNST	
PREJUDICES WHICH HAVE RETARDED THE PROGRESS OF GEOLOGY . . . . SIR CHARLES LYELL	405
UNIFORMITY IN THE SERIES OF PAST CHANGES IN THE ANIMATE AND INANIMATE WORLD SIR CHARLES LYELL	419

INTRODUCTORY NOTE

HIPPOCRATES, *the celebrated Greek physician, was a contemporary of the historian Herodotus. He was born in the island of Cos between 470 and 460 B.C., and belonged to the family that claimed descent from the mythical Æsculapius, son of Apollo. There was already a long medical tradition in Greece before his day, and this he is supposed to have inherited chiefly through his predecessor Herodicus; and he enlarged his education by extensive travel. He is said, though the evidence is unsatisfactory, to have taken part in the efforts to check the great plague which devastated Athens at the beginning of the Peloponnesian war. He died at Larissa between 380 and 360 B.C.*

The works attributed to Hippocrates are the earliest extant Greek medical writings, but very many of them are certainly not his. Some five or six, however, are generally granted to be genuine, and among these is the famous "Oath." This interesting document shows that in his time physicians were already organized into a corporation or guild, with regulations for the training of disciples, and with an esprit de corps and a professional ideal which, with slight exceptions, can hardly yet be regarded as out of date.

One saying occurring in the words of Hippocrates has achieved universal currency, though few who quote it to-day are aware that it originally referred to the art of the physician. It is the first of his "Aphorisms": "Life is short, and the Art long; the occasion fleeting; experience fallacious, and judgment difficult. The physician must not only be prepared to do what is right himself, but also to make the patient, the attendants, and externals cooperate."

THE OATH OF HIPPOCRATES

I SWEAR by Apollo the physician and Æsculapius, and Health, and All-heal, and all the gods and goddesses, that, according to my ability and judgment, I will keep this Oath and this stipulation—to reckon him who taught me this Art equally dear to me as my parents, to share my substance with him, and relieve his necessities if required; to look upon his offspring in the same footing as my own brothers, and to teach them this art, if they shall wish to learn it, without fee or stipulation; and that by precept, lecture, and every other mode of instruction, I will impart a knowledge of the Art to my own sons, and those of my teachers, and to disciples bound by a stipulation and oath according to the law of medicine, but to none others. I will follow that system of regimen which, according to my ability and judgment, I consider for the benefit of my patients, and abstain from whatever is deleterious and mischievous. I will give no deadly medicine to any one if asked, nor suggest any such counsel; and in like manner I will not give to a woman a pessary to produce abortion. With purity and with holiness I will pass my life and practice my Art. I will not cut persons labouring under the stone, but will leave this to be done by men who are practitioners of this work. Into whatever houses I enter, I will go into them for the benefit of the sick, and will abstain from every voluntary act of mischief and corruption; and, further, from the seduction of females or males, of freemen and slaves. Whatever, in connection with my professional practice, or not in connection with it, I see or hear, in the life of men, which ought not to be spoken of abroad, I will not divulge, as reckoning that all such should be kept secret. While I continue to keep this Oath unviolated, may it be granted to me to enjoy life and the practice of the art, respected by all men, in all times. But should I trespass and violate this Oath, may the reverse be my lot.

THE LAW OF HIPPOCRATES

MEDICINE is of all the arts the most noble; but, owing to the ignorance of those who practice it, and of those who, inconsiderately, form a judgment of them, it is at present far behind all the other arts. Their mistake appears to me to arise principally from this, that in the cities there is no punishment connected with the practice of medicine (and with it alone) except disgrace, and that does not hurt those who are familiar with it. Such persons are like the figures which are introduced in tragedies, for as they have the shape, and dress, and personal appearance of an actor, but are not actors, so also physicians are many in title but very few in reality.

2. Whoever is to acquire a competent knowledge of medicine, ought to be possessed of the following advantages: a natural disposition; instruction; a favorable position for the study; early tuition; love of labour; leisure. First of all, a natural talent is required; for, when Nature leads the way to what is most excellent, instruction in the art takes place, which the student must try to appropriate to himself by reflection, becoming an early pupil in a place well adapted for instruction. He must also bring to the task a love of labour and perseverance, so that the instruction taking root may bring forth proper and abundant fruits.

3. Instruction in medicine is like the culture of the productions of the earth. For our natural disposition, is, as it were, the soil; the tenets of our teacher are, as it were, the seed; instruction in youth is like the planting of the seed in the ground at the proper season; the place where the instruction is communicated is like the food imparted to vegetables by the atmosphere; diligent study is like the cultivation of the fields; and it is time which imparts strength to all things and brings them to maturity.

4. Having brought all these requisites to the study of medicine, and having acquired a true knowledge of it, we

shall thus, in travelling through the cities, be esteemed physicians not only in name but in reality. But inexperience is a bad treasure, and a bad fund to those who possess it, whether in opinion or reality, being devoid of self-reliance and contentedness, and the nurse both of timidity and audacity. For timidity betrays a want of powers, and audacity a lack of skill. They are, indeed, two things, knowledge and opinion, of which the one makes its possessor really to know, the other to be ignorant.

5. Those things which are sacred, are to be imparted only to sacred persons; and it is not lawful to impart them to the profane until they have been initiated in the mysteries of the science.

JOURNEYS IN DIVERSE PLACES

BY
AMBROISE PARE

TRANSLATED BY
STEPHEN PAGET

INTRODUCTORY NOTE

AMBROISE PARE *was born in the village of Bourg-Hersent, near Laval, in Maine, France, about 1510. He was trained as a barber-surgeon at a time when a barber-surgeon was inferior to a surgeon, and the professions of surgeon and physician were kept apart by the law of the Church that forbade a physician to shed blood. Under whom he served his apprenticeship is unknown, but by 1533 he was in Paris, where he received an appointment as house surgeon at the Hôtel Dieu. After three or four years of valuable experience in this hospital, he set up in private practise in Paris, but for the next thirty years he was there only in the intervals of peace; the rest of the time he followed the army. He became a master barber-surgeon in 1541.*

In Paré's time the armies of Europe were not regularly equipped with a medical service. The great nobles were accompanied by their private physicians; the common soldiers doctored themselves, or used the services of barber-surgeons and quacks who accompanied the army as adventurers. "When Paré joined the army," says Paget, "he went simply as a follower of Colonel Montejan, having neither rank, recognition, nor regular payment. His fees make up in romance for their irregularity: a cask of wine, fifty double ducats and a horse, a diamond, a collection of crowns and half-crowns from the ranks, other 'honorable presents and of great value'; from the King himself, three hundred crowns, and a promise he would never let him be in want; another diamond, this time from the finger of a duchess: and a soldier once offered a bag of gold to him."

When Paré was a man of seventy, the Dean of the Faculty of Medicine in Paris made an attack on him on account of his use of the ligature instead of cauterizing after amputation. In answer, Paré appealed to his successful experience, and narrated the "Journeys in Diverse Places" here printed. This entertaining volume gives a vivid picture, not merely of the condition of surgery in the sixteenth century, but of the military life of the time; and reveals incidentally a personality of remarkable vigor and charm. Paré's own achievements are recorded with modest satisfaction: "I dressed him, and God healed him," is the refrain. Paré died in Paris in December, 1590.

JOURNEYS IN DIVERSE PLACES[1]

1537-1569

THE JOURNEY TO TURIN. 1537

I WILL here shew my readers the towns and places where I found a way to learn the art of surgery: for the better instruction of the young surgeon.

And first, in the year 1536, the great King Francis sent a large army to Turin, to recover the towns and castles that had been taken by the Marquis du Guast, Lieutenant-General of the Emperor. M. the Constable, then Grand Master, was Lieutenant-General of the army, and M. de Montejan was Colonel-General of the infantry, whose surgeon I was at this time. A great part of the army being come to the Pass of Suze, we found the enemy occupying it; and they had made forts and trenches, so that we had to fight to dislodge them and drive them out. And there were many killed and wounded on both sides,—but the enemy were forced to give way and retreat into the castle, which was captured, part of it, by Captain Le Rat, who was posted on a little hill with some of his soldiers, whence they fired straight on the enemy. He received an arquebus-shot in his right ankle, and fell to the ground at once, and then said, "Now they have got the Rat." I dressed him, and God healed him.

We entered pell-mell into the city, and passed over the dead bodies, and some not yet dead, hearing them cry under our horses' feet; and they made my heart ache to hear them. And truly I repented I had left Paris to see such a pitiful spectacle. Being come into the city, I entered into a stable, thinking to lodge my own and my man's horse, and found

---

[1] The present translation is taken from Mr. Stephen Paget's "Ambroise Paré and His Times" by arrangement with Messrs. G. P. Putnam's Sons.

four dead soldiers, and three propped against the wall, their features all changed, and they neither saw, heard, nor spake, and their clothes were still smouldering where the gunpowder had burned them. As I was looking at them with pity, there came an old soldier who asked me if there were any way to cure them. I said no. And then he went up to them and cut their throats, gently, and without ill will toward them. Seeing this great cruelty, I told him he was a villain: he answered he prayed God, when he should be in such a plight, he might find someone to do the same for him, that he should not linger in misery.

To come back to my story, the enemy were called on to surrender, which they did, and left the city with only their lives saved, and the white stick in their hands; and most of them went off to the Château de Villane, where about two hundred Spaniards were stationed. M. the Constable would not leave these behind him, wishing to clear the road for our own men. The castle is seated on a small hill; which gave great confidence to those within, that we could not bring our artillery to bear upon them. They were summoned to surrender, or they would be cut in pieces: they answered that they would not, saying they were as good and faithful servants of the Emperor, as M. the Constable could be of the King his master. Thereupon our men by night hoisted up two great cannons, with the help of the Swiss soldiers and the lansquenets; but as ill luck would have it, when the cannons were in position, a gunner stupidly set fire to a bag full of gunpowder, whereby he was burned, with ten or twelve soldiers; and the flame of the powder discovered our artillery, so that all night long those within the castle fired their arquebuses at the place where they had caught sight of the cannons, and many of our men were killed and wounded. Next day, early in the morning, the attack was begun, and we soon made a breach in their wall. Then they demanded a parley: but it was too late, for meanwhile our French infantry, seeing them taken by surprise, mounted the breach, and cut them all in pieces, save one very fair young girl of Piedmont, whom a great seigneur would have. . . . The captain and the ensign were taken alive, but soon afterward hanged and strangled on the battlements of the gate of the city, to give example and fear to the Emperor's soldiers, not to be so rash and mad as to wish to hold such places against so great an army.

The soldiers within the castle, seeing our men come on them with great fury, did all they could to defend themselves, and killed and wounded many of our soldiers with pikes, arquebuses, and stones, whereby the surgeons had all their work cut out for them. Now I was at this time a fresh-water soldier; I had not yet seen wounds made by gunshot at the first dressing. It is true I had read in John de Vigo, first book, *Of Wounds in General,* eighth chapter, that wounds made by firearms partake of venenosity, by reason of the powder; and for their cure he bids you cauterise them with oil of elders scalding hot, mixed with a little treacle. And to make no mistake, before I would use the said oil, knowing this was to bring great pain to the patient, I asked first before I applied it, what the other surgeons did for the first dressing; which was to put the said oil, boiling well, into the wounds, with tents and setons; wherefore I took courage to do as they did. At last my oil ran short, and I was forced instead thereof to apply a digestive made of the yolks of eggs, oil of roses, and turpentine. In the night I could not sleep in quiet, fearing some default in not cauterising, that I should find the wounded to whom I had not used the said oil dead from the poison of their wounds; which made me rise very early to visit them, where beyond my expectation I found that those to whom I had applied my digestive medicament had but little pain, and their wounds without inflammation or swelling, having rested fairly well that night; the others, to whom the boiling oil was used, I found feverish, with great pain and swelling about the edges of their wounds. Then I resolved never more to burn thus cruelly poor men with gunshot wounds.

While I was at Turin, I found a surgeon famed above all others for his treatment of gunshot wounds; into whose favour I found means to insinuate myself, to have the recipe of his balm, as he called it, wherewith he dressed gunshot wounds. And he made me pay my court to him for two years, before I could possibly draw the recipe from him.

In the end, thanks to my gifts and presents, he gave it to me; which was to boil, in oil of lilies, young whelps just born, and earth-worms prepared with Venetian turpentine. Then I was joyful, and my heart made glad, that I had understood his remedy, which was like that which I had obtained by chance.

See how I learned to treat gunshot wounds; not by books.

My Lord Marshal Montejan remained Lieutenant-General for the King in Piedmont, having ten or twelve thousand men in garrison in the different cities and castles, who were often fighting among themselves with swords and other weapons, even with arquebuses. And if there were four wounded, I always had three of them; and if there were question of cutting off an arm or a leg, or of trepanning, or of reducing a fracture or a dislocation, I accomplished it all. The Lord Marshal sent me now here now there to dress the soldiers committed to me who were wounded in other cities beside Turin, so that I was always in the country, one way or the other.

M. the Marshal sent to Milan, to a physician of no less reputation than the late M. le Grand for his success in practice, to treat him for an hepatic flux, whereof in the end he died. This physician was some while at Turin to treat him, and was often called to visit the wounded, where always he found me; and I was used to consult with him, and with some other surgeons; and when we had resolved to do any serious work of surgery, it was Ambroise Paré that put his hand thereto, which I would do promptly and skilfully, and with great assurance, insomuch that the physician wondered at me, to be so ready in the operations of surgery, and I so young. One day, discoursing with the Lord Marshal, he said to him:

" Signor, tu hai un Chirurgico giovane di anni, ma egli è vecchio di sapere é di esperientia: Guardato bene, perche egli ti fara servicio et honore." That is to say, " Thou hast a surgeon young in age, but he is old in knowledge and experience: take good care of him, for he will do thee service and honour." But the good man did not know I had lived three years at the Hôtel Dieu in Paris, with the patients there.

In the end, M. the Marshal died of his hepatic flux. He being dead, the King sent M. the Marshal d'Annebaut to be in his place: who did me the honour to ask me to live with him, and he would treat me as well or better than M. the Marshal de Montejan. Which I would not do, for grief at the loss of my master, who loved me dearly; so I returned to Paris.

The Journey to Marolle and Low Brittany. 1543

I went to the Camp of Marolle, with the late M. de Rohan, as surgeon of his company; where was the King himself. M. d'Estampes, Governor of Brittany, had told the King how the English had hoist sail to land in Low Brittany; and had prayed him to send, to help him, MM. de Rohan and de Laval, because they were the seigneurs of that country, and by their help the country people would beat back the enemy, and keep them from landing. Having heard this, the King sent these seigneurs to go in haste to the help of their country; and to each was given as much power as to the Governor, so that they were all three the King's Lieutenants. They willingly took this charge upon them, and went off posting with good speed, and took me with them as far as Landreneau. There we found every one in arms, the tocsin sounding on every side, for a good five or six leagues round the harbours, Brest, Couquet, Crozon, le Fou, Doulac, Laudanec; each well furnished with artillery, as cannons, demi-cannons, culverins, muskets, falcons, arquebuses; in brief, all who came together were well equipped with all sorts and kinds of artillery, and with many soldiers, both Breton and French, to hinder the English from landing as they had resolved at their parting from England.

The enemy's army came right under our cannons: and when we perceived them desiring to land, we saluted them with cannon-shot, and unmasked our forces and our artillery. They fled to sea again. I was right glad to see their ships set sail, which were in good number and good order, and seemed to be a forest moving upon the sea. I saw a thing also whereat I marvelled much, which was, that the balls of the great cannons made long rebounds, and grazed over the water as they do over the earth. Now to make the matter short, our English did us no harm, and returned safe and sound into England. And they leaving us in peace, we stayed in that country in garrison until we were assured that their army was dispersed.

Now our soldiers used often to exercise themselves with running at the ring, or with fencing, so that there was always some one in trouble, and I had always something to employ me. M. d'Estampes, to make pastime and pleasure for the Seigneurs de Rohan and de Laval, and other gentlemen, got a number of village girls to come to the sports, to sing songs in the tongue of Low Brittany: wherein their harmony was like the croaking of frogs when they are in love. Moreover, he made them dance the Brittany *triori*, without moving feet or hips: he made the gentlemen see and hear many good things.

At other times they made the wrestlers of the towns and villages come, where there was a prize for the best: and the sport was not ended but that one or other had a leg or arm broken, or the shoulder or hip dislocated.

There was a little man of Low Brittany, of a square body and well set, who long held the credit of the field, and by his skill and strength threw five or six to the ground. There came against him a big man, one Dativo, a pedagogue, who was said to be one of the best wrestlers in all Brittany: he entered into the lists, having thrown off his long jacket, in hose and doublet: when he was near the little man, it looked as though the little man had been tied to his girdle. Nevertheless, when they gripped each other round the neck, they were a long time without doing anything, and we thought they would remain equal in force and skill: but the little man suddenly leaped beneath this big Dativo, and took him on his shoulder, and threw him to earth on his back all spread out like a frog; and all the company laughed at the skill and strength of the little fellow. The great Dativo was furious to have been thus thrown to earth by so small a man: he rose again in a rage, and would have his revenge. They took hold again round the neck, and were again a good while at their hold without falling to the ground: but at last the big man let himself fall upon the little, and in falling put his elbow upon the pit of his stomach, and burst his heart, and killed him stark dead. And knowing he had given him his death's blow, took again his long cassock, and went away with his tail between his legs, and eclipsed himself. Seeing the little man came not again to himself, either for wine, vinegar, or any other thing presented to him, I drew near to him and felt his pulse, which did not beat at all: then I said he was dead. Then the Bretons, who were assisting at the wrestling, said aloud in their jargon, " Andraze meuraquet enes rac un bloa so abeuduex henelep e barz an gouremon enel ma hoa engoustun." That is to say, " That is not in the sport." And someone said that this great Dativo was accustomed to do so, and but a year past he had done the same at a wrestling. I must needs open the body to know the cause of this sudden death. I found much blood in the thorax . . . I tried to find some internal opening whence it might have come, which I could not, for all the diligence that I could use. . . . The poor little wrestler was buried. I took leave of MM. de Rohan, de Laval, and d'Estampes. M. de Rohan made me a present of fifty double ducats and a horse, M. de Laval gave me a nag for my man, and M. d'Estampes gave me a diamond worth thirty crowns; and I returned to my house in Paris.

The Journey to Perpignan. 1543

Some while after, M. de Rohan took me with him posting to the camp at Perpignan. While we were there, the enemy sallied out, and surrounded three pieces of our artillery before they were beaten back to the gates of the city. Which was not done without many killed and wounded, among the others M. de Brissac, who was then grand master of the artillery, with an arquebus-shot in the shoulder. When he retired to his tent, all the wounded followed him, hoping to be dressed by the surgeons who were to dress him. Being come to his tent and laid on his bed, the bullet was searched for by three or four of the best surgeons in the army, who could not find it, but said it had entered into his body.

At last he called for me, to see if I could be more skilful

than they, because he had known me in Piedmont. Then I made him rise from his bed, and told him to put himself in the same posture that he had when he was wounded, which he did, taking a javelin in his hand just as he had held his pike to fight. I put my hand around the wound, and found the bullet. . . . Having found it, I showed them the place where it was, and it was taken out by M. Nicole Lavernot, surgeon of M. the Dauphin, who was the King's Lieutenant in that army; all the same, the honour of finding it belonged to me.

I saw one very strange thing, which was this: a soldier in my presence gave one of his fellows a blow on the head with a halbard, penetrating to the left ventricle of the brain; yet the man did not fall to the ground. He that struck him said he heard that he had cheated at dice, and he had drawn a large sum of money from him, and was accustomed to cheat. They called me to dress him; which I did, as it were for the last time, knowing that he would die soon. When I had dressed him, he returned all alone to his quarters, which were at the least two hundred paces away. I bade one of his companions send for a priest to dispose the affairs of his soul; he got one for him, who stayed with him to his last breath. The next day, the patient sent for me by his girl, dressed in boy's apparel, to come and dress him; which I would not, fearing he would die under my hands; and to be rid of the matter I told her the dressing must not be removed before the third day. But in truth he was sure to die, though he were never touched again. The third day, he came staggering to find me in my tent, and the girl with him, and prayed me most affectionately to dress him, and showed me a purse wherein might be an hundred or sixscore pieces of gold, and said he would give me my heart's desire; nevertheless, for all that, I put off the removal of the dressing, fearing lest he should die then and there. Certain gentlemen desired me to go and dress him; which I did at their request; but in dressing him he died under my hands in a convulsion. The priest stayed with him till death, and seized his purse, for fear another man should take it, saying he would say masses for his poor soul. Also he took his clothes, and everything else.

I have told this case for the wonder of it, that the soldier, having received this great blow, did not fall down, and kept his reason to the end.

Not long afterward, the camp was broken up from diverse causes: one, because we were told that four companies of Spaniards were entered into Perpignan: the other, that the plague was spreading through the camp. Moreover, the country folk warned us there would soon be a great overflowing of the sea, which might drown us all. And the presage which they had, was a very great wind from sea, which rose so high that there remained not a single tent but was broken and thrown down, for all the care and diligence we could give; and the kitchens being all uncovered, the wind raised the dust and sand, which salted and powdered our meats in such fashion that we could not eat them; and we had to cook them in pots and other covered vessels. Nor was the camp so quickly moved but that many carts and carters, mules and mule drivers, were drowned in the sea, with great loss of baggage.

When the camp was moved I returned to Paris.

The Journey to Landresy. 1544

The King raised a great army to victual Landresy. Against him the Emperor had no fewer men, but many more, to wit, eighteen thousand Germans, ten thousand Spaniards, six thousand Walloons, ten thousand English, and from thirteen to fourteen thousand horse. I saw the two armies near each other, within cannon-shot; and we thought they could not withdraw without giving battle. There were some foolish gentlemen who must needs approach the enemy's camp; the enemy fired on them with light field pieces; some died then and there, others had their arms or legs carried away. The King having done what he wished, which was to victual Landresy, withdrew his army to Guise, which was the day after All Saints, 1544; and from there I returned to Paris.

The Journey to Boulogne. 1545

A LITTLE while after, we went to Boulogne; where the English, seeing our army, left the forts which they were holding, Moulambert, le petit Paradis, Monplaisir, the fort of Chastillon, le Portet, the fort of Dardelot. One day, as I was going through the camp to dress my wounded men, the enemy who were in the Tour d' Ordre fired a cannon against us, thinking to kill two men-at-arms who had stopped to talk together. It happened that the ball passed quite close to one of them, which threw him to the ground, and it was thought the ball had touched him, which it did not; but only the wind of the ball full against his corselet, with such force that all the outer part of his thigh became livid and black, and he could hardly stand. I dressed him, and made diverse scarifications to let out the bruised blood made by the wind of the ball; and by the rebounds that it made on the ground it killed four soldiers, who remained dead where they fell.

I was not far from this shot, so that I could just feel the moved air, without its doing me any harm save a fright, which made me duck my head low enough; but the ball was already far away. The soldiers laughed at me, to be afraid of a ball which had already passed. *Mon petit maistre,* I think if you had been there, I should not have been afraid all alone, and you would have had your share of it.

Monseigneur the Duc de Guise, François de Lorraine, was wounded before Boulogne with a thrust of a lance, which entered above the right eye, toward the nose, and passed out on the other side between the ear and the back of the neck, with so great violence that the head of the lance, with a piece of the wood, was broken and remained fast; so that it could not be drawn out save with extreme force, with smith's pincers. Yet notwithstanding the great violence of the blow, which was not without fracture of bones, nerves, veins, and arteries, and other parts torn and broken, my lord, by the grace of God, was healed. He was used to go into battle always with his vizard raised: that is why the lance passed right out on the other side.

JOURNEYS IN DIVERSE PLACES

THE JOURNEY TO GERMANY. 1552

I WENT to Germany, in the year 1552, with M. de Rohan, captain of fifty men-at-arms, where I was surgeon of his company, as I have said before. On this expedition, M. the Constable was general of the army; M. de Chastillon, afterward the Admiral, was chief colonel of the infantry, with four regiments of lansquenets under Captains Recrod and Ringrave, two under each; and every regiment was of ten ensigns, and every ensign of five hundred men. And beside these were Captain Chartel, who led the troops that the Protestant princes had sent to the King (this infantry was very fine, and was accompanied by fifteen hundred men-at-arms, with a following of two archers apiece, which would make four thousand five hundred horse); and two thousand light horse, and as many mounted arquebusiers, of whom M. d'Aumalle was general; and a great number of the nobility, who were come there for their pleasure. Moreover, the King was accompanied by two hundred gentlemen of his household, under the command of the Seigneurs de Boisy and de Canappe, and by many other princes. For his following, to escort him, there were the French and Scotch and Swiss guards, amounting to six hundred foot soldiers; and the companies of MM. the Dauphin, de Guise, d'Aumalle, and Marshal Saint André, amounting to four hundred lances; which was a marvellous thing, to see such a multitude; and with this equipage the King entered into Toul and Metz.

I must not omit to say that the companies of MM. de Rohan, the Comte de Sancerre, and de Jarnac, which were each of them of fifty horse, went upon the wings of the camp. And God knows how scarce we were of victuals, and I protest before Him that at three diverse times I thought to die of hunger; and it was not for want of money, for I had enough of it; but we could not get victuals save by force, because the country people collected them all into the towns and castles.

One of the servants of the captain-ensign of the company of M. de Rohan went with others to enter a church where the peasants were retreated, thinking to get victuals by love or by force; but he got the worst of it, as they all did, and came back with seven sword-wounds on the head, the least of which penetrated to the inner table of the skull; and he had four other wounds upon the arms, and one on the right shoulder, which cut more than half of the blade-bone. He was brought back to his master's lodging, who seeing him so mutilated, and not hoping he could be cured, made him a grave, and would have cast him therein, saying that else the peasants would massacre and kill him. I in pity told him the man might still be cured if he were well dressed. Diverse gentlemen of the company prayed he would take him along with the baggage, since I was willing to dress him; to which he agreed, and after I had got the man ready, he was put in a cart, on a bed well covered and well arranged, drawn by a horse. I did him the office of physician, apothecary, surgeon, and cook. I dressed him to the end of his case, and God healed him; insomuch that all the three companies marvelled at this cure. The men-at-arms of the company of M. de Rohan, the first muster that was made, gave me each a crown, and the archers half a crown.

The Journey to Danvilliers. 1552

On his return from the expedition against the German camp, King Henry besieged Danvilliers, and those within would not surrender. They got the worst of it, but our powder failed us; so they had a good shot at our men. There was a culverin-shot passed through the tent of M. de Rohan, which hit a gentleman's leg who was of his household. I had to finish the cutting off of it, which I did without applying the hot irons.

The King sent for powder to Sedan, and when it came we began the attack more vigorously than before, so that a breach was made. MM. de Guise and the Constable, being in the King's chamber, told him, and they agreed that next day they would assault the town, and were confident they would enter into it; and it must be kept secret, for fear the enemy should come to hear of it; and each promised not to speak of it to any man. Now there was a groom of the King's chamber, who being laid under the King's camp-bed to sleep, heard they were resolved to attack the town next day. So he told the secret to a certain captain, saying that they would make the attack next day for certain, and he had heard it from the King, and prayed the said captain to speak of it to no man, which he promised; but his promise did not hold, and forthwith he disclosed it to a captain, and this captain to a captain, and the captains to some of the soldiers, saying always, "Say nothing." And it was just so much hid, that next day early in the morning there was seen the greater part of the soldiers with their boots and breeches cut loose at the knee for the better mounting of the breach. The King was told of this rumour that ran through the camp, that the attack was to be made; whereat he was astonished, seeing there were but three in that advice, who had promised each other to tell it to no man. The King sent for M. de Guise, to know if he had spoken of this attack; he swore and affirmed to him he had not told it to anybody; and M. the Constable said the same, and told the King they must know for certain who had declared this secret counsel, seeing they were but three. Inquiry was made from captain to captain. In the end they found the truth; for one said, "It was such an one told me," and another said the same, till it came to the first of all, who declared he had heard it from the groom of the King's chamber, called Guyard, a native of Blois, son of a barber of the late King Francis. The King sent for him into his tent, in the presence of MM. de Guise and the Constable, to hear from him whence he had his knowledge, and who had told him the attack was to be made; and said if he did not speak the truth he would have him hanged. Then he declared he lay down under the King's bed thinking to sleep, and so having heard the plan he revealed it to a captain who was a friend of his, to the end he might prepare himself with his soldiers to be the first at the attack. Then the King knew the truth, and told him he should never serve him again, and that he deserved to be hanged, and forbade him ever to come again to the Court.

The groom of the chamber went away with this to swallow, and slept that night with a surgeon-in-ordinary of the King, Master Louis of Saint André; and in the night he gave himself six stabs with a knife, and cut his throat. Nor did the surgeon perceive it till the morning, when he found his bed all bloody, and the dead body by him. He marvelled at this sight on his awaking, and feared they would say he was the cause of the murder; but he was soon relieved, seeing the reason, which was despair at the loss of the good friendship of the King.

So Guyard was buried. And those of Danvilliers, when they saw the breach large enough for us to enter, and our soldiers ready to assault them, surrendered themselves to the mercy of the King. Their leaders were taken prisoners, and their soldiers were sent away without arms.

The camp being dispersed, I returned to Paris with my gentleman whose leg I had cut off; I dressed him, and God healed him. I sent him to his house merry with a wooden leg; and he was content, saying he had got off cheap, not to have been miserably burned to stop the blood, as you write in your book, *mon petit maistre*.

The Journey to Chateau le Comte. 1552

Some time after, King Henry raised an army of thirty thousand men, to go and lay waste the country about Hesdin. The King of Navarre, who was then called M. de Vendosme, was chief of the army, and the King's Lieutenant. Being at St. Denis, in France, waiting while the companies passed by, he sent to Paris for me to speak with him. When I came he begged me (and his request was a command) to follow him on this journey; and I, wishing to make my excuses, saying my wife was sick in bed, he made answer there were physicians in Paris to cure her, and he, too, had left his wife, who was of as good a house as mine, and he said he would use me well, and forthwith ordered I should be attached to his household. Seeing this great desire he had to take me with him, I dared not refuse him.

I went after him to Château le Comte, within three or four leagues of Hesdin. The Emperor's soldiers were in garrison there, with a number of peasants from the country road. M. de Vendosme called on them to surrender;

they made answer that he should never take them, unless it were piecemeal; let him do his worst, and they would do their best to defend themselves. They trusted in their moats, which were full of water; but in two hours, with plenty of faggots and casks, we made a way for our infantry to pass over, when they had to advance to the assault; and the place was attacked with five cannons, and a breach was made large enough for our men to enter; where those within received the attack very valiantly, and killed and wounded a great number of our men with arquebuses, pikes, and stones. In the end, when they saw themselves overpowered, they set fire to their powder and ammunition, whereby many of our men were burned, and some of their own. And they were almost all put to the sword; but some of our soldiers had taken twenty or thirty, hoping to have ransom for them: and so soon as this was known, orders were given to proclaim by trumpet through the camp, that all soldiers who had Spaniards for prisoners must kill them, on pain of being themselves hanged and strangled: which was done in cold blood.

Thence we went and burned several villages; and the barns were all full of grain, to my very great regret. We came as far as Tournahan, where there was a large tower, whither the enemy withdrew, but we found the place empty: our men sacked it, and blew up the tower with a mine of gunpowder, which turned it upside down. After that, the camp was dispersed, and I returned to Paris. And the day after Château le Comte was taken, M. de Vendosme sent a gentleman under orders to the King, to report to him all that had happened, and among other things he told the King I had done very good work dressing the wounded, and had showed him eighteen bullets that I had taken out of their bodies, and there were many more that I had not been able to find or take out; and he spoke more good of me than there was by half. Then the King said he would take me into his service, and commnaded M. de Goguier, his first physician, to write me down in the King's service as one of his surgeons-in-ordinary, and I was to meet him at Rheims within ten or twelve days: which I did. And the King did me the honour to command me to live near him, and he would be a good friend to me. Then I thanked him most humbly for the honour he was pleased to do me, in appointing me to serve him.

The Journey to Metz. 1552

The Emperor having besieged Metz with more than an hundred and twenty thousand men, and in the hardest time of winter,—it is still fresh in the minds of all—and there were five or six thousand men in the town, and among them seven princes; MM. le Duc de Guise, the King's Lieutenant, d'Enghien, de Condé, de la Montpensier, de la Roche-sur-Yon, de Nemours, and many other gentlemen, with a number of veteran captains and officers: who often sallied out against the enemy (as I shall tell hereafter), not without heavy loss on both sides. Our wounded died almost all, and it was thought the drugs wherewith they were dressed had been poisoned. Wherefore M. de Guise, and MM. the princes, went so far as to beg the King that if it were possible I should be sent to them with a supply of drugs, and they believed their drugs were poisoned, seeing that few of their wounded escaped. My belief is that there was no poison; but the severe cutlass and arquebus wounds, and the extreme cold, were the cause why so many died. The King wrote to M. the Marshal de Saint André, who was his Lieutenant at Verdun, to find means to get me into Metz, whatever way was possible. MM. the Marshal de Saint André, and the Marshal de Vielleville, won over an Italian captain, who promised to get me into the place, which he did (and for this he had fifteen hundred crowns). The King having heard the promise that the Italian captain had made, sent for me, and commanded me to take of his apothecary, named Daigne, so many and such drugs as I should think necessary for the wounded within the town; which I did, as much as a post-horse could carry. The King gave me messages to M. de Guise, and to the princes and the captains that were in Metz.

When I came to Verdun, some days after, M. the Marshal de Saint André got horses for me and for my man, and for the Italian captain, who spoke excellent German, Spanish, and Walloon, beside his own mother-tongue. When we were within eight or ten leagues of Metz, we began to go by night only; and when we came near the enemy's camp I saw, more than a league and a half off, fires lighted all round the town, as if the whole earth were burning; and I believed we could never pass through these fires without being discovered, and therefore hanged and strangled, or cut in pieces, or made to pay a great ransom. To speak truth, I could well and gladly have wished myself back in Paris, for the great danger that I foresaw. God guided our business so well, that we entered into the town at midnight, thanks to a signal the captain had with another captain of the company of M. de Guise; to whom I went, and found him in bed, and he received me with high favour, being right glad at my coming.

I gave him my message as the King had commanded me, and told him I had a little letter for him, and the next day I would not fail to deliver it. Then he ordered me a good lodging, and that I should be well treated, and said I must not fail next morning to be upon the breach, where I should find all the princes and seigneurs, and many captains. Which I did, and they received me with great joy, and did me the honour to embrace me, and tell me I was welcome; adding they would no more be afraid of dying, if they should happen to be wounded.

M. le Prince de la Roche-sur-Yon was the first who entertained me, and inquired what they were saying at the Court concerning the town of Metz. I told him all that I chose to tell. Forthwith he begged me to go and see one of his gentlemen named M. de Magnane, now Chevalier of the Order of the King, and Lieutenant of His Majesty's Guards, who had his leg broken by a cannon-shot. I found him in bed, his leg bent and crooked, without any dressing on it, because a gentleman promised to cure him, having his name and his girdle, with certain words (and the poor patient was weeping and crying out with pain, not sleeping day or night for four days past). Then I laughed at such cheating and false promises; and I reduced and dressed his leg so skilfully that he was without pain, and slept all the night, and afterward, thanks be to God, he was healed, and is still living now, in the King's service. The Prince de la Roche-sur-Yon sent me a cask of wine, bigger than a pipe of Anjou, to my lodging, and told me when it was drunk, he would send me another; that was how he treated me, most generously.

After this, M. de Guise gave me a list of certain captains and seigneurs, and bade me tell them what the King had charged me to say; which I did, and this was to commend him to them, and give them his thanks for the duty they had done and were doing in holding his town of Metz, and that he would remember it. I was more than eight days acquitting myself of this charge, because they were many. First, to all the princes; then to others, as the Duke Horace, the Count de Martigues, and his brother M. de Baugé, the Seigneurs de Montmorency and d'Anville, now Marshal of France, M. de la Chapelle aux Ursins, Bonnivet, Carouge, now Governor of Rouen, the Vidasme de Chartres, the Count de Lude, M. de Biron, now Marshal of France, M. de Randan, la Rochefoucaut, Bordaille, d' Estrés the younger, M. de Saint Jehan en Dauphiné, and many others whom it would take too long to name; and also to many captains, who had all done their duty well for the defence of their lives and of the town. Afterward I asked M. de Guise what it pleased him I should do with the drugs I had brought with me; he bade me distribute them to the surgeons and apothecaries, and principally to the poor wounded soldiers, who were in great numbers in the Hospital. Which I did, and can truly say I could not so much as go and see all the wounded, who kept sending for me to visit and dress them.

All the seigneurs within the town asked me to give special care, above all the rest, to M. de Pienne, who had been wounded, while on the breach, by a stone shot from a cannon, on the temple, with fracture and depression of the bone. They told me that so soon as he received the blow, he fell to the ground as dead, and cast forth blood by the mouth, nose, and ears, with great vomiting, and was fourteen days without being able to speak or reason; also he had tremors of a spasmodic nature, and all his face was swelled and livid. He was trepanned at the side of the temporal muscle, over the frontal bone. I dressed him, with other surgeons, and God healed him; and to-day he is still living, thank God.

JOURNEYS IN DIVERSE PLACES

The Emperor attacked the town with forty double cannons, and the powder was not spared day or night. So soon as M. de Guise saw the artillery set and pointed to make a breach, he had the nearest houses pulled down and made into ramparts, and the beams and joists were put end to end, and between them faggots, earth, beds, and wool-packs; then they put above them other beams and joists as before. And there was plenty of wood from the houses in the suburbs; which had been razed to the ground, for fear the enemy should get under cover of them, and make use of the wood; it did very well for repairing the breach. Everybody was hard at work carrying earth to repair it, day and night; MM. the princes, the seigneurs, and captains, lieutenants, ensigns, were all carrying the basket, to set an example to the soldiers and citizens to do the like, which they did; even the ladies and girls, and those who had not baskets, made use of cauldrons, panniers, sacks, sheets, and all such things to carry the earth; so that the enemy had no sooner broken down the wall than they found behind it a yet stronger rampart. The wall having fallen, our men cried out at those outside, "Fox, fox, fox," and they vented a thousand insults against one another. M. de Guise forbade any man on pain of death to speak with those outside, for fear there should be some traitor who would betray what was being done within the town. After this order, our men tied live cats to the ends of their pikes, and put them over the wall and cried with the cats, "Miaut, Miaut."

Truly the Imperials were much enraged, having been so long making a breach, at great loss, which was eighty paces wide, that fifty men of their front rank should enter in, only to find a rampart stronger than the wall. They threw themselves upon the poor cats, and shot them with arquebuses as men shoot at the popinjay.

Our men often ran out upon them, by order of M. de Guise; a few days ago, our men had all made haste to enrol themselves in sallying-parties, chiefly the young nobility, led by experienced captains; and indeed it was doing them a great favour to let them issue from the town and run upon the enemy. They went forth always an hundred or six score men, well armed with cutlasses, arquebuses, pistols, pikes, partisans, and halbards; and advanced as far as the trenches, to take the enemy unawares. Then an alarum would be sounded all through the enemy's camp, and their drums would beat *plan, plan, ta ti ta, ta ta ti ta, tou touf touf*. Likewise their trumpets and clarions rang and sounded, *To saddle, to saddle, to saddle, to horse, to horse, to horse, to saddle, to horse, to horse*. And all their soldiers cried, "*Arm, arm, arm! to arms, to arms, to arms! arm, to arms, arm, to arms, arm*":—like the hue-and-cry after wolves; and all diverse tongues, according to their nations; and you saw them come out of their tents and little lodgings, as thick as little ants when you uncover the ant-hills, to bring help to their comrades, who were having their throats cut like sheep. Their cavalry also came from all sides at full gallop, *patati, patata, patati, patata, pa, ta, ta, patata, pata, ta,* eager to be in the thick of the fighting, to give and take their share of the blows. And when our men saw themselves hard pressed, they would turn back into the town, fighting all the way; and those pursuing them were driven back with cannon-shots, and the cannons were loaded with flint-stones and with big pieces of iron, square or three-sided. And our men on the wall fired a volley, and rained bullets on them as thick as hail, to send them back to their beds; whereas many remained dead on the field: and our men also did not all come back with whole skins, and there were always some left behind (as it were a tax levied on us) who were joyful to die on the bed of honour. And if there was a horse wounded, it was skinned and eaten by the soldiers, instead of beef and bacon; and if a man was wounded, I must run and dress him. Some days afterward there were other sallies, which infuriated the enemy, that we would not let him sleep a little in safety.

M. de Guise played a trick upon them: he sent a peasant, who was none of the wisest, with two letters to the King, and gave him ten crowns, and promised the King would give him an hundred if he got the letters to him. In the one letter M. de Guise told the King that the enemy shewed no signs of retreating, and had put forth all their strength and made a great breach, which he hoped to defend, even at the cost of his own life and of all who were in the town; and that the enemy had planted their artillery so well in a certain place (which he named) that it was with great difficulty he could keep them from entering the town, seeing it was the weakest place in the town; but soon he hoped to rebuild it well, so that they should not be able to enter. This letter was sewed in the lining of the man's doublet, and he was told to be very careful not to speak of it to any person. And the other letter was given to him, wherein M. de Guise told the King that he and all those besieged with him hoped to guard the town well; and other matters which I leave untold here. He sent out the man at night, and he was taken by the enemy's guard and brought to the Duke of Alva, that the Duke might hear what was doing in the town; and the peasant was asked if he had any letters. He said "Yes," and gave them the one; and they having seen it asked him if he had not another. He said "No." Then he was searched, and they found on him that which was sewed in his doubtlet; and the poor messenger was hanged and strangled.

The letters were taken to the Emperor, who called his council, where it was resolved, since they had been unable to do anything at the first breach, the artillery should forthwith be set against the place which they thought weakest, where they put forth all their strength to make a fresh breach; and they sapped and mined the wall, and tried hard to make a way into the Hell Tower, but dared not assault it openly.

The Duke of Alva represented to the Emperor that every day their soldiers were dying, to the number of more than two hundred, and there was so little hope of entering the town, seeing the time of year and the great number of our soldiers who were in it. The Emperor asked what men they were who were dying, and whether they were gentlemen and men of mark; answer was made to him "They were all poor soldiers." Then said he, "It was no great loss if they died," comparing them to caterpillars, grasshoppers, and cockchafers, which eat up the buds and other good things of the earth; and if they were men of any worth they would not be in his camp at six livres the month, and therefore it was no great harm if they died. Moreover, he said he would never depart from the town till he had taken it by force or by famine, though he should lose all his army; because of the great number of princes who were shut up in it, with the greater part of the nobility of France, who he hoped would pay his expenses four times over; and he would go yet again to Paris, to see the Parisians, and to make himself King of all the kingdom of France.

M. de Guise, with the princes, captains, and soldiers, and in general all the citizens of the town, having heard the Emperor's resolve to exterminate us all, forbade the soldiers and citizens, and even the princes and seigneurs, to eat fresh fish or venison, or partridges, woodcocks, larks, francolines, plovers, or other game, for fear these had acquired any pestilential air which could bring infection among us. So they had to content themselves with the fare of the army; biscuit, beef, salt cow-beef, bacon, cervelas, and Mayence hams; also fish, as haddock, salmon, shad, tunny, whale, anchovy, sardines, herrings; also peas, beans, rice, garlic, onions, prunes, cheeses, butter, oil, and salt; pepper, ginger, nutmegs and other spices to put in our pies, mostly of horses, which without the spice had a very bad taste. Many citizens, having gardens in the town, had planted them with fine radishes, turnips, carrots, and leeks, which they kept flourishing and very dear, for the extreme necessity of the famine. Now all these stores were distributed by weight, measure, and justice, according to the quality of the persons, because we knew not how long the siege would last. For after we heard the Emperor's words, how he would not depart from before Metz, till he had taken it by force or by famine, the victuals were cut down; and what they used to distribute to three soldiers was given to four; and it was forbidden to them to sell the remains which might be left after their meals; but they might give them to the rabble. And they always rose from table with an appetite, for fear they should be subject to take physick.

And before we surrendered to the mercy of the enemy, we had determined to eat the asses, mules, and horses, dogs, cats, and rats, even our boots and collars, and other skins that we could have softened and stewed. And, in a word, all the besieged were resolved to defend themselves valiantly with all instruments of war; to set the artillery at the entry of the breach, and load with balls, stones, cart-nails, bars and chains of iron; also all sorts and kinds of artificial fires, as barricadoes, grenades, stink-pots, torches, squibs, fire-traps, burning faggots; with boiling water, melted lead, and lime, to put out the enemy's eyes. Also, they were to make holes right through their houses, and put arquebusiers in them, to take the enemy in flank and hasten his going, or else give him stop then and there. Also they were to order the women to pull up the streets, and throw from their windows billets, tables, trestles, benches, and stools, to dash out the enemy's brains. Moreover, a little within the breach, there was a great stronghold full of carts and palisades, tuns and casks; and barricades of earth to serve as gabions, interlaid with falconets, falcons, field-pieces, crooked arquebuses, pistols, arquebuses, and wild-fires, to break their legs and thighs, so that they would be taken from above and on the flank and from behind; and if they had carried this stronghold, there were others where the streets crossed, every hundred paces, which would have been as bad friends to them as the first, or worse, and would have made many widows and orphans. And if fortune had been so hard on us that they had stormed and broken up our strongholds, there would yet have been seven great companies, drawn up in square and in triangle, to fight them all at once, each led by one of the princes, for the better encouragement of our men to fight and die all together, even to the last breath of their souls. And all were resolved to bring their treasures, rings, and jewels, and their best and richest and most beautiful household stuffs, and burn them to ashes in the great square, lest the enemy should take them and make trophies of them. Also there were men charged to set fire to all the stores and burn them, and to stave in all the wine-casks; others to set fire to every single house, to burn the enemy and us together. The citizens thus were all of one mind, rather than see the bloody knife at their throats, and their wives and daughters ravished and taken by the cruel savage Spaniards.

Now we had certain prisoners, who had been made secretly to understand our last determination and desperation; these prisoners M. de Guise sent away on parole, who being come to their camp, lost no time in saying what we had told them; which restrained the great and vehement desire of the enemy, so that they were no longer eager to enter the town to cut our throats and enrich themselves with the spoils. The Emperor, having heard the decision of this great warrior, M. de Guise, put water in his wine, and restrained his fury; saying that he could not enter the town save with vast butchery and carnage, and shedding of much blood, both of those defending and of those attacking, and they would be all dead together, and in the end he would get nothing but ashes; and afterward men might say it was a like destruction to that of the town of Jerusalem, made of old time by Titus and Vespasian.

The Emperor thus having heard our last resolve, and seeing how little he had gained by his attack, sappings, and mines, and the great plague that was through all his camp, and the adverse time of the year, and the want of victuals and of money, and how his soldiers were disbanding themselves and going off in great companies, decided at last to raise the siege and go away, with the cavalry of his vanguard, and the greater part of the artillery and engines of war. The Marquis of Brandebourg was the last to budge from his place; he had with him some troops of Spaniards and Bohemians, and his German regiments, and there he stopped for a day and a half, to the great regret of M. de Guise, who brought four pieces of artillery out of the town, which he fired on him this side and that, to hurry him off: and off he went, sure enough, and all his men with him.

When he was a quarter of a league from Metz, he was seized with a panic lest our cavalry should fall upon his tail; so he set fire to his store of powder, and left behind him some pieces of artillery, and a quantity of baggage, which he could not take along with him, because their vanguard and their great cannons had broken and torn up the roads. Our cavalry were longing with all their hearts to issue from the town and attack him behind; but M. de Guise would

Ambroise Paré
From the original picture, in "L'École de Médecine," at Paris

never let them, saying on the contrary we had better make their way smooth for them, and build them gold and silver bridges to let them go; like the good pastor and shepherd, who will not lose one of his sheep.

That is how our dear and well-beloved Imperials went away from Metz, which was the day after Christmas Day, to the great content of those within the walls, and the praise of the princes, seigneurs, captains, and soldiers, who had endured the travail of this siege for more than two months. Nevertheless, they did not all go: there wanted more than twenty thousand of them, who were dead, from our artillery and the fighting, or from plague, cold, and starvation (and from spite and rage that they could not get into the town to cut our throats and plunder us): and many of their horses also died, the greater part whereof they had eaten instead of beef and bacon. We went where their camp had been, where we found many dead bodies not yet buried, and the earth all worked up, as one sees in the Cemetery of the Holy Innocents during some time of many deaths. In their tents, pavilions, and lodgings were many sick people. Also cannon-shot, weapons, carts, waggons, and other baggage, with a great quantity of soldier's bread, spoiled and rotted by the snows and rains (yet the soldiers had it but by weight and measure). Also they left a good store of wood, all that remained of the houses they had demolished and broken down in the villages for two or three leagues around; also many other pleasure-houses, that had belonged to our citizens, with gardens and fine orchards full of diverse fruit-trees. And without all this, they would have been benumbed and dead of the cold, and forced to raise the siege sooner than they did.

M. de Guise had their dead buried, and their sick people treated. Also the enemy left behind them in the Abbey of Saint Arnoul many of their wounded soldiers, whom they could not possibly take with them. M. de Guise sent them all victuals enough, and ordered me and the other surgeons to go dress and physick them, which we did with good will; and I think they would not have done the like for our men. For the Spaniard is very cruel, treacherous, and inhuman, and so far enemy of all nations: which is proved by Lopez the Spaniard, and Benzo of Milan, and others who have written the history of America and the West Indies: who have had to confess that the cruelty, avarice, blasphemies, and wickedness of the Spaniards have utterly estranged the poor Indians from the religion that these Spaniards professed. And all write that they are of less worth than the idolatrous Indians, for their cruel treatment of these Indians.

And some days later M. de Guise sent a trumpet to Thionville to the enemy, that they could send for their wounded in safety: which they did with carts and waggons, but not enough. M. de Guise gave them carts and carters, to help to take them to Thionville. Our carters, when they returned, told us the roads were all paved with dead bodies, and they never got half the men there, for they died in their carts: and the Spaniards seeing them at the point of death, before they had breathed their last, threw them out of the carts and buried them in the mud and mire, saying they had no orders to bring back dead men. Moreover, our carters said they had found on the roads many carts stuck in the mud, full of baggage, for which the enemy dared not send back, lest we who were within Metz should run out upon them.

I would return to the reason why so many of them died; which was mostly starvation, the plague, and cold. For the snow was more than two feet deep upon the ground, and they were lodged in pits below the ground, covered only with a little thatch. Nevertheless, each soldier had his camp-bed, and a coverlet all strewed with stars, glittering and shining brighter than fine gold, and every day they had white sheets, and lodged at the sign of the Moon, and enjoyed themselves if only they had been able, and paid their host so well over night that in the morning they went off quits, shaking their ears: and they had no need of a comb to get the down and feathers out of their beards and hair, and they always found a white table-cloth, and would have enjoyed good meals but for want of food. Also the greater part of them had neither boots, half-boots, slippers, hose, nor shoes: and most of them would rather have none than any, because they were always in the mire up to mid-leg.

And because they went bare-foot, we called them the Emperor's Apostles.

After the camp was wholly dispersed, I distributed my patients into the hands of the surgeons of the town, to finish dressing them: then I took leave of M. de Guise, and returned to the King, who received me with great favour, and asked me how I had been able to make my way into Metz. I told him fully all that I had done. He gave me two hundred crowns, and an hundred which I had when I set out: and said he would never leave me poor. Then I thanked him very humbly for the good and the honour he was pleased to do me.

The Journey to Hesdin. 1553

The Emperor Charles laid siege to the town of Therouenne; and M. le Duc de Savoie was General of his whole army. It was taken by assault: and there was a great number of our men killed and taken prisoners.

The King, wishing to prevent the enemy from besieging the town and castle of Hesdin also, sent thither MM. le Duc de Bouillon, le Duc Horace, le Marquis de Villars, and a number of captains, and about eighteen hundred soldiers: and during the siege of Therouenne, these Seigneurs fortified the castle of Hesdin, so that it seemed to be impregnable. The King sent me to the Seigneurs, to help them with my art, if they should come to have need of it.

Soon after the capture of Therouenne, we were besieged in Hesdin. There was a clear stream of running water within shot of our cannon, and about it were fourscore or an hundred of the enemy's rabble, drawing water. I was on a rampart watching the enemy pitch their camp; and, seeing the crowd of idlers round the stream, I asked M. du Pont, commissary of the artillery, to send one cannon-shot among this *canaille:* he gave me a flat refusal, saying that all this sort of people was not worth the powder would be wasted on them. Again I begged him to level the cannon, telling him, "The more dead, the fewer enemies;" which he did for my sake: and the shot killed fifteen or sixteen, and wounded many. Our men made sorties against the enemy, wherein many were killed and wounded on both sides, with gunshot or with fighting hand to hand; and our men often sallied out before their trenches were made; so that I had my work cut out for me, and had no rest either day or night for dressing the wounded.

And here I would note that we had put many of them in a great tower, laying them on a little straw: and their pillows were stones, their coverlets were cloaks, those who had any. When the attack was made, so often as the enemy's cannons were fired, our wounded said they felt pain in their wounds, as if you had struck them with a stick: one was crying out on his head, the other on his arm, and so with the other parts of the body: and many had their wounds bleed again, even more profusely than at the time they were wounded, and then I had to run to staunch them. *Mon petit maistre,* if you had been there, you would have been much hindered with your hot irons; you would have wanted a lot of charcoal to heat them red, and sure you would have been killed like a calf for your cruelty. Many died of the diabolical storm of the echo of these engines of artillery, and the vehement agitation and severe shock of the air acting on their wounds; others because they got no rest for the shouting and crying that were made day and night, and for want of good food, and other things needful for their treatment. *Mon petit maistre,* if you had been there, no doubt you could have given them jelly, restoratives, gravies, pressed meats, broth, barley-water, almond-milk, blanc-mange, prunes, plums, and other food proper for the sick; but your diet would have been only on paper, and in fact they had nothing but beef of old shrunk cows, seized round Hesdin for our provision, salted and half-cooked, so that he who would eat it must drag at it with his teeth, as birds of prey tear their food. Nor must I forget the linen for dressing their wounds, which was only washed daily and dried at the fire, till it was as hard as parchment: I leave you to think how their wounds could do well. There were four big fat rascally women who had charge to whiten the linen, and were kept at it with the stick; and yet they had not water enough to do it, much less soap. That is how the poor patients died, for want of food and other necessary things.

One day the enemy feigned a general attack, to draw our soldiers into the breach, that they might see what we were like: every man ran thither. We had made a great store of artificial fires to defend the breach; a priest of M. le Duc de Bouillon took a grenade, thinking to throw it at the enemy, and lighted it before he ought: it burst, and set fire to all our store, which was in a house near the breach. This was a terrible disaster for us, because it burned many poor soldiers; it even caught the house, and we had all been burned, but for help given to put it out; there was only one well in the castle with any water in it, and this was almost dry, and we took beer to put it out instead of water; afterward we were in great want of water, and to drink what was left we must strain it through napkins.

The enemy, seeing the explosion and violence of the fires, which made a wonderful flame and thundering, thought we had lit them on purpose to defend the breach, and that we had many more of them. This made them change their minds, to have us some other way than by attack: they dug mines, and sapped the greater part of our walls, till they came near turning our castle altogether upside down; and when the sappers had finished their work, and their artillery was fired, all the castle shook under our feet like an earthquake, to our great astonishment. Moreover, they had levelled five pieces of artillery, which they had placed on a little hillock, so as to have us from behind when we were gone to defend the breach. M. le Duc Horace had a cannon-shot on the elbow, which carried off his arm one way and his body the other, before he could say a single word; his death was a great disaster to us, for the high rank that he held in the town. Also M. de Martigues had a gun-shot wound which pierced his lungs: I dressed him, as I shall tell hereafter.

Then we asked leave to speak with the enemy; and a trumpet was sent to the Prince of Piedmont, to know what terms he would give us. He answered that all the leaders, such as gentlemen, captains, lieutenants, and ensigns, would be taken prisoners for ransom, and the soldiers would leave the town without their arms; and if we refused this fair and honest offer, we might rest assured they would take us next day, by attack or otherwise.

A council was held, to which I was called, to know if I would sign the surrender of the town; with many captains, gentlemen, and others. I answered it was not possible to hold the town, and I would sign the surrender with my own blood, for the little hope I had we could resist the enemy's forces, and for the great longing I had to be out of this hell and utter torture; for I slept neither night nor day for the great number of the wounded, who were about two hundred. The dead were advanced in putrefaction, piled one upon the other like faggots, and not covered with earth, because we had none. And if I went into a soldier's lodging, there were soldiers waiting for me at the door when I came out, for me to dress others; it was who should have me, and they carried me like the body of a saint, with my feet off the ground, fighting for me. I could not satisfy this great number of wounded: nor had I got what I wanted for their treatment. For it is not enough that the surgeon do his duty toward his patients, but the patient also must do his; and the assistants, and external things, must work together for him: *see Hippocrates, Aphorism the First*.

Having heard that we were to surrender the place, I knew our business was not prospering; and for fear of being known, I gave a velvet coat, a satin doublet, and a cloak of fine cloth trimmed with velvet, to a soldier; who gave me a bad doublet all torn and ragged with wear, and a frayed leather collar, and a bad hat, and a short cloak; I dirtied the neck of my shirt with water mixed with a little soot, I rubbed my hose with a stone at the knees and over the heels, as though they had been long worn, I did the same to my shoes, till one would have taken me for a chimney-sweep rather than a King's surgeon. I went in this gear to M. de Martigues, and prayed him to arrange I should stop with him to dress him; which he granted very willingly, and was as glad I should be near him as I was myself.

Soon afterward, the commissioners who were to select

the prisoners entered the castle, the seventeenth day of July, 1553. They took prisoners MM. le Duc de Bouillon, le Marquis de Villars, de Roze, le Baron de Culan, M. du Pont, commissary of the artillery, and M. de Martigues; and me with him, because he asked them; and all the gentlemen who they knew could pay ransom, and most of the soldiers and the leaders of companies; so many and such prisoners as they wished. And then the Spanish soldiers entered by the breach, unresisted; our men thought they would keep their faith and agreement that all lives should be spared. They entered the town in a fury to kill, plunder, and ravage everything: they took a few men, hoping to have ransom for them. . . . If they saw they could not get it, they cruelly put them to death in cold blood. . . . And they killed them all with daggers, and cut their throats. Such was their great cruelty and treachery; let him trust them who will.

To return to my story: when I was taken from the castle into the town, with M. de Martigues, there was one of M. de Savoie's gentlemen, who asked me if M. de Martigues's wound could be cured. I told him no, that it was incurable: and off he went to tell M. le Duc de Savoie. I bethought myself they would send physicians and surgeons to dress M. de Martigues; and I argued within myself if I ought to play the simpleton, and not let myself be known for a surgeon, lest they should keep me to dress their wounded, and in the end I should be found to be the King's surgeon, and they would make me pay a big ransom. On the other hand, I feared, if I did not show I was a surgeon and had dressed M. de Martigues skilfully, they would cut my throat. Forthwith I made up my mind to show them he would not die for want of having been well dressed and nursed.

Soon after, sure enough, there came many gentlemen, with the Emperor's physician, and his surgeon, and those belonging to M. de Savoie, and six other surgeons of his army, to see M. de Martigues's wound, and to know of me how I had dressed and treated it. The Emperor's physician bade me declare the essential nature of the wound, and what I had done for it. And all his assistants kept their ears wide open, to know if the wound were or were not mortal. I commenced my discourse to them, how M. de Martigues, looking over the wall to mark those who were sapping it, was shot with an arquebus through the body, and I was called of a sudden to dress him. I found blood coming from his mouth and from his wounds. Moreover, he had a great difficulty of breathing in and out, and air came whistling from the wounds, so that it would have put out a candle; and he said he had a very great stabbing pain where the bullet had entered. . . . I withdrew some scales of bone, and put in each wound a tent with a large head, fastened with a thread, lest on inspiration it should be drawn into the cavity of the chest; which has happened with surgeons, to the detriment of the poor wounded; for being fallen in, you cannot get them out; and then they beget corruption, being foreign bodies. The tents were anointed with a preparation of yolk of egg, Venice turpentine, and a little oil of roses. . . . I put over the wounds a great plaster of diachylum, wherewith I had mixed oil of roses, and vinegar, to avoid inflammation. Then I applied great compresses steeped in oxycrate, and bandaged him, not too tight, that he might breathe easily. Next, I drew five basons of blood from his right arm, considering his youth and his sanguine temperament. . . . Fever took him, soon after he was wounded, with feebleness of the heart. . . . His diet was barley-water, prunes with sugar, at other times broth: his drink was a ptisane. He could lie only on his back. . . . What more shall I say? but that my Lord de Martigues never had an hour's rest after he was wounded. . . . These things considered, Gentlemen, no other prognosis is possible, save that he will die in a few days, to my great grief.

Having finished my discourse, I dressed him as I was accustomed. When I displayed his wounds, the physicians and surgeons, and other assistants present, knew the truth of what I had said. The physicians, having felt his pulse and seen that the vital forces were depressed and spent, agreed with me that in a few days he would die. Then they all went to the Duc de Savoie, and told him M. de Martigues would die in a short time. He answered them, "Possibly, if he had been well dressed, he might have escaped death." Then they all with one voice said he had been very well dressed and cared for altogether, and it could not be better, and it was impossible to cure him, and his wound was of necessity mortal. Then M. de Savoie was very angry with them, and cried, and asked them again if for certain they all held his case hopeless: they answered, yes.

Then a Spanish impostor came forward, who promised on his life to cure him; and if he did not, they should cut him in an hundred pieces; but he would have no physicians, nor surgeons, nor apothecaries with him: and M. le Duc de Savoie forthwith bade the physicians and surgeons not go near M. de Martigues; and sent a gentleman to bid me, under pain of death, not so much as to touch him. Which I promised, and was very glad, for now he would not die under my hands; and the impostor was told to dress him, and to have with him no other physicians or surgeons, but only himself. By and bye he came, and said to M. de Martigues, "Señor Cavallero, M. de Savoie has bid me come and dress your wound. I swear to God, before eight days I will set you on horseback, lance in hand, provided none touch you but I alone. You shall eat and drink whatever you like. I will be dieted instead of you; and you may trust me to perform what I promise. I have cured many who had worse wounds than yours." And the Seigneurs answered him, "God give you His grace for it."

He asked for a shirt of M. de Martigues, and tore it in little strips, which he laid cross-wise, muttering and murmuring certain words over the wounds: having done this much for him, he let him eat and drink all he would, saying he himself would be dieted in his stead; which he did, eating but six prunes and six morsels of bread for dinner, and drinking only beer. Nevertheless, two days later, M. de Martigues died: and my friend the Spaniard, seeing him at the point of death, eclipsed himself, and got away without good-bye to any man. And I believe if he had been caught he would have been hanged and strangled, for the false promise he made to M. le Duc de Savoie and many other gentlemen. M. de Martigues died about ten o'clock in the morning; and after dinner M. de Savoie sent the physicians and surgeons, and his apothecary, with a store of drugs to embalm him. They came with many gentlemen and captains of his army.

The Emperor's surgeon came to me, and asked me in a very friendly way to make the embalmment; which I refused, saying that I was not worthy to carry his instrument-box after him. He begged me again to do it to please him, and that he would be very glad of it. . . . Seeing his kindness, and fearing to displease him, I then decided to show them the anatomist that I was, expounding to them many things, which would here be too long to recite. . . . Our discourse finished, I embalmed the body; and it was placed in a coffin. Then the Emperor's surgeon drew me aside, and told me, if I would stop with him, he would treat me well, and give me a new suit of clothes, and set me on horseback. I gave him many thanks, and said I had no wish to serve any country but my own. Then he told me I was a fool, and if he were a prisoner as I was, he would serve a devil to get his freedom. In the end I told him flat I would not stop with him. The Emperor's physician then went back to M. de Savoie, and explained to him the causes of M. de Martigues' death, and that it was impossible for all the men in the world to have cured him; and assured him again I had done all that was to be done, and besought him to take me into his service; saying much more good of me than there was. He having been persuaded to do this, sent to me one of his stewards, M. du Bouchet, to tell me, if I would serve him, he would use me well; I sent back my very humble thanks, and that I had decided not to take service under any foreigner. When he heard my answer he was very angry, and said I ought to be sent to the galleys.

M. de Vaudeville, Governor of Graveline, and colonel of seventeen ensigns of infantry, asked him to send me to him, to dress an old ulcer on his leg, that he had had for six or seven years. M. de Savoie said he was willing, so far as I was concerned; and if I used the cautery to his leg, it would serve him right. M. de Vaudeville answered, if he saw me trying it, he would have my throat cut. Soon after, he sent for me four German halberdiers of his guard; and I was terrified, for I did not know where they were taking me: they spoke no more French than I German. When I was come to his lodging, he bade me welcome, and said, now I belonged to him; and so soon as I had healed him, he would let me go without ransom. I told him I had no means to pay any ransom. He called his physician and his surgeon-in-ordinary, to show me his leg; and when we had examined it, we withdrew into a room, where I began my discourse to them. . . . Then the physician left me with the surgeon, and went back to M. de Vaudeville, and said he was sure I could cure him, and told him all I had decided to do; which pleased him vastly. He sent for me, and asked if I thought I could cure him; I said yes, if he were obedient to what was necessary. He promised to do only what I wished and ordered; and so soon as he was healed, he would let me go home without ransom. Then I asked him to make better terms with me, saying it was too long to wait for my liberty: in fifteen days I hoped his ulcer would be less than half its present size, and give no pain; then his own surgeon and physician could finish the cure. He granted this to me. Then I took a piece of paper to measure the size of the ulcer, and gave it to him, and kept another by me; I asked him to keep his promise, when I had done my work; he swore by the faith of a gentleman he would. Then I set myself to dress him properly, after the manner of Galen. . . . He wished to know if it were true, what I said of Galen, and bade his physician look to it, for he would know it for himself; he had the book put on the table, and found that what I said was true; so the physician was ashamed, and I was glad. Within the fifteen days, it was almost all healed; and I began to feel happy about the compact made between us. He had me to eat and drink at his table, when there were no more great persons than he and I only. He gave me a big red scarf which I must wear; which made me feel something like a dog when they give him a clog, to stop him eating the grapes in the vineyards. His physician and surgeon took me through the camp to visit their wounded; and I took care to observe what our enemy was doing. I found they had no more great cannons, but only twenty-five or thirty field-pieces.

M. de Vaudeville held prisoner M. de Baugé, brother of M. de Martigues who died at Hesdin. M. de Baugé was prisoner at Château de La Motte au Bois, belonging to the Emperor; he had been captured at Theroüenne by two Spanish soldiers; and M. de Vaudeville, when he saw him there, concluded he must be some gentleman of good family: he made him pull off his stockings, and seeing his clean legs and feet, and his fine white stockings, knew he was one to pay a good ransom. He told the soldiers he would give them thirty crowns down for their prisoner: they agreed gladly, for they had no place to keep him, nor food for him, nor did they know his value: so they gave their man into his hands, and he sent him off at once, guarded by four of his own soldiers, to Château de La Motte au Bois, with others of our gentlemen who were prisoners.

M. de Baugé would not tell who he was; and endured much hardship, living on bread and water, with a little straw for his bed. When Hesdin was taken, M. de Vaudeville sent the news of it to him and to the other prisoners, and the list of the killed, and among them M. de Martigues: and when M. de Baugé heard with his own ears his brother was dead, he fell to crying, weeping, and lamentation. His guards asked him why he was so miserable: he told them, for love of M. de Martigues, his brother. When he heard this, the captain of the castle sent straight to tell M. de Vaudeville he had a good prisoner: who was delighted at this, and sent me next day with four soldiers, and his own physician, to the castle, to say that if M. de Baugé would pay him fifteen thousand crowns ransom, he would send him home free: and he asked only the security of two Antwerp merchants that he should name. M. de Vaudeville persuaded me I should commend this offer to his prisoner: that is why he sent me to the castle. He told the captain to treat him well and put him in a room with hangings, and strengthen his guard: and from that time onward they made a great deal of him, at the expense of M. de Vaudeville.

M. de Baugé answered that he could not pay his ransom himself: it depended on M. d' Estampes his uncle, and Mlle. de Bressure his aunt: he had no means to pay such a ransom. I went back with my guards, and gave this answer to M. de Vaudeville; who said, "Possibly he will not get away so cheap": which was true, for they knew who he was. Then the Queen of Hungary and M. le Duc de Savoie sent word to M. de Vaudeville that this mouthful was too big for him, and he must send his prisoner to them (which he did), and he had other prisoners enough without him. The ransom paid was forty thousand crowns, without other expenses.

On my way back to M. de Vaudeville, I passed by Saint Omer, where I saw their great cannons, most of which were fouled and broken. Also I passed by Therouenne, where I saw not one stone left on another, save a vestige of the great church: for the Emperor ordered the country people for five or six leagues round to clear and take away the stones; so that now you may drive a cart over the town: and the same at Hesdin, and no trace of castle and fortress. Such is the evil that wars bring with them.

To return to my story; M. de Vaudeville soon got the better of his ulcer, and was nearly healed: so he let me go, and sent me by a trumpet, with passport, as far as Abbeville. I posted from here, and went to find my master, King Henry, at Aufimon, who received me gladly and with good favour. He sent MM. de Guise, the Constable, and d' Estrés, to hear from me the capture of Hesdin; and I made them a true report, and assured them I had seen the great cannons they had taken to Saint Omer: and the King was glad, for he had feared the enemy would come further into France. He gave me two hundred crowns to take me home: and I was thankful to be free, out of this great torment and thunder of the diabolical artillery, and away from the soldiers, blasphemers and deniers of God. I must add that after Hesdin was taken, the King was told I was not killed but taken prisoner. He made M. Goguier, his chief physician, write to my wife that I was living, and she was not to be unhappy, and he would pay my ransom.

Battle of Saint Quentin. 1557

After the battle of Saint Quentin, the King sent me to La Fère en Tartenois, to M. le Maréchal de Bourdillon, for a passport to M. le Duc de Savoie, that I might go and dress the Constable, who had been badly wounded in the back with a pistol-shot, whereof he was like to die, and remained prisoner in the enemy's hands. But never would M. le Duc de Savoie let me go to him, saying he would not die for want of a surgeon; that he much doubted I would go there only to dress him, and not rather to take some secret information to him; and that he knew I was privy to other things besides surgery, and remembered I had been his prisoner at Hesdin. M. le Maréchal told the King of this refusal: who wrote to M. le Maréchal, that if Mme. the Constable's Lady would send some quick-witted man of her household I would give him a letter, and had also something to say to him by word of mouth, entrusted to me by the King and by M. le Cardinal de Lorraine. Two days later there came one of the Constable's gentlemen of the bedchamber, with his shirts and other linen, to whom M. le Maréchal gave a passport to go to the Constable. I was very glad, and gave him my letter, and instructed him what his master must do now he was prisoner.

I thought, having finished my mission, to return to the King; but M. le Maréchal begged me to stop at La Fère with him, to dress a very great number of wounded who had retreated there after the battle, and he would write to the King to explain why I stopped; which I did. Their wounds were very putrid, and full of worms, with gangrene, and corruption; and I had to make free play with the knife to cut off what was corrupt, which was not done without amputation of arms and legs, and also sundry trepannings. They found no store of drugs at La Fère, because the surgeons of the camp had taken them all away; but I found the waggons of the artillery there, and these had not been touched. I asked M. le Maréchal to let me have some of the drugs which were in them, which he did; and I was given the half only at one time, and five or six days later I had to take the rest; and yet it was not half enough to dress the great number of wounded. And to correct and stop the corruption, and kill the worms in their wounds, I washed them with Ægyptiacum dissolved in wine and *eau-de-vie,* and did all I could for them; but in spite of all my care many of them died.

There were at La Fère some gentlemen charged to find the dead body of M. de Bois-Dauphin the elder, who had been killed in the battle; they asked me to go with them to the camp, to pick him out, if we could, among the dead; but it was not possible to recognize him, the bodies being all far gone in corruption, and their faces changed. We saw more than half a league round us the earth all covered with the dead; and hardly stopped there, because of the stench of the dead men and their horses; and so many blue and green flies rose from them, bred of the moisture of the bodies and the heat of the sun, that when they were up in the air they hid the sun. It was wonderful to hear them buzzing; and where they settled, there they infected the air, and brought the plague with them. *Mon petit maistre,* I wish you had been there with me, to experience the smells, and make report thereof to them that were not there.

I was very weary of the place; I prayed M. le Maréchal to let me leave it, and feared I should be ill there; for the wounded men stank past all bearing, and they died nearly all, in spite of everything we did. He got surgeons to finish the treatment of them, and sent me away with his good favour. He wrote to the King of the diligence I had shown toward the poor wounded. Then I returned to Paris, where I found many more gentlemen, who had been wounded and gone thither after the battle.

The Journey to the Camp at Amiens. 1558

The King sent me to Dourlan, under conduct of Captain Gouast; with fifty men-at-arms, for fear I should be taken by the enemy; and seeing we were always in alarms on the way, I made my man get down, and made him the master; for I got on his horse, which carried my valise, and could go well if we had to make our escape, and I took his cloak and hat and gave him my mount, which was a good little mare; he being in front, you would have taken him for the master and me for the servant. The garrison inside Dourlan, when they saw us, thought we were the enemy, and fired their cannon at us. Captain Gouast, my conductor, made signs to them with his hat that we were not the enemy; at last they ceased firing, and we entered Dourlan, to our great relief.

Five or six days before this, a sortie had been made from Dourlan; wherein many captains and brave soldiers had been killed or wounded: and among the wounded was Captain Saint Aubin, *vaillant comme l' espée,* a great friend of M. de Guise: for whose sake chiefly the King had sent me there. Who, being attacked with a quartan fever, yet left his bed to command the greater part of his company. A Spaniard, seeing him in command, perceived he was a captain, and shot him through the neck with an arquebus. Captain Saint Aubin thought himself killed: and by this fright I protest to God he lost his quartan fever, and was forever free of it. I dressed him, with Antoine Portail, surgeon-in-ordinary of the King; and many other soldiers. Some died, others got off with the loss of an arm or a leg or an eye, and said they had got off cheap, to be alive at all. Then, the enemy having broken up their camp, I returned to Paris.

I say nothing here of *mon petit maistre,* who was more comfortable in his house than I at the wars.

The Journey to Bourges. 1562

The King with his camp was but a short time at Bourges, till those within the walls should surrender; and they came out with their goods saved. I know nothing worth remembering, but that a boy of the King's kitchen, having come near the walls of the town before the agreement had been signed, cried with a loud voice, "Huguenot,

Huguenot, shoot here, shoot here," having his arm thrown up and his hand spread out; a soldier shot his hand right through with a bullet. When he was thus shot, he came to find me to dress him. And the Constable seeing the boy in tears, with his hand all bloody, asked who had wounded him: then a gentleman who had seen him shot said it served him right, beause he kept calling "Huguenot, hit here, aim here." And then the Constable said, this Huguenot was a good shot and a good fellow, for most likely if he had chosen to fire at the boy's head, he would have hit it even more easily than his hand. I dressed the kitchen boy, who was very ill. He recovered, but with no power in his hand: and from that time his comrades called him "Huguenot": he is still living now.

The Journey to Rouen. 1562

Now, as for the capture of Rouen, they killed many of our men both before and at the attack: and the very next day after we had entered the town, I trepanned eight or nine of our men, who had been wounded with stones as they were on the breach. The air was so malignant, that many died, even of quite small wounds, so that some thought the bullets had been poisoned: and those within the town said the like of us; for though they had within the town all that was needful, yet all the same they died like those outside.

The King of Navarre was wounded, some days before the attack, with a bullet in the shoulder. I visited him, and helped to dress him, with one of his own surgeons, Master Gilbert, one of the chief men of Montpellier, and others. They could not find the bullet. I searched for it very accurately, and found reason to believe it had entered at the top of the arm, by the head of the bone, and had passed into the hollow part of the bone, which was why they could not find it; and most of them said it had entered his body and was lost in it. M. le Prince de La Roche-sur-Yon, who dearly loved the King of Navarre, drew me aside and asked if the wound were mortal. I told him yes, because all wounds of great joints, and especially contused wounds, were mortal, according to all those who have written about them.

He asked the others what they thought of it, and chiefly Master Gilbert, who told him he had great hope his Lord the King would recover; which made the Prince very glad.

Four days later, the King, and the Queen-mother, and M. le Cardinal de Bourbon, his brother, and M. le Prince de la Roche-sur-Yon, and M. de Guise, and other great persons, after we had dressed the King of Navarre, wished us to hold a consultation in their presence, all the physicians and surgeons together. Each of them said what he thought, and there was not one but had good hope, they said, that he would recover. I persisted always in the contrary. M. le Prince, who loved me, drew me aside, and said I was alone against the opinion of all the others, and prayed me not to be obstinate against so many good men. I answered, When I shall see good signs of recovery, I will change my mind. Many consultations were held, and I never changed what I said, and the prognosis I had made at the first dressing, and said always the arm would fall into a gangrene: which it did, for all the care they could give to it; and he rendered his spirit to God the eighteenth day after his wound.

M. le Prince, having heard of it, sent to me his surgeon, and his physician, one Lefêvre, now physician-in-ordinary to the King and Queen-mother, to say he wished to have the bullet, and we were to look for it, to see where it was. Then I was very glad, and assured them I should quickly find it; which I did in their presence, with many other gentlemen: it was just in the very middle of the bone. M. le Prince took and showed it to the King and to the Queen, who all said that my prognosis had come true. The body was laid to rest at Château Gaillard: and I returned to Paris, where I found many patients, who had been wounded on the breach at Rouen, and chiefly Italians, who were very eager I should dress them: which I did willingly. Many of them recovered: the rest died. *Mon petit maistre,* I think you were called to dress some, for the great number there was of them.

The Battle of Dreux. 1562

The day after the battle of Dreux, the King bade me go and dress M. le Comte d'Eu, who had been wounded in the right thigh, near the hip-joint, with a pistol-shot: which had smashed and broken the thigh-bone into many pieces: whereon many accidents supervened, and at last death, to my great grief. The day after I came, I would go to the camp where the battle had been, to see the dead bodies. I saw, for a long league round, the earth all covered: they estimated it at twenty-five thousand men or more; and it was all done in less than two hours. I wish, *mon petit maistre,* for the love I bear you, you had been there, to tell it to your scholars and your children.

Now while I was at Dreux, I visited and dressed a great number of gentlemen, and poor soldiers, and among the rest many of the Swiss captains. I dressed fourteen all in one room, all wounded with pistol-shots and other diabolical firearms, and not one of the fourteen died. M. le Comte d'Eu being dead, I made no long stay at Dreux. Surgeons came from Paris, who fulfilled their duty to the wounded, as Pigray, Cointeret, Hubert, and others; and I returned to Paris, where I found many wounded gentlemen who had retreated thither after the battle, to have their wounds dressed; and I was not there without seeing many of them.

The Journey to Havre de Grace. 1563

And I will not omit to tell of the camp at Havre de Grace. When our artillery came before the walls of the town, the English within the walls killed some of our men, and several pioneers who were making gabions. And seeing they were so wounded that there was no hope of curing them, their comrades stripped them, and put them still living inside the gabions, which served to fill them up. When the English saw that they could not withstand our attack, because they were hard hit by sickness, and especially by the plague, they surrendered. The King gave them ships to return to England, very glad to be out of this plague-stricken place. The greater part of them died, and they took the plague to England, and they have not got rid of it since. Captain Sarlabous, master of the camp, was left in garrison, with six ensigns of infantry, who had no fear of the plague; and they were very glad to get into the town, hoping to enjoy themselves there. *Mon petit maistre,* if you had been there, you would have done as they did.

The Journey to Bayonne. 1564

I WENT with the King on that journey to Bayonne, when we were two years and more making the tour of well-nigh all this kingdom. And in many towns and villages I was called in consultation over sundry diseases, with the late M. Chapelain, chief physician to the King, and M. Castellan, chief physician to the Queen-mother; honorable men and very learned in medicine and surgery. During this journey, I always inquired of the surgeons if they had noted anything rare in their practices, so that I might learn something new. While I was at Bayonne, two things happened worthy of remark by young surgeons. The first is, I dressed a Spanish gentleman, who had a great and enormous swelling of the throat. He had lately been touched by the deceased King Charles for the king's evil. I opened his swelling. . . . I left him in the hands of a surgeon of the town, to finish his cure. M. de Fontaine, Knight of the Order of the King, had a severe continued pestilent fever, accompanied with many inflammatory swellings in sundry parts of the body. He had bleeding at the nose for two days, without ceasing, nor could we staunch it: and after this hæmorrhage the fever ceased, with much sweating, and by and bye the swellings suppurated, and he was dressed by me, and healed by the grace of God.

Battle of Saint Denis. 1567

As for the battle of Saint Denis, there were many killed on both sides. Our wounded withdrew to Paris to be dressed, with the prisoners they had taken, and I dressed many of them. The King ordered me, at the request of Mme. the Constable's Lady, to go to her house to dress the

Constable; who had a pistol-shot in the middle of the spine of his back, whereby at once he lost all feeling and movement in his thighs and legs ... because the spinal cord, whence arise the nerves to give feeling and movement to the parts below, was crushed, broken, and torn by the force of the bullet. Also he lost understanding and reason, and in a few days he died. The surgeons of Paris were hard put to it for many days to treat all the wounded. I think, *mon petit maistre,* you saw some of them. I beseech the great God of victories, that we be never more employed in such misfortune and disaster.

Voyage of the Battle of Moncontour. 1569

During the battle of Moncontour, King Charles was at Plessis-les-Tours, where he heard the news of the victory. A great number of gentlemen and soldiers retreated into the town and suburbs of Tours, wounded, to be dressed and treated; and the King and the Queen-mother bade me do my duty by them, with other surgeons who were then on duty, as Pigray, du Bois, Portail, and one Siret, a surgeon of Tours, a man well versed in surgery, who was at this time surgeon to the King's brother. And for the multitude of bad cases we had scarce any rest, nor the physicians either.

M. le Comte de Mansfeld, Governor of the Duchy of Luxembourg, Knight of the Order of the King, was severely wounded in the battle, in the left arm, with a pistol-shot which broke a great part of his elbow; and he withdrew to Borgueil near Tours. Then he sent a gentleman to the King, to beg him to send one of his surgeons, to help him of his wound. So they debated which surgeon they should send. M. le Maréchal de Montmorency told the King and the Queen that they ought to send him their chief surgeon; and urged that M. de Mansfeld had done much toward the victory.

The King said flat, he would not have me go, and wished me to stop with himself. Then the Queen-mother told him I would but go and come back, and he must remember it was a foreign lord, who had come, at the command of the

King of Spain, to help him. Then he let me go, provided I came back very soon. So he sent for me, and the Queen-mother with him, and bade me go and find the Lord de Mansfeld, wherever he should be, to do all I could for him to heal his wound. I went to him, with a letter from Their Majesties. When he saw it, he received me with good-will, and forthwith dismissed three or four surgeons who were dressing him; which was to my very great regret, because his wound seemed to me incurable.

Now many gentlemen had retreated to Borgueil, having been wounded: for they knew that M. de Guise was there, who also had been badly wounded with a pistol-shot through the leg, and they were sure that he would have good surgeons to dress him, and would help them, as he is kindly and very generous, and would relieve their wants. This he did with a will, both for their eating and drinking, and for what else they needed: and for my part, they had the comfort and help of my art: some died, others recovered, according to their wounds. M. le Comte Ringrave died, who was shot in the shoulder, like the King of Navarre before Rouen. M. de Bassompierre, colonel of twelve hundred horse, was wounded by a similar shot, in the same place, as M. de Mansfeld: whom I dressed, and God healed. God blessed my work so well, that in three weeks I sent them back to Paris: where I had still to make incisions in M. de Mansfeld's arm, to remove some pieces of the bones, which were badly splintered, broken, and carious. He was healed by the grace of God, and made me a handsome present, so I was well content with him, and he with me; as he has shown me since. He wrote a letter to M. le Duc d' Ascot, how he was healed of his wound, and also M. de Bassompierre of his, and many others whom I had dressed after the battle of Moncontour; and advised him to ask the King of France to let me visit M. le Marquis d' Auret, his brother: which he did.

THE JOURNEY TO FLANDERS. 1569

M. LE DUC D' ASCOT did not fail to send a gentleman to the King, with a letter humbly asking he would do him

JOURNEYS IN DIVERSE PLACES

so much kindness and honour as to permit and command his chief surgeon to visit M. le Marquis d' Auret, his brother, who had received a gunshot wound near the knee, with fracture of the bone, about seven months ago, and the physicians and surgeons all this time had not been able to heal him. The King sent for me and bade me go and see M. d' Auret, and give him all the help I could, to heal him of his wound. I told him I would employ all the little knowledge it had pleased God to give me.

I went off, escorted by two gentlemen, to the Chateau d' Auret, which is a league and a half from Mons in Hainault, where M. le Marquis was lying. So soon as I had come, I visited him, and told him the King had commanded me to come and see him and dress his wound. He said he was very glad I had come, and was much beholden to the King, who had done him so much honour as to send me to him.

I found him in a high fever, his eyes deep sunken, with a moribund and yellowish face, his tongue dry and parched, and the whole body much wasted and lean, the voice low as of a man very near death: and I found his thigh much inflamed, suppurating, and ulcerated, discharging a greenish and very offensive sanies. I probed it with a silver probe, wherewith I found a large cavity in the middle of the thigh, and others round the knee, sanious and cuniculate: also several scales of bone, some loose, others not. The leg was greatly swelled, and imbued with a pituitous humor . . . and bent and drawn back. There was a large bedsore; he could rest neither day nor night; and had no appetite to eat, but very thirsty. I was told he often fell into a faintness of the heart, and sometimes as in epilepsy: and often he felt sick, with such trembling he could not carry his hands to his mouth. Seeing and considering all these great complications, and the vital powers thus broken down, truly I was very sorry I had come to him, because it seemed to me there was little hope he would escape death. All the same, to give him courage and good hope, I told him I would soon set him on his legs, by the grace of God, and the help of his physicians and surgeons.

Having seen him, I went a walk in a garden, and prayed

God He would show me this grace, that he should recover; and that He would bless our hands and our medicaments, to fight such a complication of diseases. I discussed in my mind the means I must take to do this. They called me to dinner. I came into the kitchen, and there I saw, taken out of a great pot, half a sheep, a quarter of veal, three great pieces of beef, two fowls, and a very big piece of bacon, with abundance of good herbs: then I said to myself that the broth of the pot would be full of juices, and very nourishing.

After dinner, we began our consultation, all the physicians and surgeons together, in the presence of M. le Duc d' Ascot and some gentlemen who were with him. I began to say to the surgeons that I was astonished they had not made incisions in M. le Marquis' thigh, seeing that it was all suppurating, and the thick matter in it very fœtid and offensive, showing it had long been pent up there; and that I had found with the probe caries of the bone, and scales of bone, which were already loose. They answered me: "Never would he consent to it"; indeed, it was near two months since they had been able to get leave to put clean sheets on his bed; and one scarce dared touch the coverlet, so great was his pain. Then I said, "To heal him, we must touch something else than the coverlet of his bed." Each said what he thought of the malady of the patient, and in conclusion they all held it hopeless. I told them there was still some hope, because he was young, and God and Nature sometimes do things which seem to physicians and surgeons impossible.

To restore the warmth and nourishment of the body, general frictions must be made with hot cloths, above, below, to right, to left, and around, to draw the blood and the vital spirits from within outward. . . . For the bedsore, he must be put in a fresh, soft bed, with clean shirt and sheets. . . . Having discoursed of the causes and complications of his malady, I said we must cure them by their contraries; and must first ease the pain, making openings in the thigh to let out the matter. . . . Secondly, having regard to the great swelling and coldness of the limb, we must apply hot bricks round it, and sprinkle them with a decoction of nerval herbs in wine and vinegar, and wrap them in napkins; and to his feet, an earthenware bottle filled with the decoction, corked, and wrapped in cloths. Then the thigh, and the whole of the leg, must be fomented with a decoction made of sage, rosemary, thyme, lavender, flowers of chamomile and melilot, red roses boiled in white wine, with a drying powder made of oak-ashes and a little vinegar and half a handful of salt. . . . Thirdly, we must apply to the bedsore a large plaster made of the desiccative red ointment and of *Unguentum Comitissæ,* equal parts, mixed together, to ease his pain and dry the ulcer; and he must have a little pillow of down, to keep all pressure off it. . . . And for the strengthening of his heart, we must apply over it a refrigerant of oil of water-lilies, ointment of roses, and a little saffron, dissolved in rose-vinegar and treacle, spread on a piece of red cloth. For the syncope, from exhaustion of the natural forces, troubling the brain, he must have good nourishment full of juices, as raw eggs, plums stewed in wine and sugar, broth of the meat of the great pot, whereof I have already spoken; the white meat of fowls, partridges' wings minced small, and other roast meats easy to digest, as veal, kid, pigeons, partridges, thrushes, and the like, with sauce of orange, verjuice, sorrel, sharp pomegranates; or he may have them boiled with good herbs, as lettuce, purslain, chicory, bugloss, marigold, and the like. At night he can take barley-water, with juice of sorrel and of water-lilies, of each two ounces, with four or five grains of opium, and the four cold seeds crushed, of each half an ounce; which is a good nourishing remedy and will make him sleep. His bread to be farmhouse bread, neither too stale nor too fresh. For the great pain in his head, his hair must be cut, and his head rubbed with rose-vinegar just warm, and a double cloth steeped in it and put there; also a forehead-cloth, of oil of roses and water-lilies and poppies, and a little opium and rose-vinegar, with a little camphor, and changed from time to time. Moreover, we must allow him to smell flowers of henbane and water-lilies, bruised with vinegar and rose-water, with a little camphor, all wrapped in a handkerchief, to be held some time to his nose. . . . And we must make artificial rain, pouring water from some high place into a cauldron, that he may hear the sound of it; by which means sleep shall be provoked on him. As for the contraction of his leg, there is hope of righting it when we have let out the pus and other humors pent up in the thigh, and have rubbed the whole knee with ointment of mallows, and oil of lilies, and a little *eau-de-vie,* and wrapped it in black wool with the grease left in it; and if we put under the knee a feather pillow doubled, little by little we shall straighten the leg.

This my discourse was well approved by the physicians and surgeons.

The consultation ended, we went back to the patient, and I made three openings in his thigh. . . . Two or three hours later, I got a bed made near his old one, with fair white sheets on it; then a strong man put him in it, and he was thankful to be taken out of his foul stinking bed. Soon after, he asked to sleep; which he did for near four hours: and everybody in the house began to feel happy, and especially M. le Duc d' Ascot, his brother.

The following days, I made injections, into the depth and cavities of the ulcers, of Ægyptiacum dissolved sometimes in *eau-de-vie,* other times in wine. I applied compresses to the bottom of the sinuous tracks, to cleanse and dry the soft spongy flesh, and hollow leaden tents, that the sanies might always have a way out; and above them a large plaster of Diacalcitheos dissolved in wine. And I bandaged him so skilfully that he had no pain; and when the pain was gone, the fever began at once to abate. Then I gave him wine to drink moderately tempered with water, knowing it would restore and quicken the vital forces. And all that we agreed in consultation was done in due time and order; and so soon as his pains and fever ceased, he began steadily to amend. He dismissed two of his surgeons, and one of his physicians, so that we were but three with him.

Now I stopped there about two months, not without seeing many patients, both rich and poor, who came to me from three or four leagues round. He gave food and drink to the needy, and commended them all to me, asking me to help them for his sake. I protest I refused not one, and did for them all I could, to his great pleasure. Then, when I saw him beginning to be well, I told him we must have viols and violins, and a buffoon to make him laugh: which he did. In one month, we got him into a chair, and he had himself carried about in his garden and at the door of his château, to see everybody passing by.

The villagers of two or three leagues round, now they could have sight of him, came on holidays to sing and dance, men and women, pell-mell for a frolic, rejoiced at his good convalescence, all glad to see him, not without plenty of laughter and plenty to drink. He always gave them a hogshead of beer; and they all drank merrily to his health. And the citizens of Mons in Hainault, and other gentlemen, his neighbours, came to see him for the wonder of it, as a man come out of the grave; and from the time he was well, he was never without company. When one went out, another came in to visit him; his table was always well covered. He was dearly loved both by the nobility and by the common people; as for his generosity, so for his handsome face and his courtesy: with a kind look and a gracious word for everybody, so that all who saw him had perforce to love him.

The chief citizens of Mons came one Saturday, to beg him let me go to Mons, where they wished to entertain me with a banquet, for their love of him. He told them he would urge me to go, which he did; but I said such great honour was not for me, moreover they could not feast me better than he did. Again he urged me, with much affection, to go there, to please him: and I agreed. The next day, they came to fetch me with two carriages: and when we got to Mons, we found the dinner ready, and the chief men of the town, with their ladies, who attended me with great devotion. We sat down to dinner, and they put me at the top of the table, and all drank to me, and to the health of M. le Marquis d'Auret: saying he was happy, and they with him, to have had me to put him on his legs again; and truly the whole company were full of honour and love for him. After dinner, they brought me back to the Château d'Auret, where M. le Marquis was awaiting me; who affectionately welcomed me, and would hear what we had done at our banquet; and I told him all the company had drunk many times to his health.

In six weeks he began to stand a little on crutches, and to put on fat and get a good natural colour. He would go to Beaumont, his brother's place; and was taken there in a carrying-chair, by eight men at a time. And the peasants in the villages through which we passed, knowing it was M. le Marquis, fought who should carry him, and would have us drink with them; but it was only beer. Yet I believe if they had possessed wine, even hippocras, they would have given it to us with a will. And all were right glad to see him, and all prayed God for him.

When we came to Beaumont, everybody came out to meet us and pay their respects to him, and prayed God bless him and keep him in good health. We came to the château, and found there more than fifty gentlemen whom M. le Duc d'Ascot had invited to come and be happy with his brother; and he kept open house three whole days. After dinner, the gentlemen used to tilt at the ring and play with the foils, and were full of joy at the sight of M. d'Auret, for they had heard he would never leave his bed or be healed of his wound. I was always at the upper end of the table, and everybody drank to him and to me, thinking to make me drunk, which they could not; for I drank only as I always do.

A few days later, we went back; and I took my leave of Mdme. la Duchesse d'Ascot, who drew a diamond from her finger, and gave it me in gratitude for my good care of her brother: and the diamond was worth more than fifty crowns. M. d' Auret was ever getting better, and was walking all alone on crutches round his garden. Many times I asked him to let me go back to Paris, telling him his physician and his surgeon could do all that was now wanted for his wound: and to make a beginning to get away from him, I asked him to let me go and see the town of Antwerp. To this he agreed at once, and told his steward to escort me there, with two pages. We passed through Malines and Brussels, where the chief citizens of the town begged us to let them know of it when we returned; for they too wished, like those of Mons, to have a festival for me. I gave them very humble thanks, saying I did not deserve such honour. I was two days and a half seeing the town of Antwerp, where certain merchants, knowing the steward, prayed he would let them have the honour of giving us a dinner or a supper: it was who should have us, and they were all truly glad to hear how well M. d' Auret was doing, and made more of me than I asked.

On my return, I found M. le Marquis enjoying himself: and five or six days later I asked his leave to go, which he gave, said he, with great regret. And he made me a handsome present of great value, and sent me back, with the steward, and two pages, to my house in Paris.

I forgot to say that the Spaniards have since ruined and demolished his Château d' Auret, sacked, pillaged, and burned all the houses and villages belonging to him: because he would not be of their wicked party in their assassinations and ruin of the Netherlands.

I have published this Apologia, that all men may know on what footing I have always gone: and sure there is no man so touchy not to take in good part what I have said. For I have but told the truth; and the purport of my discourse is plain for all men to see, and the facts themselves are my guarantee against all calumnies.

ON THE MOTION OF THE HEART AND BLOOD IN ANIMALS

BY
WILLIAM HARVEY

TRANSLATED BY
ROBERT WILLIS

AND REVISED BY
ALEXANDER BOWIE

INTRODUCTORY NOTE

WILLIAM HARVEY, *whose epoch-making treatise announcing and demonstrating the circulation of the blood is here printed, was born at Folkestone, Kent, England, April 1, 1578. He was educated at the King's School, Canterbury, and at Gonville and Caius College, Cambridge; and studied medicine on the Continent, receiving the degree of M.D. from the University of Padua. He took the same degree later at both the English universities. After his return to England he became Fellow of the College of Physicians, physician to St. Bartholomew's Hospital, and Lumleian lecturer at the College of Physicians. It was in this last capacity that he delivered, in 1616, the lectures in which he first gave public notice of his theories on the circulation of the blood. The notes of these lectures are still preserved in the British Museum.*

In 1618 Harvey was appointed physician extraordinary to James I, and he remained in close professional relations to the royal family until the close of the Civil War, being present at the battle of Edgehill. By mandate of Charles I, he was, for a short time, Warden of Merton College, Oxford (1645-6), and, when he was too infirm to undertake the duties, he was offered the Presidency of the College of Physicians. He died on June 3, 1657.

Harvey's famous "Exercitatio Anatomica de Motu Cordis et Sanguinis in Animalibus" was published in Latin at Frankfort in 1628. The discovery was received with great interest, and in his own country was accepted at once; on the Continent it won favor more slowly. Before his death, however, the soundness of his views was acknowledged by the medical profession throughout Europe, and "it remains to this day the greatest of the discoveries of physiology, and its whole honor belongs to Harvey."

Nach dem nun die von der religion an vil orth.	Legert sich der Prins von Conde bei S Denis.	Mit dem Connestable, der aber gar bald.	Hin vnder gzugkt, vnd todtlich gewundt
Water tod geschlagen, erwurght vnd ermordt	Da seind kummen die Papisten von Paris	Im anfang der slacht vom pferd mit gwalt.	Da von er gstorben nach wenigh stundt

Am X. Nouembr. Im iar M. D. LXVII.

Battle of Saint Denis
1567
From an engraving in the Print Room,
British Museum

DEDICATION

TO HIS VERY DEAR FRIEND,
DOCTOR ARGENT, THE EXCELLENT AND
ACCOMPLISHED PRESIDENT OF THE ROYAL COLLEGE OF PHYSICIANS,
AND TO OTHER LEARNED PHYSICIANS, HIS
MOST ESTEEMED COLLEAGUES.

I HAVE already and repeatedly presented you, my learned friends, with my new views of the motion and function of the heart, in my anatomical lectures; but having now for more than nine years confirmed these views by multiplied demonstrations in your presence, illustrated them by arguments, and freed them from the objections of the most learned and skilful anatomists, I at length yield to the requests, I might say entreaties, of many, and here present them for general consideration in this treatise.

Were not the work indeed presented through you, my learned friends, I should scarce hope that it could come out scatheless and complete; for you have in general been the faithful witnesses of almost all the instances from which I have either collected the truth or confuted error. You have seen my dissections, and at my demonstrations of all that I maintain to be objects of sense, you have been accustomed to stand by and bear me out with your testimony. And as this book alone declares the blood to course and revolve by a new route, very different from the ancient and beaten pathway trodden for so many ages, and illustrated by such a host of learned and distinguished men, I was greatly afraid lest I might be charged with presumption did I lay my work before the public at home, or send it beyond seas for impression, unless I had first proposed the subject to you, had confirmed its conclusions by ocular demonstrations in your presence, had replied to your doubts and objections, and secured the assent and support of our distinguished President. For I was most intimately persuaded, that if I could make good my proposition before you and our College, illustrious by its numerous body of learned individuals, I had less to fear from others. I even ventured to hope that I should have the comfort of finding all that you had granted me in your sheer love of truth, conceded by others who were philosophers like yourselves. True philosophers, who are only eager for truth and knowledge, never regard themselves as already so thoroughly informed, but that they welcome further information from whomsoever and from wheresoever it may come; nor are they so narrow-minded as to imagine any of the arts or sciences transmitted to us by the ancients, in such a state of forwardness or completeness, that nothing is left for the ingenuity and industry of others. On the contrary, very many maintain that all we know is still infinitely less than all that still remains unknown; nor do philosophers pin their faith to others' precepts in such wise that they lose their liberty, and cease to give credence to the conclusions of their proper senses. Neither do they swear such fealty to their mistress Antiquity, that they openly, and in sight of all, deny and desert their friend Truth. But even as they see that the credulous and vain are disposed at the first blush to accept and believe everything that is proposed to them, so do they observe that the dull and unintellectual are indisposed to see what lies before their eyes, and even deny the light of the noonday sun. They teach us in our course of philosophy to sedulously avoid the fables of the poets and the fancies of the vulgar, as the false conclusions of the sceptics. And then the studious and good and true, never suffer their minds to be warped by the passions of hatred and envy, which unfit men duly to weigh the arguments that are advanced in behalf of truth, or to appreciate the proposition that is even fairly demonstrated. Neither do they think it unworthy of them to change their opinion if truth and undoubted demonstration require them to do so. They do not esteem it discreditable to desert error, though sanctioned by the highest antiquity, for they know full well that to err, to be deceived, is human; that many things are discovered by accident and that many may be learned indifferently from any quarter, by an old man from a youth, by a person of understanding from one of inferior capacity.

My dear colleagues, I had no purpose to swell this treatise into a large volume by quoting the names and writings of anatomists, or to make a parade of the strength of my memory, the extent of my reading, and the amount of my pains; because I profess both to learn and to teach anatomy, not from books but from dissections; not from the positions of philosophers but from the fabric of nature; and then because I do not think it right or proper to strive to take from the ancients any honor that is their due, nor yet to dispute with the moderns, and enter into controversy with those who have excelled in anatomy and been my teachers. I would not charge with wilful falsehood any one who was sincerely anxious for truth, nor lay it to any one's door as a crime that he had fallen into error. I avow myself the partisan of truth alone; and I can indeed say that I have used all my endeavours, bestowed all my pains on an attempt to produce something that should be agreeable to the good, profitable to the learned, and useful to letters.

Farewell, most worthy Doctors,
  And think kindly of your Anatomist,
    WILLIAM HARVEY.

INTRODUCTION

As we are about to discuss the motion, action, and use of the heart and arteries, it is imperative on us first to state what has been thought of these things by others in their writings, and what has been held by the vulgar and by tradition, in order that what is true may be confirmed, and what is false set right by dissection, multiplied experience, and accurate observation.

Almost all anatomists, physicians, and philosophers up to the present time have supposed, with Galen, that the object of the pulse was the same as that of respiration, and only differed in one particular, this being conceived to depend on the animal, the respiration on the vital faculty; the two, in all other respects, whether with reference to purpose or to motion, comporting themselves alike. Whence it is affirmed, as by Hieronymus Fabricius of Aquapendente, in his book on "Respiration," which has lately appeared, that as the pulsation of the heart and arteries does not suffice for the ventilation and refrigeration of the blood, therefore were the lungs fashioned to surround the heart. From this it appears that whatever has hitherto been said upon the systole and diastole, or on the motion of the heart and arteries, has been said with especial reference to the lungs.

But as the structure and movements of the heart differ from those of the lungs, and the motions of the arteries from those of the chest, so it seems likely that other ends and offices will thence arise, and that the pulsations and uses of the heart, likewise of the arteries, will differ in many respects from the heavings and uses of the chest and lungs. For did the arterial pulse and the respiration serve the same ends; did the arteries in their diastole take air into their cavities, as commonly stated, and in their systole emit fuliginous vapours by the same pores of the flesh and skin; and further, did they, in the time intermediate between the diastole and the systole, contain air, and at all times either air or spirits, or fuliginous vapours, what should then be said to Galen, who wrote a book on purpose to show that by nature the arteries contained blood, and nothing but blood, and consequently neither spirits nor air, as may readily be gathered from the experiments and reasonings contained in the same book? Now, if the arteries are filled in the diastole with air then taken into them (a larger quantity of air penetrating when the pulse is large and full), it must come to pass that if you plunge into a bath of water or of oil when the pulse is strong and full, it ought forthwith to become either smaller or much slower, since the circumambient bath will render it either difficult or impossible for the air to penetrate. In like manner, as all the arteries, those that are deep-seated as well as those that are superficial, are dilated at the same instant and with the same rapidity, how is it possible that air should penetrate to the deeper parts as freely and quickly through the skin, flesh, and other structures, as through the cuticle alone? And how should the arteries of the fœtus draw air into their cavities through the abdomen of the mother and the body of the womb? And how should seals, whales, dolphins, and other cetaceans, and fishes of every description, living in the depths of the sea, take in and emit air by the diastole and systole of their arteries through the infinite mass of water? For to say that they absorb the air that is present in the water, and emit their fumes into this medium, were to utter something like a figment. And if the arteries in their systole expel fuliginous vapours from their cavities through the pores of the flesh and skin, why not the spirits, which are said to be contained in those vessels, at the same time, since spirits are much more subtile than fuliginous vapours or smoke? And if the arteries take in and cast out air in the systole and diastole, like the lungs in the process of respiration, why do they not do the same thing when a wound is made in one of them, as in the operation of arteriotomy? When the windpipe is divided, it is sufficiently obvious that the air enters and returns through the wound by two opposite movements; but when an artery is divided, it is equally manifest that blood escapes in one continuous stream, and that no air either enters or issues. If the pulsations of the arteries fan and refrigerate the several parts of the body as the lungs do the heart, how comes it, as is commonly said, that the arteries carry the vital blood into the different parts, abundantly charged with vital spirits, which cherish the heat of these parts, sustain them when asleep, and recruit them when exhausted? How should it happen that, if you tie the arteries, immediately the parts not only become torpid, and frigid, and look pale, but at length cease even to be nourished? This, according to Galen, is because they are deprived of the heat which flowed through all parts from the heart, as its source; whence it would appear that the arteries rather carry warmth to the parts than serve for any fanning or refrigeration. Besides, how can their diastole draw spirits from the heart to warm the body and its parts, and means of cooling them from without? Still further, although some affirm that the lungs, arteries, and heart have all the same offices, they yet maintain that the heart is the workshop of the spirits, and that the arteries contain and transmit them; denying, however, in opposition to the opinion of Columbus, that the lungs can either make or contain spirits. They then assert, with Galen, against Erasistratus, that it is the blood, not spirits, which is contained in the arteries.

These opinions are seen to be so incongruous and mutually subversive, that every one of them is justly brought under suspicion. That it is blood and blood alone which is contained in the arteries is made manifest by the experiment of Galen, by arteriotomy, and by wounds; for from a single divided artery, as Galen himself affirms in more than one place, the whole of the blood may be withdrawn in the course of half an hour or less. The experiment of Galen alluded to is this: "If you include a portion of an artery between two ligatures, and slit it open lengthwise you will find nothing but blood"; and thus he proves that the arteries contain only blood. And we too may be permitted to proceed by a like train of reasoning: if we find the same blood in the arteries as in the veins, after having tied them in the same way, as I have myself repeatedly ascertained, both in the dead body and in living animals, we may fairly conclude that the arteries contain the same blood as the veins, and nothing but the same blood. Some, whilst they attempt to lessen the difficulty, affirm that the blood is spirituous and arterious, and virtually concede that the office of the arteries is to carry blood from the heart into the whole of the body, and that they are therefore filled with blood; for spirituous blood is not the less blood on that account. And no one denies the blood as such, even the portion of it which flows in the veins, is imbued with spirits. But if that portion of it which is contained in the arteries be richer in spirits, it is still to be believed that these spirits are inseparable from the blood, like those in the veins; that the blood and spirits constitute one body (like whey and butter in milk, or heat in hot water), with which the arteries are charged, and for the distribution of which from the heart they are provided. This body is nothing else than blood. But if this blood be said to be drawn from the heart into the arteries by the diastole of these vessels, it is then assumed that the arteries by their distension are filled with blood, and not with the surrounding air, as heretofore; for if they be said also to become filled with air from the ambient atmosphere, how and when, I ask, can they receive blood from the heart? If it be answered: during the systole, I take it to be impossible: the arteries would then have to fill while they contracted, to fill, and yet not become distended. But if it be said: during diastole, they would then, and for two opposite purposes, be receiving both blood and air, and heat and cold, which is improbable. Further when it is affirmed that the diastole of the heart and arteries is simultaneous, and the systole of the two is also concurrent, there is another incongruity. For how can two bodies mutually connected, which are simultaneously distended, attract or draw anything from one another? or being simultaneously contracted, receive anything from each other? And then it seems impossible that one body can thus attract another body into itself, so as to become distended, seeing that to be distended is to be passive, unless, in the manner of a sponge, which has been previously compressed by an external force, it is returning to its natural state. But it is difficult to conceive that there can be anything of this kind in the arteries. The arteries dilate, because they are filled like bladders or leathern bottles; they are not filled because they expand like bellows. This I think easy of demonstration, and indeed conceive that I have already proved it. Nevertheless, in that book of Galen headed "Quod Sanguis continetur in Arteriis," he quotes an experiment to prove the contrary. An artery having been exposed, is opened longitudinally, and a reed or other pervious tube is inserted into the vessel through the opening, by which the blood is prevented from being lost, and the wound is closed. "So long," he says, "as things are thus arranged, the whole artery will pulsate; but if you now throw a ligature about the vessel and tightly compress its wall over the tube, you will no longer see the artery beating beyond the ligature." I have never performed this experiment of Galen's nor do I think that it could very well be performed in the living body, on account of the profuse flow of blood that would take place from the vessel that was operated on; neither would the tube effectually close the wound in the vessel without a ligature; and I cannot doubt but that the blood would be found to flow out between the tube and the vessel. Still Galen appears by this experiment to prove both that the pulsative property extends from the heart by the walls of the arteries, and that the arteries, whilst they dilate, are filled by that pulsific force, because they expand like bellows, and do not dilate as if they are filled like skins, But the contrary is obvious in arteriotomy and in wounds; for the blood spurting from the arteries escapes with force, now farther, now not so far, alternately, or in jets; and the jet always takes place with the diastole of the artery, never with the systole. By which it clearly appears that the artery is dilated with the impulse of the blood; for of itself it would not throw the blood to such a distance and whilst it was dilating; it ought rather to draw air into its cavity through the wound, were those things true that are commonly stated concerning the uses of the arteries. Do not let the thickness of the arterial tunics impose upon us, and lead us to conclude that the pulsative property proceeds along them from the heart. For in several animals the arteries do not apparently differ from the veins; and in extreme parts of the body where the arteries are minutely subdivided, as in the brain, the hand, etc., no one could distinguish the arteries from the veins by the dissimilar characters of their coats: the tunics of both are identical. And then, in the aneurism proceeding from a wounded or eroded artery, the pulsation is precisely the same as in the other arteries, and yet it has no proper arterial covering. To this the learned Riolanus testifies along with me, in his Seventh Book.

Nor let any one imagine that the uses of the pulse and the respiration are the same, because, under the influences of the same causes, such as running, anger, the warm bath, or any other heating thing, as Galen says, they become more frequent and forcible together. For not only is experience in opposition to this idea, though Galen endeavours to explain it away, when we see that with excessive repletion the pulse beats more forcibly, whilst the respiration is diminished in amount; but in young persons the pulse is quick, whilst respiration is slow. So it is also in alarm, and amidst care, and under anxiety of mind; sometimes, too, in fevers, the pulse is rapid, but the respiration is slower than usual.

These and other objections of the same kind may be urged against the opinions mentioned. Nor are the views that are entertained of the offices and pulse of the heart, perhaps, less bound up with great and most inextricable difficulties. The heart, it is vulgarly said, is the fountain and workshop of the vital spirits, the centre from which life is dispensed to the several parts of the body. Yet it is denied that the right ventricle makes spirits, which is rather held to supply nourishment to the lungs. For these reasons it is maintained that fishes are without any right ventricle (and indeed every animal wants a right ventricle which is unfurnished with lungs), and that the right ventricle is present solely for the sake of the lungs.

1. Why, I ask, when we see that the structure of both ventricles is almost identical, there being the same apparatus of fibres, and braces, and valves, and vessels, and auricles, and both in the same way in our dissections are found to be filled up with blood similarly black in colour, and coagulated—why, I say, should their uses be imagined to be different, when the action, motion, and pulse of both are the same? If the three tricuspid valves placed at the entrance into the right ventricle prove obstacles to the reflux of the blood into the vena cava, and if the three semilunar valves which are situated at the commencement of the pulmonary artery be there, that they may prevent the return of the blood into the ventricle; why, when we find similar structures in connexion with the left ventricle, should we deny that they are there for the same end, of preventing here the egress, there the regurgitation, of the blood?

2. And, when we have these structures, in points of size, form, and situation, almost in every respect the same in the left as in the right ventricle, why should it be said that things are arranged in the former for the egress and regress of spirits,

and in the latter or right ventricle, for the blood? The same arrangement cannot be held fitted to favour or impede the motion of the blood and of spirits indifferently.

3. And when we observe that the passages and vessels are severally in relation to one another in point of size, viz., the pulmonary artery to the pulmonary veins; why should the one be destined to a private purpose, that of furnishing the lungs, the other to a public function?

4. And as Realdus Columbus says, is it probable that such a quantity of blood should be required for the nutrition of the lungs; the vessel that leads to them, the vena arteriosa or pulmonary artery being of greater capacity than both the iliac veins?

5. And I ask, as the lungs are so close at hand, and in continual motion, and the vessel that supplies them is of such dimensions, what is the use or meaning of this pulse of the right ventricle? and why was nature reduced to the necessity of adding another ventricle for the sole purpose of nourishing the lungs?

When it is said that the left ventricle draws materials for the formation of spirits, air and blood, from the lungs and right sinuses of the heart, and in like manner sends spirituous blood into the aorta, drawing fuliginous vapours from there, and sending them by the pulmonary vein into the lungs, whence spirits are at the same time obtained for transmission into the aorta, I ask how, and by what means is the separation effected? And how comes it that spirits and fuliginous vapours can pass hither and thither without admixture or confusion? If the mitral cuspidate valves do not prevent the egress of fuliginous vapours to the lungs, how should they oppose the escape of air? And how should the semilunars hinder the regress of spirits from the aorta upon each supervening diastole of the heart? Above all, how can they say that the spirituous blood is sent from the pulmonary veins by the left ventricle into the lungs without any obstacle to its passage from the mitral valves, when they have previously asserted that the air entered by the same vessel from the lungs into the left ventricle, and have brought forward these same mitral valves as obstacles to its retrogression? Good God! how should the mitral valves prevent the regurgitation of air and not of blood?

Moreover, when they appoint the pulmonary artery, a vessel of great size, with the coverings of an artery, to none but a kind of private and single purpose, that, namely, of nourishing the lungs, why should the pulmonary vein, which is scarcely so large, which has the coats of a vein, and is soft and lax, be presumed to be made for many—three or four different—uses? For they will have it that air passes through this vessel from the lungs into the left ventricle; that fuliginous vapours escape by it from the heart into the lungs; and that a portion of the spirituous blood is distributed to the lungs for their refreshment.

If they will have it that fumes and air—fumes flowing from, air proceeding towards the heart—are transmitted by the same conduit, I reply, that nature is not wont to construct but one vessel, to contrive but one way for such contrary motions and purposes, nor is anything of the kind seen elsewhere.

If fumes or fuliginous vapours and air permeate this vessel, as they do the pulmonary bronchia, wherefore do we find neither air nor fuliginous vapours when we divide the pulmonary vein? Why do we always find this vessel full of sluggish blood, never of air, whilst in the lungs we find abundance of air remaining?

If any one will perform Galen's experiment of dividing the trachea of a living dog, forcibly distending the lungs with a pair of bellows, and then tying the trachea securely, he will find, when he has laid open the thorax, abundance of air in the lungs, even to their extreme investing tunic, but none in either the pulmonary veins or the left ventricle of the heart. But did the heart either attract air from the lungs, or did the lungs transmit any air to the heart, in the living dog, much more ought this to be the case in the experiment just referred to. Who, indeed, doubts that, did he inflate the lungs of a subject in the dissecting-room, he would instantly see the air making its way by this route, were there actually any such passage for it? But this office of the pulmonary veins, namely, the transference of air from the lungs of the heart, is held of such importance, that Hieronymus Fabricius of Aquapendente, contends that the lungs were made for the sake of this vessel, and that it constitutes the principal element in their structure.

But I should like to be informed why, if the pulmonary vein were destined for the conveyance of air, it has the structure of a blood-vessel here. Nature had rather need of annular tubes, such as those of the bronchi, in order that they might always remain open, and not be liable to collapse; and that they might continue entirely free from blood, lest the liquid should interfere with the passage of the air, as it so obviously does when the lungs labour from being either greatly oppressed or loaded in a less degree with phlegm, as they are when the breathing is performed with a sibilous or rattling noise.

Still less is that opinion to be tolerated which, as a two-fold material, one aerial, one sanguineous, is required for the composition of vital spirits, supposes the blood to ooze through the septum of the heart from the right to the left ventricle by certain hidden porosities, and the air to be attracted from the lungs through the great vessel, the pulmonary vein; and which, consequently, will have it, that there are numerous porosities in the septum of the heart adapted for the transmission of the blood. But by Hercules! no such pores can be demonstrated, nor in fact do any such exist. For the septum of the heart is of a denser and more compact structure than any portion of the body, except the bones and sinews. But even supposing that there were foramina or pores in this situation, how could one of the ventricles extract anything from the other—the left, *e.g.*, obtain blood from the right, when we see that both ventricles contract and dilate simultaneously? Why should we not rather believe that the right took spirits from the left, than that the left obtained blood from the right ventricle through these foramina? But it is certainly mysterious and incongruous that blood should be supposed to be most commodiously drawn through a set of obscure or invisible ducts, and air through perfectly open passages, at one and the same moment. And why, I ask, is recourse had to secret and invisible porosities, to uncertain and obscure channels, to explain the passage of the blood into the left ventricle, when there is so open a way through the pulmonary veins? I own it has always appeared extraordinary to me that they should have chosen to make, or rather to imagine, a way through the thick, hard, dense, and most compact septum of the heart, rather than take that by the open pulmonary vein, or even through the lax, soft and spongy substance of the lungs at large. Besides, if the blood could permeate the substance of the septum, or could be imbibed from the ventricles, what use were there for the coronary artery and vein, branches of which proceed to the septum itself, to supply it with nourishment? And what is especially worthy of notice is this: if in the fœtus, where everything is more lax and soft, nature saw herself reduced to the necessity of bringing the blood from the right to the left side of the heart by the foramen ovale, from the vena cava through the pulmonary vein, how should it be likely that in the adult she should pass it so commodiously, and without an effort through the septum of the ventricles which has now become denser by age?

Andreas Laurentius,[1] resting on the authority of Galen[2] and the experience of Hollerius, asserts and proves that the serum and pus in empyema, absorbed from the cavities of the chest into the pulmonary vein may be expelled and got rid of with the urine and fæces through the left ventricle of the heart and arteries. He quotes the case of a certain person affected with melancholia, and who suffered from repeated fainting fits, who was relieved from the paroxysms on passing a quantity of turbid, fetid and acrid urine. But he died at last, worn out by disease; and when the body came to be opened after death, no fluid like that he had micturated was discovered either in the bladder or the kidneys; but in the left ventricle of the heart and cavity of the thorax plenty of it was met with. And then Laurentius boasts that he had predicted the cause of the symptoms. For my own part, however, I cannot but wonder, since he had divined and predicted that heterogeneous matter could be discharged by the course he indicates, why he could not or would not perceive, and inform us that, in the natural state of things, the blood might be commodiously transferred from the lungs to the left ventricle of the heart by the very same route.

Since, therefore, from the foregoing considerations and many others to the same effect, it is plain that what has heretofore been said concerning the motion and function of the heart and arteries must appear obscure, inconsistent, or even impossible to him who carefully considers the entire subject, it would be proper to look more narrowly into the matter to contemplate the motion of the heart and arteries, not only in man, but in all animals that have hearts; and also, by frequent appeals to vivisection, and much ocular inspection, to investigate and discern the truth.

[1] Lib. ix, cap. xi, quest. 12.   [2] De Locis Affectis. lib. vi, cap. 7.

ON THE MOTION OF THE HEART AND BLOOD IN ANIMALS

CHAPTER I

THE AUTHOR'S MOTIVES FOR WRITING

WHEN I first gave my mind to vivisections, as a means of discovering the motions and uses of the heart, and sought to discover these from actual inspection, and not from the writings of others, I found the task so truly arduous, so full of difficulties, that I was almost tempted to think, with Fracastorius, that the motion of the heart was only to be comprehended by God. For I could neither rightly perceive at first when the systole and when the diastole took place, nor when and where dilatation and contraction occurred, by reason of the rapidity of the motion, which in many animals is accomplished in the twinkling of an eye, coming and going like a flash of lightning; so that the systole presented itself to me now from this point, now from that; the diastole the same; and then everything was reversed, the motions occurring, as it seemed, variously and confusedly together. My mind was therefore greatly unsettled nor did I know what I should myself conclude, nor what believe from others. I was not surprised that Andreas Laurentius should have written that the motion of the heart was as perplexing as the flux and reflux of Euripus had appeared to Aristotle.

At length, by using greater and daily diligence and investigation, making frequent inspection of many and various animals, and collating numerous observations, I thought that I had attained to the truth, that I should extricate myself and escape from this labyrinth, and that I had discovered what I so much desired, both the motion and the use of the heart and arteries. From that time I have not hesitated to expose my views upon these subjects, not only in private to my friends, but also in public, in my anatomical lectures, after the manner of the Academy of old.

These views as usual, pleased some more, others less; some chid and calumniated me, and laid it to me as a crime that I had dared to depart from the precepts and opinions of all anatomists; others desired further explanations of the novelties, which they said were both worthy of consideration, and might perchance be found of signal use. At length, yielding to the requests of my friends, that all might be made participators in my labors, and partly moved by the envy of others, who, receiving my views with uncandid minds and understanding them indifferently, have essayed to traduce me publicly, I have moved to commit these things to the press, in order that all may be enabled to form an opinion both of me and my labours. This step I take all the more willingly, seeing that Hieronymus Fabricius of Aquapendente, although he has accurately and learnedly delineated almost every one of the several parts of animals in a special work, has left the heart alone untouched. Finally, if any use or benefit to this department of the republic of letters should accrue from my labours, it will, perhaps, be allowed that I have not lived idly, and as the old man in the comedy says:

> For never yet hath any one attained
> To such perfection, but that time, and place,
> And use, have brought addition to his knowledge;
> Or made correction, or admonished him,
> That he was ignorant of much which he
> Had thought he knew; or led him to reject
> What he had once esteemed of highest price.

So will it, perchance, be found with reference to the heart at this time; or others, at least, starting hence, with the way pointed out to them, advancing under the guidance of a happier genius, may make occasion to proceed more fortunately, and to inquire more accurately.

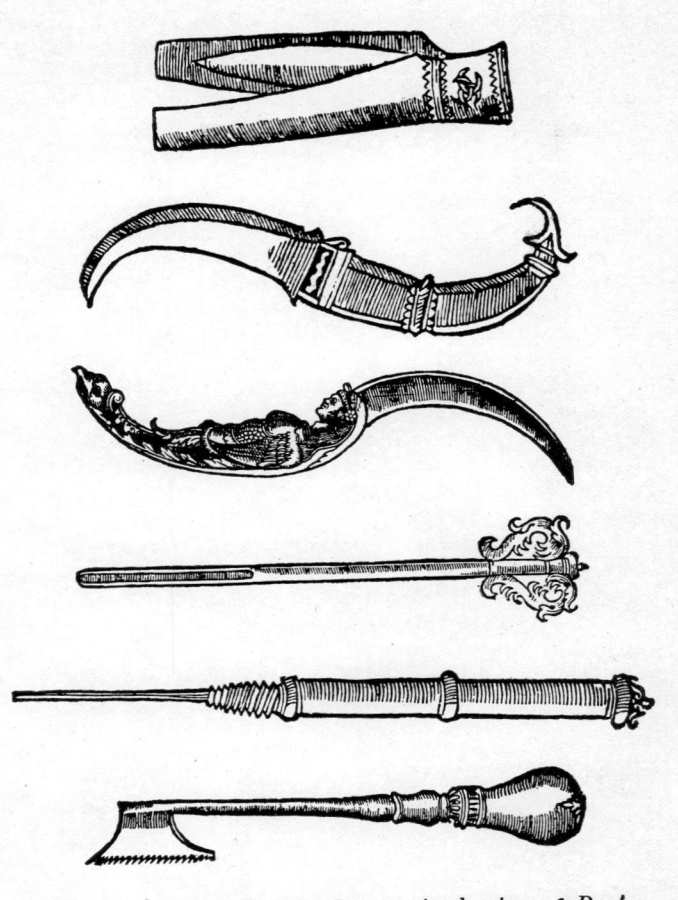

Instruments of General Surgery in the time of Paré

1. A lancet, which has on it the crest of Diane de Poitiers.
2. An incision-knife.
3. A small knife folding into a sheath.
4. A director.
5. A cataract-needle, screwing into a handle.
6. A small saw.

CHAPTER II

ON THE MOTIONS OF THE HEART AS SEEN IN THE DISSECTION OF LIVING ANIMALS

In the first place, then, when the chest of a living animal is laid open and the capsule that immediately surrounds the heart is slit up or removed, the organ is seen now to move, now to be at rest; there is a time when it moves, and a time when it is motionless.

These things are more obvious in the colder animals, such as toads, frogs, serpents, small fishes, crabs, shrimps, snails, and shell-fish. They also become more distinct in warm-blooded animals, such as the dog and hog, if they be attentively noted when the heart begins to flag, to move more slowly, and, as it were, to die: the movements then become slower and rarer, the pauses longer, by which it is made much more easy to perceive and unravel what the motions really are, and how they are performed. In the pause, as in death, the heart is soft, flaccid, exhausted, lying, as it were, at rest.

In the motion, and interval in which this is accomplished, three principal circumstances are to be noted:

1. That the heart is erected, and rises upwards to a point, so that at this time it strikes against the breast and the pulse is felt externally.

2. That it is everywhere contracted, but more especially towards the sides so that it looks narrower, relatively longer, more drawn together. The heart of an eel taken out of the body of the animal and placed upon the table or the hand, shows these particulars; but the same things are manifest in the hearts of all small fishes and of those colder animals where the organ is more conical or elongated.

3. The heart being grasped in the hand, is felt to become harder during its action. Now this hardness proceeds from tension, precisely as when the forearm is grasped, its tendons are perceived to become tense and resilient when the fingers are moved.

4. It may further be observed in fishes, and the colder blooded animals, such as frogs, serpents, etc., that the heart,

when it moves, becomes of a paler color, when quiescent of a deeper blood-red color.

From these particulars it appears evident to me that the motion of the heart consists in a certain universal tension— both contraction in the line of its fibres, and constriction in every sense. It becomes erect, hard, and of diminished size during its action; the motion is plainly of the same nature as that of the muscles when they contract in the line of their sinews and fibres; for the muscles, when in action, acquire vigor and tenseness, and from soft become hard, prominent, and thickened: and in the same manner the heart.

We are therefore authorized to conclude that the heart, at the moment of its action, is at once constricted on all sides, rendered thicker in its parietes and smaller in its ventricles, and so made apt to project or expel its charge of blood. This, indeed, is made sufficiently manifest by the preceding fourth observation in which we have seen that the heart, by squeezing out the blood that it contains, becomes paler, and then when it sinks into repose and the ventricle is filled anew with blood, that the deeper crimson colour returns. But no one need remain in doubt of the fact, for if the ventricle be pierced the blood will be seen to be forcibly projected outwards upon each motion or pulsation when the heart is tense.

These things, therefore, happen together or at the same instant: the tension of the heart, the pulse of its apex, which is felt externally by its striking against the chest, the thickening of its parietes, and the forcible expulsion of the blood it contains by the constriction of its ventricles.

Hence the very opposite of the opinions commonly received appears to be true; inasmuch as it is generally believed that when the heart strikes the breast and the pulse is felt without, the heart is dilated in its ventricles and is filled with blood; but the contrary of this is the fact, and the heart, when it contracts (and the impulse of the apex is conveyed through the chest wall), is emptied. Whence the motion which is generally regarded as the diastole of the heart, is in truth its systole. And in like manner the intrinsic motion of the heart is not the diastole but the systole; neither is it in the diastole that the heart grows firm and tense, but in the systole, for then only, when tense, is it moved and made vigorous.

Neither is it by any means to be allowed that the heart only moves in the lines of its straight fibres, although the great Vesalius giving this notion countenance, quotes a bundle of osiers bound in a pyramidal heap in illustration; meaning, that as the apex is approached to the base, so are the sides made to bulge out in the fashion of arches, the cavities to dilate, the ventricles to acquire the form of a cupping-glass and so to suck in the blood. But the true effect of every one of its fibres is to constringe the heart at the same time they render it tense; and this rather with the effect of thickening and amplifying the walls and substance of the organ than enlarging its ventricles. And, again, as the fibres run from the apex to the base, and draw the apex towards the base, they do not tend to make the walls of the heart bulge out in circles, but rather the contrary; inasmuch as every fibre that is circularly disposed, tends to become straight when it contracts; and is distended laterally and thickened, as in the case of muscular fibres in general, when they contract, that is, when they are shortened longitudinally, as we see them in the bellies of the muscles of the body at large. To all this let it be added, that not only are the ventricles contracted in virtue of the direction and condensation of their walls, but farther, that those fibres, or bands, styled nerves by Aristotle, which are so conspicuous in the ventricles of the larger animals, and contain all the straight fibres (the parietes of the heart containing only circular ones), when they contract simultaneously by an admirable adjustment all the internal surfaces are drawn together as if with cords, and so is the charge of blood expelled with force.

Neither is it true, as vulgarly believed, that the heart by any dilatation or motion of its own, has the power of drawing the blood into the ventricles; for when it acts and becomes tense, the blood is expelled; when it relaxes and sinks together it receives the blood in the manner and wise which will by-and-by be explained.

CHAPTER III

OF THE MOTIONS OF THE ARTERIES, AS SEEN IN THE DISSECTION OF LIVING ANIMALS

In connexion with the motions of the heart these things are further to be observed having reference to the motions and pulses of the arteries.

1. At the moment the heart contracts, and when the breast is struck, when in short the organ is in its state of systole, the arteries are dilated, yield a pulse, and are in the state of diastole. In like manner, when the right ventricle contracts and propels its charge of blood, the pulmonary artery is distended at the same time with the other arteries of the body.

2. When the left ventricle ceases to act, to contract, to pulsate, the pulse in the arteries also ceases; further, when this ventricle contracts languidly, the pulse in the arteries is scarcely perceptible. In like manner, the pulse in the right ventricle failing, the pulse in the pulmonary artery ceases also.

3. Further, when an artery is divided or punctured, the blood is seen to be forcibly propelled from the wound the moment the left ventricle contracts; and, again, when the pulmonary artery is wounded, the blood will be seen spouting forth with violence at the instant when the right ventricle contracts.

So also in fishes, if the vessel which leads from the heart to the gills be divided, at the moment when the heart becomes tense and contracted, at the same moment does the blood flow with force from the divided vessel.

In the same way, when we see the blood in arteriotomy projected now to a greater, now to a less distance, and that the greater jet corresponds to the diastole of the artery and to the time when the heart contracts and strikes the ribs, and is in its state of systole, we understand that the blood is expelled by the same movement.

From these facts it is manifest, in opposition to commonly received opinions, that the diastole of the arteries corresponds with the time of the heart's systole; and that the arteries are filled and distended by the blood forced into them by the contraction of the ventricles; the arteries, therefore, are distended, because they are filled like sacs or bladders, and are not filled because they expand like bellows. It is in virtue of one and the same cause, therefore, that all the arteries of the body pulsate, viz., the contraction of the left ventricle; in the same way as the pulmonary artery pulsates by the contraction of the right ventricle.

Finally, that the pulses of the arteries are due to the impulses of the blood from the left ventricle, may be illustrated by blowing into a glove, when the whole of the fingers will be found to become distended at one and the same time, and in their tension to bear some resemblance to the pulse. For in the ratio of the tension is the pulse of the heart, fuller, stronger, and more frequent as that acts more vigorously, still preserving the rhythm and volume, and order of the heart's contractions. Nor is it to be expected that because of the motion of the blood, the time at which the contraction of the heart takes place, and that at which the pulse in an artery (especially a distant one) is felt, shall be otherwise than simultaneous: it is here the same as in blowing up a glove or bladder; for in a plenum (as in a drum, a long piece of timber, etc.) the stroke and the motion occur at both extremities at the same time. Aristotle,[1] too, has said, "the blood of all animals palpitates within their veins (meaning the arteries), and by the pulse is sent everywhere simultaneously." And further,[2] "thus do all the veins pulsate together and by successive strokes, because they all depend upon the heart; and, as it is always in motion, so are they likewise always moving together, but by successive movements." It is well to observe with Galen, in this place, that the old philosophers called the arteries veins.

I happened upon one occasion to have a particular case under my care, which plainly satisfied me of the truth: A certain person was affected with a large pulsating tumour on the right side of the neck, called an aneurism, just at that part where the artery descends into the axilla, produced by an erosion of the artery itself, and daily increasing in size;

[1] De Anim., iii, cap. 9.   [2] De Respir., cap. 20.

this tumour was visibly distended as it received the charge of blood brought to it by the artery, with each stroke of the heart; the connexion of parts was obvious when the body of the patient came to be opened after his death. The pulse in the corresponding arm was small, in consequence of the greater portion of the blood being diverted into the tumour and so intercepted.

Whence it appears that whenever the motion of the blood through the arteries is impeded, whether it be by compression or infarction, or interception, there do the remote divisions of the arteries beat less forcibly, seeing that the pulse of the arteries is nothing more than the impulse or shock of the blood in these vessels.

CHAPTER IV

OF THE MOTION OF THE HEART AND ITS AURICLES, AS SEEN IN THE BODIES OF LIVING ANIMALS

BESIDES the motions already spoken of, we have still to consider those that appertain to the auricles.

Caspar Bauhin and John Riolan,[1] most learned men and skilful anatomists, inform us that from their observations, that if we carefully watch the movements of the heart in the vivisection of an animal, we shall perceive four motions distinct in time and in place, two of which are proper to the auricles, two to the ventricles. With all deference to such authority I say that there are four motions distinct in point of place, but not of time; for the two auricles move together, and so also do the two ventricles, in such wise that though the places be four, the times are only two. And this occurs in the following manner:

There are, as it were, two motions going on together: one of the auricles, another of the ventricles; these by no means taking place simultaneously, but the motion of the auricles preceding, that of the heart following; the motion appearing to begin from the auricles and to extend to the ventricles. When all things are becoming languid, and the heart is dying, as also in fishes and the colder blooded animals, there

[1] Bauhin, lib. ii, cap. 21. Riolan, lib. viii, cap. 1.

is a short pause between these two motions, so that the heart aroused, as it were, appears to respond to the motion, now more quickly, now more tardily; and at length, when near to death, it ceases to respond by its proper motion, but seems, as it were, to nod the head, and is so slightly moved that it appears rather to give signs of motion to the pulsating auricles than actually to move. The heart, therefore, ceases to pulsate sooner than the auricles, so that the auricles have been said to outlive it, the left ventricle ceasing to pulsate first of all; then its auricle, next the right ventricle; and, finally, all the other parts being at rest and dead, as Galen long since observed, the right auricle still continues to beat; life, therefore, appears to linger longest in the right auricle. Whilst the heart is gradually dying, it is sometimes seen to reply, after two or three contractions of the auricles, roused as it were to action, and making a single pulsation, slowly, unwillingly, and with an effort.

But this especially is to be noted, that after the heart has ceased to beat, the auricles however still contracting, a finger placed upon the ventricles perceives the several pulsations of the auricles, precisely in the same way and for the same reason, as we have said, that the pulses of the ventricles are felt in the arteries, to wit, the distension produced by the jet of blood. And if at this time, the auricles alone pulsating, the point of the heart be cut off with a pair of scissors, you will perceive the blood flowing out upon each contraction of the auricles. Whence it is manifest that the blood enters the ventricles, not by any attraction or dilatation of the heart, but by being thrown into them by the pulses of the auricles.

And here I would observe, that whenever I speak of pulsations as occurring in the auricles or ventricles, I mean contractions: first the auricles contract, and then and subsequently the heart itself contracts. When the auricles contract they are seen to become whiter, especially where they contain but little blood; but they are filled as magazines or reservoirs of the blood, which is tending spontaneously and, by its motion in the veins, under pressure towards the centre; the whiteness indicated is most conspicuous towards the extremities or edges of the auricles at the time of their contractions.

In fishes and frogs, and other animals which have hearts with but a single ventricle, and for an auricle have a kind of bladder much distended with blood, at the base of the organ, you may very plainly perceive this bladder contracting first, and the contraction of the heart or ventricle following afterwards.

But I think it right to describe what I have observed of an opposite character: the heart of an eel, of several fishes, and even of some (of the higher) animals taken out of the body, pulsates without auricles; nay, if it be cut in pieces the several parts may still be seen contracting and relaxing; so that in these creatures the body of the heart may be seen pulsating and palpitating, after the cessation of all motion in the auricle. But is not this perchance peculiar to animals more tenacious of life, whose radical moisture is more glutinous, or fat and sluggish, and less readily soluble? The same faculty indeed appears in the flesh of eels, which even when skinned and embowelled, and cut into pieces, are still seen to move.

Experimenting with a pigeon upon one occasion, after the heart had wholly ceased to pulsate, and the auricles too had become motionless, I kept my finger wetted with saliva and warm for a short time upon the heart, and observed that under the influence of this fomentation it recovered new strength and life, so that both ventricles and auricles pulsated, contracting and relaxing alternately, recalled as it were from death to life.

Besides this, however, I have occasionally observed, after the heart and even its right auricle had ceased pulsating,—when it was in articulo mortis in short,—that an obscure motion, an undulation or palpitation, remained in the blood itself, which was contained in the right auricle, this being apparent so long as it was imbued with heat and spirit. And, indeed, a circumstance of the same kind is extremely manifest in the course of the generation of animals, as may be seen in the course of the first seven days of the incubation of the chick: A drop of blood makes its appearance which palpitates, as Aristotle had already observed; from this, when the growth is further advanced and the chick is fashioned, the auricles of the heart are formed, which pulsating henceforth give constant signs of life. When at length, and after the lapse of a few days, the outline of the body begins to be distinguished, then is the ventricular part of the heart also produced, but it continues for a time white and apparently bloodless, like the rest of the animal; neither does it pulsate or give signs of motion. I have seen a similar condition of the heart in the human fœtus about the beginning of the third month, the heart then being whitish and bloodless, although its auricles contained a considerable quantity of purple blood. In the same way in the egg, when the chick was formed and had increased in size, the heart too increased and acquired ventricles, which then began to receive and to transmit blood.

And this leads me to remark that he who inquires very particularly into this matter will not conclude that the heart, as a whole, is the primum vivens, ultimum moriens,— the first part to live, the last to die,—but rather its auricles, or the part which corresponds to the auricles in serpents, fishes, etc., which both lives before the heart and dies after it.

Nay, has not the blood itself or spirit an obscure palpitation inherent in it, which it has even appeared to me to retain after death? and it seems very questionable whether or not we are to say that life begins with the palpitation or beating of the heart. The seminal fluid of all animals—the prolific spirit, as Aristotle observed, leaves their body with a bound and like a living thing; and nature in death, as Aristotle[2] further remarks, retracing her steps, reverts to where she had set out, and returns at the end of her course to the goal whence she had started. As animal generation proceeds from that which is not animal, entity from nonentity, so, by a retrograde course, entity, by corruption, is resolved into nonentity, whence that in animals, which was last created, fails first and that which was first, fails last.

I have also observed that almost all animals have truly a heart, not the larger creatures only, and those that have red blood, but the smaller, and pale-blooded ones also, such as slugs, snails, scallops, shrimps, crabs, crayfish, and many others; nay, even in wasps, hornets, and flies, I have, with

[2] De Motu Animal., cap. 8.

the aid of a magnifying glass, and at the upper part of what is called the tail, both seen the heart pulsating myself, and shown it to many others.

But in the pale-blooded tribes the heart pulsates sluggishly and deliberately, contracting slowly as in animals that are moribund, a fact that may readily be seen in the snail, whose heart will be found at the bottom of that orifice in the right side of the body which is seen to be opened and shut in the course of respiration, and whence saliva is discharged, the incision being made in the upper aspect of the body, near the part which corresponds to the liver.

This, however, is to be observed: that in winter and the colder season, exsanguine animals, such as the snail, show no pulsation; they seem rather to live after the manner of vegetables, or of those other productions which are therefore designated plant-animals.

It is also to be noted that all animals which have a heart have also auricles, or something analogous to auricles; and, further, that whenever the heart has a double ventricle, there are always two auricles present, but not otherwise. If you turn to the production of the chick in ovo, however, you will find at first no more a vesicle or auricle, or pulsating drop of blood; it is only by and by, when the development has made some progress, that the heart is fashioned; even so in certain animals not destined to attain to the highest perfection in their organization, such as bees, wasps, snails, shrimps, crayfish, etc., we only find a certain pulsating vesicle, like a sort of red or white palpitating point, as the beginning or principle of their life.

We have a small shrimp in these countries, which is taken in the Thames and in the sea, the whole of whose body is transparent; this creature, placed in a little water, has frequently afforded myself and particular friends an opportunity of observing the motions of the heart with the greatest distinctness, the external parts of the body presenting no obstacle to our view, but the heart being perceived as though it had been seen through a window.

I have also observed the first rudiments of the chick in the course of the fourth or fifth day of the incubation, in the guise of a little cloud, the shell having been removed and the egg immersed in clear tepid water. In the midst of the cloudlet in question there was a bloody point so small that it disappeared during the contraction and escaped the sight, but in the relaxation it reappeared again, red and like the point of a pin; so that betwixt the visible and invisible, betwixt being and not being, as it were, it gave by its pulses a kind of representation of the commencement of life.

CHAPTER V

Of the Motion, Action and Office of the Heart

From these and other observations of a similar nature, I am persuaded it will be found that the motion of the heart is as follows:

First of all, the auricle contracts, and in the course of its contraction forces the blood (which it contains in ample quantity as the head of the veins, the store-house and cistern of the blood) into the ventricle, which, being filled, the heart raises itself straightway, makes all its fibres tense, contracts the ventricles, and performs a beat, by which beat it immediately sends the blood supplied to it by the auricle into the arteries. The right ventricle sends its charge into the lungs by the vessel which is called vena arteriosa, but which in structure and function, and all other respects, is an artery. The left ventricle sends its charge into the aorta, and through this by the arteries to the body at large.

These two motions, one of the ventricles, the other of the auricles, take place consecutively, but in such a manner that there is a kind of harmony or rhythm preserved between them, the two concurring in such wise that but one motion is apparent, especially in the warmer blooded animals, in which the movements in question are rapid. Nor is this for any other reason than it is in a piece of machinery, in which, though one wheel gives motion to another, yet all the wheels seem to move simultaneously; or in that mechanical contrivance which is adapted to firearms, where, the trigger being touched, down comes the flint, strikes against the steel, elicits a spark, which falling among the powder, ignites it, when the flame extends, enters the barrel, causes the explosion, propels the ball, and the mark is attained—all of which incidents, by reason of the celerity with which they happen, seem to take place in the twinkling of an eye. So also in deglutition: by the elevation of the root of the tongue, and the compression of the mouth, the food or drink is pushed into the fauces, when the larynx is closed by its muscles and by the epiglottis. The pharynx is then raised and opened by its muscles in the same way as a sac that is to be filled is lifted up and its mouth dilated. Upon the mouthful being received, it is forced downwards by the transverse muscles, and then carried farther by the longitudinal ones. Yet all these motions, though executed by different and distinct organs, are performed harmoniously, and in such order that they seem to constitute but a single motion and act, which we call deglutition.

Even so does it come to pass with the motions and action of the heart, which constitute a kind of deglutition, a transfusion of the blood from the veins to the arteries. And if anyone, bearing these things in mind, will carefully watch the motions of the heart in the body of a living animal, he will perceive not only all the particulars I have mentioned, viz., the heart becoming erect, and making one continuous motion with its auricles; but farther, a certain obscure undulation and lateral inclination in the direction of the axis of the right ventricle, as if twisting itself slightly in performing its work. And indeed everyone may see, when a horse drinks, that the water is drawn in and transmitted to the stomach at each movement of the throat, which movement produces a sound and yields a pulse both to the ear and the touch; in the same way it is with each motion of the heart, when there is the delivery of a quantity of blood from the veins to the arteries a pulse takes place, and can be heard within the chest.

The motion of the heart, then, is entirely of this description, and the one action of the heart is the transmission of the blood and its distribution, by means of the arteries, to the very extremities of the body; so that the pulse which we feel in the arteries is nothing more than the impulse of the blood derived from the heart.

Whether or not the heart, besides propelling the blood,

giving it motion locally, and distributing it to the body, adds anything else to it—heat, spirit, perfection,—must be inquired into by-and-by, and decided upon other grounds. So much may suffice at this time, when it is shown that by the action of the heart the blood is transfused through the ventricles from the veins to the arteries, and distributed by them to all parts of the body.

The above, indeed, is admitted by all, both from the structure of the heart and the arrangement and action of its valves. But still they are like persons purblind or groping about in the dark, for they give utterance to various, contradictory, and incoherent sentiments, delivering many things upon conjecture, as we have already shown.

The grand cause of doubt and error in this subject appears to me to have been the intimate connexion between the heart and the lungs. When men saw both the pulmonary artery and the pulmonary veins losing themselves in the lungs, of course it became a puzzle to them to know how or by what means the right ventricle should distribute the blood to the body, or the left draw it from the venæ cavæ. This fact is borne witness to by Galen, whose words, when writing against Erasistratus in regard to the origin and use of the veins and the coction of the blood, are the following[1]: "You will reply," he says, "that the effect is so; that the blood is prepared in the liver, and is thence transferred to the heart to receive its proper form and last perfection; a statement which does not appear devoid of reason; for no great and perfect work is ever accomplished at a single effort, or receives its final polish from one instrument. But if this be actually so, then show us another vessel which draws the absolutely perfect blood from the heart, and distributes it as the arteries do the spirits over the whole body." Here then is a reasonable opinion not allowed, because, forsooth, besides not seeing the true means of transit, he could not discover the vessel which should transmit the blood from the heart to the body at large!

But had anyone been there in behalf of Erasistratus, and of that opinion which we now espouse, and which Galen himself acknowledges in other respects consonant with reason, to

[1] De Placitis Hippocratis et Platonis, vi.

have pointed to the aorta as the vessel which distributes the blood from the heart to the rest of the body, I wonder what would have been the answer of that most ingenious and learned man? Had he said that the artery transmits spirits and not blood, he would indeed sufficiently have answered Erasistratus, who imagined that the arteries contained nothing but spirits; but then he would have contradicted himself, and given a foul denial to that for which he had keenly contended in his writings against this very Erasistratus, to wit, that blood in substance is contained in the arteries, and not spirits; a fact which he demonstrated not only by many powerful arguments, but by experiments.

But if the divine Galen will here allow, as in other places he does, "that all the arteries of the body arise from the great artery, and that this takes its origin from the heart; that all these vessels naturally contain and carry blood; that the three semilunar valves situated at the orifice of the aorta prevent the return of the blood into the heart, and that nature never connected them with this, the most noble viscus of the body, unless for some important end"; if, I say, this father of physicians concedes all these things,—and I quote his own words,—I do not see how he can deny that the great artery is the very vessel to carry the blood, when it has attained its highest term of perfection, from the heart for distribution to all parts of the body. Or would he perchance still hesitate, like all who have come after him, even to the present hour, because he did not perceive the route by which the blood was transferred from the veins to the arteries, in consequence, as I have already said, of the intimate connexion between the heart and the lungs? And that this difficulty puzzled anatomists not a little, when in their dissections they found the pulmonary artery and left ventricle full of thick, black, and clotted blood, plainly appears, when they felt themselves compelled to affirm that the blood made its way from the right to the left ventricle by transuding through the septum of the heart. But this fancy I have already refuted. A new pathway for the blood must therefore be prepared and thrown open, and being once exposed, no further difficulty will, I believe, be experienced by anyone in admitting what I have already proposed in regard to the pulse of the heart and arteries, viz., the passage of the blood from the veins to the arteries, and its distribution to the whole of the body by means of these vessels.

CHAPTER VI

Of the Course by which the Blood is Carried from the Vena Cava into the Arteries, or from the Right into the Left Ventricle of the Heart

Since the intimate connexion of the heart with the lungs, which is apparent in the human subject, has been the probable cause of the errors that have been committed on this point, they plainly do amiss who, pretending to speak of the parts of animals generally, as anatomists for the most part do, confine their researches to the human body alone, and that when it is dead. They obviously do not act otherwise than he who, having studied the forms of a single commonwealth, should set about the composition of a general system of polity; or who, having taken cognizance of the nature of a single field, should imagine that he had mastered the science of agriculture; or who, upon the ground of one particular proposition, should proceed to draw general conclusions.

Had anatomists only been as conversant with the dissection of the lower animals as they are with that of the human body, the matters that have hitherto kept them in a perplexity of doubt would, in my opinion, have met them freed from every kind of difficulty.

And first, in fishes, in which the heart consists of but a single ventricle, being devoid of lungs, the thing is sufficiently manifest. Here the sac, which is situated at the base of the heart, and is the part analogous to the auricle in man, plainly forces the blood into the heart, and the heart, in its turn, conspicuously transmits it by a pipe or artery, or vessel analogous to an artery; these are facts which are confirmed by simple ocular inspection, as well as by a division of the vessel, when the blood is seen to be projected by each pulsation of the heart.

The same thing is also not difficult of demonstration in

those animals that have, as it were, no more than a single ventricle to the heart, such as toads, frogs, serpents, and lizards, which have lungs in a certain sense, as they have a voice. I have many observations by me on the admirable structure of the lungs of these animals, and matters appertaining, which, however, I cannot introduce in this place. Their anatomy plainly shows us that the blood is transferred in them from the veins to the arteries in the same manner as in higher animals, viz., by the action of the heart; the way, in fact, is patent, open, manifest; there is no difficulty, no room for doubt about it; for in them the matter stands precisely as it would in man were the septum of his heart perforated or removed, or one ventricle made out of two; and this being the case, I imagine that no one will doubt as to the way by which the blood may pass from the veins into the arteries.

But as there are actually more animals which have no lungs than there are furnished with them, and in like manner a greater number which have only one ventricle than there are with two, it is open to us to conclude, judging from the mass or multitude of living creatures, that for the major part, and generally, there is an open way by which the blood is transmitted from the veins through the sinuses or cavities of the heart into the arteries.

I have, however, cogitating with myself, seen further, that the same thing obtained most obviously in the embryos of those animals that have lungs; for in the fœtus the four vessels belonging to the heart, viz., the vena cava, the pulmonary artery, the pulmonary vein, and the great artery or aorta, are all connected otherwise than in the adult, a fact sufficiently known to every anatomist. The first contact and union of the vena cava with the pulmonary veins, which occurs before the cava opens properly into the right ventricle of the heart, or gives off the coronary vein, a little above its escape from the liver, is by a lateral anastomosis; this is an ample foramen, of an oval form, communicating between the cava and the pulmonary vein, so that the blood is free to flow in the greatest abundance by that foramen from the vena cava into the pulmonary vein, and left auricle, and from thence into the left ventricle.

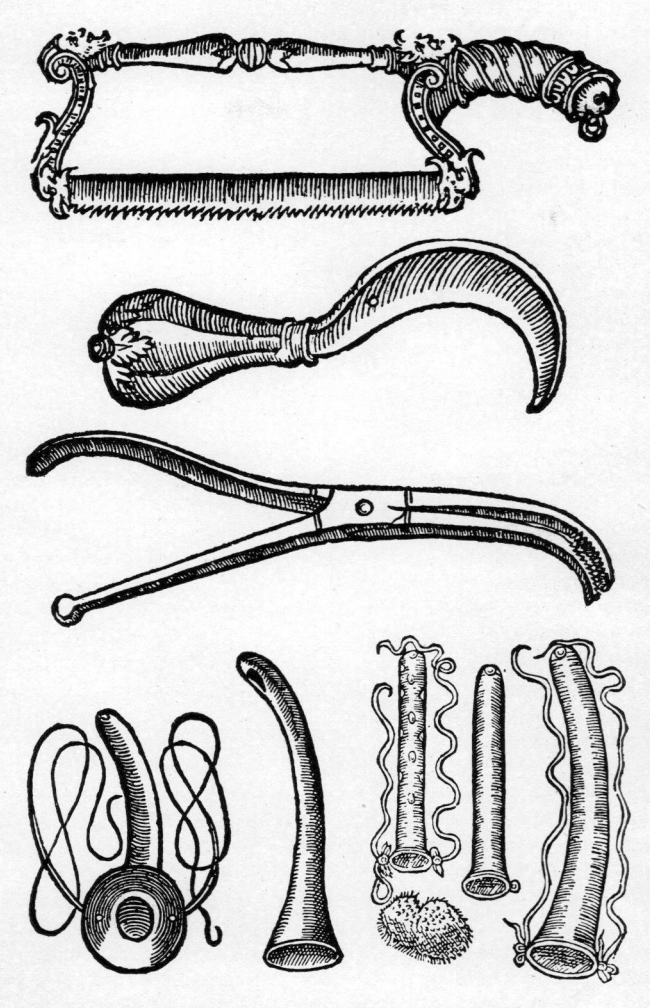

Amputating Instruments in the time of Paré

1. *An amputating saw.*
2. *An amputating knife.*
3. *A forceps.*
4. *Drainage tubes and sponge.*

Farther, in this foramen ovale, from that part which regards the pulmonary vein, there is a thin tough membrane, larger than the opening, extended like an operculum or cover; this membrane in the adult blocking up the foramen, and adhering on all sides, finally closes it up, and almost obliterates every trace of it. In the fœtus, however, this membrane is so contrived that falling loosely upon itself, it permits a ready access to the lungs and heart, yielding a passage to the blood which is streaming from the cava, and hindering the tide at the same time from flowing back into that vein. All things, in short, permit us to believe that in the embryo the blood must constantly pass by this foramen from the vena cava into the pulmonary vein, and from thence into the left auricle of the heart; and having once entered there, it can never regurgitate.

Another union is that by the pulmonary artery, and is effected when that vessel divides into two branches after its escape from the right ventricle of the heart. It is as if to the two trunks already mentioned a third were superadded, a kind of arterial canal, carried obliquely from the pulmonary artery, to perforate and terminate in the great artery or aorta. So that in the dissection of the embryo, as it were, two aortas, or two roots of the great artery, appear springing from the heart. This canal shrinks gradually after birth, and after a time becomes withered, and finally almost removed, like the umbilical vessels.

The arterial canal contains no membrane or valve to direct or impede the flow of blood in this or in that direction: for at the root of the pulmonary artery, of which the arterial canal is the continuation in the fœtus, there are three semilunar valves, which open from within outwards, and oppose no obstacle to the blood flowing in this direction or from the right ventricle into the pulmonary artery and aorta; but they prevent all regurgitation from the aorta or pulmonic vessels back upon the right ventricle; closing with perfect accuracy, they oppose an effectual obstacle to everything of the kind in the embryo. So that there is also reason to believe that when the heart contracts, the blood is regularly propelled by the canal or passage indicated from the right ventricle into the aorta.

What is commonly said in regard to these two great communications, to wit, that they exist for the nutrition of the lungs, is both improbable and inconsistent; seeing that in the adult they are closed up, abolished, and consolidated, although the lungs, by reason of their heat and motion, must then be presumed to require a larger supply of nourishment. The same may be said in regard to the assertion that the heart in the embryo does not pulsate, that it neither acts nor moves, so that nature was forced to make these communications for the nutrition of the lungs. This is plainly false; for simple inspection of the incubated egg, and of embryos just taken out of the uterus, shows that the heart moves in them precisely as in adults, and that nature feels no such necessity. I have myself repeatedly seen these motions, and Aristotle is likewise witness of their reality. "The pulse," he observes, "inheres in the very constitution of the heart, and appears from the beginning as is learned both from the dissection of living animals and the formation of the chick in the egg."[1] But we further observe that the passages in question are not only pervious up to the period of birth in man, as well as in other animals, as anatomists in general have described them, but for several months subsequently, in some indeed for several years, not to say for the whole course of life; as, for example, in the goose, snipe, and various birds and many of the smaller animals. And this circumstance it was, perhaps, that imposed upon Botallus, who thought he had discovered a new passage for the blood from the vena cava into the left ventricle of the heart; and I own that when I met with the same arrangement in one of the larger members of the mouse family, in the adult state, I was myself at first led to something of a like conclusion.

From this it will be understood that in the human embryo, and in the embryos of animals in which the communications are not closed, the same thing happens, namely, that the heart by its motion propels the blood by obvious and open passages from the vena cava into the aorta through the cavities of both the ventricles, the right one receiving the blood from the auricle, and propelling it by the pulmonary

[1] Lib. de Spiritu, cap. v.

artery and its continuation, named the ductus arteriosus, into the aorta; the left, in like manner, charged by the contraction of its auricle, which has received its supply through the foramen ovale from the vena cava, contracting, and projecting the blood through the root of the aorta into the trunk of that vessel.

In embryos, consequently, whilst the lungs are yet in a state of inaction, performing no function, subject to no motion any more than if they had not been present, nature uses the two ventricles of the heart as if they formed but one, for the transmission of the blood. The condition of the embryos of those animals which have lungs, whilst these organs are yet in abeyance and not employed, is the same as that of those animals which have no lungs.

So it clearly appears in the case of the fœtus that the heart by its action transfers the blood from the vena cava into the aorta, and that by a route as obvious and open, as if in the adult the two ventricles were made to communicate by the removal of their septum. We therefore find that in the greater number of animals—in all, indeed, at a certain period of their existence—the channels for the transmission of the blood through the heart are conspicuous. But we have to inquire why in some creatures—those, namely, that have warm blood, and that have attained to the adult age, man among the number—we should not conclude that the same thing is accomplished through the substance of the lungs, which in the embryo, and at a time when the function of these organs is in abeyance, nature effects by the direct passages described, and which, indeed, she seems compelled to adopt through want of a passage by the lungs; or why it should be better (for nature always does that which is best) that she should close up the various open routes which she had formerly made use of in the embryo and fœtus, and still uses in all other animals. Not only does she thereby open up no new apparent channels for the passages of the blood, but she even shuts up those which formerly existed.

And now the discussion is brought to this point, that they who inquire into the ways by which the blood reaches the left ventricle of the heart and pulmonary veins from the vena cava, will pursue the wisest course if they seek by dissection to discover the causes why in the larger and more perfect animals of mature age nature has rather chosen to make the blood percolate the parenchyma of the lungs, than, as in other instances, chosen a direct and obvious course—for I assume that no other path or mode of transit can be entertained. It must be because the larger and more perfect animals are warmer, and when adult their heat greater—ignited, as I might say, and requiring to be damped or mitigated, that the blood is sent through the lungs, in order that it may be tempered by the air that is inspired, and prevented from boiling up, and so becoming extinguished, or something else of the sort. But to determine these matters, and explain them satisfactorily, were to enter on a speculation in regard to the office of the lungs and the ends for which they exist. Upon such a subject, as well as upon what pertains to respiration, to the necessity and use of the air, etc., as also to the variety and diversity of organs that exist in the bodies of animals in connexion with these matters, although I have made a vast number of observations, I shall not speak till I can more conveniently set them forth in a treatise apart, lest I should be held as wandering too wide of my present purpose, which is the use and motion of the heart, and be charged with speaking of things beside the question, and rather complicating and quitting than illustrating it. And now returning to my immediate subject, I go on with what yet remains for demonstration, viz., that in the more perfect and warmer adult animals, and man, the blood passes from the right ventricle of the heart by the pulmonary artery, into the lungs, and thence by the pulmonary veins into the left auricle, and from there into the left ventricle of the heart. And, first, I shall show that this may be so, and then I shall prove that it is so in fact.

CHAPTER VII

THE BLOOD PASSES THROUGH THE SUBSTANCE OF THE LUNGS FROM THE RIGHT VENTRICLE OF THE HEART INTO THE PULMONARY VEINS AND LEFT VENTRICLE

THAT this is possible, and that there is nothing to prevent it from being so, appears when we reflect on the way in which water permeating the earth produces springs and rivulets, or when we speculate on the means by which the sweat passes through the skin, or the urine through the substance of the kidneys. It is well known that persons who use the Spa waters or those of La Madonna, in the territories of Padua, or others of an acidulous or vitriolated nature, or who simply swallow drinks by the gallon, pass all off again within an hour or two by the bladder. Such a quantity of liquid must take some short time in the concoction: it must pass through the liver (it is allowed by all that the juices of the food we consume pass twice through this organ in the course of the day); it must flow through the veins, through the tissues of the kidneys, and through the ureters into the bladder.

To those, therefore, whom I hear denying that the blood, aye, the whole mass of the blood, may pass through the substance of the lungs, even as the nutritive juices percolate the liver, asserting such a proposition to be impossible, and by no means to be entertained as credible, I reply, with the poet, that they are of that race of men who, when they will, assent full readily, and when they will not, by no manner of means; who, when their assent is wanted, fear, and when it is not, fear not to give it.

The substance of the liver is extremely dense, so is that of the kidney; the lungs, however, are of a much looser texture, and if compared with the kidneys are absolutely spongy. In the liver there is no forcing, no impelling power; in the lungs the blood is forced on by the pulse of the right ventricle, the necessary effect of whose impulse is the distension of the vessels and the pores of the lungs. And then the lungs, in respiration, are perpetually rising and falling: motions, the effect of which must needs be to open and shut the pores and vessels, precisely as in the case of a sponge, and of parts having a spongy structure, when they are alternately compressed and again are suffered to expand. The liver, on the contrary, remains at rest, and is never seen to be dilated or constricted. Lastly, if no one denies the possibility in man, oxen, and the larger animals generally, of the whole of the ingested juices passing through the liver, in order to reach the vena cava, for this reason, that if nourishment is to go on, these juices must needs get into the veins, and there is no other way but the one indicated, why should not the same arguments be held of avail for the passage of the blood in adults through the lungs? Why not maintain, with Columbus, that skilful and learned anatomist, that it must be so from the capacity and structure of the pulmonary vessels, and from the fact of the pulmonary veins and ventricle corresponding with them, being always found to contain blood, which must needs have come from the veins, and by no other passage save through the lungs? Columbus, and we also, from what precedes, from dissections, and other arguments, conceive the thing to be clear. But as there are some who admit nothing unless upon authority, let them learn that the truth I am contending for can be confirmed from Galen's own words, namely, that not only may the blood be transmitted from the pulmonary artery into the pulmonary veins, then into the left ventricle of the heart, and from thence into the arteries of the body, but that this is effected by the ceaseless pulsation of the heart and the motion of the lungs in breathing.

There are, as everyone knows, three sigmoid or semilunar valves situated at the orifice of the pulmonary artery, which effectually prevent the blood sent into the vessel from returning into the cavity of the heart. Now Galen, explaining the use of these valves, and the necessity for them, employs the following language:[1] "There is everywhere a mutual anastomosis and inosculation of the arteries with the veins, and they severally transmit both blood and spirit, by certain invisible and undoubtedly very narrow passages. Now if the mouth of the pulmonary artery had stood in

[1] De Usu partium, lib. vi, cap. 10.

like manner continually open, and nature had found no contrivance for closing it when requisite, and opening it again, it would have been impossible that the blood could ever have passed by the invisible and delicate mouths, during the contractions of the thorax, into the arteries; for all things are not alike readily attracted or repelled; but that which is light is more readily drawn in, the instrument being dilated, and forced out again when it is contracted, than that which is heavy; and in like manner is anything drawn more rapidly along an ample conduit, and again driven forth, than it is through a narrow tube. But when the thorax is contracted the pulmonary veins, which are in the lungs, being driven inwardly, and powerfully compressed on every side, immediately force out some of the spirit they contain, and at the same time assume a certain portion of blood by those subtle mouths, a thing that could never come to pass were the blood at liberty to flow back into the heart through the great orifice of the pulmonary artery. But its return through this great opening being prevented, when it is compressed on every side, a certain portion of it distils into the pulmonary veins by the minute orifices mentioned." And shortly afterwards, in the next chapter, he says: "The more the thorax contracts, the more it strives to force out the blood, the more exactly do these membranes (viz., the semilunar valves) close up the mouth of the vessel, and suffer nothing to regurgitate." The same fact he has also alluded to in a preceding part of the tenth chapter: "Were there no valves, a three-fold inconvenience would result, so that the blood would then perform this lengthened course in vain; it would flow inwards during the disastoles of the lungs and fill all their arteries; but in the systoles, in the manner of the tide, it would ever and anon, like the Euripus, flow backwards and forwards by the same way, with a reciprocating motion, which would nowise suit the blood. This, however, may seem a matter of little moment; but if it meantime appear that the function of respiration suffer, then I think it would be looked upon as no trifle, etc." Shortly afterwards he says: "And then a third inconvenience, by no means to be thought lightly of, would follow, were the blood moved backwards during the expirations, had not our Maker instituted those supplementary membranes." In the eleventh chapter he concludes: "That they (the valves) have all a common use, and that it is to prevent regurgitation or backward motion; each, however, having a proper function, the one set drawing matters from the heart, and preventing their return, the other drawing matters into the heart, and preventing their escape from it. For nature never intended to distress the heart with needless labour, neither to bring aught into the organ which it had been better to have kept away, nor to take from it again aught which it was requisite should be brought. Since, then, there are four orifices in all, two in either ventricle, one of these induces, the other educes." And again he says: "Farther, since there is one vessel, which consists of a simple covering implanted in the heart, and another which is double, extending from it (Galen is here speaking of the right side of the heart, but I extend his observations to the left side also), a kind of reservoir had to be provided, to which both belonging, the blood should be drawn in by one, and sent out by the other."

Galen adduces this argument for the transit of the blood by the right ventricle from the vena cava into the lungs; but we can use it with still greater propriety, merely changing the terms, for the passage of the blood from the veins through the heart into the arteries. From Galen, however, that great man, that father of physicians, it clearly appears that the blood passes through the lungs from the pulmonary artery into the minute branches of the pulmonary veins, urged to this both by the pulses of the heart and by the motions of the lungs and thorax; that the heart, moreover, is incessantly receiving and expelling the blood by and from its ventricles, as from a magazine or cistern, and for this end it is furnished with four sets of valves, two serving for the induction and two for the eduction of the blood, lest, like the Euripus, it should be incommodiously sent hither and thither, or flow back into the cavity which it should have quitted, or quit the part where its presence was required, and so the heart might be oppressed with labour in vain, and the office of the lungs be interfered with.[2] Finally, our position that the blood is continually permeating from the right to the left ventricle, from the vena cava into the aorta, through the porosities of the lungs, plainly appears from this, that since the blood is incessantly sent from the right ventricle into the lungs by the pulmonary artery, and in like manner is incessantly drawn from the lungs into the left ventricle, as appears from what precedes and the position of the valves, it cannot do otherwise than pass through continuously. And then, as the blood is incessantly flowing into the right ventricle of the heart, and is continually passed out from the left, as appears in like manner, and as is obvious, both to sense and reason, it is impossible that the blood can do otherwise than pass continually from the vena cava into the aorta.

Dissection consequently shows distinctly what takes place in the majority of animals, and indeed in all, up to the period of their maturity; and that the same thing occurs in adults is equally certain, both from Galen's words, and what has already been said, only that in the former the transit is effected by open and obvious passages, in the latter by the hidden porosities of the lungs and the minute inosculations of vessels. It therefore appears that, although one ventricle of the heart, the left to wit, would suffice for the distribution of the blood over the body, and its eduction from the vena cava, as indeed is done in those creatures that have no lungs, nature, nevertheless, when she ordained that the same blood should also percolate the lungs, saw herself obliged to add the right ventricle, the pulse of which should force the blood from the vena cava through the lungs into the cavity of the left ventricle. In this way, it may be said, that the right ventricle is made for the sake of the lungs, and for the transmission of the blood through them, not for their nutrition; for it were unreasonable to suppose that the lungs should require so much more copious a supply of nutriment, and that of so much purer and more spirituous a nature as coming immediately from the ventricle of the heart, that either the brain, with its peculiarly pure substance, or

[2] See the Commentary of the learned Hofmann upon the Sixth Book of Galen, "De Usu partium," a work which I first saw after I had written what precedes.

the eyes, with their lustrous and truly admirable structure, or the flesh of the heart itself, which is more suitably nourished by the coronary artery.

CHAPTER VIII

OF THE QUANTITY OF BLOOD PASSING THROUGH THE HEART FROM THE VEINS TO THE ARTERIES; AND OF THE CIRCULAR MOTION OF THE BLOOD

THUS far I have spoken of the passage of the blood from the veins into the arteries, and of the manner in which it is transmitted and distributed by the action of the heart; points to which some, moved either by the authority of Galen or Columbus, or the reasonings of others, will give in their adhesion. But what remains to be said upon the quantity and source of the blood which thus passes is of a character so novel and unheard-of that I not only fear injury to myself from the envy of a few, but I tremble lest I have mankind at large for my enemies, so much doth wont and custom become a second nature. Doctrine once sown strikes deep its root, and respect for antiquity influences all men. Still the die is cast, and my trust is in my love of truth and the candour of cultivated minds. And sooth to say, when I surveyed my mass of evidence, whether derived from vivisections, and my various reflections on them, or from the study of the ventricles of the heart and the vessels that enter into and issue from them, the symmetry and size of these conduits,—for nature doing nothing in vain, would never have given them so large a relative size without a purpose,—or from observing the arrangement and intimate structure of the valves in particular, and of the other parts of the heart in general, with many things besides, I frequently and seriously bethought me, and long revolved in my mind, what might be the quantity of blood which was transmitted, in how short a time its passage might be effected, and the like. But not finding it possible that this could be supplied by the juices of the ingested aliment without the veins on the one hand becoming drained, and the arteries on the other getting ruptured through the excessive charge of blood, unless the blood should somehow find its way from the arteries into the veins, and so return to the right side of the heart, I began to think whether there might not be a MOTION, AS IT WERE, IN A CIRCLE. Now, this I afterwards found to be true; and I finally saw that the blood, forced by the action of the left ventricle into the arteries, was distributed to the body at large, and its several parts, in the same manner as it is sent through the lungs, impelled by the right ventricle into the pulmonary artery, and that it then passed through the veins and along the vena cava, and so round to the left ventricle in the manner already indicated. This motion we may be allowed to call circular, in the same way as Aristotle says that the air and the rain emulate the circular motion of the superior bodies; for the moist earth, warmed by the sun, evaporates; the vapours drawn upwards are condensed, and descending in the form of rain, moisten the earth again. By this arrangement are generations of living things produced; and in like manner are tempests and meteors engendered by the circular motion, and by the approach and recession of the sun.

And similarly does it come to pass in the body, through the motion of the blood, that the various parts are nourished, cherished, quickened by the warmer, more perfect, vaporous, spirituous, and, as I may say, alimentive blood; which, on the other hand, owing to its contact with these parts, becomes cooled, coagulated, and so to speak effete. It then returns to its sovereign, the heart, as if to its source, or to the inmost home of the body, there to recover its state of excellence or perfection. Here it renews its fluidity, natural heat, and becomes powerful, fervid, a kind of treasury of life, and impregnated with spirits, it might be said with balsam. Thence it is again dispersed. All this depends on the motion and action of the heart.

The heart, consequently, is the beginning of life; the sun of the microcosm, even as the sun in his turn might well be designated the heart of the world; for it is the heart by whose virtue and pulse the blood is moved, perfected, and made nutrient, and is preserved from corruption and coagulation; it is the household divinity which, discharging its function, nourishes, cherishes, quickens the whole body, and is indeed the foundation of life, the source of all action. But of these things we shall speak more opportunely when we come to speculate upon the final cause of this motion of the heart.

As the blood-vessels, therefore, are the canals and agents that transport the blood, they are of two kinds, the cava and the aorta; and this not by reason of there being two sides of the body, as Aristotle has it, but because of the difference of office, not, as is commonly said, in consequence of any diversity of structure, for in many animals, as I have said, the vein does not differ from the artery in the thickness of its walls, but solely in virtue of their distinct functions and uses. A vein and an artery, both styled veins by the ancients, and that not without reason, as Galen has remarked, for the artery is the vessel which carries the blood from the heart to the body at large, the vein of the present day bringing it back from the general system to the heart; the former is the conduit from, the latter the channel to, the heart; the latter contains the cruder, effete blood, rendered unfit for nutrition; the former transmits the digested, perfect, peculiarly nutritive fluid

CHAPTER IX

That there is a Circulation of the Blood is Confirmed from the First Proposition

But lest anyone should say that we give them words only, and make mere specious assertions without any foundation, and desire to innovate without sufficient cause, three points present themselves for confirmation, which, being stated, I conceive that the truth I contend for will follow necessarily, and appear as a thing obvious to all. First, the blood is incessantly transmitted by the action of the heart from the vena cava to the arteries in such quantity that it cannot be supplied from the ingesta, and in such a manner that the whole must very quickly pass through the organ; second, the blood under the influence of the arterial pulse enters and is impelled in a continuous, equable, and incessant stream through every part and member of the body, in much larger quantity than were sufficient for nutrition, or than the whole mass of fluids could supply; third, the veins in like manner return this blood incessantly to the heart from parts and members of the body. These points proved, I conceive it will be manifest that the blood circulates, revolves, propelled and then returning, from the heart to the extremities, from the extremities to the heart, and thus that it performs a kind of circular motion.

Let us assume, either arbitrarily or from experiment, the quantity of blood which the left ventricle of the heart will contain when distended, to be, say, two ounces, three ounces, or one ounce and a half—in the dead body I have found it to hold upwards of two ounces. Let us assume further how much less the heart will hold in the contracted than in the dilated state; and how much blood it will project into the aorta upon each contraction; and all the world allows that with the systole something is always projected, a necessary consequence demonstrated in the third chapter, and obvious from the structure of the valves; and let us suppose as approaching the truth that the fourth, or fifth, or sixth, or even but the eighth part of its charge is thrown into the artery at each contraction; this would give either half an ounce, or three drachms, or one drachm of blood as propelled by the heart at each pulse into the aorta; which quantity, by reason of the valves at the root of the vessel, can by no means return into the ventricle. Now, in the course of half an hour, the heart will have made more than one thousand beats, in some as many as two, three, and even four thousand. Multiplying the number of drachms propelled by the number of pulses, we shall have either one thousand half ounces, or one thousand times three drachms, or a like proportional quantity of blood, according to the amount which we assume as propelled with each stroke of the heart, sent from this organ into the artery—a larger quantity in every case than is contained in the whole body! In the same way, in the sheep or dog, say but a single scruple of blood passes with each stroke of the heart, in one half-hour we should have one thousand scruples, or about three pounds and a half, of blood injected into the aorta; but the body of neither animal contains above four pounds of blood, a fact which I have myself ascertained in the case of the sheep.

Upon this supposition, therefore, assumed merely as a ground for reasoning, we see the whole mass of blood passing through the heart, from the veins to the arteries, and in like manner through the lungs.

But let it be said that this does not take place in half an hour, but in an hour, or even in a day; any way, it is still manifest that more blood passes through the heart in consequence of its action, than can either be supplied by the whole of the ingesta, or than can be contained in the veins at the same moment.

Nor can it be allowed that the heart in contracting sometimes propels and sometimes does not propel, or at most propels but very little, a mere nothing, or an imaginary something: all this, indeed, has already been refuted, and is, besides, contrary both to sense and reason. For if it be a necessary effect of the dilatation of the heart that its ventricles become filled with blood, it is equally so that, contracting, these cavities should expel their contents; and this not in any trifling measure. For neither are the conduits small, nor the contractions few in number, but frequent, and always in some certain proportion, whether it be a third or a sixth, or an eighth, to the total capacity of the ventricles, so that a like proportion of blood must be expelled, and a like proportion received with each stroke of the heart, the capacity of the ventricle contracted always bearing a certain relation to the capacity of the ventricle when dilated. And since, in dilating, the ventricles cannot be supposed to get filled with nothing, or with an imaginary something, so in contracting they never expel nothing or aught imaginary, but always a certain something, viz., blood, in proportion to the amount of the contraction. Whence it is to be concluded that if at one stroke the heart of man, the ox, or the sheep, ejects but a single drachm of blood and there are one thousand strokes in half an hour, in this interval there will have been ten pounds five ounces expelled; if with each stroke two drachms are expelled, the quantity would, of course, amount to twenty pounds and ten ounces; if half an ounce, the quantity would come to forty-one pounds and eight ounces; and were there one ounce, it would be as much as eighty-three pounds and four ounces; the whole of which, in the course of one-half hour, would have been transfused from the veins to the arteries. The actual quantity of blood expelled at each stroke of the heart, and the circumstances under which it is either greater or less than ordinary, I leave for particular determination afterwards, from numerous observations which I have made on the subject.

Meantime this much I know, and would here proclaim to all, that the blood is transfused at one time in larger, at another in smaller, quantity; and that the circuit of the blood is accomplished now more rapidly, now more slowly, according to the temperament, age, etc., of the individual, to external and internal circumstances, to naturals and non-naturals—sleep, rest, food, exercise, affections of the mind, and the like. But, supposing even the smallest quantity of blood to be passed through the heart and the lungs with each pulsation, a vastly greater amount would still be thrown into the arteries and whole body than could by any possibility be supplied by the food consumed. It could be furnished in no other way than by making a circuit and returning.

This truth, indeed, presents itself obviously before us when we consider what happens in the dissection of living animals; the great artery need not be divided, but a very small branch only (as Galen even proves in regard to man), to have the whole of the blood in the body, as well that of the veins as of the arteries, drained away in the course of no long time—some half-hour or less. Butchers are well aware of the fact and can bear witness to it; for, cutting the throat of an ox and so dividing the vessels of the neck, in less than a quarter of an hour they have all the vessels bloodless—the whole mass of blood has escaped. The same thing also occasionally occurs with great rapidity in performing amputations and removing tumors in the human subject.

Nor would this argument lose of its force, did any one say that in killing animals in the shambles, and performing amputations, the blood escaped in equal, if not perchance in larger quantity by the veins than by the arteries. The contrary of this statement, indeed, is certainly the truth; the veins, in fact, collapsing, and being without any propelling power, and further, because of the impediment of the valves, as I shall show immediately, pour out but very little blood; whilst the arteries spout it forth with force abundantly, impetuously, and as if it were propelled by a syringe. And then the experiment is easily tried of leaving the vein untouched and only dividing the artery in the neck of a sheep or dog, when it will be seen with what force, in what abundance, and how quickly, the whole blood in the body, of the veins as well as of the arteries, is emptied. But the arteries receive blood from the veins in no other way than by transmission through the heart, as we have already seen; so that if the aorta be tied at the base of the heart, and the carotid or any other artery be opened, no one will now be surprised to find it empty, and the veins only replete with blood.

And now the cause is manifest, why in our dissections we usually find so large a quantity of blood in the veins, so little in the arteries; why there is much in the right ventricle, little in the left, which probably led the ancients to believe that the arteries (as their name implies) contained nothing but spirits during the life of an animal. The true cause of the difference is perhaps this, that as there is no passage to the arteries, save through the lungs and heart, when an animal has ceased to breathe and the lungs to move, the blood in the pulmonary artery is prevented from passing into the pulmonary veins, and from thence into the left ventricle of the heart; just as we have already seen the same transit prevented in the embryo, by the want of movement in the lungs and the alternate opening and shutting of their hidden and invisible porosities and apertures. But the heart not ceasing to act at the same precise moment as the lungs, but surviving them and continuing to pulsate for a time, the left ventricle and arteries go on distributing their blood to the body at large and sending it into the veins; receiving none from the lungs, however, they are soon exhausted, and left, as it were, empty. But even this fact confirms our views, in no trifling manner, seeing that it can be ascribed to no other than the cause we have just assumed.

Moreover, it appears from this that the more frequently or forcibly the arteries pulsate, the more speedily will the body be exhausted of its blood during hemorrhage. Hence, also, it happens, that in fainting fits and in states of alarm, when the heart beats more languidly and less forcibly, hemorrhages are diminished and arrested.

Still further, it is from this, that after death, when the heart has ceased to beat, it is impossible, by dividing either the jugular or femoral veins and arteries, by any effort, to force out more than one-half of the whole mass of the blood. Neither could the butchers ever bleed the carcass effectually did he neglect to cut the throat of the ox which he has knocked on the head and stunned, before the heart had ceased beating.

Finally, we are now in a condition to suspect wherefore it is that no one has yet said anything to the purpose upon the anastomosis of the veins and arteries, either as to where or how it is effected, or for what purpose. I now enter upon the investigation of the subject.

CHAPTER X

THE FIRST POSITION: OF THE QUANTITY OF BLOOD PASSING FROM THE VEINS TO THE ARTERIES. AND THAT THERE IS A CIRCUIT OF THE BLOOD, FREED FROM OBJECTIONS, AND FARTHER CONFIRMED BY EXPERIMENT

So far our first position is confirmed, whether the thing be referred to calculation or to experiment and dissection, viz., that the blood is incessantly poured into the arteries in larger quantities than it can be supplied by the food; so that the whole passing over in a short space of time, it is matter of necessity that the blood perform a circuit, that it return to whence it set out.

But if anyone shall here object that a large quantity may pass through and yet no necessity be found for a circulation, that all may come from the meat and drink consumed, and quote as an illustration the abundant supply of milk in the mammæ—for a cow will give three, four, and even seven gallons and more in a day, and a woman two or three pints whilst nursing a child or twins, which must manifestly be derived from the food consumed; it may be answered that the heart by computation does as much and more in the course of an hour or two.

And if not yet convinced, he shall still insist that when an artery is divided, a preternatural route is, as it were, opened, and that so the blood escapes in torrents, but that the same thing does not happen in the healthy and uninjured body when no outlet is made; and that in arteries filled, or in their natural state, so large a quantity of blood cannot pass in so short a space of time as to make any return necessary—to all this it may be answered that, from the calculation already made, and the reasons assigned, it appears that by so much as the heart in its dilated state contains, in addition to its contents in the state of constriction, so much in a general way must it emit upon each pulsation, and in such quantity must the blood pass, the body being entire and naturally constituted.

But in serpents, and several fishes, by tying the veins some way below the heart you will perceive a space between the ligature and the heart speedily to become empty; so that, unless you would deny the evidence of your senses, you must needs admit the return of the blood to the heart. The same thing will also plainly appear when we come to discuss our second position.

Let us here conclude with a single example, confirming all that has been said, and from which everyone may obtain conviction through the testimony of his own eyes.

If a live snake be laid open, the heart will be seen pulsating quietly, distinctly, for more than an hour, moving like a worm, contracting in its longitudinal dimensions, (for it is of an oblong shape), and propelling its contents. It becomes of a paler colour in the systole, of a deeper tint in the diastole; and almost all things else are seen by which I have already said that the truth I contend for is established, only that here everything takes place more slowly, and is more distinct. This point in particular may be observed more clearly than the noonday sun: the vena cava enters the heart at its lower part, the artery quits it at the superior part; the vein being now seized either with forceps or between the finger and the thumb, and the course of the blood for some space below the heart interrupted, you will perceive the part that intervenes between the fingers and the heart almost immediately to become empty, the blood being exhausted by the action of the heart; at the same time the heart will become of a much paler colour, even in its state of dilatation, than it was before; it is also smaller than at first, from wanting blood: and then it begins to beat more slowly, so that it seems at length as if it were about to die. But the impediment to the flow of blood being removed, instantly the colour and the size of the heart are restored.

If, on the contrary, the artery instead of the vein be compressed or tied, you will observe the part between the obstacle and the heart, and the heart itself, to become inordinately distended, to assume a deep purple or even livid colour, and at length to be so much oppressed with blood that you will believe it about to be choked; but the obstacle removed, all things immediately return to their natural state and colour, size, and impulse.

Here then we have evidence of two kinds of death: extinction from deficiency, and suffocation from excess. Examples of both have now been set before you, and you have had opportunity of viewing the truth contended for with your own eyes in the heart.

CHAPTER XI

The Second Position is Demonstrated

THAT this may the more clearly appear to everyone, I have here to cite certain experiments, from which it seems obvious that the blood enters a limb by the arteries, and returns from it by the veins; that the arteries are the vessels carrying the blood from the heart, and the veins the returning channels of the blood to the heart; that in the limbs and extreme parts of the body the blood passes either immediately by anastomosis from the arteries into the veins, or mediately by the porosities of the flesh, or in both ways, as has already been said in speaking of the passage of the blood through the lungs whence it appears manifest that in the circuit the blood moves from that place to this place, and from that point to this one; from the centre to the extremities, to wit; and from the extreme parts back to the centre. Finally, upon grounds of calculation, with the same elements as before, it will be obvious that the quantity can neither be accounted for by the ingesta, nor yet be held necessary to nutrition.

The same thing will also appear in regard to ligatures, and wherefore they are said to *draw;* though this is neither from the heat, nor the pain, nor the vacuum they occasion, nor indeed from any other cause yet thought of; it will also explain the uses and advantages to be derived from ligatures in medicine, the principle upon which they either suppress or occasion hemorrhage; how they induce sloughing and more extensive mortification in extremities; and how they act in the castration of animals and the removal of warts and fleshy tumours. But it has come to pass, from no one having duly weighed and understood the cause and rationale of these various effects, that though almost all, upon the faith of the old writers, recommend ligatures in the treatment of disease, yet very few comprehend their proper employment, or derive any real assistance from them in effecting cures.

Ligatures are either very tight or of medium tightness. A ligature I designate as tight or perfect when it so constricts an extremity that no vessel can be felt pulsating beyond it. Such a ligature we use in amputations to control the flow of blood; and such also are employed in the castration of animals and the ablation of tumours. In the latter instances, all afflux of nutriment and heat being prevented by the ligature, we see the testes and large fleshy tumours dwindle, die, and finally fall off.

Ligatures of medium tightness I regard as those which compress a limb firmly all round, but short of pain, and in such a way as still suffers a certain degree of pulsation to be felt in the artery beyond them. Such a ligature is in use in blood-letting, an operation in which the fillet applied above the elbow is not drawn so tight but that the arteries at the wrist may still be felt beating under the finger.

Now let anyone make an experiment upon the arm of a man, either using such a fillet as is employed in blood-letting, or grasping the limb lightly with his hand, the best subject for it being one who is lean, and who has large veins, and the best time after exercise, when the body is warm, the pulse is full, and the blood carried in larger quantity to the extremities, for all then is more conspicuous; under such circumstances let a ligature be thrown about the extremity, and drawn as tightly as can be borne, it will first be perceived that beyond the ligature, neither in the wrist nor anywhere else, do the arteries pulsate, at the same time that immediately above the ligature the artery begins to rise higher at each diastole, to throb more violently, and to swell in its vicinity with a kind of tide, as if it strove to break through and overcome the obstacle to its current; the artery here, in short, appears as if it were preternaturally full. The hand under such circumstances retains its natural colour and appearance; in the course of time it begins to fall somewhat in temperature, indeed, but nothing is *drawn* into it.

After the bandage has been kept on for some short time in this way, let it be slackened a little, brought to that state or term of medium tightness which is used in bleeding, and it will be seen that the whole hand and arm will instantly become deeply coloured and distended, and the veins show themselves tumid and knotted; after ten or twelve pulses of the artery, the hand will be perceived excessively distended, injected, gorged with blood, *drawn,* as it is said, by this medium ligature, without pain, or heat, or any horror of a vacuum, or any other cause yet indicated.

If the finger be applied over the artery as it is pulsating by the edge of the fillet, at the moment of slackening it, the blood will be felt to glide through, as it were, underneath the finger; and he, too, upon whose arm the experiment is made, when the ligature is slackened, is distinctly conscious of a sensation of warmth, and of something, viz., a stream of blood suddenly making its way along the course of the vessels and diffusing itself through the hand, which at the same time begins to feel hot, and becomes distended.

As we had noted, in connexion with the tight ligature, that the artery above the bandage was distended and pulsated, not below it, so, in the case of the moderately tight bandage, on the contrary, do we find that the veins below, never above, the fillet, swell, and become dilated, whilst the arteries shrink; and such is the degree of distension of the veins here, that it is only very strong pressure that will force the blood beyond the fillet, and cause any of the veins in the upper part of the arm to rise.

From these facts it is easy for every careful observer to learn that the blood enters an extremity by the arteries; for when they are effectually compressed nothing is *drawn* to the member; the hand preserves its colour; nothing flows into it, neither is it distended; but when the pressure is diminished, as it is with the bleeding fillet, it is manifest that the blood is instantly thrown in with force, for then the hand begins to swell; which is as much as to say, that when the arteries pulsate the blood is flowing through them, as it is when the moderately tight ligature is applied; but where they do not pulsate, as, when a tight ligature is used, they cease from transmitting anything, they are only distended above the part where the ligature is applied. The veins again being compressed, nothing can flow through them; the certain indication of which is, that below the ligature they are much more tumid than above it, and than they usually appear when there is no bandage upon the arm.

It therefore plainly appears that the ligature prevents the return of the blood through the veins to the parts above it, and maintains those beneath it in a state of permanent distension. But the arteries, in spite of its pressure, and under the force and impulse of the heart, send on the blood from the internal parts of the body to the parts beyond the ligature. And herein consists the difference between the tight and the medium ligature, that the former not only prevents the passage of the blood in the veins, but in the arteries also; the latter, however, whilst it does not prevent the force of the pulse from extending beyond it, and so propelling the blood to the extremities of the body, compresses the veins, and greatly or altogether impedes the return of the blood through them.

Seeing, therefore, that the moderately tight ligature renders the veins turgid and distended, and the whole hand full of blood, I ask, whence is this? Does the blood accumulate below the ligature coming through the veins, or through the arteries, or passing by certain hidden porosities? Through the veins it cannot come; still less can it come through invisible channels; it must needs, then, arrive by the arteries, in conformity with all that has been already said. That it cannot flow in by the veins appears plainly enough from the fact that the blood cannot be forced towards the heart unless the ligature be removed; when this is done suddenly all the veins collapse, and disgorge themselves of their contents into the superior parts, the hand at the same time resumes its natural pale colour, the tumefaction and the stagnating blood having disappeared.

Moreover, he whose arm or wrist has thus been bound for some little time with the medium bandage, so that it has not only got swollen and livid but cold, when the fillet is undone is aware of something cold making its way upwards along with the returning blood, and reaching the elbow or the axilla. And I have myself been inclined to think that this cold blood rising upwards to the heart was the cause of the fainting that often occurs after blood-letting: fainting frequently supervenes even in robust subjects, and mostly at the moment of undoing the fillet, as the vulgar say, from the turning of the blood.

Farther, when we see the veins below the ligature instantly swell up and become gorged, when from extreme tightness it is somewhat relaxed, the arteries meantime continuing unaffected, this is an obvious indication that the blood passes from the arteries into the veins, and not from the veins into the arteries, and that there is either an anastomosis of the two orders of vessels, or porosities in the flesh and solid parts generally that are permeable to the blood. It is farther an indication that the veins have frequent communications with one another, because they all become turgid together, whilst under the medium ligature applied above the elbow; and if any single small vein be pricked with a lancet, they all speedily shrink, and disburthening themselves into this they subside almost simultaneously.

These considerations will enable anyone to understand the nature of the attraction that is exerted by ligatures, and perchance of fluxes generally; how, for example, when the veins are compressed by a bandage of medium tightness applied above the elbow, the blood cannot escape, whilst it still continues to be driven in, by the forcing power of the heart, by which the parts are of necessity filled, gorged with blood. And how should it be otherwise? Heat and pain and a vacuum draw, indeed; but in such wise only that parts are filled, not preternaturally distended or gorged, and not so suddenly and violently overwhelmed with the charge of blood forced in upon them, that the flesh is lacerated and the vessels ruptured. Nothing of the kind as an effect of heat, or pain, or the vacuum force, is either credible or demonstrable.

Besides, the ligature is competent to occasion the afflux in question without either pain, or heat, or a vacuum. Were pain in any way the cause, how should it happen that, with the arm bound above the elbow, the hand and fingers should swell below the bandage, and their veins become distended? The pressure of the bandage certainly prevents the blood from getting there by the veins. And then, wherefore is there neither swelling nor repletion of the veins, nor any sign or symptom of attraction or afflux, above the ligature? But this is the obvious cause of the preternatural attraction and swelling below the bandage, and in the hand and fingers, that the blood is entering abundantly, and with force, but cannot pass out again.

Now is not this the cause of all tumefaction, as indeed Avicenna has it, and of all oppressive redundancy in parts, that the access to them is open, but the egress from them is closed? Whence it comes that they are gorged and tumefied. And may not the same thing happen in local inflammations, where, so long as the swelling is on the increase, and has not reached its extreme term, a full pulse is felt in the part, especially when the disease is of the more acute kind, and the swelling usually takes place most rapidly. But these are matters for after discussion. Or does this, which occurred in my own case, happen from the same cause? Thrown from a carriage upon one occasion, I struck my forehead a blow upon the place where a twig of the artery advances from the temple, and immediately, within the time in which twenty beats could have been made I felt a tumour the size of an egg developed, without either heat or any great pain: the near vicinity of the artery had caused the blood to be effused into the bruised part with unusual force and velocity.

And now, too, we understand why in phlebotomy we apply our ligature above the part that is punctured, not below it; did the flow come from above, not from below, the constriction in this case would not only be of no service, but would prove a positive hindrance; it would have to be applied below the orifice, in order to have the flow more free, did the blood descend by the veins from superior to inferior parts; but as it is elsewhere forced through the extreme arteries into the extreme veins, and the return in these last is opposed by the ligature, so do they fill and swell, and being thus filled and distended, they are made capable of projecting their charge with force, and to a distance, when any one of them is suddenly punctured; but the ligature being slackened, and the returning channels thus left open, the blood forthwith no longer escapes, save by drops; and, as all the world knows, if in performing phlebotomy the bandage be either slackened too much or the limb be bound too tightly, the blood escapes without force, because in the one case the returning channels are not adequately obstructed; in the other the channels of influx, the arteries, are impeded.

CHAPTER XII

THAT THERE IS A CIRCULATION OF THE BLOOD IS SHOWN FROM THE SECOND POSITION DEMONSTRATED

If these things be so, another point which I have already referred to, viz., the continual passage of the blood through the heart will also be confirmed. We have seen, that the blood passes from the arteries into the veins, not from the veins into the arteries; we have seen, farther, that almost the whole of the blood may be withdrawn from a puncture made in one of the cutaneous veins of the arm if a bandage properly applied be used; we have seen, still farther, that the blood flows so freely and rapidly that not only is the whole quantity which was contained in the arm beyond the ligature, and before the puncture was made, discharged, but the whole which is contained in the body, both that of the arteries and that of the veins.

Whence we must admit, first, that the blood is sent along with an impulse, and that it is urged with force below the ligature; for it escapes with force, which force it receives from the pulse and power of the heart; for the force and motion of the blood are derived from the heart alone. Second, that the afflux proceeds from the heart, and through the heart by a course from the great veins; for it gets into the parts below the ligature through the arteries, not through the veins; and the arteries nowhere receive blood from the veins, nowhere receive blood save and except from the left ventricle of the heart. Nor could so large a quantity of blood be drawn from one vein (a ligature having been duly applied), nor with such impetuousity, such readiness, such celerity, unless through the medium of the impelling power of the heart.

But if all things be as they are now represented, we shall feel ourselves at liberty to calculate the quantity of the blood, and to reason on its circular motion. Should anyone, for instance, performing phlebotomy, suffer the blood to flow in the manner it usually does, with force and freely, for some half hour or so, no question but that the greatest part of the blood being abstracted, faintings and syncopes would ensue, and that not only would the arteries but the great veins also be nearly emptied of their contents. It is only consonant with reason to conclude that in the course of the half hour hinted at, so much as has escaped has also passed from the great veins through the heart into the aorta. And further, if we calculate how many ounces flow through one arm, or how many pass in twenty or thirty pulsations under the medium ligature, we shall have some grounds for estimating how much passes through the other arm in the same space of time: how much through both lower extremities, how much through the neck on either side, and through all the other arteries and veins of the body, all of which have been supplied with fresh blood, and as this blood must have passed through the lungs and ventricles of the heart, and must have come from the great veins,— we shall perceive that a circulation is absolutely necessary, seeing that the quantities hinted at cannot be supplied immediately from the ingesta, and are vastly more than can be requisite for the mere nutrition of the parts.

It is still further to be observed, that in practising phlebotomy the truths contended for are sometimes confirmed in another way; for having tied up the arm properly, and made the puncture duly, still, if from alarm or any other causes, a state of faintness supervenes, in which the heart always pulsates more languidly, the blood does not flow freely, but distils by drops only. The reason is, that with a somewhat greater than usual resistance offered to the transit of the blood by the bandage, coupled with the weaker action of the heart, and its diminished impelling power, the stream cannot make its way under the ligature; and farther, owing to the weak and languishing state of the heart, the blood is not transferred in such quantity as wont from the veins to the arteries through the sinuses of that organ. So also, and for the same reasons, are the menstrual fluxes of women, and indeed hemorrhages of every kind, controlled. And now, a contrary state of things occurring, the patient getting rid of his fear and recovering his courage, the pulse strength is increased, the arteries begin again to beat with greater force, and to drive the blood even into the part that is bound; so that the blood now springs from the puncture in the vein, and flows in a continuous stream.

CHAPTER XIII

The Third Position is Confirmed: and the Circulation of the Blood is Demonstrated from It

Thus far we have spoken of the quantity of blood passing through the heart and the lungs in the centre of the body, and in like manner from the arteries into the veins in the peripheral parts and the body at large. We have yet to explain, however, in what manner the blood finds its way back to the heart from the extremities by the veins, and how and in what way these are the only vessels that convey the blood from the external to the central parts; which done, I conceive that the three fundamental propositions laid down for the circulation of the blood will be so plain, so well established, so obviously true, that they may claim general credence. Now the remaining position will be made sufficiently clear from the valves which are found in the cavities of the veins themselves, from the uses of these, and from experiments cognizable by the senses.

The celebrated Hieronymus Fabricius of Aquapendente, a most skilful anatomist, and venerable old man, or, as the learned Riolan will have it, Jacobus Silvius, first gave representations of the valves in the veins, which consist of raised or loose portions of the inner membranes of these vessels, of extreme delicacy, and a sigmoid or semilunar shape. They are situated at different distances from one another, and diversely in different individuals; they are connate at the sides of the veins; they are directed upwards towards the trunks of the veins; the two—for there are for the most part two together—regard each other, mutually touch, and are so ready to come into contact by their edges, that if anything attempts to pass from the trunks into the branches of the veins, or from the greater vessels into the less, they completely prevent it; they are farther so arranged, that the horns of those that succeed are opposite the middle of the convexity of those that precede, and so on alternately.

The discoverer of these valves did not rightly understand their use, nor have succeeding anatomists added anything to our knowledge: for their office is by no means explained when we are told that it is to hinder the blood, by its weight, from all flowing into inferior parts; for the edges of the valves in the jugular veins hang downwards, and are so contrived that they prevent the blood from rising upwards; the valves, in a word, do not invariably look upwards, but always toward the trunks of the veins, invariably towards the seat of the heart. I, and indeed others, have sometimes found valves in the emulgent veins, and in those of the mesentery, the edges of which were directed towards the vena cava and vena portæ. Let it be added that there are no valves in the arteries, and that dogs, oxen, etc., have invariably valves at the divisions of their crural veins, in the veins that meet towards the top of the os sacrum, and in those branches which come from the haunches, in which no such effect of gravity from the erect position was to be apprehended. Neither are there valves in the jugular veins for the purpose of guarding against apoplexy, as some have said; because in sleep the head is more apt to be influenced by the contents of the carotid arteries. Neither are the valves present, in order that the blood may be retained in the divarications or smaller trunks and minuter branches, and not be suffered to flow entirely into the more open and capacious channels; for they occur where there are no divarications; although it must be owned that they are most frequent at the points where branches join. Neither do they exist for the purpose of rendering the current of blood more slow from the centre of the body; for it seems likely that the blood would be disposed to flow with sufficient slowness of its own accord, as it would have to pass from larger into continually smaller vessels, being separated from the mass and fountain head, and attaining from warmer into colder places.

But the valves are solely made and instituted lest the blood should pass from the greater into the lesser veins, and either rupture them or cause them to become varicose; lest, instead of advancing from the extreme to the central parts of the body, the blood should rather proceed along the veins from the centre to the extremities; but the delicate valves, while they readily open in the right direction, entirely prevent all such contrary motion, being so situated and arranged, that if anything escapes, or is less perfectly obstructed by the cornua of the one above, the fluid passing, as it were, by the chinks between the cornua, it is immediately received on the convexity of the one beneath, which is placed transversely with reference to the former, and so is effectually hindered from getting any farther.

And this I have frequently experienced in my dissections of the veins: if I attempted to pass a probe from the trunk of the veins into one of the smaller branches, whatever care I took I found it impossible to introduce it far any way, by reason of the valves; whilst, on the contrary, it was most easy to push it along in the opposite direction, from without inwards, or from the branches towards the trunks and roots. In many places two valves are so placed and fitted, that when raised they come exactly together in the middle of the vein, and are there united by the contact of their margins; and so accurate is the adaptation, that neither by the eye nor by any other means of examination, can the slightest chink along the line of contact be perceived. But if the probe be now introduced from the extreme towards the more central parts, the valves, like the floodgates of a river, give way, and are most readily pushed aside. The effect of this arrangement plainly is to prevent all motion of the blood from the heart and vena cava, whether it be upwards towards the head, or downwards towards the feet, or to either side towards the arms, not a drop can pass; all motion of the blood, beginning in the larger and tending towards the smaller veins, is opposed and resisted by them; whilst the motion that proceeds from the lesser to end in the larger branches is favoured, or, at all events, a free and open passage is left for it.

But that this truth may be made the more apparent, let an arm be tied up above the elbow as if for phlebotomy (A, A, fig. 1). At intervals in the course of the veins, especially in labouring people and those whose veins are large, certain knots or elevations (B, C, D, E, F) will be perceived, and this not only at the places where a branch is received (E. F), but also where none enters (C, D): these knots or risings are all formed by valves, which thus show themselves externally. And now if you press the blood from the space above one of the valves, from H to O, (fig. 2,) and keep the point of a finger upon the vein inferiorly, you will see no influx of blood from above; the portion of the vein between the point of the finger and the valve O will be obliterated; yet will the vessel continue sufficiently distended above the valve (O, G). The blood being thus pressed out, and the vein emptied, if you now apply a finger of the other hand upon the distended part of the vein above the valve O, (fig. 3,) and press downwards, you will find that you cannot force the blood through or beyond the valve; but the greater effort you use, you will only see the portion of vein that is between the finger and the valve become more distended, that portion of the vein which is below the valve remaining all the while empty (H, O, fig. 3).

It would therefore appear that the function of the valves in the veins is the same as that of the three sigmoid valves which we find at the commencement of the aorta and pulmonary artery, viz., to prevent all reflux of the blood that is passing over them.

[NOTE.—Woodcuts of the veins of the arm to which these letters and figures refer appear here in the original.— C. N. B. C.]

Farther, the arm being bound as before, and the veins looking full and distended, if you press at one part in the course of a vein with the point of a finger (L, fig. 4), and then with another finger streak the blood upwards beyond the next valve (N), you will perceive that this portion of the vein continues empty (L. N), and that the blood cannot retrograde, precisely as we have already seen the case to be in fig. 2; but the finger first applied (H, fig. 2, L, fig. 4), being removed, immediately the vein is filled from below, and the arm becomes as it appears at D C, fig. 1. That the blood in the veins therefore proceeds from inferior or more remote parts, and towards the heart, moving in these vessels in this and not in the contrary direction, appears most obviously. And although in some places the valves, by not acting with such perfect accuracy, or where there is but a single valve, do not seem totally to prevent the passage of the blood from the centre, still the greater number of them plainly do so; and then, where things appear contrived more negligently, this is compensated either by the more frequent occurrence or more perfect action of the succeeding valves, or in some other way: the veins in short, as they are the free and open conduits of the blood returning *to* the heart, so are they effectually prevented from serving as its channels of distribution *from* the heart.

But this other circumstance has to be noted: The arm being bound, and the veins made turgid, and the valves prominent, as before, apply the thumb or finger over a vein in the situation of one of the valves in such a way as to compress it, and prevent any blood from passing upwards from the hand; then, with a finger of the other hand, streak the blood in the vein upwards till it has passed the next valve above (N, fig. 4), the vessel now remains empty; but the finger at L being removed for an instant, the vein is immediately filled from below; apply the finger again, and having in the same manner streaked the blood upwards, again remove the finger below, and again the vessel becomes distended as before; and this repeat, say a thousand times, in a short space of time. And now compute the quantity of blood which you have thus pressed up beyond the valve, and then multiplying the assumed quantity by one thousand, you will find that so much blood has passed through a certain portion of the vessel; and I do now believe that you will find yourself convinced of the circulation of the blood, and of its rapid motion. But if in this experiment you say that a violence is done to nature, I do not doubt but that, if you proceed in the same way, only taking as great a length of vein as possible, and merely remark with what rapidity the blood flows upwards, and fills the vessel from below, you will come to the same conclusion.

CHAPTER XIV

CONCLUSION OF THE DEMONSTRATION OF THE CIRCULATION

AND now I may be allowed to give in brief my view of the circulation of the blood, and to propose it for general adoption.

Since all things, both argument and ocular demonstration, show that the blood passes through the lungs, and heart by the force of the ventricles, and is sent for distribution to all parts of the body, where it makes its way into the veins and porosities of the flesh, and then flows by the veins from the circumference on every side to the centre, from the lesser to the greater veins, and is by them finally discharged into the vena cava and right auricle of the heart, and this in such a quantity or in such a flux and reflux thither by the arteries, hither by the veins, as cannot possibly be supplied by the ingesta, and is much greater than can be required for mere purposes of nutrition; it is absolutely necessary to conclude that the blood in the animal body is impelled in a circle, and is in a state of ceaseless motion; that this is the act or function which the heart performs by means of its pulse; and that it is the sole and only end of the motion and contraction of the heart.

CHAPTER XV

THE CIRCULATION OF THE BLOOD IS FURTHER CONFIRMED BY PROBABLE REASONS

IT will not be foreign to the subject if I here show further, from certain familiar reasonings, that the circulation is matter both of convenience and necessity. In the first place, since death is a corruption which takes place through deficiency of heat,[1] and since all living things are warm, all dying things cold, there must be a particular seat and fountain, a kind of home and hearth, where the cherisher of nature, the original of the native fire, is stored and preserved; from which heat and life are dispensed to all

[1] Aristoteles De Respiratione, lib. ii et iii: De Part. Animal. et alibi.

parts as from a fountain head; from which sustenance may be derived; and upon which concoction and nutrition, and all vegetative energy may depend. Now, that the heart is this place, that the heart is the principle of life, and that all passes in the manner just mentioned, I trust no one will deny.

The blood, therefore, required to have motion, and indeed such a motion that it should return again to the heart; for sent to the external parts of the body far from its fountain, as Aristotle says, and without motion, it would become congealed. For we see motion generating and keeping up heat and spirits under all circumstances, and rest allowing them to escape and be dissipated. The blood, therefore, becoming thick or congealed by the cold of the extreme and outward parts, and robbed of its spirits, just as it is in the dead, it was imperative that from its fount and origin, it should again receive heat and spirits, and all else requisite to its preservation—that, by returning, it should be renovated and restored.

We frequently see how the extremities are chilled by the external cold, how the nose and cheeks and hands look blue, and how the blood, stagnating in them as in the pendent or lower parts of a corpse, becomes of a dusky hue; the limbs at the same time getting torpid, so that they can scarcely be moved, and seem almost to have lost their vitality. Now they can by no means be so effectually, and especially so speedily restored to heat and colour and life, as by a new efflux and contact of heat from its source. But how can parts attract in which the heat and life are almost extinct? Or how should they whose passages are filled with condensed and frigid blood, admit fresh aliment—renovated blood—unless they had first got rid of their old contents? Unless the heart were truly that fountain where life and heat are restored to the refrigerated fluid, and whence new blood, warm, imbued with spirits, being sent out by the arteries, that which has become cooled and effete is forced on, and all the particles recover their heat which was failing, and their vital stimulus wellnigh exhausted.

Hence it is that if the heart be unaffected, life and health may be restored to almost all the other parts of the body;

but if the heart be chilled, or smitten with any serious disease, it seems matter of necessity that the whole animal fabric should suffer and fall into decay. When the source is corrupted, there is nothing, as Aristotle says,[2] which can be of service either to it or aught that depends on it. And hence, by the way, it may perchance be why grief, and love, and envy, and anxiety, and all affections of the mind of a similar kind are accompanied with emaciation and decay, or with disordered fluids and crudity, which engender all manner of diseases and consume the body of man. For every affection of the mind that is attended with either pain or pleasure, hope or fear, is the cause of an agitation whose influence extends to the heart, and there induces change from the natural constitution, in the temperature, the pulse and the rest, which impairing all nutrition in its source and abating the powers at large, it is no wonder that various forms of incurable disease in the extremities and in the trunk are the consequence, inasmuch as in such circumstances the whole body labours under the effects of vitiated nutrition and a want of native heat.

Moreover, when we see that all animals live through food digested in their interior, it is imperative that the digestion and distribution be perfect, and, as a consequence, that there be a place and receptacle where the aliment is perfected and whence it is distributed to the several members. Now this place is the heart, for it is the only organ in the body which contains blood for the general use; all the others receive it merely for their peculiar or private advantage, just as the heart also has a supply for its own especial behoof in its coronary veins and arteries. But it is of the store which the heart contains in its auricles and ventricles that I here speak. Then the heart is the only organ which is so situated and constituted that it can distribute the blood in due proportion to the several parts of the body, the quantity sent to each being according to the dimensions of the artery which supplies it, the heart serving as a magazine or fountain ready to meet its demands.

[2] De Part. Animal., iii.

Further, a certain impulse or force, as well as an impeller or forcer, such as the heart, was required to effect this distribution and motion of the blood; both because the blood is disposed from slight causes, such as cold, alarm, horror, and the like, to collect in its source, to concentrate like parts to a whole, or the drops of water spilt upon a table to the mass of liquid; and because it is forced from the capillary veins into the smaller ramifications, and from these into the larger trunks by the motion of the extremities and the compression of the muscles generally. The blood is thus more disposed to move from the circumference to the centre than in the opposite direction, even were there no valves to oppose its motion; wherefore, that it may leave its source and enter more confined and colder channels, and flow against the direction to which it spontaneously inclines, the blood requires both force and impelling power. Now such is the heart and the heart alone, and that in the way and manner already explained.

CHAPTER XVI

The Circulation of the Blood is Further Proved from Certain Consequences

There are still certain problems, which, taken as consequences of this truth assumed as proven, are not without their use in exciting belief, as it were, *a posteriore;* and which, although they may seem to be involved in much doubt and obscurity, nevertheless readily admit of having reasons and causes assigned for them. Of such a nature are those that present themselves in connexion with contagions, poisoned wounds, the bites of serpents and rabid animals, lues venerea and the like. We sometimes see the whole system contaminated, though the part first infected remains sound; the lues venerea has occasionally made its attack with pains in the shoulders and head, and other symptoms, the genital organs being all the while unaffected; and then we know that the wound made by a rabid dog having healed, fever and a train of disastrous symptoms may nevertheless supervene. Whence it appears that the contagion impressed upon or deposited in a particular part, is by-and-by carried by the returning current of blood to the heart, and by that organ is sent to contaminate the whole body.

In tertian fever, the morbific cause seeking the heart in the first instance, and hanging about the heart and lungs, renders the patient short-winded, disposed to sighing, and indisposed to exertion, because the vital principle is oppressed and the blood forced into the lungs and rendered thick. It does not pass through them, (as I have myself seen in opening the bodies of those who had died in the beginning of the attack,) when the pulse is always frequent, small, and occasionally irregular; but the heat increasing, the matter becoming attenuated, the passages forced, and the transit made, the whole body begins to rise in temperature, and the pulse becomes fuller and stronger. The febrile paroxysm is fully formed, whilst the preternatural heat kindled in the heart is thence diffused by the arteries through the whole body along with the morbific matter, which is in this way overcome and dissolved by nature.

When we perceive, further, that medicines applied externally exert their influence on the body just as if they had been taken internally, the truth we are contending for is confirmed. Colocynth and aloes in this way move the belly, cantharides excites the urine, garlic applied to the soles of the feet assists expectoration, cordials strengthen, and an infinite number of examples of the same kind might be cited. Perhaps it will not, therefore, be found unreasonable, if we say that the veins, by means of their orifices, absorb some of the things that are applied externally and carry this inwards with the blood, not otherwise, it may be, than those of the mesentery imbibe the chyle from the intestines and carry it mixed with the blood to the liver. For the blood entering the mesentery by the cœliac artery, and the superior and inferior mesenterics, proceeds to the intestines, from which, along with the chyle that has been attracted into the veins, it returns by their numerous ramifications into the vena portæ of the liver, and from this into the vena cava, and this in such wise that the blood in these veins has the same colour and consistency as in other veins, in opposition to what many believe to be the fact. Nor indeed can we imagine two contrary motions in any capillary system—the chyle upwards, the blood downwards. This could scarcely take place, and must be held as altogether improbable. But is not the thing rather arranged as it is by the consummate providence of nature? For were the chyle mingled with the blood, the crude with the digested, in equal proportions, the result would not be concoction, transmutation, and sanguification, but rather, and because they are severally active and passive, a mixture or combination, or medium compound of the two, precisely as happens when wine is mixed with water and syrup. But when a very minute quantity of chyle is mingled with a very large quantity of circulating blood, a quantity of chyle that bears no kind of proportion to the mass of blood, the effect is the same, as Aristotle says, as when a drop of water is added to a cask of wine, or the contrary; the mass does not then present itself as a mixture, but is still sensibly either wine or water.

So in the mesenteric veins of an animal we do not find either chyme or chyle and blood, blended together or distinct, but only blood, the same in colour, consistency, and other sensible properties, as it appears in the veins generally. Still as there is a certain though small and inappreciable portion of chyle or incompletely digested matter mingled with the blood, nature has interposed the liver, in whose meandering channels it suffers delay and undergoes additional change, lest arriving prematurely and crude at the heart, it should oppress the vital principle. Hence in the embryo, there is almost no use for the liver, but the umbilical vein passes directly through, a foramen or an anastomosis existing from the vena portæ. The blood returns from the intestines of the fœtus, not through the liver, but into the umbilical vein mentioned, and flows at once into the heart, mingled with the natural blood which is returning from the placenta; whence also it is that in the development of the fœtus the liver is one of the organs that is last formed. I have observed all the members perfectly marked out in the human fœtus, even the genital organs, whilst there was yet scarcely any trace of the liver. And indeed at the period when all the parts, like the heart itself in the beginning, are still white, and except in the veins there is no appearance of redness, you shall see nothing in the seat of the liver but a shapeless collection, as it were, of extravasated blood, which you might take for the effects of a contusion or ruptured vein.

But in the incubated egg there are, as it were, two umbilical vessels, one from the albumen passing entire through the liver, and going straight to the heart; another from the yelk, ending in the vena portæ; for it appears that the chick, in the first instance, is entirely formed and nourished by the white; but by the yelk after it has come to perfection and is excluded from the shell; for this part may still be found in the abdomen of the chick many days after its exclusion, and is a substitute for the milk to other animals.

But these matters will be better spoken of in my observations on the formation of the fœtus, where many propositions, the following among the number, will be discussed: Wherefore is this part formed or perfected first, that last, and of the several members, what part is the cause of another? And there are many points having special reference to the heart, such as wherefore does it first acquire consistency, and appear to possess life, motion, sense, before any other part of the body is perfected, as Aristotle says in his third book, "De partibus Animalium"? And so also of the blood, wherefore does it precede all the rest? And in what way does it possess the vital and animal principle, and show a tendency to motion, and to be impelled hither and thither, the end for which the heart appears to be made? In the same way, in considering the pulse, why should one kind of pulse indicate death, another recovery? And so of all the other kinds of pulse, what may be the cause and indication of each? Likewise we must consider the reason of crises and natural critical discharges; of nutrition, and especially the distribution of the nutriment; and of defluxions of every description. Finally, reflecting on every part of medicine, physiology, pathology, semeiotics and therapeutics, when I see how many questions can be answered, how many doubts resolved, how much obscurity illustrated by the truth we have declared, the light we have made to shine, I see a field of such vast extent in which I might proceed so far, and expatiate so widely, that this my tractate would not only swell out into a volume, which was beyond my purpose, but my whole life, perchance, would not suffice for its completion.

In this place, therefore, and that indeed in a single chapter, I shall only endeavour to refer the various particulars that present themselves in the dissection of the heart and arteries to their several uses and causes; for so I shall meet with many things which receive light from the truth I have been contending for, and which, in their turn, render it more obvious. And indeed I would have it confirmed and illustrated by anatomical arguments above all others.

There is but a single point which indeed would be more correctly placed among our observations on the use of the spleen, but which it will not be altogether impertinent to notice in this place incidentally. From the splenic branch which passes into the pancreas, and from the upper part, arise the posterior coronary, gastric, and gastroepiploic veins, all of which are distributed upon the stomach in numerous branches and twigs, just as the mesenteric vessels are upon the intestines. In a similar way, from the inferior part of the same splenic branch, and along the back of the colon and rectum proceed the hemorrhoidal veins. The blood returning by these veins, and bringing the cruder juices along with it, on the one hand from the stomach, where they are thin, watery, and not yet perfectly chylified; on the other thick and more earthy, as derived from the fæces, but all poured into this splenic branch, are duly tempered by the admixture of contraries; and nature mingling together these two kinds of juices, difficult of coction by reason of most opposite defects, and then diluting them with a large quantity of warm blood, (for we see that the quantity returned from the spleen must be very large when we contemplate the size of its arteries,) they are brought to the porta of the liver in a state of higher preparation. The defects of either extreme are supplied and compensated by this arrangement of the veins.

CHAPTER XVII

THE MOTION AND CIRCULATION OF THE BLOOD ARE CONFIRMED FROM THE PARTICULARS APPARENT IN THE STRUCTURE OF THE HEART, AND FROM THOSE THINGS WHICH DISSECTION UNFOLDS

I DO not find the heart as a distinct and separate part in all animals; some, indeed, such as the zoöphytes, have no heart; this is because these animals are coldest, of one great bulk, of soft texture, or of a certain uniform sameness or simplicity of structure; among the number I may instance grubs and earth-worms, and those that are engendered of putrefaction and do not preserve their species. These have no heart, as not requiring any impeller of nourishment into the extreme parts; for they have bodies which are connate and homogeneous and without limbs; so that by the contraction and relaxation of the whole body they assume and expel, move and remove, the aliment. Oysters, mussels, sponges, and the whole genus of zoöphytes or plant-animals have no heart, for the whole body is used as a heart, or the whole animal is a heart. In a great number of animals,—almost the whole tribe of insects— we cannot see distinctly by reason of the smallness of the body; still in bees, flies, hornets, and the like we can perceive something pulsating with the help of a magnifying-glass; in pediculi, also, the same thing may be seen, and as the body is transparent, the passage of the food through the intestines, like a black spot or stain, may be perceived by the aid of the same magnifying-glass.

But in some of the pale-blooded and colder animals, as in snails, whelks, shrimps, and shell-fish, there is a part which pulsates,—a kind of vesicle or auricle without a heart,—slowly, indeed, and not to be perceived except in the warmer season of the year. In these creatures this part is so contrived that it shall pulsate, as there is here a necessity for some impulse to distribute the nutritive fluid, by reason of the variety of organic parts, or of the density of the substance; but the pulsations occur unfrequently, and sometimes in consequence of the cold not at all, an arrangement the best adapted to them as being of a doubtful nature, so that sometimes they appear to live, sometimes to die; sometimes they show the vitality of an animal, sometimes of a vegetable. This seems also to be the case with the insects which conceal themselves in winter, and lie, as it were, defunct, or merely manifesting a kind of vegetative existence. But whether the same thing happens in the case of certain animals that have red blood, such as frogs, tortoises, serpents, swallows, may be very properly doubted.

In all the larger and warmer animals which have red blood, there was need of an impeller of the nutritive fluid, and that, perchance, possessing a considerable amount of power. In fishes, serpents, lizards, tortoises, frogs, and others of the same kind there is a heart present, furnished with both an auricle and a ventricle, whence it is perfectly true, as Aristotle has observed,[1] that no sanguineous animal is without a heart, by the impelling power of which the nutritive fluid is forced, both with greater vigour and rapidity, to a greater distance; and not merely agitated by an auricle, as it is in lower forms. And then in regard to animals that are yet larger, warmer, and more perfect, as they abound in blood, which is always hotter and more spirituous, and which possess bodies of greater size and consistency, these require a larger, stronger, and more fleshy heart, in order that the nutritive fluid may be propelled with yet greater force and celerity. And further, inasmuch as the more perfect animals require a still more perfect nutrition, and a larger supply of native heat, in order that the aliment may be thoroughly concocted and acquire the last degree of perfection, they required both lungs and a second ventricle, which should force the nutritive fluid through them.

Every animal that has lungs has, therefore, two ventricles to its heart—one right, the other left; and wherever there is a right, there also is there a left ventricle; but

[1] De Part. Animal., lib. iii.

the contrary of this does not hold good: where there is a left there is not always a right ventricle. The left ventricle I call that which is distinct in office, not in place from the other, that one, namely, which distributes the blood to the body at large, not to the lungs only. Hence the left ventricle seems to form the principle part of the heart; situated in the middle, more strongly marked, and constructed with greater care, the heart seems formed for the sake of the left ventricle, and the right but to minister to it. The right neither reaches to the apex of the heart nor is it nearly of such strength, being three times thinner in its walls, and in some sort jointed on to the left (as Aristotle says), though, indeed, it is of greater capacity, inasmuch as it has not only to supply material to the left ventricle, but likewise to furnish aliment to the lungs.

It is to be observed, however, that all this is otherwise in the embryo, where there is not such a difference between the two ventricles. There, as in a double nut, they are nearly equal in all respects, the apex of the right reaching to the apex of the left, so that the heart presents itself as a sort of double-pointed cone. And this is so, because in the fœtus, as already said, whilst the blood is not passing through the lungs from the right to the left cavities of the heart, it flows by the foramen ovale and ductus arteriosus directly from the vena cava into the aorta, whence it is distributed to the whole body. Both ventricles have, therefore, the same office to perform, whence their equality of constitution. It is only when the lungs come to be used and it is requisite that the passages indicated should be blocked up that the difference in point of strength and other things between the two ventricles begins to be apparent. In the altered circumstances the right has only to drive the blood through the lungs, whilst the left has to propel it through the whole body.

There are, moreover, within the heart numerous braces, in the form of fleshy columns and fibrous bands, which Aristotle, in his third book on "Respiration," and the "Parts of Animals," entitles nerves. These are variously extended, and are either distinct or contained in grooves in the walls and partition, where they occasion numerous pits or depressions. They constitute a kind of small muscles, which are superadded and supplementary to the heart, assisting it to execute a more powerful and perfect contraction, and so proving subservient to the complete expulsion of the blood. They are, in some sort, like the elaborate and artful arrangement of ropes in a ship, bracing the heart on every side as it contracts, and so enabling it more effectually and forcibly to expel the charge of blood from its ventricles. This much is plain, at all events, that in some animals they are less strongly marked than in others; and, in all that have them, they are more numerous and stronger in the left than in the right ventricle; and while some have them present in the left, yet they are absent in the right ventricle. In man they are more numerous in the left than in the right ventricle, more abundant in the ventricles than in the auricles; and occasionally there appear to be none present in the auricles. They are numerous in the large, more muscular and hardier bodies of countrymen, but fewer in more slender frames and in females.

In those animals in which the ventricles of the heart are smooth within and entirely without fibres of muscular bands, or anything like hollow pits, as in almost all the smaller birds, the partridge and the common fowl, serpents, frogs, tortoises, and most fishes, there are no chordæ tendineæ, nor bundles of fibres, neither are there any tricuspid valves in the ventricles.

Some animals have the right ventricle smooth internally, but the left provided with fibrous bands, such as the goose, swan, and larger birds; and the reason is the same here as elsewhere. As the lungs are spongy and loose and soft, no great amount of force is required to force the blood through them; therefore the right ventricle is either without the bundles in question, or they are fewer and weaker, and not so fleshy or like muscles. Those of the left ventricle, however, are both stronger and more numerous, more fleshy and muscular, because the left ventricle requires to be stronger, inasmuch as the blood which it propels has to be driven through the whole body. And this, too, is the reason why the left ventricle occupies the middle of the heart, and has parietes three times thicker and stronger than those of the right. Hence all animals—and among men it is similar—

CIRCULATION OF THE BLOOD

that are endowed with particularly strong frames, and with large and fleshy limbs at a great distance from the heart, have this central organ of greater thickness, strength, and muscularity. This is manifest and necessary. Those, on the contrary, that are of softer and more slender make have the heart more flaccid, softer, and internally either less or not at all fibrous. Consider, farther, the use of the several valves, which are all so arranged that the blood, once received into the ventricles of the heart, shall never regurgitate; once forced into the pulmonary artery and aorta, shall not flow back upon the ventricles. When the valves are raised and brought together, they form a three-cornered line, such as is left by the bite of a leech; and the more they are forced, the more firmly do they oppose the passage of the blood. The tricuspid valves are placed, like gate-keepers, at the entrance into the ventricles from the venæ cavæ and pulmonary veins, lest the blood when most forcibly impelled should flow back. It is for this reason that they are not found in all animals, nor do they appear to have been constructed with equal care in all animals in which they are found. In some they are more accurately fitted, in others more remissly or carelessly contrived, and always with a view to their being closed under a greater or a slighter force of the ventricle. In the left ventricle, therefore, in order that the occlusion may be the more perfect against the greater impulse, there are only two valves, like a mitre, and produced into an elongated cone, so that they come together and touch to their middle; a circumstance which perhaps led Aristotle into the error of supposing this ventricle to be double, the division taking place transversely. For the same reason, and that the blood may not regurgitate upon the pulmonary veins, and thus the force of the ventricle in propelling the blood through the system at large come to be neutralized, it is that these mitral valves excel those of the right ventricle in size and strength and exactness of closing. Hence it is essential that there can be no heart without a ventricle, since this must be the source and store-house of the blood. The same law does not hold good in reference to the brain. For almost no genus of birds has a ventricle in the brain, as is obvious in the goose and swan, the brains of which nearly equal that of a rabbit in size; now rabbits have ventricles in the brain, whilst the goose has none. In like manner, wherever the heart has a single ventricle, there is an auricle appended, flaccid, membranous, hollow, filled with blood; and where there are two ventricles, there are likewise two auricles. On the other hand, some animals have an auricle without any ventricle; or, at all events, they have a sac analogous to an auricle; or the vein itself, dilated at a particular part, performs pulsations, as is seen in hornets, bees, and other insects, which certain experiments of my own enable me to demonstrate, have not only a pulse, but a respiration in that part which is called the tail, whence it is that this part is elongated and contracted now more rarely, now more frequently, as the creature appears to be blown and to require a large quantity of air. But of these things, more in our "Treatise on Respiration."

It is in like manner evident that the auricles pulsate, contract, as I have said before, and throw the blood into the ventricles; so that wherever there is a ventricle, an auricle is necessary, not merely that it may serve, according to the general belief, as a source and magazine for the blood: for what were the use of its pulsations had it only to contain?

The auricles are prime movers of the blood, especially the right auricle, which, as already said, is "the first to live, the last to die"; whence they are subservient to sending the blood into the ventricles, which, contracting continuously, more readily and forcibly expel the blood already in motion; just as the ball-player can strike the ball more forcibly and further if he takes it on the rebound than if he simply threw it. Moreover, and contrary to the general opinion, neither the heart nor anything else can dilate or distend itself so as to draw anything into its cavity during the diastole, unless, like a sponge, it has been first compressed and is returning to its primary condition. But in animals all local motion proceeds from, and has its origin in, the contraction of some part; consequently it is by the contraction of the auricles that the blood is thrown into the ventricles, as I have already shown, and from there, by the contraction of the ventricles, it is propelled and distributed. Concerning local motions, it is true that the immediate moving organ in every motion of an animal primarily endowed with a motive spirit (as Aristotle has it[2]) is contractile; in which way the word νεῦρον is derived from νεύω, nuto, contraho; and if I am permitted to proceed in my purpose of making a particular demonstration of the organs of motion in animals from observations in my possession, I trust I shall be able to make sufficiently plain how Aristotle was acquainted with the muscles, and advisedly referred all motion in animals to the nerves, or to the contractile element, and, therefore, called those little bands in the heart nerves.

But that we may proceed with the subject which we have in hand, viz., the use of the auricles in filling the ventricles, we should expect that the more dense and compact the heart, the thicker its parietes, the stronger and more muscular must be the auricle to force and fill it, and vice versâ. Now this is actually so: in some the auricle presents itself as a sanguinolent vesicle, as a thin membrane containing blood, as in fishes, in which the sac that stands in lieu of the auricles is of such delicacy and ample capacity that it seems to be suspended or to float above the heart. In those fishes in which the sac is somewhat more fleshy, as in the carp, barbel, tench, and others, it bears a wonderful and strong resemblance to the lungs.

In some men of sturdier frame and stouter make the right auricle is so strong, and so curiously constructed on its inner surface of bands and variously interlacing fibres, that it seems to equal in strength the ventricle of the heart in other subjects; and I must say that I am astonished to find such diversity in this particular in different individuals. It is to be observed, however, that in the fœtus the auricles are out of all proportion large, which is because they are present before the heart makes its appearance or suffices for its office even when it has appeared, and they, therefore, have, as it were, the duty of the whole heart committed to them, as has already been demonstrated. But what I have observed in the formation of the fœtus, as before remarked (and Aristotle had already confirmed all in studying the incubated egg), throws the greatest light and likelihood upon the point. Whilst the fœtus is yet in the form of a soft worm, or, as is commonly said, in the milk, there is a mere bloody

[2] In the book de Spiritu, and elsewhere.

point or pulsating vesicle, a portion apparently of the umbilical vein, dilated at its commencement or base. Afterwards, when the outline of the fœtus is distinctly indicated and it begins to have greater bodily consistence, the vesicle in question becomes more fleshy and stronger, changes its position, and passes into the auricles, above which the body of the heart begins to sprout, though as yet it apparently performs no office. When the fœtus is farther advanced, when the bones can be distinguished from the fleshy parts and movements take place, then it also has a heart which pulsates, and, as I have said, throws blood by either ventricle from the vena cava into the arteries.

Thus nature, ever perfect and divine, doing nothing in vain, has neither given a heart where it was not required, nor produced it before its office had become necessary; but by the same stages in the development of every animal, passing through the forms of all, as I may say (ovum, worm, fœtus), it acquires perfection in each. These points will be found elsewhere confirmed by numerous observations on the formation of the fœtus.

Finally, it is not without good grounds that Hippocrates in his book, "De Corde," entitles it a muscle; its action is the same; so is its functions, viz., to contract and move something else—in this case the charge of the blood.

Farther, we can infer the action and use of the heart from the arrangement of its fibres and its general structures, as in muscles generally. All anatomists admit with Galen that the body of the heart is made up of various courses of fibres running straight, obliquely, and transversely, with reference to one another; but in a heart which has been boiled, the arrangement of the fibres is seen to be different. All the fibres in the parietes and septum are circular, as in the sphincters; those, again, which are in the columns extend lengthwise, and are oblique longitudinally; and so it comes to pass that when all the fibres contract simultaneously, the apex of the cone is pulled towards its base by the columns, the walls are drawn circularly together into a globe—the whole heart, in short, is contracted and the ventricles narrowed. It is, therefore, impossible not to perceive that,

CIRCULATION OF THE BLOOD

as the action of the organ is so plainly contraction, its function is to propel the blood into the arteries.

Nor are we the less to agree with Aristotle in regard to the importance of the heart, or to question if it receives sense and motion from the brain, blood from the liver, or whether it be the origin of the veins and of the blood, and such like. They who affirm these propositions overlook, or do not rightly understand, the principal argument, to the effect that the heart is the first part which exists, and that it contains within itself blood, life, sensation, and motion, before either the brain or the liver were created or had appeared distinctly, or, at all events, before they could perform any function. The heart, ready furnished with its proper organs of motion, like a kind of internal creature, existed before the body. The first to be formed, nature willed that it should afterwards fashion, nourish, preserve, complete the entire animal, as its work and dwelling-place: and as the prince in a kingdom, in whose hands lie the chief and highest authority, rules over all, the heart is the source and foundation from which all power is derived, on which all power depends in the animal body.

Many things having reference to the arteries farther illustrate and confirm this truth. Why does not the pulmonary vein pulsate, seeing that it is numbered among the arteries? Or wherefore is there a pulse in the pulmonary artery? Because the pulse of the arteries is derived from the impulse of the blood. Why does an artery differ so much from a vein in the thickness and strength of its coats? Because it sustains the shock of the impelling heart and streaming blood. Hence, as perfect nature does nothing in vain, and suffices under all circumstances, we find that the nearer the arteries are to the heart, the more do they differ from the veins in structure; here they are both stronger and more ligamentous, whilst in extreme parts of the body, such as the feet and hands, the brain, the mesentery, and the testicles, the two orders of vessels are so much alike that it is impossible to distinguish between them with the eye. Now this is for the following very sufficient reasons: the more remote the vessels are from the heart, with so much the less force are they distended by the stroke of the heart, which is broken by the great distance at which it is given. Add to this that the impulse of the heart exerted upon the mass of blood, which must needs fill the trunks and branches of the arteries, is diverted, divided, as it were, and diminished at every subdivision, so that the ultimate capillary divisions of the arteries look like veins, and this not merely in constitution, but in function. They have either no perceptible pulse, or they rarely exhibit one, and never except where the heart beats more violently than usual, or at a part where the minute vessel is more dilated or open than elsewhere. It, therefore, happens that at times we are aware of a pulse in the teeth, in inflammatory tumours, and in the fingers; at another time we feel nothing of the sort. By this single symptom I have ascertained for certain that young persons whose pulses are naturally rapid were labouring under fever; and in like manner, on compressing the fingers in youthful and delicate subjects during a febrile paroxysm, I have readily perceived the pulse there. On the other hand, when the heart pulsates more languidly, it is often impossible to feel the pulse not merely in the fingers, but the wrist, and even at the temple, as in persons afflicted with lipothymiæ asphyxia, or hysterical symptoms, and in the debilitated and moribund.

Here surgeons are to be advised that, when the blood escapes with force in the amputation of limbs, in the removal of tumours, and in wounds, it constantly comes from an artery; not always indeed per saltum, because the smaller arteries do not pulsate, especially if a tourniquet has been applied.

For the same reason the pulmonary artery not only has the structure of an artery, but it does not differ so widely from the veins in the thickness of its walls as does the aorta. The aorta sustains a more powerful shock from the left than the pulmonary artery does from the right ventricle, and the walls of this last vessel are thinner and softer than those of the aorta in the same proportion as the walls of the right ventricle of the heart are weaker and thinner than those of the left ventricle. In like manner the lungs are softer and laxer in structure than the flesh and other constituents of the body, and in a similar way the walls of the branches of the pulmonary artery differ from those of the vessels derived from the aorta. And the same proportion in these particulars is universally preserved. The more muscular and powerful men are, the firmer their flesh; the stronger, thicker, denser, and more fibrous their hearts, the thicker, closer, and stronger are the auricles and arteries. Again, in those animals the ventricles of whose hearts are smooth on their inner surface, without villi or valves, and the walls of which are thin, as in fishes, serpents, birds, and very many genera of animals, the arteries differ little or nothing in the thickness of their coats from the veins.

Moreover, the reason why the lungs have such ample vessels, both arteries and veins (for the capacity of the pulmonary veins exceeds that of both crural and jugular vessels), and why they contain so large a quantity of blood, as by experience and ocular inspection we know they do, admonished of the fact indeed by Aristotle, and not led into error by the appearances found in animals which have been bled to death, is, because the blood has its fountain, and storehouse, and the workshop of its last perfection, in the heart and lungs. Why, in the same way, we find in the course of our anatomical dissections the pulmonary vein and left ventricle so full of blood, of the same black colour and clotted character as that with which the right ventricle and pulmonary artery are filled, is because the blood is incessantly passing from one side of the heart to the other through the lungs. Wherefore, in fine, the pulmonary artery has the structure of an artery, and the pulmonary veins have the structure of veins. In function and constitution and everything else the first is an artery, the others are veins, contrary to what is commonly believed; and the reason why the pulmonary artery has so large an orifice is because it transports much more blood than is requisite for the nutrition of the lungs.

All these appearances, and many others, to be noted in the course of dissection, if rightly weighed, seem clearly to illustrate and fully to confirm the truth contended for throughout these pages, and at the same time to oppose the vulgar opinion; for it would be very difficult to explain in any other way to what purpose all is constructed and arranged as we have seen it to be.

THE THREE ORIGINAL PUBLICATIONS ON VACCINATION AGAINST SMALLPOX

BY
EDWARD JENNER

INTRODUCTORY NOTE

EDWARD JENNER was born at his father's vicarage at Berkeley, Gloucestershire, England, on May 17, 1749. After leaving school, he was apprenticed to a local surgeon, and in 1770 he went to London and became a resident pupil under the great surgeon and anatomist, John Hunter, with whom he remained on intimate terms for the rest of Hunter's life. In 1773 he took up practise at Berkeley, where, except for numerous visits to London, he spent the rest of his life. He died of apoplexy on January 26, 1823.

Jenner's scientific interests were varied, but the importance of his work in vaccination has overshadowed his other results. Early in his career he had begun to observe the phenomena of cowpox, a disease common in the rural parts of the western counties of England, and he was familiar with the belief, current among the peasantry, that a person who had suffered from the cowpox could not take smallpox. Finally, in 1796, he made his first experiment in vaccination, inoculating a boy of eight with cowpox, and, after his recovery, with smallpox; with the result that the boy did not take the latter disease.

Jenner's first paper on his discovery was never printed; but in 1798 appeared the first of the following treatises. Its reception by the medical profession was highly discouraging; but progress began when Cline, the surgeon of St. Thomas's Hospital, used the treatment with success. Jenner continued his investigations, publishing his results from time to time, and gradually gaining recognition; though opposition to his theory and practise was at first vehement, and has never entirely disappeared. In 1802, Parliament voted him £10,000, and in 1806, £20,000, in recognition of the value of his services, and the sacrifices they had entailed. As early as 1807, Bavaria made vaccination compulsory; and since that date most of the European governments have officially encouraged or compelled the practise; and smallpox has ceased to be the almost universal scourge it was before Jenner's discovery.

To
C. H. PARRY, M.D.
AT BATH

MY DEAR FRIEND:

In the present age of scientific investigation it is remarkable that a disease of so peculiar a nature as the cow-pox, which has appeared in this and some of the neighbouring counties for such a series of years, should so long have escaped particular attention. Finding the prevailing notions on the subject, both among men of our profession and others, extremely vague and indeterminate, and conceiving that facts might appear at once both curious and useful, I have instituted as strict an inquiry into the causes and effects of this singular malady as local circumstances would admit.

The following pages are the result, which, from motives of the most affectionate regard, are dedicated to you, by

Your sincere friend,

EDWARD JENNER.

BERKELEY, GLOUCESTERSHIRE,
June 21st, 1798.

VACCINATION AGAINST SMALLPOX

I

AN INQUIRY INTO THE CAUSES AND EFFECTS OF THE VARIOLÆ VACCINÆ, OR COW-POX. 1798

THE deviation of man from the stage in which he was originally placed by nature seems to have proved to him a prolific source of diseases. From the love of splendour, from the indulgences of luxury, and from his fondness for amusement he has familiarised himself with a great number of animals, which may not originally have been intended for his associates.

The wolf, disarmed of ferocity, is now pillowed in the lady's lap.[1] The cat, the little tiger of our island, whose natural home is the forest, is equally domesticated and caressed. The cow, the hog, the sheep, and the horse, are all, for a variety of purposes, brought under his care and dominion.

There is a disease to which the horse, from his state of domestication, is frequently subject. The farriers have called it the grease. It is an inflammation and swelling in the heel, from which issues matter possessing properties of a very peculiar kind, which seems capable of generating a disease in the human body (after it has undergone the modification which I shall presently speak of), which bears so strong a resemblance to the smallpox that I think it highly probable it may be the source of the disease.

In this dairy country a great number of cows are kept, and the office of milking is performed indiscriminately by

---

[1] The late Mr. John Hunter proved, by experiments, that the dog is the wolf in a degenerate state.

men and maid servants. One of the former having been appointed to apply dressings to the heels of a horse affected with the grease, and not paying due attention to cleanliness, incautiously bears his part in milking the cows, with some particles of the infectious matter adhering to his fingers. When this is the case, it commonly happens that a disease is communicated to the cows, and from the cows to the dairymaids, which spreads through the farm until the most of the cattle and domestics feel its unpleasant consequences. This disease has obtained the name of the cow-pox. It appears on the nipples of the cows in the form of irregular pustules. At their first appearance they are commonly of a palish blue, or rather of a colour somewhat approaching to livid, and are surrounded by an erysipelatous inflammation. These pustules, unless a timely remedy be applied, frequently degenerate into phagedenic ulcers, which prove extremely troublesome.[2] The animals become indisposed, and the secretion of milk is much lessened. Inflamed spots now begin to appear on different parts of the hands of the domestics employed in milking, and sometimes on the wrists, which quickly run on to suppuration, first assuming the appearance of the small vesications produced by a burn. Most commonly they appear about the joints of the fingers and at their extremities; but whatever parts are affected, if the situation will admit, these superficial suppurations put on a circular form, with their edges more elevated than their centre, and of a colour distantly approaching to blue. Absorption takes place, and tumours appear in each axilla. The system becomes affected—the pulse is quickened; and shiverings, succeeded by heat, with general lassitude and pains about the loins and limbs, with vomiting, come on. The head is painful, and the patient is now and then even affected with delirium. These symptoms, varying in their degrees of violence, generally continue from one day to three or four, leaving ulcerated sores about the hands, which, from the sensibility of the parts, are very troublesome, and commonly heal slowly, frequently becoming phagedenic, like

[2] They who attend sick cattle in this country find a speedy remedy for stopping the progress of this complaint in those applications which act chemically upon the morbid matter, such as the solutions of the vitriolum zinci and the vitriolum cupri, etc.

those from whence they sprung. The lips, nostrils, eyelids, and other parts of the body are sometimes affected with sores; but these evidently arise from their being heedlessly rubbed or scratched with the patient's infected fingers. No eruptions on the skin have followed the decline of the feverish symptoms in any instance that has come under my inspection, one only excepted, and in this case a very few appeared on the arms: they were very minute, of a vivid red colour, and soon died away without advancing to maturation; so that I cannot determine whether they had any connection with the preceding symptoms.

Thus the disease makes its progress from the horse[3] to the nipple of the cow, and from the cow to the human subject.

Morbid matter of various kinds, when absorbed into the system, may produce effects in some degree similar; but what renders the cow-pox virus so extremely singular is that the person who has been thus affected is forever after secure from the infection of the smallpox; neither exposure to the variolous effluvia, nor the insertion of the matter into the skin, producing this distemper.

In support of so extraordinary a fact, I shall lay before my reader a great number of instances.[4]

CASE I.—Joseph Merret, now an under gardener to the Earl of Berkeley, lived as a servant with a farmer near this place in the year 1770, and occasionally assisted in milking his master's cows. Several horses belonging to the farm

[3] Jenner's conclusion that "grease" and cow-pox were the same disease has since been proved erroneous; but this error has not invalidated his main conclusion as to the relation of cow-pox and smallpox.—EDITOR.

[4] It is necessary to observe that pustulous sores frequently appear spontaneously on the nipples of cows, and instances have occurred, though very rarely, of the hands of the servants employed in milking being affected with sores in consequence, and even of their feeling an indisposition from absorption. These pustules are of a much milder nature than those which arise from that contagion which constitutes the true cow-pox. They are always free from the bluish or livid tint so conspicuous in the pustules in that disease. No erysipelas attends them, nor do they shew any phagedenic disposition as in the other case, but quickly terminate in a scab without creating any apparent disorder in the cow. This complaint appears at various seasons of the year, but most commonly in the spring, when the cows are first taken from their winter food and fed with grass. It is very apt to appear also when they are suckling their young. But this disease is not to be considered as similar in any respect to that of which I am treating, as it is incapable of producing any specific effects on the human constitution. However, it is of the greatest consequence to point it out here, lest the want of discrimination should occasion an idea of security from the infection of the smallpox, which might prove delusive.

began to have sore heels, which Merret frequently attended. The cows soon became affected with the cow-pox, and soon after several sores appeared on his hands. Swellings and stiffness in each axilla followed, and he was so much indisposed for several days as to be incapable of pursuing his ordinary employment. Previously to the appearance of the distemper among the cows there was no fresh cow brought into the farm, nor any servant employed who was affected with the cow-pox.

In April, 1795, a general inoculation taking place here, Merret was inoculated with his family; so that a period of twenty-five years had elapsed from his having the cow-pox to this time. However, though the variolous matter was repeatedly inserted into his arm, I found it impracticable to infect him with it; an efflorescence only, taking on an erysipelatous look about the centre, appearing on the skin near the punctured parts. During the whole time that his family had the smallpox, one of whom had it very full, he remained in the house with them, but received no injury from exposure to the contagion.

It is necessary to observe that the utmost care was taken to ascertain, with the most scrupulous precision, that no one whose case is here adduced had gone through the smallpox previous to these attempts to produce that disease.

Had these experiments been conducted in a large city, or in a populous neighbourhood, some doubts might have been entertained; but here, where population is thin, and where such an event as a person's having had the smallpox is always faithfully recorded, no risk of inaccuracy in this particular can arise.

CASE II.—Sarah Portlock, of this place, was infected with the cow-pox when a servant at a farmer's in the neighbourhood, twenty-seven years ago.[5]

In the year 1792, conceiving herself, from this circumstance, secure from the infection of the smallpox, she nursed one of her own children who had accidentally caught the

---

[5] I have purposely selected several cases in which the disease had appeared at a very distant period previous to the experiments made with variolous matter, to shew that the change produced in the constitution is not affected by time.

disease, but no indisposition ensued. During the time she remained in the infected room, variolous matter was inserted into both her arms, but without any further effect than in the preceding case.

Case III.—John Phillips, a tradesman of this town, had the cow-pox at so early a period as nine years of age. At the age of sixty-two I inoculated him, and was very careful in selecting matter in its most active state. It was taken from the arm of a boy just before the commencement of the eruptive fever, and instantly inserted. It very speedily produced a sting-like feel in the part. An efflorescence appeared, which on the fourth day was rather extensive, and some degree of pain and stiffness were felt about the shoulder: but on the fifth day these symptoms began to disappear, and in a day or two after went entirely off, without producing any effect on the system.

Case IV.—Mary Barge, of Woodford, in this parish, was inoculated with variolous matter in the year 1791. An efflorescence of a palish red colour soon appeared about the parts where the matter was inserted, and spread itself rather extensively, but died away in a few days without producing any variolous symptoms.[6] She has since been repeatedly employed as a nurse to smallpox patients, without experiencing any ill consequences. This woman had the cowpox when she lived in the service of a farmer in this parish thirty-one years before.

Case V.—Mrs. H——, a respectable gentlewoman of this town, had the cow-pox when very young. She received the infection in rather an uncommon manner: it was given by means of her handling some of the same utensils[7] which

[6] It is remarkable that variolous matter, when the system is disposed to reject it, should excite inflammation on the part to which it is applied more speedily than when it produces the smallpox. Indeed, it becomes almost a criterion by which we can determine whether the infection will be received or not. It seems as if a change, which endures through life, had been produced in the action, or disposition to action, in the vessels of the skin; and it is remarkable, too, that whether this change has been effected by the smallpox or the cow-pox that the disposition to sudden cuticular inflammation is the same on the application of variolous matter.

[7] When the cow-pox has prevailed in the dairy, it has often been communicated to those who have not milked the cows, by the handle of the milk pail.

were in use among the servants of the family, who had the disease from milking infected cows. Her hands had many of the cow-pox sores upon them, and they were communicated to her nose, which became inflamed and very much swollen. Soon after this event Mrs. H—— was exposed to the contagion of the smallpox, where it was scarcely possible for her to have escaped, had she been susceptible of it, as she regularly attended a relative who had the disease in so violent a degree that it proved fatal to him.

In the year 1778 the smallpox prevailed very much at Berkeley, and Mrs. H——, not feeling perfectly satisfied respecting her safety (no indisposition having followed her exposure to the smallpox), I inoculated her with active variolous matter. The same appearance followed as in the preceding cases—an efflorescence on the arm without any effect on the constitution.

CASE VI.—It is a fact so well known among our dairy farmers that those who have had the smallpox either escape the cow-pox or are disposed to have it slightly, that as soon as the complaint shews itself among the cattle, assistants are procured, if possible, who are thus rendered less susceptible of it, otherwise the business of the farm could scarcely go forward.

In the month of May, 1796, the cow-pox broke out at Mr. Baker's, a farmer who lives near this place. The disease was communicated by means of a cow which was purchased in an infected state at a neighbouring fair, and not one of the farmer's cows (consisting of thirty) which were at that time milked escaped the contagion. The family consisted of a man servant, two dairymaids, and a servant boy, who, with the farmer himself, were twice a day employed in milking the cattle. The whole of this family, except Sarah Wynne, one of the dairymaids, had gone through the smallpox. The consequence was that the farmer and the servant boy escaped the infection of the cow-pox entirely, and the servant man and one of the maid servants had each of them nothing more then a sore on one of their fingers, which produced no disorder in the system. But the other dairymaid, Sarah Wynne, who never had the smallpox, did not escape in so easy a manner. She caught the complaint from the cows, and was affected with the symptoms described on page 154 in so violent a degree that she was confined to her bed, and rendered incapable for several days of pursuing her ordinary vocations in the farm.

March 28, 1797, I inoculated this girl and carefully rubbed the variolous matter into two slight incisions made upon the left arm. A little inflammation appeared in the usual manner around the parts where the matter was inserted, but so early as the fifth day it vanished entirely without producing any effect on the system.

CASE VII.—Although the preceding history pretty clearly evinces that the constitution is far less susceptible of the contagion of the cow-pox after it has felt that of the smallpox, and although in general, as I have observed, they who have had the smallpox, and are employed in milking cows which are infected with the cow-pox, either escape the disorder, or have sores on the hands without feeling any general indisposition, yet the animal economy is subject to some variation in this respect, which the following relation will point out:

In the summer of the year 1796 the cow-pox appeared at the farm of Mr. Andrews, a considerable dairy adjoining to the town of Berkeley. It was communicated, as in the preceding instance, by an infected cow purchased at a fair in the neighbourhood. The family consisted of the farmer, his wife, two sons, a man and a maid servant; all of whom, except the farmer (who was fearful of the consequences), bore a part in milking the cows. The whole of them, exclusive of the man servant, had regularly gone through the smallpox; but in this case no one who milked the cows escaped the contagion. All of them had sores upon their hands, and some degree of general indisposition, preceded by pains and tumours in the axillæ: but there was no comparison in the severity of the disease as it was felt by the servant man, who had escaped the smallpox, and by those of the family who had not, for, while he was confined to his bed, they were able, without much inconvenience, to follow their ordinary business.

February the 13th, 1797, I availed myself of an opportunity of inoculating William Rodway, the servant man above alluded to. Variolous matter was inserted into both his arms: in the right, by means of superficial incisions, and into the left by slight punctures into the cutis. Both were perceptibly inflamed on the third day. After this the inflammation about the punctures soon died away, but a small appearance of erysipelas was manifest about the edges of the incisions till the eighth day, when a little uneasiness was felt for the space of half an hour in the right axilla. The inflammation then hastily disappeared without producing the most distant mark of affection of the system.

CASE VIII.—Elizabeth Wynne, aged fifty-seven, lived as a servant with a neighbouring farmer thirty-eight years ago. She was then a dairymaid, and the cow-pox broke out among the cows. She caught the disease with the rest of the family, but, compared with them, had it in a very slight degree, one very small sore only breaking out on the little finger of her left hand, and scarcely any perceptible indisposition following it.

As the malady had shewn itself in so slight a manner, and as it had taken place at so distant a period of her life, I was happy with the opportunity of trying the effects of variolous matter upon her constitution, and on the 28th of March, 1797, I inoculated her by making two superficial incisions on the left arm, on which the matter was cautiously rubbed. A little efflorescence soon appeared, and a tingling sensation was felt about the parts where the matter was inserted until the third day, when both began to subside, and so early as the fifth day it was evident that no indisposition would follow.

CASE IX.—Although the cow-pox shields the constitution from the smallpox, and the smallpox proves a protection against its own future poison, yet it appears that the human body is again and again susceptible of the infectious matter of the cow-pox, as the following history will demonstrate.

William Smith, of Pyrton in this parish, contracted this disease when he lived with a neighbouring farmer in the

Edward Jenner
From the painting by Sir T. Lawrence, P. R. A.

year 1780. One of the horses belonging to the farm had sore heels, and it fell to his lot to attend him. By these means the infection was carried to the cows, and from the cows it was communicated to Smith. On one of his hands were several ulcerated sores, and he was affected with such symptoms as have been before described.

In the year 1791 the cow-pox broke out at another farm where he then lived as a servant, and he became affected with it a second time; and in the year 1794 he was so unfortunate as to catch it again. The disease was equally as severe the second and third time as it was on the first.[8]

In the spring of the year 1795 he was twice inoculated, but no affection of the system could be produced from the variolous matter; and he has since associated with those who had the smallpox in its most contagious state without feeling any effect from it.

CASE X.—Simon Nichols lived as a servant with Mr. Bromedge, a gentleman who resides on his own farm in this parish, in the year 1782. He was employed in applying dressings to the sore heels of one of his master's horses, and at the same time assisted in milking the cows. The cows became affected in consequence, but the disease did not shew itself on their nipples till several weeks after he had begun to dress the horse. He quitted Mr. Bromedge's service, and went to another farm without any sores upon him; but here his hands soon began to be affected in the common way, and he was much indisposed with the usual symptoms. Concealing the nature of the malady from Mr. Cole, his new master, and being there also employed in milking, the cow-pox was communicated to the cows.

Some years afterward Nichols was employed in a farm where the smallpox broke out, when I inoculated him with several other patients, with whom he continued during the whole time of their confinement. His arm inflamed, but neither the inflammation nor his associating with the inoculated family produced the least effect upon his constitution.

---

[8] This is not the case in general—a second attack is commonly very slight, and so, I am informed, it is among the cows.

CASE XI.—William Stinchcomb was a fellow servant with Nichols at Mr. Bromedge's farm at the time the cattle had the cow-pox, and he was, unfortunately, infected by them. His left hand was very severely affected with several corroding ulcers, and a tumour of considerable size appeared in the axilla of that side. His right hand had only one small tumour upon it, and no sore discovered itself in the corresponding axilla.

In the year 1792 Stinchcomb was inoculated with variolous matter, but no consequences ensued beyond a little inflammation in the arm for a few days. A large party were inoculated at the same time, some of whom had the disease in a more violent degree than is commonly seen from inoculation. He purposely associated with them, but could not receive the smallpox.

During the sickening of some of his companions their symptoms so strongly recalled to his mind his own state when sickening with the cow-pox that he very pertinently remarked their striking similarity.

CASE XII.—The paupers of the village of Tortworth, in this county, were inoculated by Mr. Henry Jenner, Surgeon, of Berkeley, in the year 1795. Among them, eight patients presented themselves who had at different periods of their lives had the cow-pox. One of them, Hester Walkley, I attended with that disease when she lived in the service of a farmer in the same village in the year 1782; but neither this woman, nor any other of the patients who had gone through the cow-pox, received the variolous infection either from the arm or from mixing in the society of the other patients who were inoculated at the same time. This state of security proved a fortunate circumstance, as many of the poor women were at the same time in a state of pregnancy.

CASE XIII.—One instance has occurred to me of the system being affected from the matter issuing from the heels of horses, and of its remaining afterwards unsusceptible of the variolous contagion; another, where the smallpox appeared obscurely; and a third, in which its complete existence was positively ascertained.

First, Thomas Pearce is the son of a smith and farrier near to this place. He never had the cow-pox; but, in consequence of dressing horses with sore heels at his father's, when a lad, he had sores on his fingers which suppurated, and which occasioned a pretty severe indisposition. Six years afterwards I inserted variolous matter into his arm repeatedly, without being able to produce any thing more than slight inflammation, which appeared very soon after the matter was applied, and afterwards I exposed him to the contagion of the smallpox with as little effect.[*]

CASE XIV.—Secondly, Mr. James Cole, a farmer in this parish, had a disease from the same source as related in the preceding case, and some years after was inoculated with variolous matter. He had a little pain in the axilla and felt a slight indisposition for three or four hours. A few eruptions shewed themselves on the forehead, but they very soon disappeared without advancing to maturation.

CASE XV.—Although in the former instances the system seemed to be secured, or nearly so, from variolous infection, by the absorption of matter from the sores produced by the diseased heels of horses, yet the following case decisively proves that this cannot be entirely relied upon until a disease has been generated by the morbid matter from the horse on the nipple of the cow, and passed through that medium to the human subject.

Mr. Abraham Riddiford, a farmer at Stone in this parish, in consequence of dressing a mare that had sore heels, was affected with very painful sores in both his hands, tumours in each axilla, and severe and general indisposition. A surgeon in the neighbourhood attended him, who knowing the similarity between the appearance of the sores upon his hands and those produced by the cow-pox, and being acquainted also with the effects of that disease on the human constitution, assured him that he never need to fear the infection of the smallpox; but this assertion proved fallacious,

---

[*] It is a remarkable fact, and well known to many, that we are frequently foiled in our endeavours to communicate the smallpox by inoculation to blacksmiths, who in the country are farriers. They often, as in the above instance, either resist the contagion entirely, or have the disease anomalously. Shall we not be able to account for this on a rational principle?

for, on being exposed to the infection upwards of twenty years afterwards, he caught the disease, which took its regular course in a very mild way. There certainly was a difference perceptible, although it is not easy to describe it, in the general appearance of the pustules from that which we commonly see. Other practitioners who visited the patient at my request agreed with me in this point, though there was no room left for suspicion as to the reality of the disease, as I inoculated some of his family from the pustules, who had the smallpox, with its usual appearances, in consequence.

CASE XVI.—Sarah Nelmes, a dairymaid at a farmer's near this place, was infected with the cow-pox from her master's cows in May, 1796. She received the infection on a part of her hand which had been previously in a slight degree injured by a scratch from a thorn. A large pustulous sore and the usual symptoms accompanying the disease were produced in consequence. The pustule was so expressive of the true character of the cow-pox, as it commonly appears upon the hand, that I have given a representation of it in the annexed plate. The two small pustules on the wrists arose also from the application of the virus to some minute abrasions of the cuticle, but the livid tint, if they ever had any, was not conspicuous at the time I saw the patient. The pustule on the forefinger shews the disease in an earlier stage. It did not actually appear on the hand of this young woman, but was taken from that of another, and is annexed for the purpose of representing the malady after it has newly appeared.

CASE XVII.—The more accurately to observe the progress of the infection I selected a healthy boy, about eight years old, for the purpose of inoculation for the cow-pox. The matter was taken from a sore on the hand of a dairymaid,[10] who was infected by her master's cows, and it was inserted, on the 14th of May, 1796, into the arm of the boy by means of two superficial incisions, barely penetrating the cutis, each about half an inch long.

[10] From the sore on the hand of Sarah Nelmes. See the preceding case.

On the seventh day he complained of uneasiness in the axilla, and on the ninth he became a little chilly, lost his appetite, and had a slight headache. During the whole of this day he was perceptibly indisposed, and spent the night with some degree of restlessness, but on the day following he was perfectly well.

The appearance of the incisions in their progress to a state of maturation were much the same as when produced in a similar manner by variolous matter. The only difference which I perceived was in the state of the limpid fluid arising from the action of the virus, which assumed rather a darker hue, and in that of the efflorescence spreading round the incisions, which had more of an erysipelatous look than we commonly perceive when variolous matter has been made use of in the same manner; but the whole died away (leaving on the inoculated parts scabs and subsequent eschars) without giving me or my patient the least trouble.

In order to ascertain whether the boy, after feeling so slight an affection of the system from the cow-pox virus, was secure from the contagion of the smallpox, he was inoculated the 1st of July following with variolous matter, immediately taken from a pustule. Several slight punctures and incisions were made on both his arms, and the matter was carefully inserted, but no disease followed. The same appearances were observable on the arms as we commonly see when a patient has had variolous matter applied, after having either the cow-pox or smallpox. Several months afterwards he was again inoculated with variolous matter, but no sensible effect was produced on the constitution.

Here my researches were interrupted till the spring of the year 1798, when, from the wetness of the early part of the season, many of the farmers' horses in this neighbourhood were affected with sore heels, in consequence of which the cow-pox broke out among several of our dairies, which afforded me an opportunity of making further observations upon this curious disease.

A mare, the property of a person who keeps a dairy in a neighbouring parish, began to have sore heels the latter end of the month of February, 1798, which were occasionally washed by the servant men of the farm, Thomas Virgoe,

William Wherret, and William Haynes, who in consequence became affected with sores in their hands, followed by inflamed lymphatic glands in the arms and axillæ, shiverings succeeded by heat, lassitude, and general pains in the limbs. A single paroxysm terminated the disease; for within twenty-four hours they were free from general indisposition, nothing remaining but the sores on their hands. Haynes and Virgoe, who had gone through the smallpox from inoculation, described their feelings as very similar to those which affected them on sickening with that malady. Wherret never had had the smallpox. Haynes was daily employed as one of the milkers at the farm, and the disease began to shew itself among the cows about ten days after he first assisted in washing the mare's heels. Their nipples became sore in the usual way, with bluish pustules; but as remedies were early applied, they did not ulcerate to any extent.

CASE XVIII.—John Baker, a child of five years old, was inoculated March 16, 1798, with matter taken from a pustule on the hand of Thomas Virgoe, one of the servants who had been infected from the mare's heels. He became ill on the sixth day with symptoms similar to those excited by cowpox matter. On the eighth day he was free from indisposition.

There was some variation in the appearance of the pustule on the arm. Although it somewhat resembled a smallpox pustule, yet its similitude was not so conspicuous as when excited by matter from the nipple of the cow, or when the matter has passed from thence through the medium of the human subject.

This experiment was made to ascertain the progress and subsequent effects of the disease when thus propagated. We have seen that the virus from the horse, when it proves infectious to the human subject, is not to be relied upon as rendering the system secure from variolous infection, but that the matter produced by it upon the nipple of the cow is perfectly so. Whether its passing from the horse through the human constitution, as in the present instance, will produce a similar effect, remains to be decided. This would now have been effected, but the boy was rendered unfit for inoculation from having felt the effects of a contagious fever in a workhouse soon after this experiment was made.

CASE XIX.—William Summers, a child of five years and a half old, was inoculated the same day with Baker, with matter taken from the nipples of one of the infected cows, at the farm alluded to. He became indisposed on the sixth day, vomited once, and felt the usual slight symptoms till the eighth day, when he appeared perfectly well. The progress of the pustule, formed by the infection of the virus, was similar to that noticed in Case XVII, with this exception, its being free from the livid tint observed in that instance.

CASE XX.—From William Summers the disease was transferred to William Pead, a boy of eight years old, who was inoculated March 28th. On the sixth day he complained of pain in the axilla, and on the seventh was affected with the common symptoms of a patient sickening with the smallpox from inoculation, which did not terminate till the third day after the seizure. So perfect was the similarity to the variolous fever that I was induced to examine the skin, conceiving there might have been some eruptions, but none appeared. The efflorescent blush around the part punctured in the boy's arm was so truly characteristic of that which appears on variolous inoculation that I have given a representation of it. The drawing was made when the pustule was beginning to die away and the areola retiring from the centre.

CASE XXI.—April 5th: Several children and adults were inoculated from the arm of William Pead. The greater part of them sickened on the sixth day, and were well on the seventh, but in three of the number a secondary indisposition arose in consequence of an extensive erysipelatous inflammation which appeared on the inoculated arms. It seemed to arise from the state of the pustule, which spread out, accompanied with some degree of pain, to about half the diameter of a sixpence. One of these patients was an infant of half a year old. By the application of mercurial ointment to the inflamed parts (a treatment recommended under similar circumstances in the inoculated smallpox) the complaint subsided without giving much trouble.

Hannah Excell, an healthy girl of seven years old, and one of the patients above mentioned, received the infection from the insertion of the virus under the cuticle of the arm in three distinct points. The pustules which arose in consequence so much resembled, on the twelfth day, those appearing from the infection of variolous matter, that an experienced inoculator would scarcely have discovered a shade of difference at that period. Experience now tells me that almost the only variation which follows consists in the pustulous fluids remaining limpid nearly to the time of its total disappearance; and not, as in the direct smallpox, becoming purulent.

CASE XXII.—From the arm of this girl matter was taken and inserted April 12th into the arms of John Macklove, one year and a half old, Robert F. Jenner, eleven months old, Mary Pead, five years old, and Mary James, six years old.

Among these, Robert F. Jenner did not receive the infection. The arms of the other three inflamed properly and began to affect the system in the usual manner; but being under some apprehensions from the preceding cases that a troublesome erysipelas might arise, I determined on making an experiment with the view of cutting off its source. Accordingly, after the patients had felt an indisposition of about twelve hours, I applied in two of these cases out of the three, on the vesicle formed by the virus, a little mild caustic, composed of equal parts of quick-lime and soap, and suffered it to remain on the part six hours.[11] It seemed to give the children but little uneasiness, and effectually answered my intention in preventing the appearance of erysipelas. Indeed, it seemed to do more, for in half an hour after its application the indisposition of the children ceased.[12] These precautions were perhaps unnecessary, as the arm of the third child, Mary Pead, which was suffered to take its common course, scabbed quickly, without any erysipelas.

[11] Perhaps a few touches with the lapis septicus would have proved equally efficacious.
[12] What effect would a similar treatment produce in inoculation for the smallpox?

CASE XXIII.—From this child's arm matter was taken and transferred to that of J. Barge, a boy of seven years old. He sickened on the eighth day, went through the disease with the usual slight symptoms, and without any inflammation on the arm beyond the common efflorescence surrounding the pustule, an appearance so often seen in inoculated smallpox.

After the many fruitless attempts to give the smallpox to those who had had the cow-pox, it did not appear necessary, nor was it convenient to me, to inoculate the whole of those who had been the subjects of these late trials; yet I thought it right to see the effects of variolous matter on some of them, particularly William Summers, the first of these patients who had been infected with matter taken from the cow. He was, therefore, inoculated with variolous matter from a fresh pustule; but, as in the preceding cases, the system did not feel the effects of it in the smallest degree. I had an opportunity also of having this boy and William Pead inoculated by my nephew, Mr. Henry Jenner, whose report to me is as follows: "I have inoculated Pead and Barge, two of the boys whom you lately infected with the cow-pox. On the second day the incisions were inflamed and there was a pale inflammatory stain around them. On the third day these appearances were still increasing and their arms itched considerably. On the fourth day the inflammation was evidently subsiding, and on the sixth day it was scarcely perceptible. No symptom of indisposition followed.

"To convince myself that the variolous matter made use of was in a perfect state I at the same time inoculated a patient with some of it who never had gone through the cow-pox, and it produced the smallpox in the usual regular manner."

These experiments afforded me much satisfaction; they proved that the matter, in passing from one human subject to another, through five gradations, lost none of its original properties, J. Barge being the fifth who received the infection successively from William Summers, the boy to whom it was communicated from the cow.

I shall now conclude this inquiry with some general observations on the subject, and on some others which are interwoven with it.

Although I presume it may be unnecessary to produce further testimony in support of my assertion "that the cow-pox protects the human constitution from the infection of the smallpox," yet it affords me considerable satisfaction to say that Lord Somerville, the President of the Board of Agriculture, to whom this paper was shewn by Sir Joseph Banks, has found upon inquiry that the statements were confirmed by the concurring testimony of Mr. Dolland, a surgeon, who resides in a dairy country remote from this, in which these observations were made. With respect to the opinion adduced "that the source of the infection is a peculiar morbid matter arising in the horse," although I have not been able to prove it from actual experiments conducted immediately under my own eye, yet the evidence I have adduced appears sufficient to establish it.

They who are not in the habit of conducting experiments may not be aware of the coincidence of circumstances necessary for their being managed so as to prove perfectly decisive; nor how often men engaged in professional pursuits are liable to interruptions which disappoint them almost at the instant of their being accomplished: however, I feel no room for hesitation respecting the common origin of the disease, being well convinced that it never appears among the cows (except it can be traced to a cow introduced among the general herd which has been previously infected, or to an infected servant) unless they have been milked by some one who, at the same time, has the care of a horse affected with diseased heels.

The spring of the year 1797, which I intended particularly to have devoted to the completion of this investigation, proved, from its dryness, remarkably adverse to my wishes; for it frequently happens, while the farmers' horses are exposed to the cold rains which fall at that season, that their heels become diseased, and no cow-pox then appeared in the neighbourhood.

The active quality of the virus from the horses' heels is greatly increased after it has acted on the nipples of the cow, as it rarely happens that the horse affects his dresser with sores, and as rarely that a milkmaid escapes the infection when she milks infected cows. It is most active at the commencement of the disease, even before it has acquired a pus-like appearance; indeed, I am not confident whether this property in the matter does not entirely cease as soon as it is secreted in the form of pus. I am induced to think it does cease,[13] and that it is the thin, darkish-looking fluid only, oozing from the newly-formed cracks in the heels, similar to what sometimes appears from erysipelatous blisters, which gives the disease. Nor am I certain that the nipples of the cows are at all times in a state to receive the infection. The appearance of the disease in the spring and the early part of the summer, when they are disposed to be affected with spontaneous eruptions so much more frequently than at other seasons, induces me to think that the virus from the horse must be received upon them when they are in this state, in order to produce effects: experiments, however, must determine these points. But it is clear that when the cow-pox virus is once generated, that the cows cannot resist the contagion, in whatever state their nipples may chance to be, if they are milked with an infected hand.

Whether the matter, either from the cow or the horse, will affect the sound skin of the human body, I cannot positively determine; probably it will not, unless on those parts where the cuticle is extremely thin, as on the lips, for example. I have known an instance of a poor girl who produced an ulceration on her lip by frequently holding her finger to her mouth to cool the raging of a cow-pox sore by blowing upon it. The hands of the farmers' servants here, from the nature of their employments, are constantly exposed to those injuries which occasion abrasions of the cuticle, to punctures from thorns, and such like accidents; so that they are always in a state to feel the consequence of exposure to infectious matter.

It is singular to observe that the cow-pox virus, although

[13] It is very easy to procure pus from old sores on the heels of horses. This I have often inserted into scratches made with a lancet, on the sound nipples of cows, and have seen no other effects from it than simple inflammation.

it renders the constitution unsusceptible of the variolous, should nevertheless, leave it unchanged with respect to its own action. I have already produced an instance [14] to point out this, and shall now corroborate it with another.

Elizabeth Wynne, who had the cow-pox in the year 1759, was inoculated with variolous matter, without effect, in the year 1797, and again caught the cow-pox in the year 1798. When I saw her, which was on the eighth day after she received the infection, I found her affected with general lassitude, shiverings, alternating with heat, coldness of the extremities, and a quick and irregular pulse. These symptoms were preceded by a pain in the axilla. On her hand was one large pustulous sore, which resembled that delineated in Plate No. 1. (Plate appears in original.)

It is curious also to observe that the virus, which with respect to its effects is undetermined and uncertain previously to its passing from the horse through the medium of the cow, should then not only become more active, but should invariably and completely possess those specific properties which induce in the human constitution symptoms similar to those of the variolous fever, and effect in it that peculiar change which for ever renders it unsusceptible of the variolous contagion.

May it not then be reasonably conjectured that the source of the smallpox is morbid matter of a peculiar kind, generated by a disease in the horse, and that accidental circumstances may have again and again arisen, still working new changes upon it until it has acquired the contagious and malignant form under which we now commonly see it making its devastations amongst us? And, from a consideration of the change which the infectious matter undergoes from producing a disease on the cow, may we not conceive that many contagious diseases, now prevalent among us, may owe their present appearance not to a simple, but to a compound, origin? For example, is it difficult to imagine that the measles, the scarlet fever, and the ulcerous sore throat with a spotted skin have all sprung from the same source, assuming some variety in their forms according to the nature of their new

[14] See Case IX.

combinations? The same question will apply respecting the origin of many other contagious diseases which bear a strong analogy to each other.

There are certainly more forms than one, without considering the common variation between the confluent and distinct, in which the smallpox appears in what is called the natural way. About seven years ago a species of smallpox spread through many of the towns and villages of this part of Gloucestershire: it was of so mild a nature that a fatal instance was scarcely ever heard of, and consequently so little dreaded by the lower orders of the community that they scrupled not to hold the same intercourse with each other as if no infectious disease had been present among them. I never saw nor heard of an instance of its being confluent. The most accurate manner, perhaps, in which I can convey an idea of it is by saying that had fifty individuals been taken promiscuously and infected by exposure to this contagion, they would have had as mild and light a disease as if they had been inoculated with variolous matter in the usual way. The harmless manner in which it shewed itself could not arise from any peculiarity either in the season or the weather, for I watched its progress upwards of a year without perceiving any variation in its general appearance. I consider it then as a *variety* of the smallpox.[15]

In some of the preceding cases I have noticed the attention that was paid to the state of the variolous matter previous to the experiment of inserting it into the arms of those who had gone through the cow-pox. This I conceived to be of great importance in conducting these experiments, and, were it always properly attended to by those who inoculate for the smallpox, it might prevent much subsequent mischief and confusion. With the view of enforcing so necessary a precaution I shall take the liberty of digressing so far as to point out some unpleasant facts relative to mismanagement in this particular, which have fallen under my own observation.

[15] My friend, Dr. Hicks, of Bristol, who, during the prevalence of this distemper, was resident at Gloucester, and physician of the hospital there (where it was seen soon after its first appearance in this country), had opportunities of making numerous observations upon it, which it is his intention to communicate to the public.

A medical gentleman (now no more), who for many years inoculated in this neighbourhood, frequently preserved the variolous matter intended for his use on a piece of lint or cotton, which, in its fluid state, was put into a vial, corked, and conveyed into a warm pocket; a situation certainly favourable for speedily producing putrefaction in it. In this state (not unfrequently after it had been taken several days from the pustules) it was inserted into the arms of his patients, and brought on inflammation of the incised parts, swellings of the axillary glands, fever, and sometimes eruptions. But what was this disease? Certainly not the smallpox; for the matter having from putrefaction lost or suffered a derangement in its specific properties, was no longer capable of producing that malady, those who had been inoculated in this manner being as much subject to the contagion of the smallpox as if they had never been under the influence of this artificial disease; and many, unfortunately, fell victims to it, who thought themselves in perfect security. The same unfortunate circumstance of giving a disease, supposed to be the smallpox, with inefficacious variolous matter, having occurred under the direction of some other practitioners within my knowledge, and probably from the same incautious method of securing the variolous matter, I avail myself of this opportunity of mentioning what I conceive to be of great importance; and, as a further cautionary hint, I shall again digress so far as to add another observation on the subject of inoculation.

Whether it be yet ascertained by experiment that the quantity of variolous matter inserted into the skin makes any difference with respect to the subsequent mildness or violence of the disease, I know not; but I have the strongest reason for supposing that if either the punctures or incisions be made so deep as to go *through* it and wound the adipose membrane, that the risk of bringing on a violent disease is greatly increased. I have known an inoculator whose practice was "to cut deep enough (to use his own expression) to see a bit of fat," and there to lodge the matter. The great number of bad cases, independent of inflammations and abscesses on the arms, and the fatality which attended this practice, was almost inconceivable; and I cannot account for it on any other principle than that of the matter being placed in this situation instead of the skin.

It was the practice of another, whom I well remember, to pinch up a small portion of the skin on the arms of his patients and to pass through it a needle, with a thread attached to it previously dipped in variolous matter. The thread was lodged in the perforated part, and consequently left in contact with the cellular membrane. This practice was attended with the same ill success as the former. Although it is very improbable that any one would now inoculate in this rude way by design, yet these observations may tend to place a double guard over the lancet, when infants, whose skins are comparatively so very thin, fall under the care of the inoculator.

A very respectable friend of mine, Dr. Hardwicke, of Sodbury, in this county, inoculated great numbers of patients previous to the introduction of the more modern method by Sutton, and with such success that a fatal instance occurred as rarely as since that method has been adopted. It was the doctor's practice to make as slight an incision as possible *upon* the skin, and there to lodge a thread saturated with the variolous matter. When his patients became indisposed, agreeably to the custom then prevailing, they were directed to go to bed and were kept moderately warm. Is it not probable then that the success of the modern practice may depend more upon the method of invariably depositing the virus in or upon the skin, than on the subsequent treatment of the disease?

I do not mean to insinuate that exposure to cool air, and suffering the patient to drink cold water when hot and thirsty, may not moderate the eruptive symptoms and lessen the number of pustules; yet, to repeat my former observation, I cannot account for the uninterrupted success, or nearly so, of one practitioner, and the wretched state of the patients under the care of another, where, in both instances, the general treatment did not differ essentially, without conceiving it to arise from the different modes of inserting the matter for the purpose of producing the disease. As it is not the identical matter inserted which is absorbed into the constitution, but that which is, by some peculiar process in the animal economy, generated by it, is it not probable that different parts of the human body may prepare or modify the virus differently? Although the skin, for example, adipose membrane, or mucous membranes are all capable of producing the variolous virus by the stimulus given by the particles originally deposited upon them, yet I am induced to conceive that each of these parts is capable of producing some variation in the qualities of the matter previous to its affecting the constitution. What else can constitute the difference between the smallpox when communicated casually or in what has been termed the natural way, or when brought on artificially through the medium of the skin?

After all, are the variolous particles, possessing their true specific and contagious principles, ever taken up and conveyed by the lymphatics unchanged into the blood vessels? I imagine not. Were this the case, should we not find the blood sufficiently loaded with them in some stages of the smallpox to communicate the disease by inserting it under the cuticle, or by spreading it on the surface of an ulcer? Yet experiments have determined the impracticability of its being given in this way; although it has been proved that variolous matter, when much diluted with water and applied to the skin in the usual manner, will produce the disease. But it would be digressing beyond a proper boundary to go minutely into this subject here.

At what period the cow-pox was first noticed here is not upon record. Our oldest farmers were not unacquainted with it in their earliest days, when it appeared among their farms without any deviation from the phænomena which it now exhibits. Its connection with the smallpox seems to have been unknown to them. Probably the general introduction of inoculation first occasioned the discovery.

Its rise in this country may not have been of very remote date, as the practice of milking cows might formerly have been in the hands of women only; which I believe is the case now in some other dairy countries, and, consequently, that the cows might not in former times have been exposed to the contagious matter brought by the men servants from the heels of horses.[16] Indeed, a knowledge of the source of the

[16] I have been informed from respectable authority that in Ireland, al-

infection is new in the minds of most of the farmers in this neighbourhood, but it has at length produced good consequences; and it seems probable, from the precautions they are now disposed to adopt, that the appearance of the cowpox here may either be entirely extinguished or become extremely rare.

Should it be asked whether this investigation is a matter of mere curiosity, or whether it tends to any beneficial purpose, I should answer that, notwithstanding the happy effects of inoculation, with all the improvements which the practice has received since its first introduction into this country, it not very unfrequently produces deformity of the skin, and sometimes, under the best management, proves fatal.

These circumstances must naturally create in every instance some degree of painful solicitude for its consequences. But as I have never known fatal effects arise from the cowpox, even when impressed in the most unfavourable manner, producing extensive inflammations and suppurations on the hands; and as it clearly appears that this disease leaves the constitution in a state of perfect security from the infection of the smallpox, may we not infer that a mode of inoculation may be introduced preferable to that at present adopted, especially among those families which, from previous circumstances, we may judge to be predisposed to have the disease unfavourably? It is an excess in the number of pustules which we chiefly dread in the smallpox; but in the cow-pox no pustules appear, nor does it seem possible for the contagious matter to produce the disease from effluvia, or by any other means than contact, and that probably not simply between the virus and the cuticle; so that a single individual in a family might at any time receive it without the risk of infecting the rest or of spreading a distemper that fills a country with terror.

Several instances have come under my observation which justify the assertion that the disease cannot be propagated by effluvia. The first boy whom I inoculated with the matter

though dairies abound in many parts of the island, the disease is entirely unknown. The reason seems obvious. The business of the dairy is conducted by women only. Were the meanest vassal among the men employed there as a milker at a dairy, he would feel his situation unpleasant beyond all endurance.

of cow-pox slept in a bed, while the experiment was going forward, with two children who never had gone through either that disease or the smallpox, without infecting either of them.

A young woman who had the cow-pox to a great extent, several sores which maturated having appeared on the hands and wrists, slept in the same bed with a fellow-dairymaid who never had been infected with either the cow-pox or the smallpox, but no indisposition followed.

Another instance has occurred of a young woman on whose hands were several large suppurations from the cow-pox, who was at the same time a daily nurse to an infant, but the complaint was not communicated to the child.

In some other points of view the inoculation of this disease appears preferable to the variolous inoculation.

In constitutions predisposed to scrophula, how frequently we see the inoculated smallpox rouse into activity that distressful malady! This circumstance does not seem to depend on the manner in which the distemper has shewn itself, for it has as frequently happened among those who have had it mildly as when it has appeared in the contrary way.

There are many who, from some peculiarity in the habit, resist the common effects of variolous matter inserted into the skin, and who are in consequence haunted through life with the distressing idea of being insecure from subsequent infection. A ready mode of dissipating anxiety originating from such a cause must now appear obvious. And, as we have seen that the constitution may at any time be made to feel the febrile attack of cow-pox, might it not, in many chronic diseases, be introduced into the system, with the probability of affording relief, upon well-known physiological principles?

Although I say the system may at any time be made to feel the febrile attack of cow-pox, yet I have a single instance before me where the virus acted locally only, but it is not in the least probable that the same person would resist the action both of the cow-pox virus and the variolous.

Elizabeth Sarfenet lived as a dairymaid at Newpark farm, in this parish. All the cows and the servants employed in milking had the cow-pox; but this woman, though she had several sores upon her fingers, felt no tumours in the axillæ, nor any general indisposition. On being afterwards casually exposed to variolous infection, she had the smallpox in a mild way. Hannah Pick, another of the dairymaids who was a fellow-servant with Elizabeth Sarfenet when the distemper broke out at the farm, was, at the same time, infected; but this young woman had not only sores upon her hands, but felt herself also much indisposed for a day or two. After this, I made several attempts to give her the smallpox by inoculation, but they all proved fruitless. From the former case then we see that the animal economy is subject to the same laws in one disease as the other.

The following case, which has very lately occurred, renders it highly probable that not only the heels of the horse, but other parts of the body of that animal, are capable of generating the virus which produces the cow-pox.

An extensive inflammation of the erysipelatous kind appeared without any apparent cause upon the upper part of the thigh of a sucking colt, the property of Mr. Millet, a farmer at Rockhampton, a village near Berkeley. The inflammation continued several weeks, and at length terminated in the formation of three or four small abscesses. The inflamed parts were fomented, and dressings were applied by some of the same persons who were employed in milking the cows. The number of cows milked was twenty-four, and the whole of them had the cow-pox. The milkers, consisting of the farmer's wife, a man and a maidservant, were infected by the cows. The man-servant had previously gone through the smallpox, and felt but little of the cow-pox. The servant maid had some years before been infected with the cow-pox, and she also felt it now in a slight degree; but the farmer's wife, who never had gone through either of the diseases, felt its effects very severely.

That the disease produced upon the cows by the colt and from thence conveyed to those who milked them was the *true* and not the *spurious* cow-pox, there can be scarcely any room for suspicion; yet it would have been more completely satisfactory had the effects of variolous matter been ascertained on the farmer's wife, but there was a peculiarity in her situation which prevented my making the experiment.

Thus far have I proceeded in an inquiry founded, as it must appear, on the basis of experiment; in which, however, conjecture has been occasionally admitted in order to present to persons well situated for such discussions objects for a more minute investigation. In the mean time I shall myself continue to prosecute this inquiry, encouraged by the hope of its becoming essentially beneficial to mankind.

II

FURTHER OBSERVATIONS ON THE VARIOLÆ VACCINÆ, OR COW-POX. 1799

ALTHOUGH it has not been in my power to extend the inquiry into the causes and effects of the variolæ vaccinæ much beyond its original limits, yet, perceiving that it is beginning to excite a general spirit of investigation, I think it of importance, without delay, to communicate such facts as have since occurred, and to point out the fallacious sources from whence a disease imitative of the true variolæ vaccinæ might arise, with the view of preventing those who may inoculate from producing a spurious disease; and, further, to enforce the precaution suggested in the former treatise on the subject, of subduing the inoculated pustule as soon as it has sufficiently produced its influence on the constitution. From a want of due discrimination of the real existence of the disease, either in the brute or in the human subject, and also of that stage of it in which it is capable of producing the change in the animal economy which renders it unsusceptible of the contagion of the smallpox, unpleasant consequences might ensue, the source of which, perhaps, might not be suspected by one inexperienced in conducting such experiments.

My late publication contains a relation of most of the facts which had come under my own inspection at the time it was written, interspersed with some conjectural observations. Since then Dr. G. Pearson has established an inquiry into the validity of my principal assertion, the result of which cannot but be highly flattering to my feelings. It contains not a single case which I think can be called an exception to the fact I was so firmly impressed with—that the cow-pox protects the human body from the smallpox. I have myself received some further confirmations, which shall be subjoined. I have lately also been favoured with a letter from a gentleman of great respectability (Dr. Ingenhousz), informing me that, on making an inquiry into the subject in the county of Wilts, he discovered that a farmer near Calne had been infected with the smallpox after having had the cow-pox, and that the disease in each instance was so strongly characterized as to render the facts incontrovertible. The cow-pox, it seems, from the doctor's information, was communicated to the farmer from his cows at the time that they gave out *an offensive stench from their udders*.

Some other instances have likewise been represented to me of the appearance of the disease, apparently marked with its characteristic symptoms, and yet that the patients have afterwards had the smallpox. On these cases I shall, for the present, suspend any particular remarks, but hope that the general observations I have to offer in the sequel will prove of sufficient weight to render the idea of their ever having had existence, but as cases of spurious cow-pox, extremely doubtful.

Ere I proceed let me be permitted to observe that truth, in this and every other physiological inquiry that has occupied my attention, has ever been the object of my pursuit, and should it appear in the present instance that I have been led into error, fond as I may appear of the offspring of my labours, I had rather see it perish at once than exist and do a public injury.

I shall proceed to enumerate the sources, or what appear to me as such, of a spurious cow-pox.

First: That arising from pustules on the nipples or udder of the cow; which pustules contain no specific virus.

Secondly: From matter (although originally possessing the specific virus) which has suffered a decomposition, either from putrefaction or from any other cause less obvious to the senses.

Thirdly: From matter taken from an ulcer in an advanced stage, which ulcer arose from a true cow pock.

Fourthly: From matter produced on the human skin from contact with some peculiar morbid matter generated by a horse.

On these subjects I shall offer some comments: First, to what length pustulous diseases of the udder and nipples of the cow may extend it is not in my power to determine; but certain it is that these parts of the animal are subject to some variety of maladies of this nature; and as many of these eruptions (probably all of them) are capable of giving a disease to the human body, would it not be discreet for those engaged in this investigation to suspend controversy and cavil until they can ascertain with precision what *is* and what *is not* the cow-pox?

For example: A farmer who is not conversant with any of these maladies, but who may have heard of the cow-pox in general terms, may acquaint a neighbouring surgeon that the distemper appears at his farm. The surgeon, eager to make an experiment, takes away matter, inoculates, produces a sore, uneasiness in the axilla, and perhaps some affection of the system. This is one way in which a fallacious idea of security both in the mind of the inoculator and the patient may arise; for a disease may thus have been propagated from a simple eruption only.

One of the first objects then of this pursuit, as I have observed, should be, to learn how to distinguish with accuracy between that peculiar pustule which is the *true* cow pock, and that which is spurious. Until experience has determined this, we view our object through a mist. Let us, for instance, suppose that the smallpox and the chicken-pox were at the same time to spread among the inhabitants of a country which had never been visited by either of these distempers, and where they were quite unknown before: what confusion would arise! The resemblance between the symptoms of the eruptive fever and between the pustules in either case would be so striking that a patient who had gone through the chicken-pox to any extent would feel equally easy with regard to his future security from the smallpox as the person who had actually passed through that disease. Time and future observation would draw the line of distinction.

So I presume it will be with the cow-pox until it is more

generally understood. All cavilling, therefore, on the mere report of those who *tell us* they have had this distemper, and are afterwards found susceptible of the smallpox, should be suspended. To illustrate this I beg leave to give the following history:

Sarah Merlin, of the parish of Eastington in this county, when about thirteen or fourteen years of age lived as a servant with farmer Clarke, who kept a dairy consisting of about eighteen cows at Stonehouse, a neighbouring village. The nipples and udders of three of the cows were extensively affected with large white blisters. These cows the girl milked daily, and at the time she assisted, with two others, in milking the rest of the herd. It soon appeared that the disease was communicated to the girl. The rest of the cows escaped the infection, although they were milked several days after the three above specified, had these eruptions on the nipples and udders, and even after the girl's hand became sore. The two others who were engaged in milking, although they milked the cows indiscriminately, received no injury. On the fingers of each of the girl's hands there appeared several large white blisters—she supposes about three or four on each finger. The hands and arms inflamed and swelled, but no constitutional indisposition followed. The sores were anointed with some domestic ointment and got well without ulcerating.

As this malady was called the cow-pox, and recorded as such in the mind of the patient, she became regardless of the smallpox; but, on being exposed to it some years afterwards she was infected, and had a full burthen.

Now had any one conversant with the habits of the disease heard this history, they would have had no hesitation in pronouncing it a case of spurious cow-pox; considering its deviation in the *numerous* blisters which appeared on the girl's hands; their termination without ulceration; its not proving more generally contagious at the farm, either among the cattle or those employed in milking; and considering also that *the patient felt no general indisposition, although there was so great a number of vesicles.*

This is perhaps the most deceptious form in which an eruptive disease can be communicated from the cow, and it certainly requires some attention in discriminating it. The most perfect criterion by which the judgment may be guided is perhaps that adopted by those who attend infected cattle. These white blisters on the nipples, they say, *never eat into the fleshy parts* like those which are commonly of a bluish cast, and which constitute the *true cow-pox,* but that they affect the skin only, quickly end in scabs, and are not nearly so infectious.

That which appeared to me as one cause of spurious eruptions, I have already remarked in the former treatise, namely, the transition that the cow makes in the spring from a poor to a nutritious diet, and from the udder's becoming at this time more vascular than usual for the supply of milk. But there is another source of inflammation and pustules which I believe is not uncommon in all the dairy counties in the west of England. A cow intended to be exposed for sale, having naturally a small udder, is previously for a day or two neither milked artificially nor is her calf suffered to have access to her. Thus the milk is preternaturally accumulated, and the udder and nipples become greatly distended. The consequences frequently are inflammation and eruptions which maturate.

Whether a disease generated in this way has the power of affecting the constitution in any *peculiar* manner I cannot presume positively to determine. It has been conjectured to have been a cause of the true cow-pox, though my inquiries have not led me to adopt this supposition in any one instance; on the contrary, I have known the milkers affected by it, but always found that an affection thus induced left the system as susceptible of the smallpox as before.

What is advanced in my second position I consider also of very great importance, and I could wish it to be strongly impressed on the minds of all who may be disposed to conclude hastily on my observations, whether engaged in their investigation by experiments or not. To place this in its clearest point of view (as the similarity between the action of the smallpox and the cow-pox matter is so obvious) it will be necessary to consider what we sometimes observe to take place in inoculation for the smallpox when imperfect variolous matter is made use of. The concise history on this subject that was brought forward respecting what I had observed in this neighbourhood[1] I perceive, by a reference since made to the Memoirs of the Medical Society of London, may be considered as no more than a corroboration of the facts very clearly detailed by Mr. Kite.[2] To this copious evidence I have to add still more in the following communications from Mr. Earle, surgeon, of Frampton-upon-Severn, in this county, which I deem the more valuable, as he has with much candour permitted me to make them public:

"SIR:

"I have read with satisfaction your late publication on the Variolæ Vaccinæ, and being, among many other curious circumstances, particularly struck with that relating to the inefficacy of smallpox matter in a particular state, I think it proper to lay before you the following facts which came within my own knowledge, and which certainly tend to strengthen the opinions advanced in pages 56 and 57 of your treatise.

"In March, 1784, a general inoculation took place at Arlingham in this county. I inoculated several patients with active variolous matter, all of whom had the disease in a favourable way; but the matter being all used, and not being able to procure any more in the state I wished, I was under the necessity of taking it from a pustule which, experience has since proved, was advanced too far to answer the purpose I intended. Of five persons inoculated with this last matter, four took the smallpox afterwards in the natural way, one of whom died, three recovered, and the other, being cautioned by me to avoid as much as possible the chance of catching it, escaped from the disease through life. He died of another disorder about two years ago.

"Although one of these cases ended unfortunate, yet I cannot suppose that any medical man will think me careless or inattentive in their management; for I conceive the appearances were such as might have induced any one to sup-

---

[1] Inquiry into the Causes and Effects of the Variolæ Vaccinæ, p. 56 of the original article.
[2] See an account of some anomalous appearances consequent to the inoculation of the smallpox, by Charles Kite, Surgeon, of Gravesend, in the Memoirs of the Medical Society of London, vol. iv, p. 114.

pose that the persons were perfectly safe from future infection. Inflammation in every case took place in the arm, and fever came on with a considerable degree of pain in the axilla. In some of their arms the inflammation and suppuration were more violent than is commonly observed when perfect matter is made use of; in one there was an ulcer which cast off several large sloughs. About the ninth day eruptions appeared, which died away earlier than common without maturation. From these circumstances I should suppose that no medical practitioner would scarcely have entertained a doubt but that these patients had been infected with a true smallpox; yet I must confess that some small degree of doubt presented itself to me at the speedy disappearance of the eruptions; and in order, as far as I could, to ascertain their safety, I sent one of them to a much older practitioner than myself. This gentleman, on hearing the circumstances of the case, pronounced the patient perfectly secure from future infection.

"The following facts are also a striking proof of the truth of your observations on this subject:

"In the year 1789 I inoculated three children of Mr. Coaley, of Hurst farm in this county. The arms inflamed properly, fever and pain in the axillæ came on precisely the same as in the former cases, and in ten days eruptions appeared, which disappeared in the course of two days. I must observe that the matter here made use of was procured for me by a friend; but no doubt it was in an improper state; for, from the similarity of these cases to those which happened at Arlingham five years before, I was somewhat alarmed for their safety, and desired to inoculate them again: which being permitted, I was particularly careful to procure matter in its most perfect state. All the children took the smallpox from this second inoculation, and all had a very full burthen. These facts I conceive strikingly corroborate your opinion relative to the different states of matter; for in both instances that I have mentioned it was capable of producing something strongly resembling the true smallpox, although it afterwards proved not to be so.

"As I think the communication of these cases is a duty

I owe to the public, you are at liberty to make what use you please of this letter.   I remain, &c.,
"John Earle.
"FRAMPTON-UPON SEVERN, GLOUCESTERSHIRE, November 10, 1798.

"P. S. I think it necessary to observe that I can pronounce, with the greatest certainty, that the matter with which the Arlingham patients were inoculated was taken from a true smallpox pustule. I took it myself from a subject that had a very full burthen."

Certain then it is that variolous matter may undergo such a change from the putrefactive process, as well as from some of the more obscure and latent processes of nature, as will render it incapable of giving the smallpox in such a manner as to secure the human constitution from future infection, although we see at the same time it is capable of exciting a disease which bears so strong a resemblance to it as to produce inflammation and matter in the incised skin (frequently, indeed, more violent than when it produces its effects perfectly), swelling of the axillary glands, general indisposition, and eruptions. So strongly persuaded was the gentleman, whose practice I have mentioned in page 56 of the late treatise, that he could produce a mild smallpox by his mode of managing the matter, that he spoke of it as a useful discovery until convinced of his error by the fatal consequence which ensued.

After this ought we to be in the smallest degree surprised to find, among a great number of individuals who, by living in dairies, have been casually exposed to the cow-pox virus when in a state analogous to that of the smallpox above described, some who may have had the disease so imperfectly as not to render them secure from variolous attacks? For the matter, when burst from the pustules on the nipples of the cow, by being exposed, from its lodgment there, to the heat of an inflamed surface, and from being at the same time in a situation to be occasionally moistened with milk, is often likely to be in a state conducive to putrefaction; and thus, under some modification of decomposition, it must, of course, sometimes find access to the hand of the milker in such a way as to infect him. What confusion should we have were there no other mode of inoculating the smallpox than such as would happen from handling the diseased skin of a person labouring under that distemper in some of its advanced and loathsome stages! It must be observed that every case of cow-pox in the human species, whether communicated by design or otherwise, is to be considered as a case of inoculation. And here I may be allowed to make an observation on the case of the farmer communicated to me by Dr. Ingenhousz. That he was exposed to the matter when it had undergone the putrefactive change is highly probable from the doctor's observing that the sick cows at the farm gave out an *offensive stench from their udders.* However, I must remark that it is unusual for cattle to suffer to such an extent, when disordered with the cow-pox, as to make a bystander sensible of any ill smell. I have often stood among a herd which had the distemper without being conscious of its presence from any particular effluvia. Indeed, in this neighbourhood it commonly receives an early check from escharotic applications of the *cow leech.* It has been conceived to be contagious without contact; but this idea cannot be well founded because the cattle in one meadow do not infect those in another (although there may be no other partition than a hedge) unless they be handled or milked by those who bring the infectious matter with them; and of course, the smallest particle imaginable, when applied to a part susceptible of its influence, may produce the effect. Among the human species it appears to be very clear that the disease is produced by contact only. All my attempts, at least, to communicate it by effluvia have hitherto proved ineffectual.

As well as the perfect change from that state in which variolous matter is capable of producing full and decisive effects on the constitution, to that wherein its specific properties are entirely lost, it may reasonably be supposed that it is capable of undergoing a variety of intermediate changes. The following singular occurrences in ten cases of inoculation, obligingly communicated to me by Mr. Trye, Senior Surgeon to the Infirmary at Glocester, seem to indicate that the variolous matter, previously to its being taken from the patient for the intended purpose, was beginning to part with some of its original properties, or, in other words, that it had suffered a partial decomposition. Mr. Trye says: " I inoculated ten children with matter taken at one time and from the same subject. I observed no peculiarity in any of them previously to their inoculation, nor did any thing remarkable appear in their arms till after the decline of the disease. Two infants of three months old had erysipelas about the incisions, in one of them extending from the shoulders to the fingers' ends. Another infant had abscesses in the cellular substance in the neighbourhood of the incisions, and five or six of the rest had axillary abscesses. The matter was taken from the distinct smallpox late in its progress, and when some pustules had been dried. It was received upon glass and slowly dried by the fire. All the children had pustules which maturated, so that I suppose them all secure from future infection; at least, as secure as any others whom I have ever inoculated. My practice never afforded a sore arm before."

In regard to my former observation on the improper and dangerous mode of preserving variolous matter, I shall here remark that it seems not to have been clearly understood. Finding that it has been confounded with the more eligible modes of preservation, I will explain myself further. When the matter is taken from a fit pustule and properly prepared for preservation, it may certainly be kept without losing its specific properties a great length of time; for instance, when it is previously dried in the open air on some compact body, as a quill or a piece of glass, and afterwards secured in a small vial.[3] But when kept several days in a state of moisture, and during that time exposed to a warm temperature, I do not think it can be relied upon as capable of giving a *perfect* disease, although, as I have before observed, the progress of the symptoms arising from the action of the imperfect matter bear so strong a resemblance to the smallpox when excited completely.

Thirdly. That the first formed virus, or what constitutes the true cow-pox pustule, invariably possesses the power I

[3] Thus prepared, the cow-pox virus was found perfectly active, and possessing all its specific properties, at the end of three months.

have ascribed to it, namely, that of affecting the constitution with a specific disease, is a truth that no subsequent occurrence has yet led me to doubt. But as I am now endeavouring to guard the public as much as possible against erroneous conclusions, I shall observe that when this pustule has degenerated into an ulcer (to which state it is often disposed to pass unless timely checked), I suspect that matter possessing very different properties may sooner or later be produced; and although it may have passed that stage wherein the specific properties of the matter secreted are no longer present in it, yet when applied to a sore (as in the casual way) it might dispose that sore to ulcerate, and from its irritation the system would probably become affected; and thus, by assuming some of its strongest characters, it would imitate the genuine cow-pox.

From the preceding observations on the matter of smallpox when decomposed it must, I conceive, be admitted that cow-pox matter in the state now described may produce a disease, the effects of which may be felt both locally and generally, yet that the disease thus induced may not be effectual in obviating the future effects of variolous contagion. In the case of Mary Miller, related by Mr. Kite in the volume above alluded to, it appears that the inflammation and suppuration of the inoculated arm were more than usually severe, although the system underwent no specific change from the action of the virus; which appears from the patient's sickening seven weeks afterwards with the natural smallpox, which went through its course. Some of the cases communicated by Mr. Earle tend further to confirm this fact, as the matter there manifestly produced ulceration on the inoculated part to a considerable extent.

Fourthly. Whether the cow-pox is a spontaneous disease in the cow, or is to be attributed to matter conveyed to the animal, as I have conceived, from the horse, is a question which, though I shall not attempt now fully to discuss, yet I shall digress so far as to adduce some further observations, and to give my reasons more at large for taking up an opinion that to some had appeared fanciful. The aggregate of these observations, though not amounting to positive proof, forms presumptive evidence of so forcible a kind that I imagine it might, on any other person, have made the same impression it did on me, without fixing the imputation of credulity.

First: I conceived this was the source, from observing that where the cow-pox had appeared among the dairies here (unless it could be traced to the introduction of an infected cow or servant) it had been preceded at the farm by a horse diseased in the manner already described, which horse had been attended by some of the milkers.

Secondly: From its being a popular opinion throughout this great dairy country, and from its being insisted on by those who here attend sick cattle.

Thirdly: From the total absence of the disease in Ireland and Scotland, where the men-servants are not employed in the dairies.[4]

Fourthly: From having observed that morbid matter generated by the horse frequently communicates, in a casual way, a disease to the human subject so like the cow-pox that, in many cases, it would be difficult to make the distinction between one and the other.[5]

Fifthly: From being induced to suppose, from experiments, that some of those who had been thus affected from the horse resisted the smallpox.

Sixthly: From the progress and general appearance of the pustule on the arm of the boy whom I inoculated with matter taken from the hand of a man infected by a horse; and from the similarity to the cow-pox of general constitutional symptoms which followed.[6]

I fear it would be trespassing too far to adduce the general testimony of our farmers in support of this opinion; yet I beg leave to introduce an extract of a letter on this

---

[4] This information was communicated to me from the first authority.
[5] The sound skin does not appear to be susceptible of this virus when inserted into it, but, when previously diseased from little accidents, its effects are often conspicuous.
[6] This case (on which I laid no inconsiderable stress in my late treatise, as presumptive evidence of the fact adduced) seems to have been either mistaken or overlooked by those who have commented upon it. (See Case XVIII, p. 36.) The boy, unfortunately, died of a fever at a parish workhouse before I had an opportunity of observing what effects would have been produced by the matter of smallpox

subject from the Rev. Mr. Moore, of Chalford Hill, in this county:

"In the month of November, 1797, my horse had diseased heels, which was certainly what is termed the grease; and at a short subsequent period my cow was also affected with what a neighbouring farmer (who was conversant with the complaints of cattle) pronounced to be the cow-pox, which he at the same time observed my servant would be infected with: and this proved to be the case; for he had eruptions on his hands, face, and many parts of the body, the pustules appearing large, and not much like the smallpox, for which he had been inoculated a year and a half before, and had then a very heavy burthen. The pustules on the face might arise from contact with his hands, as he had a habit of rubbing his forehead, where the sores were the largest and the thickest.

"The boy associated with the farmer's sons during the continuance of the disease, neither of whom had had the smallpox, but they felt no ill effects whatever. He was not much indisposed, as the disease did not prevent him from following his occupations as usual. No other person attended the horse or milked the cow but the lad above mentioned. I am firmly of opinion that the disease in the heels of the horse, which was a virulent grease, was the origin of the servant's and the cow's malady."

But to return to the more immediate object of this proposition.

From the similarity of symptoms, both constitutional and local, between the cow-pox and the disease received from morbid matter generated by a horse, the common people in this neighbourhood, when infected with this disease, through a strange perversion of terms, frequently call it the cow-pox. Let us suppose, then, such a malady to appear among some of the servants at a farm, and at the same time that the cow-pox were to break out among the cattle; and let us suppose, too, that some of the servants were infected in this way, and that others received the infection from the cows. It would be recorded at the farm, and among the servants themselves wherever they might afterwards be dispersed, that they had all had the cow-pox. But it is clear that an individual thus infected from the horse would neither be for a certainty secure himself, nor would he impart security to others were they inoculated by virus thus generated. He still would be in danger of taking the smallpox. Yet were this to happen before the nature of the cowpox be more maturely considered by the public my evidence on the subject might be depreciated unjustly. For an exemplification of what is here advanced relative to the nature of the infection when received directly from the horse see Inquiry into the Causes and Effects of the Variolæ Vaccinæ, pp. 27, 28, 29, 30, and p. 35; and by way of further example, I beg leave to subjoin the following intelligence received from Mr. Fewster, Surgeon, of Thornbury, in this county, a gentleman perfectly well acquainted with the appearances of the cow-pox on the human subject:

"William Morris, aged thirty-two, servant to Mr. Cox of Almondsbury, in this county, applied to me the 2d of April, 1798. He told me that, four days before, he found a stiffness and swelling in both his hands, which were so painful it was with difficulty he continued his work; that he had been seized with pain in his head, small of the back, and limbs, and with frequent chilly fits succeeded by fever. On examination I found him still affected with these symptoms, and that there was a great prostration of strength. Many parts of his hands on the inside were chapped, and on the middle joint of the thumb of the right hand there was a small phagedenic ulcer, about the size of a large pea, discharging an ichorous fluid. On the middle finger of the same hand there was another ulcer of a similar kind. These sores were of a *circular* form, and he described their first appearance as being somewhat like blisters arising from a burn. He complained of excessive pain, which extended up his arm into the axilla. These symptoms and appearances of the sores were so exactly like the cow-pox that I pronounced he had taken the distemper from milking cows. He assured me he had not milked a cow for more than half a year, and that his master's cows had nothing the matter with them. I then asked him if his master had a *greasy* horse, which he answered in the affirmative, and further said that he had constantly dressed him twice a day for the last three weeks or more, and remarked that the smell of his hands was much like that of the horses's heels. On the 5th of April I again saw him, and found him still complaining of pain in both hands, nor were his febrile symptoms at all relieved. The ulcers had now spread to the size of a seven-shilling gold coin, and another ulcer, which I had not noticed before, appeared on the first joint of the forefinger of the left hand, equally painful with that on the right. I ordered him to bathe his hands in warm bran and water, applied escharotics to the ulcers, and wrapped his hands up in a soft cataplasm. The next day he was much relieved, and in something more than a fortnight got well. He lost his nails from the thumb and fingers that were ulcerated."

The sudden disappearance of the symptoms in this case after the application of the escharotics to the sores is worthy of observation; it seems to show that they were kept up by the irritation of the ulcers.

The general symptoms which I have already described of the cow-pox, when communicated in a casual way to any great extent, will, I am convinced, from the many cases I have seen, be found accurate; but from the very slight indisposition which ensues in cases of inoculation, where the pustule, after affecting the constitution, quickly runs into a scab spontaneously, or is artificially suppressed by some proper application, I am induced to believe that the violence of the symptoms may be ascribed to the inflammation and irritation of the ulcers (when ulceration takes place to any extent, as in the casual cow-pox), and that the constitutional symptoms which appear during the presence of the sore, while it assumes the character of a pustule only, are felt but in a very trifling degree. This mild affection of the system happens when the disease makes but a slight local impression on those who have been accidentally infected by cows; and, as far as I have seen, it has uniformly happened among those who have been inoculated, when a pustule only and no great degree of inflammation or any ulceration has taken place from the inoculation. The following cases will strengthen this opinion.

The cow-pox appeared at a farm in the village of Stonehouse, in this county, about Michaelmas last, and continued gradually to pass from one cow to another till the end of November. On the twenty-sixth of that month some ichorous matter was taken from a cow and dried upon a quill. On the 2d of December some of it was inserted into a scratch, made so superficial that no blood appeared, on the arms of Susan Phipps, a child seven years old. The common inflammatory appearances took place in consequence, and advanced till the fifth day, when they had so much subsided that I did not conceive any thing further would ensue.

6th: Appearances stationary.

7th: The inflammation began to advance.

8th: A vesication, perceptible on the edges, forming, as in the inoculated smallpox, an appearance not unlike a grain of wheat, with the cleft, or indentation in the centre.

9th: Pain in the axilla.

10th: A little headache; pulse, 110; tongue not discoloured; countenance in health.

11th, 12th: No perceptible illness; pulse about 100.

13th: The pustule was now surrounded by an efflorescence, interspersed with very minute confluent pustules to the extent of about an inch. Some of these pustules advanced in size and maturated. So exact was the resemblance of the arm at this stage to the general appearance of the inoculated smallpox that Mr. D., a neighbouring surgeon, who took some matter from it, and who had never seen the cow-pox before, declared he could not perceive any difference.[7] The child's arm now shewed a disposition to scab, and remained nearly stationary for two or three days, when it began to run into an ulcerous state, and *then* commenced a febrile indisposition accompanied with an increase of axillary tumour. The ulcer continued spreading near a week, during which time the child continued ill, when

---

[7] That the cow-pox was a supposed guardian of the constitution from the action of the smallpox has been a prevalent idea for a long time past; but the similarity in the constitutional effects between one disease and the other could never have been so accurately observed had not the inoculation of the cow-pox placed it in a new and stronger point of view. This practice, too, has shewn us, what before lay concealed, the rise and progress of the pustule formed by the insertion of the virus, which places in a most conspicuous light its striking resemblance to the pustule formed from the inoculated smallpox.

it increased to a size nearly as large as a shilling. It began now to discharge pus; granulations sprang up, and it healed. This child had before been of a remarkably sickly constitution, but is now in very high health.

Mary Hearn, twelve years of age, was inoculated with matter taken from the arm of Susan Phipps.

6th day: A pustule beginning to appear, slight pain in the axilla.

7th: A distinct vesicle formed.

8th: The vesicle increasing; edges very red; no deviation in its appearance at this time from the inoculated smallpox.

9th: No indisposition; pustule advancing.

10th: The patient felt this evening a slight febrile attack.

11th: Free from indisposition.

12th, 13th: The same.

14th: An efflorescence of a faint red colour extending several inches round the arm. The pustule, beginning to shew a disposition to spread, was dressed with an ointment composed of *hydrarg. nit. rub. and ung. ceræ*. The efflorescence itself was covered with a plaster of *ung. hydr. fort*. In six hours it was examined, when it was found that the efflorescence had totally disappeared.

The application of the ointment with the *hydr. nit. rub.* was made use of for three days, when, the state of the pustule remaining stationary, it was exchanged for the *ung. hydr. nit.* This appeared to have a more active effect than the former, and in two or three days the virus seemed to be subdued, when a simple dressing was made use of; but the sore again shewing a disposition to inflame, the *ung. hydr. nit.* was again applied, and soon answered the intended purpose effectually. The girl, after the tenth day, when, as has been observed, she became a little ill, shewed not the least symptom of indisposition. She was afterwards exposed to the action of variolous matter, and completely resisted it. Susan Phipps also went through a similar trial. Conceiving these cases to be important, I have given them in detail: first, to urge the precaution of using such means as may stop the progress of the pustule; and, secondly, to point out (what appears to be the fact) that the most material indisposition, or at least that which is felt most sensibly, *does not arise primarily from the first action of the virus on the constitution, but that it often comes on, if the pustule is left to chance, as a secondary disease.* This leads me to conjecture, what experiment must finally determine, that they who have had the smallpox are not afterwards susceptible of the primary action of the cow-pox virus; for seeing that the simple virus itself, when it has not passed beyond the boundary of a vesicle, excites in the system so little commotion, is it not probable the trifling illness thus induced may be lost in that which so quickly, and oftentimes so severely, follows in the casual cow-pox from the presence of corroding ulcers? This consideration induces me to suppose that I may have been mistaken in my former observation on this subject.

In this respect, as well as many others, a parallel may be drawn between this disease and the smallpox. In the latter, the patient first feels the effect of what is called the absorption of the virus. The symptoms then often nearly retire, when a fresh attack commences, different from the first, and the illness keeps pace with the progress of the pustules through their different stages of maturation, ulceration, etc.

Although the application I have mentioned in the case of Mary Hearn proved sufficient to check the progress of ulceration and prevent any secondary symptoms, yet, after the pustule has duly exerted its influence, I should prefer the destroying it quickly and effectually to any other mode. The term caustic to a tender ear (and I conceive none feel more interested in this inquiry than the anxious guardians of a nursery) may sound harsh and unpleasing, but every solicitude that may arise on this account will no longer exist when it is understood that the pustule, in a state fit to be acted upon, is then quite superficial, and that it does not occupy the space of a silver penny.[8]

As a proof of the efficacy of this practice, even before the virus has fully exerted itself on the system, I shall lay before my reader the following history:

[8] I mention escharotics for stopping the progress of the pustule because I am acquainted with their efficacy; probably more simple means might answer the purpose quite as well, such as might be found among the mineral and vegetable astringents.

By a reference to the treatise on the Variolæ Vaccinæ it will be seen that, in the month of April, 1798, four children were inoculated with the matter of cow-pox, and that in two of these cases the virus on the arm was destroyed soon after it had produced a perceptible sickening. Mary James, aged seven years, one of the children alluded to, was inoculated in the month of December following with fresh variolous matter, and at the same time was exposed to the effluvia of a patient affected with the smallpox. The appearance and progress of the infected arm was, in every respect, similar to that which we generally observe when variolous matter has been inserted into the skin of a person who has not previously undergone either the cow-pox or the smallpox. On the eighth day, conceiving there was infection in it, she was removed from her residence among those who had not had the smallpox. I was now anxiously waiting the result, conceiving, from the state of the girl's arm, she would fall sick about this time. On visiting her on the evening of the following day (the ninth) all I could learn from the woman who attended her was that she felt somewhat hotter than usual during the night, but was not restless; and that in the morning there was the faint appearance of a rash about her wrists. This went off in a few hours, and was not at all perceptible to me on my visit in the evening. Not a single eruption appeared, the skin having been repeatedly and carefully examined. The inoculated arm continued to make the usual progress to the end, through all the stages of inflammation, maturation, and scabbing.

On the eighth day matter was taken from the arm of this girl (Mary James) and inserted into the arms of her mother and brother (neither of whom had had either the smallpox or the cow-pox), the former about fifty years of age, the latter six.

On the eighth day after the insertion the boy felt indisposed, and continued unwell two days, when a measles-like rash appeared on his hands and wrists, and was thinly scattered over his arms. The day following his body was marbled over with an appearance somewhat similar, but he did not complain, nor did he appear indisposed. A few pustules now appeared, the greater part of which went away without maturating.

On the ninth day the mother began to complain. She was a little chilly and had a headache for two days, but *no pustule appeared on the skin,* nor had she any appearance of a rash.

The family was attended by an elderly woman as a nurse, who in her infancy had been exposed to the contagion of the smallpox, but had resisted it. This woman was now infected, but had the disease in the slightest manner, a very few eruptions appearing, two or three of which only maturated.

From a solitary instance like that adduced of Mary James, whose constitution appears to have resisted the action of the variolous virus, after the influence of the cow-pox virus had been so soon arrested in its progress, no positive conclusion can be fairly drawn; nor from the history of the three other patients who were subsequently infected, but, nevertheless, the facts collectively may be deemed interesting.

That one mild variety of the smallpox has appeared I have already plainly shewn;[9] and by the means now mentioned we probably have it in our power to produce at will another.

At the time when the pustule was destroyed in the arm of Mary James I was informed she had been indisposed about twelve hours; but I am now assured by those who were with her that the space of time was much less. Be that as it may, in cases of cow-pox inoculation I would not recommend any application to subdue the action of the pustule until convincing proofs had appeared of the patient's having felt its effects at least twelve hours. No harm, indeed, could ensue were a longer period to elapse before the application was made use of. In short, it should be suffered to have as full an effect as it could, consistently with the state of the arm.

As the cases of inoculation multiply, I am more and more convinced of the extreme mildness of the symptoms arising

[9] See Inquiry into the Causes and Effects of the Variolæ Vaccinæ, p. 54 (of original article).

merely from the primary action of the virus on the constitution, and that those symptoms which, as in the accidental cow-pox, affect the patient with severity, are entirely secondary, excited by the irritating processes of inflammation and ulceration; and it appears to me that this singular virus possesses an irritating quality of a peculiar kind, but as a single cow-pox pustule is all that is necessary to render the variolous virus ineffectual, and as we possess the means of allaying the irritation, should any arise, it becomes of little or no consequence.

It appears then, as far as an inference can be drawn from the present progress of cow-pox inoculation, that it is an accidental circumstance only which can render this a violent disease, and a circumstance of that nature which, fortunately, it is in the power of almost every one to avoid. I allude to the communication of the disease from cows. In this case, should the hands of the milker be affected with little accidental sores to any extent, every sore would become the nidus of infection and feel the influence of the virus; and the degree of violence in the constitutional symptoms would be in proportion to the number and to the state of these local affections. Hence it follows that a person, either by accident or design, might be so filled with these wounds from contact with the virus that the constitution might sink under the pressure.

Seeing that we possess the means of rendering the action of the sores mild, which, when left to chance, are capable of producing violent effects; and seeing, too, that these sores bear a resemblance to the smallpox, especially the confluent, should it not encourage the hope that some topical application might be used with advantage to counteract the fatal tendency of that disease, when it appears in this terrific form? At what stage or stages of the disease this may be done with the most promising expectation of success I will not pretend now to determine. I only throw out this idea as the basis of further reasoning and experiment.

I have often been foiled in my endeavours to communicate the cow-pox by inoculation. An inflammation will sometimes succeed the scratch or puncture, and in a few days disappear without producing any further effect. Some-

VACCINATION AGAINST SMALLPOX

times it will even produce an ichorous fluid, and yet the system will not be affected. The same thing we know happens with the smallpox virus.

Four or five servants were inoculated at a farm contiguous to this place, last summer, with matter just taken from an infected cow. A little inflammation appeared on all their arms, but died away without producing a pustule; yet all these servants caught the disease within a month afterwards from milking the infected cows, and some of them had it severely. At present no other mode than that commonly practiced for inoculating the smallpox has been used for giving the cow-pox; but it is probable this might be varied with advantage. We should imitate the casual communication more clearly were we first, by making the smallest superficial incision or puncture on the skin, to produce a little scab, and then, removing it, to touch the abraded part with the virus. A small portion of a thread imbrued in the virus (as in the old method of inoculating the smallpox) and laid upon the slightly incised skin might probably prove a successful way of giving the disease; or the cutis might be exposed in a minute point by an atom of blistering plaster, and the virus brought in contact with it. In the cases just alluded to, where I did not succeed in giving the disease constitutionally, the experiment was made with matter taken in a purulent state from a pustule on the nipple of a cow.

Is *pure pus*, though contained in a smallpox pustule, ever capable of producing the smallpox perfectly? I suspect it is not. Let us consider that it is always preceded by the limpid fluid, which, in constitutions susceptible of variolous contagion, is always infectious; and though, on opening a pustule, its contents may appear perfectly purulent, yet a given quantity of the limpid fluid may, at the same time, be blended with it, though it would be imperceptible to the only test of our senses, the eye. The presence, then, of this fluid, or its mechanical diffusion through pus, may at all times render active what is apparently *mere pus*, while its total absence (as in stale pustules) may be attended with the imperfect effects we have seen.

It would be digressing too widely to go far into the

doctrine of secretion, but as it will not be quite extraneous, I shall just observe that I consider both the pus and the limpid fluid of the pustule as secretions, but that the organs established by nature to perform the office of secreting these fluids may differ essentially in their mechanical structure. What but a difference in the organization of glandular bodies constitutes the difference in the qualities of the fluids secreted? From some peculiar derangement in the structure or, in other words, some deviation in the natural action of a gland destined to create a mild, innoxious fluid, a poison of the most deadly nature may be created; for example: That gland, which in its sound state secretes pure saliva, may, from being thrown into diseased action, produce a poison of the most destructive quality. Nature appears to have no more difficulty in forming minute glands among the vascular parts of the body than she has in forming blood vessels, and millions of these can be called into existence, when inflammation is excited, in a few hours.[10]

In the present early stage of the inquiry (for early it certainly must be deemed), before we know for an absolute certainty how soon the virus of the cow-pox may suffer a change in its specific properties, after it has quitted the limpid state it possesses when forming a pustule, it would be prudent for those who have been inoculated with it to submit to variolous inoculation. No injury or inconvenience can accrue from this; and were the same method practiced among those who, from inoculation, have felt the smallpox in an unsatisfactory manner at any period of their lives, it might appear that I had not been too officious in offering a cautionary hint in recommending a second inoculation with matter in its most perfect state.

And here let me suppose, for argument's sake (not from conviction), that one person in an hundred after having had the cow-pox should be found susceptible of the smallpox, would this invalidate the utility of the practice? For, waiving all other considerations, who will deny that the inoculated smallpox, although abstractedly it may be considered as

[10] Mr. Home, in his excellent dissertation on pus and mucus, justifies this assertion.

harmless, does not involve in itself something that in numberless instances proves baneful to the human frame.

That in delicate constitutions it sometimes excites scrofula is a fact that must generally be subscribed to, as it is so obvious to common observation. This consideration is important.

As the effects of the smallpox inoculation on those who have had the cow-pox will be watched with the most scrupulous eye by those who prosecute this inquiry, it may be proper to bring to their recollection some facts relative to the smallpox, which I must consider here as of consequence, but which hitherto seem not to have made a due impression.

It should be remembered that the constitution cannot, by previous infection, be rendered totally unsusceptible of the variolous poison; neither the casual nor the inoculated smallpox, whether it produces the disease in a mild or in a violent way, can perfectly extinguish the susceptibility. The skin, we know, is ever ready to exhibit, though often in a very limited degree, the effects of the poison when inserted there; and how frequently do we see, among nurses, when much exposed to the contagion, eruptions, and these sometimes preceded by sensible illness! yet should any thing like an eruption appear, or the smallest degree of indisposition, upon the insertion of the variolous matter on those who have gone through the cow-pox, my assertions respecting the peculiarities of the disease might be unjustly discredited.

I know a gentleman who, many years ago, was inoculated for the smallpox, but having no pustules, or scarcely any constitutional affection that was perceptible, he was dissatisfied, and has since been repeatedly inoculated. A vesicle has always been produced in the arm in consequence, with axillary swelling and a slight indisposition; this is by no means a rare occurrence. It is probable that fluid thus excited upon the skin would always produce the smallpox.

On the arm of a person who had gone through the cow-pox many years before I once produced a vesication by the insertion of variolous matter, and, with a little of the fluid, inoculated a young woman who had a mild, but very efficacious, smallpox in consequence, although no constitutional effect was produced on the patient from whom the matter was taken. The following communication from Mr. Fewster affords a still clearer elucidation of this fact. Mr. Fewster says: "On the 3d of April, 1797, I inoculated Master H——, aged fourteen months, for the smallpox. At the usual time he sickened, had a plentiful eruption, particularly on his face, and got well. His nursemaid, aged twenty-four, had many years before gone through the smallpox, in the natural way, which was evident from her being much pitted with it. She had used the child to sleep on her left arm, with her left cheek in contact with his face, and during his inoculation he had mostly slept in that manner. About a week after the child got well she (the nurse) desired me to look at her face, which she said was very painful. There was a plentiful eruption on the left cheek, *but not on any other part of the body,* which went on to maturation.

"On enquiry I found that three days before the appearance of the eruption she was taken with slight chilly fits, pain in her head and limbs, and some fever. On the appearance of the eruption these pains went off, and now, the second day of the eruption, she complains of a little sore throat. Whether the above symptoms are the effects of the smallpox or a recent cold I do not know. On the fifth day of the eruption I charged a lancet from two of the pustules, and on the next day I inoculated two children, one two years, the other four months old, with the matter. At the same time I inoculated the mother and eldest sister with variolous matter taken from Master H——. On the fifth day of their inoculation *all* their arms were inflamed alike; and on the eighth day the eldest of those inoculated from the nurse sickened, and the youngest on the eleventh. They had both a plentiful eruption, from which I inoculated several others, who had the disease very favourably. The mother and the other child sickened about the same time, and likewise had a plentiful eruption.

"Soon after, a man in the village sickened with the smallpox and had a confluent kind. To be convinced that the children had had the disease effectually I took them to his house and inoculated them in both arms with matter taken from him, but without effect."

These are not brought forward as uncommon occurrences,

but as exemplifications of the human system's susceptibility of the variolous contagion, although it has been previously sensible of its action.

Happy is it for mankind that the appearance of the smallpox a second time on the same person, beyond a trivial extent, is so extremely rare that it is looked upon as a phænomenon! Indeed, since the publication of Dr. Heberden's paper on the *Varicellæ,* or chicken-pox, the idea of such an occurrence, in deference to authority so truly respectable, has been generally relinquished. This I conceive has been without just reason; for after we have seen, among many others, so strong a case as that recorded by Mr. Edward Withers, Surgeon, of Newbury, Berks, in the fourth volume of the Memoirs of the Medical Society of London (from which I take the following extracts), no one, I think, will again doubt the fact.

"Mr. Richard Langford, a farmer of West Shefford, in this county (Berks), about fifty years of age, when about a month old had the smallpox at a time when three others of the family had the same disease, one of whom, a servant man, died of it. Mr. Langford's countenance was strongly indicative of the malignity of the distemper, his face being so remarkably pitted and seamed as to attract the notice of all who saw him, so that no one could entertain a doubt of his having had that disease in a most inveterate manner." Mr. Withers proceeds to state that Mr. Langford was seized a second time, had a bad confluent smallpox, and died on the twenty-first day from the seizure; and that four of the family, as also a sister of the patient's, to whom the disease was conveyed by her son's visiting his uncle, falling down with the smallpox, fully satisfied the country with regard to the nature of the disease, which nothing short of this would have done; the sister died.

"This case was thought so extraordinary a one as to induce the rector of the parish to record the particulars in the parish register."

It is singular that in most cases of this kind the disease in the first instance has been confluent; so that the extent of the ulceration on the skin (as in the cow-pox) is not the process in nature which affords security to the constitution.

As the subject of the smallpox is so interwoven with that which is the more immediate object of my present concern, it must plead my excuse for so often introducing it. At present it must be considered as a distemper not well understood. The inquiry I have instituted into the nature of the cow-pox will probably promote its more perfect investigation.

The inquiry of Dr. Pearson into the history of the cow-pox having produced so great a number of attestations in favour of my assertion that it proves a protection to the human body from the smallpox, I have not been assiduous in seeking for more; but as some of my friends have been so good as to communicate the following, I shall conclude these observations with their insertion.

Extract of a letter from Mr. Drake, Surgeon, at Stroud, in this county, and late Surgeon to the North Gloucester Regiment of Militia:

"In the spring of the year 1796 I inoculated men, women, and children to the amount of about seventy. Many of the men did not receive the infection, although inoculated at least three times and kept in the same room with those who actually underwent the disease during the whole time occupied by them in passing through it. Being anxious they should, in future, be secure against it, I was very particular in my inquiries to find out whether they ever had previously had it, or at any time been in the neighbourhood of people labouring under it. But, after all, the only satisfactory information I could obtain was that they had had the cow-pox. As I was then ignorant of such a disease affecting the human subject, I flattered myself what they imagined to be the cow-pox was in reality the smallpox in a very slight degree. I mentioned the circumstance in the presence of the officers, at the time expressing my doubts if it were not smallpox, and was not a little surprised when I was told by the Colonel that he had frequently heard you mention the cow-pox as a disease endemial to Gloucestershire, and that if a person were ever affected by it, you supposed him afterwards secure from the smallpox. This excited my curiosity, and when I visited Gloucestershire I was very inquisitive concerning the subject, and from the information I have since received, both from your publication and from conversation with medical men of the greatest accuracy in their observations, I am fully convinced that what the men supposed to be cow-pox was actually so, and I can safely affirm that they effectually resisted the smallpox."

Mr. Fry, Surgeon, at Dursley in this county, favours me with the following communication:

"During the spring of the year 1797 I inoculated fourteen hundred and seventy-five patients, of all ages, from a fortnight old to seventy years; amongst whom there were many who had previously gone through the cow-pox. The exact number I cannot state; but if I say there were nearly thirty, I am certainly within the number. There was not a single instance of the variolous matter producing any constitutional effect on these people, nor any greater degree of local inflammation than it would have done in the arm of a person who had before gone through the smallpox, notwithstanding it was invariably inserted four, five, and sometimes six different times, to satisfy the minds of the patients. In the common course of inoculation previous to the general one scarcely a year passed without my meeting with one or two instances of persons who had gone through the cow-pox, resisting the action of the variolous contagion. I may fairly say that the number of people I have seen inoculated with the smallpox who, at former periods, had gone through the cow-pox, are not less than forty; and in no one instance have I known a patient receive the smallpox, notwithstanding they invariably continued to associate with other inoculated patients during the progress of the disease, and many of them purposely exposed themselves to the contagion of the natural smallpox; whence I am fully convinced that a person who had *fairly* had the cow-pox is no longer capable of being acted upon by the variolous matter.

"I also inoculated a very considerable number of those who had had a disease which ran through the neighbourhood a few years ago, and was called by the common people the *swine-pox*, not one of whom received the smallpox.[11]

"There were about half a dozen instances of people who never had either the cow- or swine-pox, yet did not receive

[11] This was that mild variety of the smallpox which I have noticed in the late Treatise on the Cow-Pox (p. 233).

the smallpox, the system not being in the least deranged, or the arms inflamed, although they were repeatedly inoculated, and associated with others who were labouring under the disease; one of them was the son of a farrier."

Mr. Tierny, Assistant Surgeon of the South Gloucester Regiment of Militia, has obliged me with the following information:

"That in the summer of the year of 1798 he inoculated a great number of the men belonging to the regiment, and that among them he found eleven who, from having lived in dairies, had gone through the cow-pox. That all of them resisted the smallpox except one, but that on making the most rigid and scrupulous enquiry at the farm in Gloucestershire, where the man said he lived when he had the disease, and among those with whom, at the same time, he declared he had associated, and particularly of a person in the parish, whom he said had dressed his fingers, it most clearly appeared that he aimed at an imposition, and that he never had been affected with the cow-pox."[12] Mr. Tierny remarks that the arms of many who were inoculated after having had the cow-pox inflamed very quickly, and that in several a little ichorous fluid was formed.

Mr. Cline, who in July last was so obliging at my request as to try the efficacy of the cow-pox virus, was kind enough to give me a letter on the result of it, from which the following is an extract:

"MY DEAR SIR:
"The cow-pox experiment has succeeded admirably. The child sickened on the seventh day, and the fever, which was moderate, subsided on the eleventh. The inflammation arising from the insertion of the virus extended to about four inches in diameter, and then gradually subsided, without having been attended with pain or other inconvenience. There were no eruptions.

"I have since inoculated him with smallpox matter in three places, which were slightly inflamed on the third day, and then subsided.

---

[12] The public cannot be too much upon their guard respecting persons of this description.

"Dr. Lister, who was formerly physician to the Smallpox Hospital, attended the child with me, and he is convinced that it is not possible to give him the smallpox. I think the substituting the cow-pox poison for the smallpox promises to be one of the greatest improvements that has ever been made in medicine; and the more I think on the subject, the more I am impressed with its importance.

"With great esteem
"I am, etc.,
"HENRY CLINE.

"Lincoln's Inn Fields,
August 2, 1798."

From communications, with which I have been favoured from Dr. Pearson, who has occasionally reported to me the result of his private practice with the vaccine virus in London, and from Dr. Woodville, who also has favoured me with an account of his more extensive inoculation with the same virus at the Smallpox Hospital, it appears that many of their patients have been affected with eruptions, and that these eruptions have maturated in a manner very similar to the variolous. The matter they made use of was taken in the first instance from a cow belonging to one of the great milk farms in London. Having never seen maturated pustules produced either in my own practice among those who were casually infected by cows, or those to whom the disease had been communicated by inoculation, I was desirous of seeing the effect of the matter generated in London, on subjects living in the country. A thread imbrued in some of this matter was sent to me, and with it two children were inoculated, whose cases I shall transcribe from my notes.

Stephen Jenner, three years and a half old.

3d day: The arm shewed a proper and decisive inflammation.

6th: A vesicle arising.

7th: The pustule of a cherry colour.

8th: Increasing in elevation. A few spots now appear on each arm near the insertion of the inferior tendons of the biceps muscles. They are very small and of a vivid red colour. The pulse natural; tongue of its natural hue; no loss of appetite or any symptom of indisposition.

9th: The inoculated pustule on the arm this evening began to inflame, and gave the child uneasiness; he cried and pointed to the seat of it, and was immediately afterwards affected with febrile symptoms. At the expiration of two hours after the seizure a plaster of *ung. hydrarg. fort.* was applied, and its effect was very quickly perceptible, for in ten minutes he resumed his usual looks and playfulness. On examining the arm about three hours after the application of the plaster its effects in subduing the inflammation were very manifest.

10th: The spots on the arms have disappeared, but there are three visible in the face.

11th: Two spots on the face are gone; the other barely perceptible.

13th: The pustule delineated in the second plate in the Treatise on the Variolæ Vaccinæ is a correct representation of that on the child's arm as it appears at this time.

14th: Two fresh spots appear on the face. The pustule on the arm nearly converted into a scab. As long as any fluid remained in it it was limpid.

James Hill, four years old, was inoculated on the same day, and with part of the same matter which infected Stephen Jenner. It did not appear to have taken effect till the fifth day.

7th: A perceptible vesicle: this evening the patient became a little chilly; no pain or tumour discoverable in the axilla.

8th: Perfectly well.

9th: The same.

10th: The vesicle more elevated than I have been accustomed to see it, and assuming more perfectly the variolous character than is common with the cow-pox at this stage.

11th: Surrounded by an inflammatory redness, about the size of a shilling, studded over with minute vesicles. The pustule contained a limpid fluid till the fourteenth day, after which it was incrusted over in the usual manner; but this incrustation or scab being accidentally rubbed off, it was slow in healing.

VACCINATION AGAINST SMALLPOX

These children were afterwards fully exposed to the smallpox contagion without effect.

Having been requested by my friend, Mr. Henry Hicks, of Eastington, in this county, to inoculate two of his children, and at the same time some of his servants and the people employed in his manufactory, matter was taken from the arm of this boy for the purpose. The numbers inoculated were eighteen. They all took the infection, and either on the fifth or sixth day a vesicle was perceptible on the punctured part. Some of them began to feel a little unwell on the eighth day, but the greater number on the ninth. Their illness, as in the former cases described, was of short duration, and not sufficient to interrupt, but at very short intervals, the children from their amusements, or the servants and manufacturers from following their ordinary business.

Three of the children whose employment in the manufactory was in some degree laborious had an inflammation on their arms beyond the common boundary about the eleventh or twelfth day, when the feverish symptoms, which before were nearly gone off, again returned, accompanied with increase of axillary tumour. In these cases (clearly perceiving that the symptoms were governed by the state of the arms) I applied on the inoculated pustules, and renewed the application three or four times within an hour, a pledget of lint, previously soaked in *aqua lythargyri acetati*,[13] and covered the hot efflorescence surrounding them with cloths dipped in cold water.

The next day I found this simple mode of treatment had succeeded perfectly. The inflammation was nearly gone off, and with it the symptoms which it had produced.

Some of these patients have since been inoculated with variolous matter, without any effect beyond a little inflammation on the part where it was inserted.

Why the arms of those inoculated with the vaccine matter in the country should be more disposed to inflame than those inoculated in London it may be difficult to determine. From comparing my own cases with some transmitted to

[13] Goulard's extract of Saturn.

me by Dr. Pearson and Dr. Woodville, this appears to be the fact; and what strikes me as still more extraordinary with respect to those inoculated in London is the appearance of maturating eruptions. In the two instances only which I have mentioned (the one from the inoculated, the other from the casual, cow-pox) a few red spots appeared, which quickly went off without maturating. The case of the Rev. Mr. Moore's servant may, indeed, seem like a deviation from the common appearances in the country, but the nature of these eruptions was not ascertained beyond their not possessing the property of communicating the disease by their effluvia. Perhaps the difference we perceive may be owing to some variety in the mode of action of the virus upon the skin of those who breathe the air of London and those who live in the country. That the erysipelas assumes a different form in London from what we see it put on in this country is a fact very generally acknowledged. In calling the inflammation that is excited by the cow-pox virus erysipelatous, perhaps I may not be critically exact, but it certainly approaches near to it. Now, as the diseased action going forward in the part infected with the virus may undergo different modifications according to the peculiarities of the constitution on which it is to produce its effect, may it not account for the variation which has been observed?

To this it may probably be objected that some of the patients inoculated, and who had pustules in consequence, were newly come from the country; but I conceive that the changes wrought in the human body through the medium of the lungs may be extremely rapid. Yet, after all, further experiments made in London with vaccine virus generated in the country must finally throw a light on what now certainly appears obscure and mysterious.

The principal variation perceptible to me in the action of the vaccine virus generated in London from that produced in the country was its proving more certainly infectious and giving a less disposition in the arm to inflame. There appears also a greater elevation of the pustule above the surrounding skin. In my former cases the pustule produced by the insertion of the virus was more like one of those which are so thickly spread over the body in a bad kind of confluent smallpox. This was more like a pustule of the distinct smallpox, except that I saw no instance of pus being formed in it, the matter remaining limpid till the period of scabbing.

Wishing to see the effects of the disease on an infant newly born, my nephew, Mr. Henry Jenner, at my request, inserted the vaccine virus into the arm of a child about twenty hours old. His report to me is that the child went through the disease without apparent illness, yet that it was found effectually to resist the action of variolous matter with which it was subsequently inoculated.

I have had an opportunity of trying the effects of the cow-pox matter on a boy, who, the day preceding its insertion, sickened with the measles. The eruption of the measles, attended with cough, a little pain in the chest, and the usual symptoms accompanying the disease, appeared on the third day and spread all over him. The disease went through its course without any deviation from its usual habits; and, notwithstanding this, the cow-pox virus excited its common appearances, both on the arm and on the constitution, without any febrile interruption; on the sixth day there was a vesicle.

8th: Pain in the axilla, chilly, and affected with headache.

9th: Nearly well.

12th: The pustule spread to the size of a large split-pea, but without any surrounding efflorescence. It soon afterwards scabbed, and the boy recovered his general health rapidly. But it should be observed that before it scabbed the efflorescence which had suffered a temporary suspension advanced in the usual manner.

Here we see a deviation from the ordinary habits of the smallpox, as it has been observed that the presence of the measles suspends the action of the variolous matter.

The very general investigation that is now taking place, chiefly through inoculation (and I again repeat my earnest hope that it may be conducted with that calmness and moderation which should ever accompany a philosophical research), must soon place the vaccine disease in its just point of view. The result of all my trials with the virus on the human subject has been uniform. In every instance the patient who has felt its influence, has completely lost the susceptibility for the variolous contagion; and as these instances are now become numerous, I conceive that, joined to the observations in the former part of this paper, they sufficiently preclude me from the necessity of entering into controversies with those who have circulated reports adverse to my assertions, on no other evidence than what has been casually collected.

III

A Continuation of Facts and Observations Relative to the Variolæ Vaccinæ, or Cow-pox. 1800

Since my former publications on the vaccine inoculation I have had the satisfaction of seeing it extend very widely. Not only in this country is the subject pursued with ardour, but from my correspondence with many respectable medical gentlemen on the Continent (among whom are Dr. De Carro, of Vienna, and Dr. Ballhorn, of Hanover) I find it is as warmly adopted abroad, where it has afforded the greatest satisfaction. I have the pleasure, too, of seeing that the feeble efforts of a few individuals to depreciate the new practice are sinking fast into contempt beneath the immense mass of evidence which has arisen up in support of it.

Upwards of six thousand persons have now been inoculated with the virus of cow-pox, and the far greater part of them have since been inoculated with that of smallpox, and exposed to its infection in every rational way that could be devised, without effect.

It was very improbable that the investigation of a disease so analogous to the smallpox should go forward without engaging the attention of the physician of the Smallpox Hospital in London.

Accordingly, Dr. Woodville, who fills that department with so much respectability, took an early opportunity of instituting an inquiry into the nature of the cow-pox. This inquiry was begun in the early part of the present year, and in May, Dr. Woodville published the result, which differs essentially from mine in a point of much importance. It appears that three-fifths of the patients inoculated were affected with eruptions, for the most part so perfectly resembling the smallpox as not to be distinguished from them. On this subject it is necessary that I should make some comments.

When I consider that out of the great number of cases of casual inoculation immediately from cows which from time to time presented themselves to my observation, and the many similar instances which have been communicated to me by medical gentlemen in this neighbourhood; when I consider, too, that the matter with which my inoculations were conducted in the years 1797, '98, and '99, was taken from some different cows, and that in no instance any thing like a variolous pustule appeared, I cannot feel disposed to imagine that eruptions, similar to those described by Dr. Woodville, have ever been produced by the *pure uncontaminated cow-pock virus;* on the contrary, I do suppose that those which the doctor speaks of originated in the action of variolous matter which crept into the constitution with the vaccine. And this I presume happened from the inoculation of a great number of the patients with variolous matter (some on the third, others on the fifth, day) after the vaccine had been applied; and it should be observed that the matter thus propagated became the source of future inoculations in the hands of many medical gentlemen who appeared to have been previously unacquainted with the nature of the cow-pox.

Another circumstance strongly, in my opinion, supporting this supposition is the following: The cow-pox has been known among our dairies time immemorial. If pustules, then, like the variolous, were to follow the communication of it from the cow to the milker, would not such a fact have been known and recorded at our farms? Yet neither our farmers nor the medical people of the neighbourhood have noticed such an occurrence.

A few scattered pimples I have sometimes, though very rarely, seen, the greater part of which have generally disappeared quickly, but some have remained long enough to suppurate at their apex. That local cuticular inflammation, whether springing up spontaneously or arising from the application of acrid substances, such for instance, as *cantharides, pix Burgundica, antimonium tartarizatum,* etc., will often produce cutaneous affections, not only near the seat of the inflammation, but on some parts of the skin far beyond its boundary, is a well-known fact. It is, doubtless, on this principle that the inoculated cow-pock pustule and its concomitant efflorescence may, in very irritable constitutions, produce this affection. The eruption I allude to has commonly appeared some time in the third week after inoculation. But this appearance is too trivial to excite the least regard.

The change which took place in the general appearance during the progress of the vaccine inoculation at the Smallpox Hospital should likewise be considered.

Although at first it took on so much of the variolous character as to produce pustules in three cases out of five, yet in Dr. Woodville's last report, published in June, he says: "Since the publication of my reports of inoculations for the cow-pox, upwards of three hundred cases have been under my care; and out of this number only thirty-nine had pustules that suppurated; viz., out of the first hundred, nineteen had pustules; out of the second, thirteen; and out of the last hundred and ten, only seven had pustules. Thus it appears that the disease has become considerably milder; which I am inclined to attribute to a greater caution used in the choice of the matter, with which the infection was communicated; for, lately, that which has been employed for this purpose has been taken only from those patients in whom the cow-pox proved very mild and well characterized."[1]

The inference I am induced to draw from these premises is very different. The decline, and, finally, the total extinction nearly, of these pustules, in my opinion, are more fairly attributable to the cow-pox virus, assimilating the variolous,[2] the former probably being the original, the lat-

[1] In a few weeks after the cow-pox inoculation was introduced at the Smallpox Hospital I was favoured with some virus from this stock. In the first instance it produced a few pustules, which did not maturate; but in the subsequent cases none appeared.—E. J.

[2] In my first publication on this subject I expressed an opinion that the smallpox and the cow-pox were the same diseases under different modifica-

ter the same disease under a peculiar, and at present an inexplicable, modification.

One experiment tending to elucidate the point under discussion I had myself an opportunity of instituting. On the supposition of its being possible that the cow which ranges over the fertile meadows in the vale of Gloucester might generate a virus differing in some respects in its qualities from that produced by the animal artificially pampered for the production of milk for the metropolis, I procured, during my residence there in the spring, some cow pock virus from a cow at one of the London milk-farms.[3] It was immediately conveyed into Gloucestershire to Dr. Marshall, who was then extensively engaged in the inoculation of the cow-pox, the general result of which, and of the inoculation in particular with this matter, I shall lay before my reader in the following communication from the doctor:

"DEAR SIR:

"My neighbour, Mr. Hicks, having mentioned your wish to be informed of the progress of the inoculation here for the cow-pox, and he also having taken the trouble to transmit to you my minutes of the cases which have fallen under my care, I hope you will pardon the further trouble I now give you in stating the observations I have made upon the subject. When first informed of it, having two children who had not had the smallpox, I determined to inoculate them for the cow-pox whenever I should be so fortunate as to procure matter proper for the purpose. I was, therefore, particularly happy when I was informed that I could procure matter from some of those whom you had inoculated. In the first instance I had no intention of extending the disease further than my own family, but the very extensive influence which the conviction of its efficacy in resisting the smallpox has had upon the minds of the people in general has rendered that intention nugatory, as

---

tions. In this opinion Dr. Woodville has concurred. The axiom of the immortal Hauter, that *two diseased actions cannot take place at the same time in one and the same part,* will not be injured by the admission of this theory.

[3] It was taken by Mr. Tanner, then a student at the Veterinary College, from a cow at Mr. Clark's farm at Kentish Town.

you will perceive, by the continuation of my cases enclosed in this letter,[4] by which it will appear that since the 22d of March I have inoculated an hundred and seven persons; which, considering the retired situation I resided in, is a very great number. There are also other considerations which, besides that of its influence in resisting the smallpox, appear to have had their weight; the peculiar mildness of the disease, the known safety of it, and its not having in any instance prevented the patient from following his ordinary business. In all the cases under my care there have only occurred two or three which required any application, owing to erysipelatous inflammation on the arm, and they immediately yielded to it. In the remainder the constitutional illness has been slight but sufficiently marked, and considerably less than I ever observed in the same number inoculated with the smallpox. In only one or two of the cases have any other eruptions appeared than those around the spot where the matter was inserted, and those near the infected part. Neither does there appear in the cow-pox to be the least exciting cause to any other disease, which in the smallpox has been frequently observed, the constitution remaining in as full health and vigour after the termination of the disease as before the infection. Another important consideration appears to be the impossibility of the disease being communicated except by the actual contact of the matter of the pustule, and consequently the perfect safety of the remaining part of the family, supposing only one or two should wish to be inoculated at the same time.

"Upon the whole, it appears evident to me that the cow-pox is a pleasanter, shorter, and infinitely more safe disease than the inoculated smallpox when conducted in the most careful and approved manner; neither is the local affection of the inoculated part, or the constitutional illness, near so violent. I speak with confidence on the subject, having had an opportunity of observing its effects upon a variety of constitutions, from three months old to sixty years; and to which I have paid particular at-

---

[4] Doctor Marshall has detailed these cases with great accuracy, but their publication would now be deemed superfluous.—E. J.

tention. In the cases alluded to here you will observe that the removal from the original source of the matter had made no alteration or change in the nature or appearance of the disease, and that it may be continued, *ad infinitum* (I imagine), from one person to another (if care be observed in taking the matter at a proper period) without any necessity of recurring to the original matter of the cow.

"I should be happy if any endeavours of mine could tend further to elucidate the subject, and shall be much gratified is sending you any further observations I may be enabled to make.

"I have the pleasure to subscribe myself,
"Dear sir, etc.,
"JOSEPH H. MARSHALL.
"EASTINGTON, GLOUCESTERSHIRE, April 26, 1799."

The gentleman who favoured me with the above account has continued to prosecute his inquiries with unremitting industry, and has communicated the result in another letter, which at his request I lay before the public without abbreviation.

Dr. Marshall's second letter:

"DEAR SIR:
"Since the date of my former letter I have continued to inoculate with the cow-pox virus. Including the cases before enumerated, the number now amounts to four hundred and twenty-three. It would be tedious and useless to detail the progress of the disease in each individual— it is sufficient to observe that I noticed no deviation in any respect from the cases I formerly adduced. The general appearances of the arm exactly corresponded with the account given in your first publication. When they were disposed to become troublesome by erysipelatous inflammation, an application of equal parts of vinegar and water always answered the desired intention. I must not omit to inform you that when the disease had duly acted upon the constitution I have frequently used the vitriolic acid. A portion of a drop applied with the head of a probe or

any convenient utensil upon the pustule, suffered to remain about forty seconds, and afterwards washed off with sponge and water, never failed to stop its progress and expedite the formation of a scab.

"I have already subjected two hundred and eleven of my patients to the action of variolous matter, *but every one resisted it*.

"The result of my experiments (which were made with every requisite caution) has fully convinced me that the *true cow-pox* is a safe and infallible preventive from the smallpox; that in no case which has fallen under my observation has it been in any considerable degree troublesome, much less have I seen any thing like danger; for in no instance were the patients prevented from following their ordinary employments.

"In Dr. Woodville's publication on the cow-pox I notice an extraordinary fact. He says that the generality of his patients had pustules. It certainly appears extremely extraordinary that in all my cases there never was but one pustule, which appeared on a patient's elbow on the inoculated arm, and maturated. It appeared exactly like that on the incised part.

"The whole of my observations, founded as it appears on an extensive experience, leads me to these obvious conclusions; that those cases which have been or may be adduced against the preventive powers of the cow-pox could not have been those of the true kind, since it must appear to be absolutely impossible that I should have succeeded in such a number of cases without a single exception if such a preventive power did not exist. I cannot entertain a doubt that the inoculated cow-pox must quickly supersede that of the smallpox. If the many important advantages which must result from the new practice are duly considered, we may reasonably infer that public benefit, the sure test of the real merit of discoveries, will render it generally extensive.

"To you, Sir, as the discoverer of this highly beneficial practice, mankind are under the highest obligations. As a private individual I participate in the general feeling; more particularly as you have afforded me an opportunity of noticing the effects of a singular disease, and of viewing the progress of the most curious experiment that ever was recorded in the history of physiology.

"I remain, dear sir, etc.,
"Joseph H. Marshall."

"P.S. I should have observed that, of the patients I inoculated and enumerated in my letter, one hundred and twenty-seven were infected with the matter you sent me from the London cow. I discovered no dissimilarity of symptoms in these cases from those which I inoculated from matter procured in this country. No pustules have occurred, except in one or two cases, where a single one appeared on the inoculated arm. No difference was apparent in the local inflammation. There was no suspension of ordinary employment among the labouring people, nor was any medicine required.

"I have frequently inoculated one or two in a family, and the remaining part of it some weeks afterwards. The uninfected have slept with the infected during the whole course of the disease without being affected; so that I am fully convinced that the disease cannot be taken but by actual contact with the matter.

"A curious fact has lately fallen under my observation, on which I leave you to comment.

"I visited a patient with the confluent smallpox and charged a lancet with some of the matter. Two days afterwards I was desired to inoculate a woman and four children with the cow-pox, and I inadvertently took the vaccine matter on the same lancet which was before charged with that of smallpox. In three days I discovered the mistake, and fully expected that my five patients would be infected with smallpox; but I was agreeably surprised to find the disease to be genuine cow-pox, which proceeded without deviating in any particular from my former cases. I afterwards inoculated these patients with variolous matter, but all of them resisted its action.

"I omitted mentioning another great advantage that now occurs to me in the inoculated cow-pox; I mean the safety with which pregnant women may have the disease communicated to them. I have inoculated a great number of females in that situation, and never observed their cases to differ in any respect from those of my other patients. Indeed, the disease is so mild that it seems as if it might at all times be communicated with the most perfect safety."

I shall here take the oportunity of thanking Dr. Marshall and those other gentlemen who have obligingly presented me with the result of their inoculations; but, as they all agree in the same point as that given in the above communication, namely, the security of the patient from the effects of the smallpox after the cow-pox, their perusal, I presume, would afford us no satisfaction that has not been amply given already. Particular occurrences I shall, of course, detail. Some of my correspondents have mentioned the appearance of smallpox-like eruptions at the commencement of their inoculations; but in these cases the matter was derived from the original stock at the Smallpox Hospital.

I have myself inoculated a very considerable number from the matter produced by Dr. Marshall's patients, originating in the London cow, without observing pustules of any kind, and have dispersed it among others who have used it with a similar effect. From this source Mr. H. Jenner informs me he has inoculated above an hundred patients without observing eruptions. Whether the nature of the virus will undergo any change from being farther removed from its original source in passing successively from one person to another time alone can determine. That which I am now employing has been in use near eight months, and not the least change is perceptible in its mode of action either locally or constitutionally. There is, therefore, every reason to expect that its effects will remain unaltered and that we shall not be under the necessity of seeking fresh supplies from the cow.

The following observations were obligingly sent me by Mr. Tierny, Assistant Surgeon to the South Gloucester Regiment of Militia, to whom I am indebted for a former report on this subject:

"I inoculated with the cow-pox matter from the eleventh to the latter part of April, twenty-five persons, including women and children. Some on the eleventh were inoculated with the matter Mr. Shrapnell (surgeon to the regiment) had from you, the others with matter taken from these. The progress of the puncture was accurately observed, and its appearance seemed to differ from the smallpox in having less inflammation around its basis on the first days—that is, from the third to the seventh; but after this the inflammation increased, extending on the tenth or eleventh day to a circle of an inch and a half from its centre, and threatening very sore arms; but this I am happy to say was not the case; for, by applying mercurial ointment to the inflamed part, which was repeated daily until the inflammation went off, the arm got well without any further application or trouble. The constitutional symptoms which appeared on the eighth or ninth day after inoculation scarcely deserved the name of disease, as they were so slight as to be scarcely perceptible, except that I could connect a slight headache and languor, with a stiffness and rather painful sensation in the axilla. This latter symptom was the most striking—it remained from twelve to forty-eight hours. In no case did I observe the smallest pustule, or even discolouration of the skin, like an incipient pustule, except about the part where the virus has been applied.

"After all these symptoms had subsided and the arms were well, I inoculated four of this number with variolous matter, taken from a patient in another regiment. In each of these it was inserted several times under the cuticle, producing slight inflammation on the second or third day, and always disappearing before the fifth or sixth, except in one who had the cow-pox in Gloucestershire before he joined us, and who also received it at this time by inoculation. In this man the puncture inflamed and his arm was much sorer than from the insertion of the cow-pox virus; but there was no pain in the axilla, nor could any constitutional affection be observed.

"I have only to add that I am now fully satisfied of the efficacy of the cow-pox in preventing the appearance of the smallpox, and that it is a most happy and salutary substitute for it.   I remain, etc.,

"M. J. TIERNY."

Although the susceptibility of the virus of the cow-pox is, for the most part, lost in those who have had the smallpox, yet in some constitutions it is only partially destroyed, and in others it does not appear to be in the least diminished.

By far the greater number on whom trials were made resisted it entirely; yet I found some on whose arm the pustule from inoculation was formed completely, but without producing the common efflorescent blush around it, or any constitutional illness, while others have had the disease in the most perfect manner. A case of the latter kind having been presented to me by Mr. Fewster, Surgeon, of Thornbury, I shall insert it:

"Three children were inoculated with the vaccine matter you obligingly sent me. On calling to look at their arms three days after I was told that John Hodges, one of the three, had been inoculated with the smallpox when a year old, and that he had a full burthen, of which his face produced plentiful marks, a circumstance I was not before made acquainted with. On the sixth day the arm of the boy appeared as if inoculated with variolous matter, but the pustule was rather more elevated. On the ninth day he complained of violent pain in his head and back, accompanied with vomiting and much fever. The next day he was very well and went to work as usual. The punctured part began to spread, and there was the areola around the inoculated part to a considerable extent.

"As this is contrary to an assertion made in the Medical and Physical Journal, No. 8, I thought it right to give you this information, and remain,

"Dear sir, etc.,
"J. FEWSTER."

It appears, then, that the animal economy with regard to the action of this virus is under the same laws as it is with respect to the variolous virus, after previously feeling its influence, as far as comparisons can be made between the two diseases.

Some striking instances of the power of the cow-pox in

VACCINATION AGAINST SMALLPOX

suspending the progress of the smallpox after the patients had been several days casually exposed to the infection have been laid before me by Mr. Lyford, Surgeon, of Winchester, and my nephew, the Rev. G. C. Jenner. Mr. Lyford, after giving an account of his extensive and successful practice in the vaccine inoculation in Hampshire, writes as follows:

"The following case occurred to me a short time since, and may probably be worth your notice. I was sent for to a patient with the smallpox, and on inquiry found that five days previous to my seeing him the eruption began to appear. During the whole of this time two children who had not had the smallpox, were constantly in the room with their father, and frequently on the bed with him. The mother consulted me on the propriety of inoculating them, but objected to my taking the matter from their father, as he was subject to erysipelas. I advised her by all means to have them inoculated at that time, as I could not procure any variolous matter elsewhere. However, they were inoculated with vaccine matter, but I cannot say I flattered myself with its proving successful, as they had previously been so long and still continued to be exposed to the variolous infection. Notwithstanding this I was agreeably surprised to find the vaccine disease advance and go through its regular course; and, if I may be allowed the expression, to the total extinction of the smallpox."

Mr. Jenner's cases were not less satisfactory. He writes as follows:

"A son of Thomas Stinchcomb, of Woodford, near Berkeley, was infected with the natural smallpox at Bristol, and came home to his father's cottage. Four days after the eruptions had appeared upon the boy, the family (none of which had ever had the smallpox), consisting of the father, mother, and five children, was inoculated with vaccine virus. On the arm of the mother it failed to produce the least effect, and she, of course, had the smallpox,[5] but the rest of the family had the cow-pox in the usual way, and were not affected with the smallpox, although they were in the same room, and the children slept in the same bed with their brother

[5] Under similar circumstances I think it would be advisable to insert the matter into each arm, which would be more likely to insure the success of the operation.—E. J.

who was confined to it with the natural smallpox; and subsequently with their mother.

"I attended this family with my brother, Mr. H. Jenner."

The following cases are of too singular a nature to remain unnoticed.

Miss R——, a young lady about five years old, was seized on the evening of the eighth day after inoculation with vaccine virus, with such symptoms as commonly denote the accession of violent fever. Her throat was also a little sore, and there were some uneasy sensations about the muscles of the neck. The day following a rash was perceptible on her face and neck, so much resembling the efflorescence of the *scarlatina anginosa* that I was induced to ask whether Miss R—— had been exposed to the contagion of that disease. An answer in the affirmative, and the rapid spreading of the redness over the skin, at once relieved me from much anxiety respecting the nature of the malady, which went through its course in the ordinary way, but not without symptoms which were alarming both to myself and Mr. Lyford, who attended with me. There was no apparent deviation in the ordinary progress of the pustule to a state of maturity from what we see in general; yet there was a total suspension of the *areola* or florid discolouration around it, until the *scarlatina* had retired from the constitution. As soon as the patient was freed from this disease this appearance advanced in the usual way.[6]

The case of Miss H—— R—— is not less interesting than that of her sister, above related. She was exposed to the contagion of the *scarlatina* at the same time, and sickened almost at the same hour. The symptoms continued severe about twelve hours, when the scarlatina-rash shewed itself faintly upon her face, and partly upon her neck. After remaining two or three hours it suddenly disappeared, and she became perfectly free from every complaint. My surprise at this sudden transition from extreme sickness to health in great measure ceased when I observed that the inoculated pustule had occasioned, in this case, the common efflorescent

---

[6] I witnessed a similar fact in a case of measles. The pustule from the cow-pock virus advanced to maturity, while the measles existed in the constitution, but no *efflorescence* appeared around it until the measles had ceased to exert its influence.

appearance around it, and that as it approached the centre it was nearly in an erysipelatous state. But the most remarkable part of this history is that, on the fourth day afterwards, so soon as the efflorescence began to die away upon the arm and the pustule to dry up, the *scarlatina* again appeared, her throat became sore, the rash spread all over her. She went fairly through the disease with its common symptoms.

That these were actually cases of *scarlatina* was rendered certain by two servants in the family falling ill at the same time with the distemper, who had been exposed to the infection with the young ladies.

Some there are who suppose the security from the smallpox obtained through the cow-pox will be of a temporary nature only. This supposition is refuted not only by analogy with respect to the habits of diseases of a similar nature, but by incontrovertible facts, which appear in great numbers against it. To those already adduced in the former part of my first treatise[7] many more might be adduced were it deemed necessary; but among the cases I refer to, one will be found of a person who had the cow-pox fifty-three years before the effect of the smallpox was tried upon him. As he completely resisted it, the intervening period I conceive must necessarily satisfy any reasonable mind. Should further evidence be thought necessary, I shall observe that, among the cases presented to me by Mr. Fry, Mr. Darke, Mr. Tierny, Mr. H. Jenner, and others, there were many whom they inoculated ineffectually with variolous matter, who had gone through the cow-pox many years before this trial was made.

It has been imagined that the cow-pox is capable of being communicated from one person to another by effluvia without the intervention of inoculation. My experiments, made with the design of ascertaining this important point, all tend to establish my original position, that it is not infectious except by contact. I have never hesitated to suffer those on whose arms there were pustules exhaling the effluvia from associating or even sleeping with others who never had experienced either the cow-pox or the smallpox. And, further, I have repeatedly, among children, caused the uninfected to breathe

[7] See pages 217, 218, 219, 221, 223, etc.

over the inoculated vaccine pustules during their whole progress, yet these experiments were tried without the least effect. However, to submit a matter so important to a still further scrutiny, I desired Mr. H. Jenner to make any further experiments which might strike him as most likely to establish or refute what had been advanced on this subject. He has since informed me "that he inoculated children at the breast, whose mothers had not gone through either the smallpox or the cow-pox; that he had inoculated mothers whose sucking infants had never undergone either of these diseases; that the effluvia from the inoculated pustules, in either case, had been inhaled from day to day during the whole progress of their maturation, and that there was not the least perceptible effect from these exposures. One woman he inoculated about a week previous to her *accouchement,* that her infant might be the more fully and conveniently exposed to the pustule; but, as in the former instances, no infection was given, although the child frequently slept on the arm of its mother with its nostrils and mouth exposed to the pustule in the fullest state of maturity. In a word, is it not impossible for the cow-pox, whose *only* manifestation appears to consist in the pustules *created by contact,* to produce *itself* by effluvia?

In the course of a late inoculation I observed an appearance which it may be proper here to relate. The punctured part on a boy's arm (who was inoculated with fresh limpid virus) on the sixth day, instead of shewing a beginning vesicle, which is usual in the cow-pox at that period, was encrusted over with a rugged, amber-coloured scab. The scab continued to spread and increase in thickness for some days, when, at its edges, a vesicated ring appeared, and the disease went through its ordinary course, the boy having had soreness in the axilla and some slight indisposition. With the fluid matter taken from his arm five persons were inoculated. In one it took no effect. In another it produced a perfect pustule without any deviation from the common appearance; but in the other three the progress of the inflammation was exactly similar to the instance which afforded the virus for their inoculation; there was a creeping scab of a loose texture, and subsequently the formation of limpid fluid at its edges. As these people were all employed in laborious exercises, it is possible that these anomalous appearances might owe their origin to the friction of the clothes on the newly inflamed part of the arm. I have not yet had an opportunity of exposing them to the smallpox.

In the early part of this inquiry I felt far more anxious respecting the inflammation of the inoculated arm than at present; yet that this affection will go on to a greater extent than could be wished is a circumstance sometimes to be expected. As this can be checked, or even entirely subdued, by very simple means, I see no reason why the patient should feel an uneasy hour because an application may not be absolutely necessary. About the tenth or eleventh day, if the pustule has proceeded regularly, the appearance of the arm will almost to a certainty indicate whether this is to be expected or not. Should it happen, nothing more need be done than to apply a single drop of the *aqua lythargyri acetati*[8] upon the pustule, and, having suffered it to remain two or three minutes, to cover the efflorescence surrounding the pustule with a piece of linen dipped in the *aqua lythargyri compos.*[9] The former may be repeated twice or thrice during the day, the latter as often as it may feel agreeable to the patient.

When the scab is prematurely rubbed off (a circumstance not unfrequent among children and working people), the application of a little *aqua lythargyri acet.* to the part immediately coagulates the surface, which supplies its place, and prevents a sore.

In my former treatises on this subject I have remarked that the human constitution frequently retains its susceptibility to the smallpox contagion (both from effluvia and contact) after previously feeling its influence. In further corroboration of this declaration many facts have been communicated to me by various correspondents. I shall select one of them.

"DEAR SIR:

"Society at large must, I think, feel much indebted to you for your Inquiries and Observations on the Nature and Effects of the Variolæ Vaccinæ, etc., etc. As I conceive

[8] Extract of Saturn.
[9] Goulard water. For further information on this subject see the first Treatise on the Var. Vac., Dr. Marshall's letters, etc.

what I am now about to communicate to be of some importance, I imagine it cannot be uninteresting to you, especially as it will serve to corroborate your assertion of the susceptibility of the human system of the variolous contagion, although it has previously been made sensible of its action. In November, 1793, I was desired to inoculate a person with the smallpox. I took the variolous matter from a child under the disease in the natural way, who had a large burthen of distinct pustules. The mother of the child being desirous of seeing my method of communicating the disease by inoculation, after having opened a pustule, I introduced the point of my lancet in the usual way on the back part of my own hand, and thought no more of it until I felt a sensation in the part which reminded me of the transaction. This happened upon the third day; on the fourth there were all the appearances common to inoculation, at which I was not at all surprised, nor did I feel myself uneasy upon perceiving the inflammation continue to increase to the sixth and seventh day, accompanied with a very small quantity of fluid, repeated experiments having taught me it might happen so with persons who had undergone the disease, and yet would escape any constitutional affection; but I was not so fortunate; for on the eighth day I was seized with all the symptoms of the eruptive fever, but in a much more violent degree than when I was before inoculated, which was about eighteen years previous to this, when I had a considerable number of pustules. I must confess I was now greatly alarmed, although I had been much engaged in the smallpox, having at different times inoculated not less than two thousand persons. I was convinced my present indisposition proceeded from the insertion of the variolous matter, and, therefore, anxiously looked for an eruption. On the tenth day I felt a very unpleasant sensation of stillness and heat on each side of my face near my ear, and the fever began to decline. The affection in my face soon terminated in three or four pustules attended with inflammation, but which did not maturate, and I was presently well.

"I remain, dear sir, etc.,
"THOMAS MILES."

This inquiry is not now so much in its infancy as to restrain me from speaking more positively than formerly on the important point of scrophula as connected with the smallpox.

Every practitioner in medicine who has extensively inoculated with the smallpox, or has attended many of those who have had the distemper in the natural way, must acknowledge that he has frequently seen scrophulous affections, in some form or another, sometimes rather quickly shewing themselves after the recovery of the patients. Conceiving this fact to be admitted, as I presume it must be by all who have carefully attended to the subject, may I not ask whether it does not appear probable that the general introduction of the smallpox into Europe has not been among the most conductive means in exciting that formidable foe to health? Having attentively watched the effects of the cow-pox in this respect, I am happy in being able to declare that the disease does not appear to have the least tendency to produce this destructive malady.

The scepticism that appeared, even among the most enlightened of medical men when my sentiments on the important subject of the cow-pox were first promulgated, was highly laudable. To have admitted the truth of a doctrine, at once so novel and so unlike any thing that ever had appeared in the annals of medicine, without the test of the most rigid scrutiny, would have bordered upon temerity; but now, when that scrutiny has taken place, not only among ourselves, but in the first professional circles in Europe, and when it has been uniformly found in such abundant instances that the human frame, when once it has felt the influence of the genuine cow-pox in the way that has been described, is never afterwards at any period of its existence assailable by the smallpox, may I not with perfect confidence congratulate my country and society at large on their beholding, in the mild form of the cow-pox, an antidote that is capable of extirpating from the earth a disease which is every hour devouring its victims; a disease that has ever been considered as the severest scourge of the human race!

THE CONTAGIOUSNESS OF PUERPERAL FEVER

BY
OLIVER WENDELL HOLMES

INTRODUCTORY NOTE

OLIVER WENDELL HOLMES was born in Cambridge, Massachusetts, August 29, 1809, and educated at Phillips Academy, Andover, and Harvard College. After graduation, he entered the Law School, but soon gave up law for medicine. He studied first in Boston, and later spent two years in medical schools in Europe, mainly in Paris. On his return he began to practise in Boston, but in two years he was appointed professor of anatomy at Dartmouth College, a position which he held from 1838 to 1840, when he again took up his Boston practise. It was soon after this, in 1843, that he published his essay on the "Contagiousness of Puerperal Fever," his only contribution of high distinction to medical science. From 1847 to 1882 he was Parkman professor of anatomy and physiology in the Harvard Medical School. He died in Boston, October 7, 1894.

In spite of the importance of the paper here printed, Holmes's reputation as a scientist was overshadowed by that won by him as a wit and a man of letters. When he was only twenty-one his "Old Ironsides" brought him into notice; and through his poetry and fiction, and the sparkling talk of the "Breakfast Table" series, he took a high place among the most distinguished group of writers that America has yet produced.

THE CONTAGIOUSNESS OF PUERPERAL FEVER

IN collecting, enforcing and adding to the evidence accumulated upon this most serious subject, I would not be understood to imply that there exists a doubt in the mind of any well-informed member of the medical profession as to the fact that puerperal fever is sometimes communicated from one person to another, both directly and indirectly. In the present state of our knowledge upon this point I should consider such doubts merely as a proof that the sceptic had either not examined the evidence, or, having examined it, refused to accept its plain and unavoidable consequences. I should be sorry to think, with Dr. Rigby, that it was a case of "oblique vision"; I should be unwilling to force home the *argumentum ad hominem* of Dr. Blundell, but I would not consent to make a *question* of a momentous fact which is no longer to be considered as a subject for trivial discussions, but to be acted upon with silent promptitude. It signifies nothing that wise and experienced practitioners have sometimes doubted the reality of the danger in question; no man has the right to doubt it any longer. No negative facts, no opposing opinions, be they what they may, or whose they may, can form any answer to the series of cases now within the reach of all who choose to explore the records of medical science.

If there are some who conceive that any important end would be answered by recording such opinions, or by collecting the history of all the cases they could find in which no evidence of the influence of contagion existed, I believe they are in error. Suppose a few writers of authority can

Note.—This essay appeared first in 1843, in *The New England Quarterly Journal of Medicine,* and was reprinted in the "Medical Essays" in 1855.

be found to profess a disbelief in contagion,—and they are very few compared with those who think differently,—is it quite clear that they formed their opinions on a view of all the facts, or is it not apparent that they relied mostly on their own solitary experience? Still further, of those whose names are quoted, is it not true that scarcely a single one could, by any possibility, have known the half or the tenth of the facts bearing on the subject which have reached such a frightful amount within the last few years? Again, as to the utility of negative facts, as we may briefly call them,—instances, namely, in which exposure has not been followed by disease,—although, like other truths, they may be worth knowing, I do not see that they are like to shed any important light upon the subject before us. Every such instance requires a good deal of circumstantial explanation before it can be accepted. It is not enough that a practitioner should have had a single case of puerperal fever not followed by others. It must be known whether he attended others while this case was in progress, whether he went directly from one chamber to others, whether he took any, and what, precautions. It is important to know that several women were exposed to infection derived from the patient, so that allowance may be made for want of predisposition. Now, if of negative facts so sifted there could be accumulated a hundred for every one plain instance of communication here recorded, I trust it need not be said that we are bound to guard and watch over the hundredth tenant of our fold, though the ninety and nine may be sure of escaping the wolf at its entrance. If any one is disposed, then, to take a hundred instances of lives, endangered or sacrificed out of those I have mentioned, and make it reasonably clear that within a similar time and compass *ten thousand* escaped the same exposure, I shall thank him for his industry, but I must be permitted to hold to my own practical conclusions, and beg him to adopt or at least to examine them also. Children that walk in calico before open fires are not always burned to death; the instances to the contrary may be worth recording; but by no means if they are to be used as arguments against woollen frocks and high fenders.

I am not sure that this paper will escape another remark which it might be wished were founded in justice. It may be said that the facts are too generally known and acknowledged to require any formal argument or exposition, that there is nothing new in the positions advanced, and no need of laying additional statements before the profession. But on turning to two works, one almost universally, and the other extensively, appealed to as authority in this country, I see ample reason to overlook this objection. In the last edition of Dewees's Treatise on the "Diseases of Females" it is expressly said, "In this country, under no circumstance that puerperal fever has appeared hitherto, does it afford the slightest ground for the belief that it is contagious." In the "Philadelphia Practice of Midwifery" not one word can be found in the chapter devoted to this disease which would lead the reader to suspect that the idea of contagion had ever been entertained. It seems proper, therefore, to remind those who are in the habit of referring to the works for guidance that there may possibly be some sources of danger they have slighted or omitted, quite as important as a trifling irregularity of diet, or a confined state of the bowels, and that whatever confidence a physician may have in his own mode of treatment, his services are of questionable value whenever he carries the bane as well as the antidote about his person.

The practical point to be illustrated is the following: *The disease known as puerperal fever is so far contagious as to be frequently carried from patient to patient by physicians and nurses.*

Let me begin by throwing out certain incidental questions, which, without being absolutely essential, would render the subject more complicated, and by making such concessions and assumptions as may be fairly supposed to be without the pale of discussion.

1. It is granted that all the forms of what is called puerperal fever may not be, and probably are not, equally contagious or infectious. I do not enter into the distinctions which have been drawn by authors, because the facts do not appear to me sufficient to establish any absolute line of demarcation between such forms as may be propagated by contagion and

those which are never so propagated. This general result I shall only support by the authority of Dr. Ramsbotham, who gives, as the result of his experience, that the same symptoms belong to what he calls the infectious and the sporadic forms of the disease, and the opinion of Armstrong in his original Essay. If others can show any such distinction, I leave it to them to do it. But there are cases enough that show the prevalence of the disease among the patients of a single practitioner when it was in no degree epidemic, in the proper sense of the term. I may refer to those of Mr. Roberton and of Dr. Peirson, hereafter to be cited, as examples.

2. I shall not enter into any dispute about the particular *mode* of infection, whether it be by the atmosphere the physician carries about him into the sick-chamber, or by the direct application of the virus to the absorbing surfaces with which his hand comes in contact. Many facts and opinions are in favour of each of these modes of transmission. But it is obvious that, in the majority of cases, it must be impossible to decide by which of these channels the disease is conveyed, from the nature of the intercourse between the physician and the patient.

3. It is not pretended that the contagion of puerperal fever must always be followed by the disease. It is true of all contagious diseases that they frequently spare those who appear to be fully submitted to their influence. Even the vaccine virus, fresh from the subject, fails every day to produce its legitimate effect, though every precaution is taken to insure its action. This is still more remarkably the case with scarlet fever and some other diseases.

4. It is granted that the disease may be produced and variously modified by many causes besides contagion, and more especially by epidemic and endemic influences. But this is not peculiar to the disease in question. There is no doubt that smallpox is propagated to a great extent by contagion, yet it goes through the same records of periodical increase and diminution which have been remarked in puerperal fever. If the question is asked how we are to reconcile the great variations in the mortality of puerperal fever in different seasons and places with the supposition of contagion, I will answer it by another question from Mr. Farr's

letter to the Registrar-General. He makes the statement that "*five* die weekly of smallpox in the metropolis when the disease is not epidemic," and adds, "The problem for solution is, Why do the five deaths become 10, 15, 20, 31, 58, 88, weekly, and then progressively fall through the same measured steps?"

5. I take it for granted that if it can be shown that great numbers of lives have been and are sacrificed to ignorance or blindness on this point, no other error of which physicians or nurses may be occasionally suspected will be alleged in palliation of this; but that whenever and wherever they can be shown to carry disease and death instead of health and safety, the common instincts of humanity will silence every attempt to explain away their responsibility.

The treatise of Dr. Gordon, of Aberdeen, was published in the year 1795, being among the earlier special works upon the disease. A part of his testimony has been occasionally copied into other works, but his expressions are so clear, his experience is given with such manly distinctness and disinterested honesty, that it may be quoted as a model which might have been often followed with advantage.

"This disease seized such women only as were visited or delivered by a practitioner, or taken care of by a nurse, who had previously attended patients affected with the disease."

"I had evident proofs of its infectious nature, and that the infection was as readily communicated as that of the smallpox or measles, and operated more speedily than any other infection with which I am acquainted."

"I had evident proofs that every person who had been with a patient in the puerperal fever became charged with an atmosphere of infection, which was communicated to every pregnant woman who happened to come within its sphere. This is not an assertion, but a fact, admitting of demonstration, as may be seen by a perusal of the foregoing table"—referring to a table of seventy-seven cases, in many of which the channel of propagation was evident.

He adds: "It is a disagreeable declaration for me to mention, that I myself was the means of carrying the infection to a great number of women." He then enumerates a number of instances in which the disease was conveyed by midwives and others to the neighboring villages, and declares that " these facts fully prove that the cause of the puerperal fever, of which I treat, was a specific contagion, or infection, altogether unconnected with a noxious constitution of the atmosphere."

But his most terrible evidence is given in these words: " I ARRIVED AT THAT CERTAINTY IN THE MATTER THAT I COULD VENTURE TO FORETELL WHAT WOMEN WOULD BE AFFECTED WITH THE DISEASE, UPON HEARING BY WHAT MIDWIFE THEY WERE TO BE DELIVERED, OR BY WHAT NURSE THEY WERE TO BE ATTENDED, DURING THEIR LYING-IN: AND ALMOST IN EVERY INSTANCE MY PREDICTION WAS VERIFIED."

Even previously to Gordon, Mr. White, of Manchester, had said: " I am acquainted with two gentlemen in another town, where the whole business of midwifery is divided betwixt them, and it is very remarkable that one of them loses several patients every year of the puerperal fever, and the other never so much as meets with the disorder "— a difference which he seems to attribute to their various modes of treatment.[1]

Dr. Armstrong has given a number of instances in his Essay on Puerperal Fever of the prevalence of the disease among the patients of a single practitioner. At Sunderland, " in all, forty-three cases occurred from the 1st of January to the 1st of October, when the disease ceased; and of this number, forty were witnessed by Mr. Gregson and his assistant, Mr. Gregory, the remainder having been separately seen by three accoucheurs." There is appended to the London edition of this Essay a letter from Mr. Gregson, in which that gentleman says, in reference to the great number of cases occurring in his practice, " The cause of this I cannot pretend fully to explain, but I should be wanting in common liberality if I were to make any hesitation in asserting that the disease which appeared in my practice was highly contagious, and communicable from one puerperal woman to another." " It is customary among the lower and middle ranks of people to make frequent personal visits

[1] *On the Management of Lying-in Women*, p. 120.

to puerperal women resident in the same neighborhood, and I have ample evidence for affirming that the infection of the disease was often carried about in that manner; and, however painful to my feelings, I must in candour declare that it is very probable the contagion was conveyed, in some instances, by myself, though I took every possible care to prevent such a thing from happening the moment that I ascertained that the distemper was infectious." Dr. Armstrong goes on to mention six other instances within his knowledge, in which the disease had at different times and places been limited, in the same singular manner, to the practice of individuals, while it existed scarcely, if at all, among the patients of others around them. Two of the gentlemen became so convinced of their conveying the contagion that they withdrew for a time from practice.

I find a brief notice, in an American journal, of another series of cases, first mentioned by Mr. Davies, in the "Medical Repository." This gentleman stated his conviction that the disease is contagious.

"In the autumn of 1822 he met with twelve cases, while his medical friends in the neighbourhood did not meet with any, 'or at least very few.' He could attribute this circumstance to no other cause than his having been present at the examination after death, of two cases, some time previous, and of his having imparted the disease to his patients, notwithstanding every precaution."[2]

Dr. Gooch says: "It is not uncommon for the greater number of cases to occur in the practice of one man, whilst the other practitioners of the neighborhood, who are not more skilful or more busy, meet with few or none. A practitioner opened the body of a woman who had died of puerperal fever, and continued to wear the same clothes. A lady whom he delivered a few days afterwards was attacked with and died of a similar disease; two more of his lying-in patients, in rapid succession, met with the same fate; struck by the thought that he might have carried contagion in his clothes, he instantly changed them, and met with no more cases of the kind.[3] A woman in the country who

[2] *Philad. Med. Journal* for 1825, p. 408.
[3] A similar anecdote is related by Sir Benjamin Brodie, of the late Dr. John Clark, *Lancet*, May 2, 1840.

was employed as washerwoman and nurse washed the linen of one who had died of puerperal fever; the next lying-in patient she nursed died of the same disease; a third nursed by her met the same fate, till the neighbourhood, getting afraid of her, ceased to employ her."[4]

In the winter of the year 1824, "several instances occurred of its prevalence among the patients of particular practitioners, whilst others who were equally busy met with few or none. One instance of this kind was very remarkable. A general practitioner, in large midwifery practice, lost so many patients from puerperal fever that he determined to deliver no more for some time, but that his partner should attend in his place. This plan was pursued for one month, during which not a case of the disease occurred in their practice. The elder practitioner, being then sufficiently recovered, returned to his practice, but the first patient he attended was attacked by the disease and died. A physician who met him in consultation soon afterwards, about a case of a different kind, and who knew nothing of his misfortune, asked him whether puerperal fever was at all prevalent in his neighbourhood, on which he burst into tears, and related the above circumstances.

"Among the cases which I saw this season in consultation, four occurred in one month in the practice of one medical man, and all of them terminated fatally."[5]

Dr. Ramsbotham asserted, in a lecture at the London Hospital, that he had known the disease spread through a particular district, or be confined to the practice of a particular person, almost every patient being attacked with it, while others had not a single case. It seemed capable, he thought, of conveyance, not only by common modes, but through the dress of the attendants upon the patient.[6]

In a letter to be found in the "London Medical Gazette" for January, 1840, Mr. Roberton, of Manchester, makes the statement which I here give in a somewhat condensed form.

A midwife delivered a woman on the 4th of December, 1830, who died soon after with the symptoms of puerperal fever. In one month from this date the same midwife de-

[4] *An Account of Some of the Most Important Diseases Peculiar to Women*. p. 4.   [5] Gooch, *op. cit.*, p. 71.   [6] *Lond. Med. Gaz.*, May 2, 1835.

livered thirty women, residing in different parts of an extensive suburb, of which number sixteen caught the disease and all died. These were the only cases which had occurred for a considerable time in Manchester. The other midwives connected with the same charitable institution as the woman already mentioned are twenty-five in number, and deliver, on an average, ninety women a week, or about three hundred and eighty a month. None of these women had a case of puerperal fever. "Yet all this time this woman was crossing the other midwives in every direction, scores of the patients of the charity being delivered by them in the very same quarters where her cases of fever were happening."

Mr. Roberton remarks that little more than half the women she delivered during this month took the fever; that on some days all escaped, on others only one or more out of three or four; a circumstance similar to what is seen in other infectious maladies.

Dr. Blundell says: "Those who have never made the experiment can have but a faint conception how difficult it is to obtain the exact truth respecting any occurrence in which feelings and interests are concerned. Omitting particulars, then, I content myself with remarking, generally, that from more than one district I have received accounts of the prevalence of puerperal fever in the practice of some individuals, while its occurrence in that of others, in the same neighborhood, was not observed. Some, as I have been told, have lost ten, twelve, or a greater number of patients, in scarcely broken succession; like their evil genius, the puerperal fever has seemed to stalk behind them wherever they went. Some have deemed it prudent to retire for a time from practice. In fine, that this fever may occur spontaneously, I admit; that its infectious nature may be plausibly disputed, I do not deny; but I add, considerately, that in my own family I had rather that those I esteemed the most should be delivered, unaided, in a stable, by the mangerside, than that they should receive the best help, in the fairest apartment, but exposed to the vapors of this pitiless disease. Gossiping friends, wet-nurses, monthly nurses, the practitioner himself, these are the channels by which, as I suspect, the infection is principally conveyed."[7]

At a meeting of the Royal Medical and Chirurgical Society Dr. King mentioned that some years since a practitioner at Woolwich lost sixteen patients from puerperal fever in the same year. He was compelled to give up practice for one or two years, his business being divided among the neighboring practitioners. No case of puerperal fever occurred afterwards, neither had any of the neighboring surgeons any cases of this disease.

At the same meeting Mr. Hutchinson mentioned the occurrence of three consecutive cases of puerperal fever, followed subsequently by two others, all in the practice of one accoucheur.[8]

Dr. Lee makes the following statement: " In the last two weeks of September, 1827, five fatal cases of uterine inflammation came under our observation. All the individuals so attacked had been attended in labor by the same midwife, and no example of a febrile or inflammatory disease of a serious nature occurred during that period among the other patients of the Westminster General Dispensary, who had been attended by the other midwives belonging to that institution."[9]

The recurrence of long series of cases like those I have cited, reported by those most interested to disbelieve in contagion, scattered along through an interval of half a century, might have been thought sufficient to satisfy the minds of all inquirers that here was something more than a singular coincidence. But if, on a more extended observation, it should be found that the same ominous groups of cases clustering about individual practitioners were observed in a remote country, at different times, and in widely separated regions, it would seem incredible that any should be found too prejudiced or indolent to accept the solemn truth knelled into their ears by the funeral bells from both sides of the ocean—the plain conclusion that the physician and the disease entered, hand in hand, into the chamber of the unsuspecting patient.

[7] *Lect. on Midwifery*, p. 395. [8] *Lancet*, May 2, 1840.
[9] *Lond. Cyc. of Pract. Med.*, art., " Fever, Puerperal."

That such series of cases have been observed in this country, and in this neighborhood, I proceed to show.

In Dr. Francis's "Notes to Denman's Midwifery" a passage is cited from Dr. Hosack in which he refers to certain puerperal cases which proved fatal to several lying-in women, and in some of which the disease was supposed to be conveyed by the accoucheurs themselves.[10]

A writer in the "New York Medical and Physical Journal" for October, 1829, in speaking of the occurrence of puerperal fever confined to one man's practice, remarks: "We have known cases of this kind occur, though rarely, in New York."

I mention these little hints about the occurrence of such cases partly because they are the first I have met with in American medical literature, but more especially because they serve to remind us that behind the fearful array of published facts there lies a dark list of similar events, unwritten in the records of science, but long remembered by many a desolated fireside.

Certainly nothing can be more open and explicit than the account given by Dr. Peirson, of Salem, of the cases seen by him. In the first nineteen days of January, 1829, he had five consecutive cases of puerperal fever, every patient he attended being attacked, and the three first cases proving fatal. In March of the same year he had two moderate cases, in June, another case, and in July, another, which proved fatal. "Up to this period," he remarks, "I am not informed that a single case had occurred in the practice of any other physician. Since that period I have had no fatal case in my practice, although I have had several dangerous cases. I have attended in all twenty cases of this disease, of which four have been fatal. I am not aware that there has been any other case in the town of distinct puerperal peritonitis, although I am willing to admit my information may be very defective on this point. I have been told of some 'mixed cases,' and 'morbid affections after delivery.'"[11]

In the "Quarterly Summary of the Transactions of the

---

[10] *Denman's Midwifery*, p. 673, third Am. ed.
[11] *Remarks on Puerperal Fever*, pp. 12 and 13.

College of Physicians of Philadelphia"[12] may be found some most extraordinary developments respecting a series of cases occurring in the practice of a member of that body.

Dr. Condie called the attention of the Society to the prevalence, at the present time, of puerperal fever of a peculiarly insidious and malignant character. "In the practice of one gentleman extensively engaged as an obstetrician nearly every female he has attended in confinement, during several weeks past, within the above limits" (the southern sections and neighboring districts), "had been attacked by the fever."

"An important query presents itself, the doctor observed, in reference to the particular form of fever now prevalent. Is it, namely, capable of being propagated by contagion, and is a physician who has been in attendance upon a case of the disease warranted in continuing, without interruption, his practice as an obstetrician? Dr. C., although not a believer in the contagious character of many of those affections generally supposed to be propagated in this manner, has, nevertheless, become convinced by the facts that have fallen under his notice that the puerperal fever now prevailing is capable of being communicated by contagion. How, otherwise, can be explained the very curious circumstance of the disease in one district being exclusively confined to the practice of a single physician, a Fellow of this College, extensively engaged in obstetrical practice, while no instance of the disease has occurred in the patients under the care of any other accoucheur practising within the same district; scarcely a female that has been delivered for weeks past has escaped an attack?"

Dr. Rutter, the practitioner referred to, "observed that, after the occurrence of a number of cases of the disease in his practice, he had left the city and remained absent for a week, but, on returning, no article of clothing he then wore having been used by him before, one of the very first cases of parturition he attended was followed by an attack of the fever and terminated fatally; he cannot readily, therefore, believe in the transmission of the disease from female to female in the person or clothes of the physician."

[12] For May, June, and July, 1842.

The meeting at which these remarks were made was held on the 3d of May, 1842. In a letter dated December 20, 1842, addressed to Dr. Meigs, and to be found in the "Medical Examiner,"[13] he speaks of "those horrible cases of puerperal fever, some of which you did me the favor to see with me during the past summer," and talks of his experience in the disease, "now numbering nearly seventy cases, all of which have occurred within less than a twelve-month past."

And Dr. Meigs asserts, on the same page, "Indeed, I believe that his practice in that department of the profession was greater than that of any other gentleman, which was probably the cause of his seeing a greater number of the cases." This from a professor of midwifery, who some time ago assured a gentleman whom he met in consultation that the night on which they met was the eighteenth in succession that he himself had been summoned from his repose,[14] seems hardly satisfactory.

I must call the attention of the inquirer most particularly to the Quarterly Report above referred to, and the letters of Dr. Meigs and Dr. Rutter, to be found in the "Medical Examiner." Whatever impression they may produce upon his mind, I trust they will at least convince him that there is some reason for looking into this apparently uninviting subject.

At a meeting of the College of Physicians just mentioned Dr. Warrington stated that a few days after assisting at an autopsy of puerperal peritonitis, in which he laded out the contents of the abdominal cavity with his hands, he was called upon to deliver three women in rapid succession. All of these women were attacked with different forms of what is commonly called puerperal fever. Soon after these he saw two other patients, both on the same day, with the same disease. Of these five patients, two died.

At the same meeting Dr. West mentioned a fact related to him by Dr. Samuel Jackson, of Northumberland. Seven females, delivered by Dr. Jackson in rapid succession, while practising in Northumberland County, were all attacked

[13] For January 21, 1843. [14] *Medical Examiner* for December 10, 1842.

with puerperal fever, and five of them died. "Women," he said, "who had expected me to attend upon them, now becoming alarmed, removed out of my reach, and others sent for a physician residing several miles distant. These women, as well as those attended by midwives, all did well; nor did we hear of any deaths in child-bed within a radius of fifty miles, excepting two, and these I afterwards ascertained to have been caused by other diseases." He underwent, as he thought, a thorough purification, and still his next patient was attacked with the disease and died. He was led to suspect that the contagion might have been carried in the gloves which he had worn in attendance upon the previous cases. Two months or more after this he had two other cases. He could find nothing to account for these unless it were the instruments for giving enemata, which had been used in two of the former cases and were employed by these patients. When the first case occurred, he was attending and dressing a limb extensively mortified from erysipelas, and went immediately to the accouchement with his clothes and gloves most thoroughly imbued with its effluvia. And here I may mention that this very Dr. Samuel Jackson, of Northumberland, is one of Dr. Dewees's authorities against contagion.

The three following statements are now for the first time given to the public. All of the cases referred to occurred within this State, and two of the three series in Boston and its immediate vicinity.

I. The first is a series of cases which took place during the last spring in a town at some distance from this neighborhood. A physician of that town, Dr. C., had the following consecutive cases:

No. 1, delivered March 20, died March 24.
" 2,   "   April 9, " April 14.
" 3,   "   "   10, "   "   14.
" 4,   "   "   11, "   "   18.
" 5,   "   "   27, " May   3.
" 6,   "   "   28, had some symptoms, recovered.
" 7,   "   May   8, had some symptoms, also recovered.

These were the only cases attended by this physician during the period referred to. "They were all attended by him until their termination, with the exception of the patient No. 6, who fell into the hands of another physician on the 2d of May." (Dr. C. left town for a few days at this time.) Dr. C. attended cases immediately before and after the above-named periods, none of which, however, presented any peculiar symptoms of the disease.

About the 1st of July he attended another patient in a neighboring village, who died two or three days after delivery.

The first patient, it is stated, was delivered on the 20th of March. "On the 19th Dr. C. made the autopsy of a man who had died suddenly, sick only forty-eight hours; had œdema of the thigh and gangrene extending from a little above the ankle into the cavity of the abdomen." Dr. C. wounded himself very slightly in the right hand during the autopsy. The hand was quite painful the night following, during his attendance on the patient No. 1. He did not see this patient after the 20th, being confined to the house, and very sick from the wound just mentioned, from this time until the 3d of April.

Several cases of erysipelas occurred in the house where the autopsy mentioned above took place, soon after the examination. There were also many cases of erysipelas in town at the time of the fatal puerperal cases which have been mentioned.

The nurse who laid out the body of the patient No. 3 was taken on the evening of the same day with sore throat and erysipelas, and died in ten days from the first attack.

The nurse who laid out the body of the patient No. 4 was taken on the day following with symptoms like those of this patient, and died in a week, without any external marks of erysipelas.

"No other cases of similar character with those of Dr. C. occurred in the practice of any of the physicians in the town or vicinity at the time. Deaths following confinement have occurred in the practice of other physicians during the past year, but they were not cases of puerperal fever. No post-mortem examinations were held in any of these puerperal cases."

Some additional statements in this letter are deserving of insertion:

"A physician attended a woman in the immediate neighborhood of the cases numbered 2, 3, and 4. This patient was confined the morning of March 1st, and died on the night of March 7th. It is doubtful whether this should be considered a case of puerperal fever. She had suffered from canker, indigestion, and diarrhœa for a year previous to her delivery. Her complaints were much aggravated for two or three months previous to delivery; she had become greatly emaciated, and weakened to such an extent that it had not been expected that she would long survive her confinement, if indeed she reached that period. Her labor was easy enough; she flowed a good deal, seemed exceedingly prostrated, had ringing in her ears, and other symptoms of exhaustion; the pulse was quick and small. On the second and third day there was some tenderness and tumefaction of the abdomen, which increased somewhat on the fourth and fifth. He had cases in midwifery before and after this, which presented nothing peculiar.

It is also mentioned in the same letter that another physician had a case during the last summer and another last fall, both of which recovered.

Another gentleman reports a case last December, a second case five weeks, and another three weeks, since. All these recovered. A case also occurred very recently in the practice of a physician in the village where the eighth patient of Dr. C. resides, which proved fatal. "This patient had some patches of erysipelas on the legs and arms. The same physician has delivered three cases since, which have all done well. There have been no other cases in this town or its vicinity recently. There have been some few cases of erysipelas." It deserves notice that the partner of Dr. C., who attended the autopsy of the man above mentioned and took an active part in it, who also suffered very slightly from a prick under the thumb-nail received during the examination, had twelve cases of midwifery between March 26th and April 12th, all of which did well, and presented no peculiar symptoms. It should also be stated that during these seventeen days he was in attendance on all the cases of erysipelas in the house where the autopsy had been performed. I owe these facts to the prompt kindness of a gentleman whose intelligence and character are sufficient guaranty for their accuracy.

The two following letters were addressed to my friend Dr. Storer by the gentleman in whose practice the cases of puerperal fever occurred. His name renders it unnecessary to refer more particularly to these gentlemen, who on their part have manifested the most perfect freedom and courtesy in affording these accounts of their painful experience.

"January 28, 1843.

II. . . . "The time to which you allude was in 1830. The first case was in February, during a very cold time. She was confined the 4th, and died the 12th. Between the 10th and 28th of this month I attended six women in labor, all of whom did well except the last, as also two who were confined March 1st and 5th. Mrs. E., confined February 28th, sickened, and died March 8th. The next day, 9th, I inspected the body, and the night after attended a lady, Mrs. B., who sickened, and died 16th. The 10th, I attended another, Mrs. G., who sickened, but recovered. March 16th I went from Mrs. G.'s room to attend a Mrs. H., who sickened, and died 21st. The 17th, I inspected Mrs. B. On the 19th, I went directly from Mrs. H.'s room to attend another lady, Mrs. G., who also sickened, and died 22d. While Mrs. B. was sick, on 15th, I went directly from her room a few rods, and attended another woman, who was not sick. Up to 20th of this month I wore the same clothes. I now refused to attend any labor, and did not till April 21st, when, having thoroughly cleansed myself, I resumed my practice, and had no more puerperal fever.

"The cases were not confined to a narrow space. The two nearest were half a mile from each other, and half that distance from my residence. The others were from two to three miles apart, and nearly that distance from my residence. There were no other cases in their immediate vicinity which came to my knowledge. The general health of all the women was pretty good, and all the labors as good as common, except the first. This woman, in consequence of my not arriving in season, and the child being half-born at some time before I arrived, was very much exposed to the cold at the time of confinement, and afterwards, being confined in a very open, cold room. Of the six cases, you perceive only one recovered.

" In the winter of 1817 two of my patients had puerperal fever, one very badly, the other not so badly. Both recovered. One other had swelled leg or phlegmasia dolens, and one or two others did not recover as well as usual.

" In the summer of 1835 another disastrous period occurred in my practice. July 1st I attended a lady in labor, who was afterwards quite ill and feverish; but at the time I did not consider her case a decided puerperal fever. On the 8th I attended one who did well. On the 12th, one who was seriously sick. This was also an equivocal case, apparently arising from constipation and irritation of the rectum. These women were ten miles apart and five from my residence. On 15th and 20th two who did well. On 25th I attended another. This was a severe labor, and followed by unequivocal puerperal fever, or peritonitis. She recovered. August 2d and 3d, in about twenty-four hours, I attended four persons. Two of them did very well; one was attacked with some of the common symptoms, which, however, subsided in a day or two, and the other had decided puerperal fever, but recovered. This woman resided five miles from me. Up to this time I wore the same coat. All my other clothes had frequently been changed. On 6th, I attended two women, one of whom was not sick at all; but the other, Mrs. L., was afterwards taken ill. On 10th, I attended a lady, who did very well. I had previously changed all my clothes, and had no garment on which had been in a puerperal room. On 12th, I was called to Mrs. S., in labor. While she was ill, I left her to visit Mrs. L., one of the ladies who was confined on 6th. Mrs. L. had been more unwell than usual, but I had not considered her case anything more than common till this visit. I had on a surtout at this visit, which, on my return to Mrs. S., I left in another room. Mrs. S. was delivered on 13th with forceps. These women both died of decided puerperal fever.

"While I attended these women in their fevers I changed my clothes, and washed my hands in a solution of chloride of lime after each visit. I attended seven women in labor during this period, all of whom recovered without sickness.

"In my practice I have had several single cases of puerperal fever, some of whom have died and some have recovered. Until the year 1830 I had no suspicion that the disease could be communicated from one patient to another by a nurse or midwife; but I now think the foregoing facts strongly favor that idea. I was so much convinced of this fact that I adopted the plan before related.

"I believe my own health was as good as usual at each of the above periods. I have no recollection to the contrary.

"I believe I have answered all your questions. I have been more particular on some points perhaps than necessary; but I thought you could form your own opinion better than to take mine. In 1830 I wrote to Dr. Channing a more particular statement of my cases. If I have not answered your questions sufficiently, perhaps Dr. C. may have my letter to him, and you can find your answer there."[15]

"BOSTON, February 3, 1843.

III. "MY DEAR SIR: I received a note from you last evening requesting me to answer certain questions therein proposed, touching the cases of puerperal fever which came under my observation the past summer. It gives me pleasure to comply with your request, so far as it is in my power so to do, but, owing to the hurry in preparing for a journey, the notes of the cases I had then taken were lost or mislaid. The principal *facts,* however, are too vivid upon my recollection to be soon forgotten. I think, therefore, that I shall be able to give you all the information you may require.

[15] In a letter to myself this gentleman also stated, "I do not recollect that there was any erysipelas or any other disease particularly prevalent at the time."

"All the cases that occurred in my practice took place between the 7th of May and the 17th of June, 1842.

"They were not confined to any particular part of the city. The first two cases were patients residing at the South End, the next was at the extreme North End, one living in Sea Street and the other in Roxbury. The following is the order in which they occurred:

"CASE 1.—Mrs. —— was confined on the 7th of May, at 5 o'clock, P. M., after a natural labor of six hours. At 12 o'clock at night, on the 9th (thirty-one hours after confinement), she was taken with severe chill, previous to which she was as comfortable as women usually are under the circumstances. She died on the 10th.

"CASE 2.—Mrs. —— was confined on the 10th of June (four weeks after Mrs. C.), at 11 A. M., after a natural, but somewhat severe, labor of five hours. At 7 o'clock, on the morning of the 11th, she had a chill. Died on the 12th.

"CASE 3.—Mrs. ——, confined on the 14th of June, was comfortable until the 18th, when symptoms of puerperal fever were manifest. She died on the 20th.

"CASE 4.—Mrs. ——, confined June 17th, at 5 o'clock, A. M., was doing well until the morning of the 19th. She died on the evening of the 21st.

"CASE 5.—Mrs. —— was confined with her *fifth* child on the 17th of June, at 6 o'clock in the evening. This patient had been attacked with puerperal fever, at three of her previous confinements, but the disease yielded to depletion and other remedies without difficulty. This time, I regret to say, I was not so fortunate. She was not attacked, as were the other patients, with a chill, but complained of extreme pain in the abdomen, and tenderness on pressure, almost from the moment of her confinement. In this, as in the other cases, the disease resisted all remedies, and she died in great distress on the 22d of the same month. Owing to the extreme heat of the season and my own indisposition, none of the subjects were examined after death. Dr. Channing, who was in attendance with me on the three last cases, proposed to have a *post-mortem* examination of the subject of case No. 5, but from some cause which I do not now recollect it was not obtained.

"You wish to know whether I wore the same clothes when attending the different cases. I cannot positively say, but I should think I did not, as the weather became warmer after the first two cases; I therefore think it probable that I made a change of at least a *part* of my dress. I have had no other case of puerperal fever in my own practice for three years, save those above related, and I do not remember to have lost a patient before with this disease. While absent, last July, I visited two patients sick with puerperal fever, with a friend of mine in the country. Both of them recovered.

"The cases that I have recorded were not confined to any particular constitution or temperament, but it seized upon the strong and the weak, the old and the young—one being over forty years, and the youngest under eighteen years of age. . . . If the disease is of an erysipelatous nature, as many suppose, contagionists may perhaps find some ground for their belief in the fact that, for two weeks previous to my first case of puerperal fever, I had been attending a severe case of erysipelas, and the infection may have been conveyed through me to the patient; but, on the other hand, why is not this the case with other physicians, or with the same physician at all times, for since my return from the country I have had a more inveterate case of erysipelas than ever before, and no difficulty whatever has attended any of my midwifery cases?"

I am assured, on unquestionable authority, that "about three years since a gentleman in extensive midwifery business, in a neighboring State, lost in the course of a few weeks eight patients in child-bed, seven of them being undoubted cases of puerperal fever. No other physician of the town lost a single patient of this disease during the same period." And from what I have heard in conversation with some of our most experienced practitioners, I am inclined to think many cases of the kind might be brought to light by extensive inquiry.

This long catalogue of melancholy histories assumes a still darker aspect when we remember how kindly nature deals with the parturient female, when she is not immersed in the virulent atmosphere of an impure lying-in hospital, or poisoned in her chamber by the unsuspected breath of contagion. From all causes together not more than four deaths in a thousand births and miscarriages happened in England and Wales during the period embraced by the first Report of the Registrar-General.[16] In the second Report the mortality was shown to be about five in one thousand.[17] In the Dublin Lying-in Hospital, during the seven years of Dr. Collins's mastership, there was one case of puerperal fever to 178 deliveries, or less than six to the thousand, and one death from this disease in 278 cases, or between three and four to the thousand.[18] Yet during this period the disease was endemic in the hospital, and might have gone on to rival the horrors of the pestilence of the Maternité, had not the poison been destroyed by a thorough purification.

In private practice, leaving out of view the cases that are to be ascribed to the self-acting system of propagation, it would seem that the disease must be far from common. Mr. White, of Manchester, says: "Out of the whole number of lying-in patients whom I have delivered (and I may safely call it a great one), I have never lost one, nor to the best of my recollection has one been greatly endangered, by the puerperal, miliary, low nervous, putrid malignant, or milk fever."[19] Dr. Joseph Clarke informed Dr. Collins that in the course of *forty-five* years' most extensive practice he lost but *four* patients from this disease.[20] One of the most eminent practitioners of Glasgow who has been engaged in very extensive practice for upwards of a quarter of a century testifies that he never saw more than twelve cases of real puerperal fever.[21]

I have myself been told by two gentlemen practicing in this city, and having for many years a large midwifery business, that they had neither of them lost a patient from this disease, and by one of them that he had only seen it in consultation with other physicians. In five hundred cases of midwifery, of which Dr. Storer has given an abstract in the first number of this journal, there was only one instance of fatal puerperal peritonitis.

[16] First Report, p. 105. [17] Second Report, p. 73.
[18] Collins's *Treatise on Midwifery*, p. 228, etc. [19] *Op. cit.*, p. 115.
[20] *Op. cit.*, p. 228. [21] *Lancet*, May 4, 1833.

In the view of these facts it does appear a singular coincidence that one man or woman should have ten, twenty, thirty, or seventy cases of this rare disease following his or her footsteps with the keenness of a beagle, through the streets and lanes of a crowded city, while the scores that cross the same paths on the same errands know it only by name. It is a series of similar coincidences which has led us to consider the dagger, the musket, and certain innocent-looking white powders as having some little claim to be regarded as dangerous. It is the practical inattention to similar coincidences which has given rise to the unpleasant but often necessary documents called *indictments*, which has sharpened a form of the cephalotome sometimes employed in the case of adults, and adjusted that modification of the fillet which delivers the world of those who happen to be too much in the way while such striking coincidences are taking place.

I shall now mention a few instances in which the disease appears to have been conveyed by the process of direct inoculation.

Dr. Campbell, of Edinburgh, states that in October, 1821, he assisted at the post-mortem examination of a patient who died with puerperal fever. He carried the pelvic viscera in his pocket to the class-room. The same evening he attended a woman in labor without previously changing his clothes; this patient died. The next morning he delivered a woman with the forceps; she died also, and of many others who were seized with the disease within a few weeks, three shared the same fate in succession.

In June, 1823, he assisted some of his pupils at the autopsy of a case of puerperal fever. He was unable to wash his hands with proper care, for want of the necessary accommodations. On getting home he found that two patients required his assistance. He went without further ablution or changing his clothes; both these patients died with puerperal fever.[22] This same Dr. Campbell is one of Dr. Churchill's authorities against contagion.

Mr. Roberton says that in one instance within his knowledge a practitioner passed the catheter for a patient with puerperal fever late in the evening; the same night he at-

[22] *Lond. Med. Gazette,* December 10, 1831.

tended a lady who had the symptoms of the disease on the second day. In another instance a surgeon was called while in the act of inspecting the body of a woman who had died of this fever, to attend a labor; within forty-eight hours this patient was seized with the fever.[23]

On the 16th of March, 1831, a medical practitioner examined the body of a woman who had died a few days after delivery, from puerperal peritonitis. On the evening of the 17th he delivered a patient, who was seized with puerperal fever on the 19th, and died on the 24th. Between this period and the 6th of April the same practitioner attended two other patients, both of whom were attacked with the same disease and died.[24]

In the autumn of 1829 a physician was present at the examination of a case of puerperal fever, dissected out the organs, and assisted in sewing up the body. He had scarcely reached home when he was summoned to attend a young lady in labor. In sixteen hours she was attacked with the symptoms of puerperal fever, and narrowly escaped with her life.[25]

In December, 1830, a midwife, who had attended two fatal cases of puerperal fever at the British Lying-in Hospital, examined a patient who had just been admitted, to ascertain if labor had commenced. This patient remained two days in the expectation that labor would come on, when she returned home and was then suddenly taken in labor and delivered before she could set out for the hospital. She went on favorably for two days, and was then taken with puerperal fever and died in thirty-six hours.[26]

"A young practitioner, contrary to advice, examined the body of a patient who had died from puerperal fever; there was no epidemic at the time; the case appeared to be purely sporadic. He delivered three other women shortly afterwards; they all died with puerperal fever, the symptoms of which broke out very soon after labor. The patients of his colleague did well, except one, where he assisted to remove some coagula from the uterus; she was attacked in the same manner as those whom he had attended, and died also." The

[23] *Ibid.* for January, 1832.
[24] *London Cyc. of Pract. Med.*, art., "Fever, Puerperal."
[25] *Ibid.*   [26] *Ibid.*

writer in the "British and Foreign Medical Review," from whom I quote this statement,—and who is no other than Dr. Rigby,—adds: "We trust that this fact alone will forever silence such doubts, and stamp the well-merited epithet of 'criminal,' as above quoted, upon such attempts.["][27]

From the cases given by Mr. Ingleby I select the following: Two gentlemen, after having been engaged in conducting the *post-mortem* examination of a case of puerperal fever, went in the same dress, each respectively, to a case of midwifery. "The one patient was seized with the rigor about thirty hours afterwards. The other patient was seized with a rigor the third morning after delivery. *One recovered, one died.*"[28] One of these same gentlemen attended another woman in the same clothes two days after the autopsy referred to. "The rigor did not take place until the evening of the fifth day from the first visit. *Result fatal.*" These cases belonged to a series of seven, the first of which was thought to have originated in a case of erysipelas. "Several cases of a mild character followed the foregoing seven, and their nature being now most unequivocal, my friend declined visiting all midwifery cases for a time, and there was no recurrence of the disease." These cases occurred in 1833. Five of them proved fatal. Mr. Ingleby gives another series of seven cases which occurred to a practitioner in 1836, the first of which was also attributed to his having opened several erysipelatous abscesses a short time previously.

I need not refer to the case lately read before this society, in which a physician went, soon after performing an autopsy of a case of puerperal fever, to a woman in labor, who was seized with the same disease and perished. The forfeit of that error has been already paid.

At a meeting of the Medical and Chirurgical Society before referred to, Dr. Merriman related an instance occurring in his own practice, which excites a reasonable suspicion that two lives were sacrificed to a still less dangerous experiment. He was at the examination of a case of puerperal fever at two o'clock in the afternoon. *He took care not to touch the body.* At nine o'clock the same evening he attended a woman

[27] *Brit. and For. Medical Review* for January, 1842, p. 112.
[28] *Edin. Med. and Surg. Journal*, April, 1838.

in labor; she was so nearly delivered that he had scarcely anything to do. The next morning she had severe rigors, and in forty-eight hours she was a corpse. Her infant had erysipelas and died in two days.[29]

In connection with the facts which have been stated it seems proper to allude to the dangerous and often fatal effects which have followed from wounds received in the postmortem examination of patients who have died of puerperal fever. The fact that such wounds are attended with peculiar risk has been long noticed. I find that Chaussier was in the habit of cautioning his students against the danger to which they were exposed in these dissections.[30] The head *pharmacien* of the Hôtel Dieu, in his analysis of the fluid effused in puerperal peritonitis, says that practitioners are convinced of its deleterious qualities, and that it is very dangerous to apply it to the denuded skin.[31] Sir Benjamin Brodie speaks of it as being well known that the inoculation of lymph or pus from the peritoneum of a puerperal patient is often attended with dangerous and even fatal symptoms. Three cases in confirmation of this statement, two of them fatal, have been reported to this society within a few months.

Of about fifty cases of injuries of this kind, of various degrees of severity, which I have collected from different sources, at least twelve were instances of infection from puerperal peritonitis. Some of the others are so stated as to render it probable that they may have been of the same nature. Five other cases were of peritoneal inflammation; three in males. Three were what was called enteritis, in one instance complicated with erysipelas; but it is well known that this term has been often used to signify inflammation of the peritoneum covering the intestines. On the other hand, no case of typhus or typhoid fever is mentioned as giving rise to dangerous consequences, with the exception of the single instance of an undertaker mentioned by Mr. Travers, who seems to have been poisoned by a fluid which exuded from the body. The other accidents were produced by dissection, or some other mode of contact with bodies of patients who had died of various affections. They also differed much

[29] *Lancet*, May 2, 1840.
[30] Stein, *L'Art d'Accoucher*, 1794; *Dict. des Sciences Médicales*, art.: "Puerperal." [31] *Journal de Pharmacie*, January, 1836.

in severity, the cases of puerperal origin being among the most formidable and fatal. Now a moment's reflection will show that the number of cases of serious consequences ensuing from the dissection of the bodies of those who had perished of puerperal fever is so vastly disproportioned to the relatively small number of autopsies made in this complaint as compared with typhus or pneumonia (from which last disease not one case of poisoning happened), and still more from all diseases put together, that the conclusion is irresistible that a most fearful morbid poison is often generated in the course of this disease. Whether or not it is *sui generis* confined to this disease, or produced in some others, as, for instance, erysipelas, I need not stop to inquire.

In connection with this may be taken the following statement of Dr. Rigby: "That the discharges from a patient under puerperal fever are in the highest degree contagious we have abundant evidence in the history of lying-in hospitals. The puerperal abscesses are also contagious, and may be communicated to healthy lying-in women by washing with the same sponge; this fact has been repeatedly proved in the Vienna Hospital; but they are equally communicable to women not pregnant; on more than one occasion the women engaged in washing the soiled bed-linen of the General Lying-in Hospital have been attacked with abscesses in the fingers or hands, attended with rapidly spreading inflammation of the cellular tissue."[32]

Now add to all this the undisputed fact that within the walls of lying-in hospitals there is often generated a miasm, palpable as the chlorine used to destroy it, tenacious so as in some cases almost to defy extirpation, deadly in some institutions as the plague; which has killed women in a private hospital of London so fast that they were buried two in one coffin to conceal its horrors; which enabled Tonnellé to record two hundred and twenty-two autopsies at the Maternité of Paris; which has led Dr. Lee to express his deliberate conviction that the loss of life occasioned by these institutions completely defeats the objects of their founders; and out of this train of cumulative evidence, the multiplied groups of cases clustering about individuals, the

[32] *System of Midwifery*, p. 292.

deadly results of autopsies, the inoculation by fluids from the living patient, the murderous poison of hospitals—does there not result a conclusion that laughs all sophistry to scorn, and renders all argument an insult?

I have had occasion to mention some instances in which there was an apparent relation between puerperal fever and erysipelas. The length to which this paper has extended does not allow me to enter into the consideration of this most important subject. I will only say that the evidence appears to me altogether satisfactory that some most fatal series of puerperal fever have been produced by an infection originating in the matter or effluvia of erysipelas. In evidence of some connection between the two diseases, I need not go back to the older authors, as Pouteau or Gordon, but will content myself with giving the following references, with their dates; from which it will be seen that the testimony has been constantly coming before the profession for the last few years:

"London Cyclopædia of Practical Medicine," article *Puerperal Fever,* 1833.

Mr. Ceeley's Account of the Puerperal Fever at Aylesbury, "Lancet," 1835.

Dr. Ramsbotham's Lecture, "London Medical Gazette," 1835.

Mr. Yates Ackerly's Letter in the same journal, 1838.

Mr. Ingleby on Epidemic Puerperal Fever, "Edinburgh Medical and Surgical Journal," 1838.

Mr. Paley's Letter, "London Medical Gazette," 1839.

Remarks at the Medical and Chirurgical Society, "Lancet," 1840.

Dr. Rigby's "System of Midwifery," 1841.

"Nunneley on Erysipelas," a work which contains a large number of references on the subject, 1841.

"British and Foreign Quarterly Review," 1842.

Dr. S. Jackson, of Northumberland, as already quoted from the Summary of the College of Physicians, 1842.

And, lastly, a startling series of cases by Mr. Storrs, of Doncaster, to be found in the "American Journal of the Medical Sciences" for January, 1843.

The relation of puerperal fever with other continued

fevers would seem to be remote and rarely obvious. Hey refers to two cases of synochus occurring in the Royal Infirmary of Edinburgh, in women who had attended upon puerperal patients. Dr. Collins refers to several instances in which puerperal fever has appeared to originate from a continued proximity to patients suffering with typhus.[33]

Such occurrences as those just mentioned, though most important to be remembered and guarded against, hardly attract our notice in the midst of the gloomy facts by which they are surrounded. Of these facts, at the risk of fatiguing repetitions, I have summoned a sufficient number, as I believe, to convince the most incredulous that every attempt to disguise the truth which underlies them all is useless.

It is true that some of the historians of the disease, especially Hulme, Hull, and Leake, in England; Tonnellé, Dugès, and Baudelocque, in France, profess not to have found puerperal fever contagious. At the most they give us mere negative facts, worthless against an extent of evidence which now overlaps the widest range of doubt, and doubles upon itself in the redundancy of superfluous demonstration. Examined in detail, this and much of the show of testimony brought up to stare the daylight of conviction out of countenance, proves to be in a great measure unmeaning and inapplicable, as might be easily shown were it necessary. Nor do I feel the necessity of enforcing the conclusion which arises spontaneously from the facts which have been enumerated by formally citing the opinions of those grave authorities who have for the last half-century been sounding the unwelcome truth it has cost so many lives to establish.

"It is to the British practitioner," says Dr. Rigby, "that we are indebted for strongly insisting upon this important and dangerous character of puerperal fever."[34]

The names of Gordon, John Clarke, Denman, Burns, Young,[35] Hamilton,[36] Haighton,[37] Good,[38] Waller,[39] Blundell,

[33] *Treatise on Midwifery*, p. 228.
[34] *British and Foreign Med. Rev.* for January, 1842.
[35] *Encyc. Britannica*, xiii, 467, art., "Medicine."
[36] *Outlines of Midwifery*, p. 109.   [37] *Oral Lectures*, etc.
[38] *Study of Medicine*, ii, 195.
[39] *Medical and Physical Journal*, July, 1830.

Gooch, Ramsbotham, Douglas,[40] Lee, Ingleby, Locock,[41] Abercrombie,[42] Alison,[43] Travers,[44] Rigby, and Watson[45] many of whose writings I have already referred to, may have some influence with those who prefer the weight of authorities to the simple deductions of their own reason from the facts laid before them. A few Continental writers have adopted similar conclusions.[46] It gives me pleasure to remember that, while the doctrine has been unceremoniously discredited in one of the leading journals,[47] and made very light of by teachers in two of the principal medical schools of this country, Dr. Channing has for many years inculcated, and enforced by examples, the danger to be apprehended and the precautions to be taken in the disease under consideration.

I have no wish to express any harsh feeling with regard to the painful subject which has come before us. If there are any so far excited by the story of these dreadful events that they ask for some word of indignant remonstrance to show that science does not turn the hearts of its followers into ice or stone, let me remind them that such words have been uttered by those who speak with an authority I could not claim.[48] It is as a lesson rather than as a reproach that I call up the memory of these irreparable errors and wrongs. No tongue can tell the heart-breaking calamity they have caused; they have closed the eyes just opened upon a new world of love and happiness; they have bowed the strength of manhood into the dust; they have cast the helplessness of infancy into the stranger's arms, or bequeathed it, with less cruelty, the death of its dying parent. There is no tone deep enough for regret, and no voice loud enough for warning. The woman about to become a mother, or with her new-born infant upon her bosom, should be the object of trembling care and sympathy wherever she bears her tender burden or stretches her aching limbs. The very

[40] *Dublin Hospital Reports* for 1822.
[41] *Library of Practical Medicine*, i, 373.
[42] *Researches on Diseases of the Stomach*, etc., p. 181.
[43] *Library of Practical Medicine*, i, 96.
[44] *Further Researches on Constitutional Irritation*, p. 128.
[45] *London Medical Gazette*, February, 1842.
[46] See *British and Foreign Medical Review*, vol. iii, p. 525, and vol. iv, p. 517. Also *Ed. Med. and Surg. Journal* for July, 1824, and *American Journal of Med. Sciences* for January, 1841.
[47] *Phil. Med. Journal*, vol. xii, p. 364.
[48] Dr. Blundell and Dr. Rigby in the works already cited.

outcast of the streets has pity upon her sister in degradation when the seal of promised maternity is impressed upon her. The remorseless vengeance of the law, brought down upon its victim by a machinery as sure as destiny, is arrested in its fall at a word which reveals her transient claim for mercy. The solemn prayer of the liturgy singles out her sorrows from the multiplied trials of life, to plead for her in the hour of peril. God forbid that any member of the profession to which she trusts her life, doubly precious at that eventful period, should hazard it negligently, unadvisedly, or selfishly!

There may be some among those whom I address who are disposed to ask the question, What course are we to follow in relation to this matter? The facts are before them, and the answer must be left to their own judgment and conscience. If any should care to know my own conclusions, they are the following; and in taking the liberty to state them very freely and broadly, I would ask the inquirer to examine them as freely in the light of the evidence which has been laid before him.

1. A physician holding himself in readiness to attend cases of midwifery should never take any active part in the post-mortem examination of cases of puerperal fever.

2. If a physician is present at such autopsies, he should use thorough ablution, change every article of dress, and allow twenty-four hours or more to elapse before attending to any case of midwifery. It may be well to extend the same caution to cases of simple peritonitis.

3. Similar precautions should be taken after the autopsy or surgical treatment of cases of erysipelas, if the physician is obliged to unite such offices with his obstetrical duties, which is in the highest degree inexpedient.

4. On the occurrence of a single case of puerperal fever in his practice, the physician is bound to consider the next female he attends in labor, unless some weeks at least have elapsed, as in danger of being infected by him, and it is his duty to take every precaution to diminish her risk of disease and death.

5. If within a short period two cases of puerperal fever happen close to each other, in the practice of the same

physician, the disease not existing or prevailing in the neighborhood, he would do wisely to relinquish his obstetrical practice for at least one month, and endeavor to free himself by every available means from any noxious influence he may carry about with him.

6. The occurrence of three or more closely connected cases, in the practice of one individual, no others existing in the neighborhood, and no other sufficient cause being alleged for the coincidence, is *primâ facie* evidence that he is the vehicle of contagion.

7. It is the duty of the physician to take every precaution that the disease shall not be introduced by nurses or other assistants, by making proper inquiries concerning them, and giving timely warning of every suspected source of danger.

8. Whatever indulgence may be granted to those who have heretofore been the ignorant causes of so much misery, the time has come when the existence of a *private pestilence* in the sphere of a single physician should be looked upon, not as a misfortune, but a crime; and in the knowledge of such occurrences the duties of the practitioner to his profession should give way to his paramount obligations to society.

ADDITIONAL REFERENCES AND CASES.

Fifth Annual Report of the Registrar-General of England, 1843. Appendix. Letter from William Farr, Esq.—Several new series of cases are given in the letter of Mr. Storrs, contained in the appendix to this report. Mr. Storrs suggests precautions similar to those I have laid down, and these precautions are strongly enforced by Mr. Farr, who is, therefore, obnoxious to the same criticisms as myself.

Hall and Dexter, in Am. Journal of Med. Sc. for January, 1844.—Cases of puerperal fever seeming to originate in erysipelas.

Elkington, of Birmingham, in Provincial Med. Journal, cited in Am. Journ. Med. Sc. for April, 1844.—Six cases in less than a fortnight, seeming to originate in a case of erysipelas.

West's Reports, in Brit. and For. Med. Review for October, 1845, and January, 1847.—Affection of the arm, resembling malignant pustule, after removing the placenta of a patient who died from puerperal fever. Reference to cases at Wurzburg, as proving contagion, and to Keiller's cases in the Monthly Journal for February, 1846, as showing connection of puerperal fever and erysipelas.

Kneeland.—Contagiousness of Puerperal Fever. Am. Jour. Med. Sc., January, 1846. Also, Connection between Puerperal Fever and Epidemic Erysipelas. *Ibid.,* April, 1846.

Robert Storrs.—Contagious Effects of Puerperal Fever on the Male Subject; or on Persons not Child-bearing. (From Provincial Med. and Surg. Journal.) Am. Jour. Med. Sc., January, 1846 Numerous cases. See also Dr. Reid's case in same journal for April, 1846.

Routh's paper in Proc. of Royal Med. Chir. Soc., Am. Jour. Med Sc., April, 1849, also in B. and F. Med. Chir. Review, April, 1850.

Hill, of Leuchars.—A Series of Cases Illustrating the Contagious Nature of Erysipelas and Puerperal Fever, and their Intimate Pathological Connection. (From Monthly Journal of Med. Sc.) Am. Jour. Med. Sc., July, 1850.

Skoda on the Causes of Puerperal Fever. (Peritonitis in rabbits, from inoculation with different morbid secretions.) Am. Jour. Med. Sc., October, 1850.

Arneth.—Paper read before the National Academy of Medicine. Annales d'Hygiène, Tome LXV. 2e Partie. (Means of Disinfection proposed by M. " Semmeliveis." Semmelweiss.) Lotions of chloride of lime and use of nail-brush before admission to lying-in wards. Alleged sudden and great decrease of mortality from puerperal fever. Cause of disease attributed to inoculation with cadaveric matters.) See also *Routh's* paper, mentioned above.

Moir.—Remarks at a meeting of the Edinburgh Medico-chirurgical Society. Refers to cases of Dr. Kellie, of Leith. *Sixteen* in succession, *all fatal.* Also to several instances of individual pupils having had a succession of cases in various quarters of the town, while others, practising as extensively in the same localities, had none. Also to several special cases not mentioned elsewhere. Am. Jour. Med. Sc. for October, 1851. (From New Monthly Journal of Med. Science.)

Simpson.—Observations at a Meeting of the Edinburgh Obstetrical Society. (An " eminent gentleman," according to Dr. Meigs, whose " name is as well known in America as in (his) native land," Obstetrics, Phil., 1852, pp. 368, 375.) The student is referred to this paper for a valuable *résumé* of many of the facts, and the necessary inferences, relating to this subject. Also for another series of cases, Mr. Sidey's, five or six in rapid succession. Dr. Simpson attended the dissection of two of Dr. Sidey's cases, and freely handled the diseased parts. His next four child-bed patients were affected with puerperal fever, and it was the first time he had seen it in practice. As Dr. Simpson is *a gentleman* (Dr. Meigs, as above), and as " a gentleman's hands are clean " (Dr. Meigs' sixth letter), it follows that a gentleman with clean hands may carry the disease. Am. Jour. Med. Sc., October, 1851.

Peddie.—The five or six cases of Dr. Sidey, followed by the four of Dr. Simpson, did not end the series. A practitioner in Leith having examined in Dr. Simpson's house, a portion of the uterus obtained from one of the patients, had immediately afterwards three fatal cases of puerperal fever. Dr. Peddie referred to two distinct series of consecutive cases in his own practice. He had since taken precautions, and not met with any such cases. Am. Jour. Med Sc., October, 1851.

Copland.—Considers it proved that puerperal fever may be propagated by the hands and the clothes, or either, of a third person, the bed-clothes or body-clothes of a patient. Mentions a new series of cases, one of which he saw, with the practitioner who had attended them. She was *the sixth* he had had within a few days. *All died.* Dr. Copland insisted that contagion had caused these cases; advised precautionary measures, and the practitioner had no other cases for a considerable time. Considers it *criminal,* after the evidence adduced,—which he could have quadrupled,—and the weight of authority brought forward, for a practitioner to be the medium of transmitting contagion and death to his patients. Dr. Copland lays down rules similar to those suggested by myself, and is therefore entitled to the same epithet for so doing. Medical Dictionary, New York, 1852. Article, *Puerperal States and Diseases.*

If there is any appetite for facts so craving as to be yet unappeased,—*lassata, necdum satiata,*—more can be obtained. Dr. Hodge remarks that "the frequency and importance of this singular circumstance (that the disease is occasionally more prevalent with one practitioner than another) has been exceedingly overrated." More than thirty strings of cases, more than two hundred and fifty sufferers from puerperal fever, more than one hundred and thirty deaths, appear as the results of a sparing estimate of such among the facts I have gleaned as could be numerically valued. These facts constitute, we may take it for granted, but a small fraction of those that have actually occurred. The number of them might be greater, but "'t is enough, 't will serve," in Mercutio's modest phrase, so far as frequency is concerned. For a just estimate of the importance of the singular circumstance, it might be proper to consult the languid survivors, the widowed husbands, and the motherless children, as well as "the unfortunate accoucheur."

ON THE ANTISEPTIC PRINCIPLE OF THE PRACTICE OF SURGERY

BY
JOSEPH LISTER

INTRODUCTORY NOTE

JOSEPH LISTER was born at Upton, Essex, England, in 1827, and received his general education at the University of London. After graduation he studied medicine in London and Edinburgh, and became lecturer in surgery at the University in the latter city. Later he was professor of surgery at Glasgow, at Edinburgh, and at King's College Hospital, London, and surgeon to Queen Victoria. He was made a baronet in 1883; retired from teaching in 1893; and was raised to the peerage in 1897, with the title of Baron Lister.

Even before the work of Pasteur on fermentation and putrefaction, Lister had been convinced of the importance of scrupulous cleanliness and the usefulness of deodorants in the operating room; and when, through Pasteur's researches, he realized that the formation of pus was due to bacteria, he proceeded to develop his antiseptic surgical methods. The immediate success of the new treatment led to its general adoption, with results of such beneficence as to make it rank as one of the great discoveries of the age.

ON THE ANTISEPTIC PRINCIPLE OF THE PRACTICE OF SURGERY
(1867)

IN the course of an extended investigation into the nature of inflammation, and the healthy and morbid conditions of the blood in relation to it, I arrived several years ago at the conclusion that the essential cause of suppuration in wounds is decomposition brought about by the influence of the atmosphere upon blood or serum retained within them, and, in the case of contused wounds, upon portions of tissue destroyed by the violence of the injury.

To prevent the occurrence of suppuration with all its attendant risks was an object manifestly desirable, but till lately apparently unattainable, since it seemed hopeless to attempt to exclude the oxygen which was universally regarded as the agent by which putrefaction was effected. But when it had been shown by the researches of Pasteur that the septic properties of the atmosphere depended not on the oxygen, or any gaseous constituent, but on minute organisms suspended in it, which owed their energy to their vitality, it occurred to me that decomposition in the injured part might be avoided without excluding the air, by applying as a dressing some material capable of destroying the life of the floating particles. Upon this principle I have based a practice of which I will now attempt to give a short account.

The material which I have employed is carbolic or phenic acid, a volatile organic compound, which appears to exercise a peculiarly destructive influence upon low forms of life, and hence is the most powerful antiseptic with which we are at present acquainted.

The first class of cases to which I applied it was that

of compound fractures, in which the effects of decomposition in the injured part were especially striking and pernicious. The results have been such as to establish conclusively the great principle that all local inflammatory mischief and general febrile disturbances which follow severe injuries are due to the irritating and poisonous influence of decomposing blood or sloughs. For these evils are entirely avoided by the antiseptic treatment, so that limbs which would otherwise be unhesitatingly condemned to amputation may be retained, with confidence of the best results.

In conducting the treatment, the first object must be the destruction of any septic germs which may have been introduced into the wounds, either at the moment of the accident or during the time which has since elapsed. This is done by introducing the acid of full strength into all accessible recesses of the wound by means of a piece of rag held in dressing forceps and dipped into the liquid.[1] This I did not venture to do in the earlier cases; but experience has shown that the compound which carbolic acid forms with the blood, and also any portions of tissue killed by its caustic action, including even parts of the bone, are disposed of by absorption and organisation, provided they are afterwards kept from decomposing. We are thus enabled to employ the antiseptic treatment efficiently at a period after the occurrence of the injury at which it would otherwise probably fail. Thus I have now under my care, in Glasgow Infirmary, a boy who was admitted with compound fracture of the leg as late as eight and one-half hours after the accident, in whom, nevertheless, all local and constitutional disturbance was avoided by means of carbolic acid, and the bones were soundly united five weeks after his admission.

The next object to be kept in view is to guard effectually against the spreading of decomposition into the wound along the stream of blood and serum which oozes out during the first few days after the accident, when the acid originally applied has been washed out or dissipated by

[1] The addition of a few drops of water to a considerable quantity of the acid, induces it to assume permanently the liquid form.

absorption and evaporation. This part of the treatment has been greatly improved during the past few weeks. The method which I have hitherto published (see Lancet for Mar. 16th, 23rd, 30th, and April 27th of the present year) consisted in the application of a piece of lint dipped in the acid, overlapping the sound skin to some extent and covered with a tin cap, which was daily raised in order to touch the surface of the lint with the antiseptic. This method certainly succeeded well with wounds of moderate size; and indeed I may say that in all the many cases of this kind which have been so treated by myself or my house-surgeons, not a single failure has occurred. When, however, the wound is very large, the flow of blood and serum is so profuse, especially during the first twenty-four hours, that the antiseptic application cannot prevent the spread of decomposition into the interior unless it overlaps the sound skin for a very considerable distance, and this was inadmissible by the method described above, on account of the extensive sloughing of the surface of the cutis which it would involve. This difficulty has, however, been overcome by employing a paste composed of common whiting (carbonate of lime), mixed with a solution of one part of carbolic acid in four parts of boiled linseed oil so as to form a firm putty. This application contains the acid in too dilute a form to excoriate the skin, which it may be made to cover to any extent that may be thought desirable, while its substance serves as a reservoir of the antiseptic material. So long as any discharge continues, the paste should be changed daily, and, in order to prevent the chance of mischief occurring during the process, a piece of rag dipped in the solution of carbolic acid in oil is put on next the skin, and maintained there permanently, care being taken to avoid raising it along with the putty. This rag is always kept in an antiseptic condition from contact with the paste above it, and destroys any germs which may fall upon it during the short time that should alone be allowed to pass in the changing of the dressing. The putty should be in a layer about a quarter of an inch thick, and may be advantageously applied rolled out between two pieces of thin calico, which maintain it in the form of a continuous sheet, which may be wrapped in a moment round the whole circumference of a limb if this be thought desirable, while the putty is prevented by the calico from sticking to the rag which is next the skin.[2] When all discharge has ceased, the use of the paste is discontinued, but the original rag is left adhering to the skin till healing by scabbing is supposed to be complete. I have at present in the hospital a man with severe compound fracture of both bones of the left leg, caused by direct violence, who, after the cessation of the sanious discharge under the use of the paste, without a drop of pus appearing, has been treated for the last two weeks exactly as if the fracture was a simple one. During this time the rag, adhering by means of a crust of inspissated blood collected beneath it, has continued perfectly dry, and it will be left untouched till the usual period for removing the splints in a simple fracture, when we may fairly expect to find a sound cicatrix beneath it.

We cannot, however, always calculate on so perfect a result as this. More or less pus may appear after the lapse of the first week, and the larger the wound, the more likely this is to happen. And here I would desire earnestly to enforce the necessity of persevering with the antiseptic application in spite of the appearance of suppuration, so long as other symptoms are favorable. The surgeon is extremely apt to suppose that any suppuration is an indication that the antiseptic treatment has failed, and that poulticing or water dressing should be resorted to. But such a course would in many cases sacrifice a limb or a life. I cannot, however, expect my professional brethren to follow my advice blindly in such a matter, and therefore I feel it necessary to place before them, as shortly as I can, some pathological principles intimately connected, not only with the point we are immediately considering, but with the whole subject of this paper.

If a perfectly healthy granulating sore be well washed and

[2] In order to prevent evaporation of the acid, which passes readily through any organic tissue, such as oiled silk or gutta percha, it is well to cover the paste with a sheet of block tin, or tinfoil strengthened with adhesive plaster. The thin sheet lead used for lining tea chests will also answer the purpose, and may be obtained from any wholesale grocer.

covered with a plate of clean metal, such as block tin, fitting its surface pretty accurately, and overlapping the surrounding skin an inch or so in every direction and retained in position by adhesive plaster and a bandage, it will be found, on removing it after twenty-four or forty-eight hours, that little or nothing that can be called pus is present, merely a little transparent fluid, while at the same time there is an entire absence of the unpleasant odour invariably perceived when water dressing is changed. Here the clean metallic surface presents no recesses like those of porous lint for the septic germs to develope in, the fluid exuding from the surface of the granulations has flowed away undecomposed, and the result is the absence of suppuration. This simple experiment illustrates the important fact that granulations have no inherent tendency to form pus, but do so only when subjected to preternatural stimulus. Further, it shows that the mere contact of a foreign body does not of itself stimulate granulations to suppurate; whereas the presence of decomposing organic matter does. These truths are even more strikingly exemplified by the fact that I have elsewhere recorded (Lancet, March 23rd, 1867), that a piece of dead bone free from decomposition may not only fail to induce the granulations around it to suppurate, but may actually be absorbed by them; whereas a bit of dead bone soaked with putrid pus infallibly induces suppuration in its vicinity.

Another instructive experiment is, to dress a granulating sore with some of the putty above described, overlapping the sound skin extensively; when we find, in the course of twenty-four hours, that pus has been produced by the sore, although the application has been perfectly antiseptic; and, indeed, the larger the amount of carbolic acid in the paste, the greater is the quantity of pus formed, provided we avoid such a proportion as would act as a caustic. The carbolic acid, though it prevents decomposition, induces suppuration —obviously by acting as a chemical stimulus; and we may safely infer that putrescent organic materials (which we know to be chemically acrid) operate in the same way.

In so far, then, carbolic acid and decomposing substances are alike; viz., that they induce suppuration by chemical stimulation, as distinguished from what may be termed simple inflammatory suppuration, such as that in which ordinary abscesses originate—where the pus appears to be formed in consequence of an excited action of the nerves, independently of any other stimulus. There is, however, this enormous difference between the effects of carbolic acid and those of decomposition; viz., that carbolic acid stimulates only the surface to which it is at first applied, and every drop of discharge that forms weakens the stimulant by diluting it; but decomposition is a self-propagating and self-aggravating poison, and, if it occur at the surface of a severely injured limb, it will spread into all its recesses so far as any extravasated blood or shreds of dead tissue may extend, and lying in those recesses, it will become from hour to hour more acrid, till it requires the energy of a caustic sufficient to destroy the vitality of any tissues naturally weak from inferior vascular supply, or weakened by the injury they sustained in the accident.

Hence it is easy to understand how, when a wound is very large, the crust beneath the rag may prove here and there insufficient to protect the raw surface from the stimulating influence of the carbolic acid in the putty; and the result will be first the conversion of the tissues so acted on into granulations, and subsequently the formation of more or less pus. This, however, will be merely superficial, and will not interfere with the absorption and organisation of extravasated blood or dead tissues in the interior. But, on the other hand, should decomposition set in before the internal parts have become securely consolidated, the most disastrous results may ensue.

I left behind me in Glasgow a boy, thirteen years of age, who, between three and four weeks previously, met with a most severe injury to the left arm, which he got entangled in a machine at a fair. There was a wound six inches long and three inches broad, and the skin was very extensively undermined beyond its limits, while the soft parts were generally so much lacerated that a pair of dressing forceps introduced at the wound and pushed directly inwards appeared beneath the skin at the opposite aspect of the limb. From this wound several tags of muscle were hanging, and among them was one consisting of about three inches of the triceps in almost its entire thickness; while the lower fragment of the bone, which was broken high up, was protruding four inches and a half, stripped of muscle, the skin being tucked in under it. Without the assistance of the antiseptic treatment, I should certainly have thought of nothing else but amputation at the shoulder-joint; but, as the radial pulse could be felt and the fingers had sensation, I did not hesitate to try to save the limb and adopted the plan of treatment above described, wrapping the arm from the shoulder to below the elbow in the antiseptic application, the whole interior of the wound, together with the protruding bone, having previously been freely treated with strong carbolic acid. About the tenth day, the discharge, which up to that time had been only sanious and serous, showed a slight admixture of slimy pus; and this increased till (a few days before I left) it amounted to about three drachms in twenty-four hours. But the boy continued as he had been after the second day, free from unfavorable symptoms, with pulse, tongue, appetite, and sleep natural and strength increasing, while the limb remained as it had been from the first, free from swelling, redness, or pain. I, therefore, persevered with the antiseptic dressing; and, before I left, the discharge was already somewhat less, while the bone was becoming firm. I think it likely that in that boy's case, I should have found merely a superficial sore had I taken off all the dressings at the end of the three weeks; though, considering the extent of the injury, I thought it prudent to let the month expire before disturbing the rag next the skin. But I feel sure that, if I had resorted to ordinary dressing when the pus first appeared, the progress of the case would have been exceedingly different.

The next class of cases to which I have applied the antiseptic treatment is that of abscesses. Here also the results have been extremely satisfactory, and in beautiful harmony with the pathological principles indicated above. The pyogenic membrane, like the granulations of a sore, which it resembles in nature, forms pus, not from any inherent disposition to do so, but only because it is subjected to some preternatural stimulation. In an ordinary abscess, whether acute or chronic, before it is opened the stimulus which maintains the suppuration is derived from the presence of pus pent up within the cavity. When a free opening is made in the ordinary way, this stimulus is got rid of, but the atmosphere gaining access to the contents, the potent stimulus of decomposition comes into operation, and pus is generated in greater abundance than before. But when the evacuation is effected on the antiseptic principle, the pyogenic membrane, freed from the influence of the former stimulus without the substitution of a new one, ceases to suppurate (like the granulations of a sore under metallic dressing), furnishing merely a trifling amount of clear serum, and, whether the opening be dependent or not, rapidly contracts and coalesces. At the same time any constitutional symptoms previously occasioned by the accumulation of the matter are got rid of without the slightest risk of the irritative fever or hectic hitherto so justly dreaded in dealing with large abscesses.

In order that the treatment may be satisfactory, the abscess must be seen before it is opened. Then, except in very rare and peculiar cases,[3] there are no septic organisms in the contents, so that it is needless to introduce carbolic acid into the interior. Indeed, such a procedure would be objectionable, as it would stimulate the pyogenic membrane to unnecessary suppuration. All that is requisite is to guard against the introduction of living atmospheric germs from without, at the same time that free opportunity is afforded for the escape of the discharge from within.

I have so lately given elsewhere a detailed account of the method by which this is effected (Lancet, July 27th, 1867), that I shall not enter into it at present further than to say that the means employed are the same as those described above for the superficial dressing of compound fractures; viz., a piece of rag dipped into the solution of carbolic acid in oil to serve as an antiseptic curtain, under cover of which the abscess is evacuated by free incision, and the antiseptic paste to guard against decomposition occurring

[3] As an instance of one of these exceptional cases, I may mention that of an abcess in the vicinity of the colon, and afterwards proved by postmortem examination to have once communicated with it. Here the pus was extremely offensive when evacuated, and exhibited vibrios under the microscope.

in the stream of pus that flows out beneath it; the dressing being changed daily until the sinus is closed.

The most remarkable results of this practice in a pathological point of view have been afforded by cases where the formation of pus depended on disease of bone. Here the abscesses, instead of forming exceptions to the general class in the obstinacy of the suppuration, have resembled the rest in yielding in a few days only a trifling discharge, and frequently the production of pus has ceased from the moment of the evacuation of the original contents. Hence it appears that caries, when no longer labouring as heretofore under the irritation of decomposing matter, ceases to be an opprobrium of surgery, and recovers like other inflammatory affections. In the publication before alluded to, I have mentioned the case of a middle-aged man with a psoas abscess depending in diseased bone, in whom the sinus finally closed after months of patient perseverance with the antiseptic treatment. Since that article was written I have had another instance of abscess equally gratifying, but the differing in the circumstance that the disease and the recovery were more rapid in their course. The patient was a blacksmith, who had suffered four and a half months before I saw him from symptoms of ulceration of cartilage in the left elbow. These had latterly increased in severity so as to deprive him entirely of his night's rest and of appetite. I found the region of the elbow greatly swollen, and on careful examination found a fluctuating point at the outer aspect of the articulation. I opened it on the antiseptic principle, the incision evidently penetrating to the joint, giving exit to a few drachms of pus. The medical gentleman under whose care he was (Dr. Macgregor, of Glasgow) supervised the daily dressing with the carbolic acid paste till the patient went to spend two or three weeks at the coast, when his wife was entrusted with it. Just two months after I opened the abscess, he called to show me the limb, stating that the discharge had been, for at least two weeks, as little as it was then, a trifling moisture upon the paste, such as might be accounted for by the little sore caused by the incision. On applying a probe guarded with an antiseptic rag, I found that the sinus was soundly closed, while the limb was free from swelling or tenderness; and, although he had not attempted to exercise it much, the joint could already be moved through a considerable angle. Here the antiseptic principle had effected the restoration of a joint, which, on any other known system of treatment, must have been excised.

Ordinary contused wounds are, of course, amenable to the same treatment as compound fractures, which are a complicated variety of them. I will content myself with mentioning a single instance of this class of cases. In April last, a volunteer was discharging a rifle when it burst, and blew back the thumb with its metacarpal bone, so that it could be bent back as on a hinge at the trapezial joint, which had evidently been opened, while all the soft parts between the metacarpal bones of the thumb and forefinger were torn through. I need not insist before my present audience on the ugly character of such an injury. My house-surgeon, Mr. Hector Cameron, applied carbolic acid to the whole raw surface, and completed the dressing as if for compound fracture. The hand remained free from pain, redness or swelling, and with the exception of a shallow groove, all the wound consolidated without a drop of matter, so that if it had been a clean cut, it would have been regarded as a good example of primary union. The small granulating surface soon healed, and at present a linear cicatrix alone tells of the injury he has sustained, while his thumb has all its movements and his hand a fine grasp.

If the severest forms of contused and lacerated wounds heal thus kindly under the antiseptic treatment, it is obvious that its application to simple incised wounds must be merely a matter of detail. I have devoted a good deal of attention to this class, but I have not as yet pleased myself altogether with any of the methods I have employed. I am, however, prepared to go so far as to say that a solution of carbolic acid in twenty parts of water, while a mild and cleanly application, may be relied on for destroying any septic germs that may fall upon the wound during the performance of an operation; and also that, for preventing the subsequent introduction of others, the paste above described, applied as for compound fractures, gives excellent results. Thus I have had a case of strangulated inguinal hernia in which it was necessary to take away half a pound of thickened omentum, heal without any deep-seated suppuration or any tenderness of the sac or any fever; and amputations, including one immediately below the knee, have remained absolutely free from constitutional symptoms.

Further, I have found that when the antiseptic treatment is efficiently conducted, ligatures may be safely cut short and left to be disposed of by absorption or otherwise. Should this particular branch of the subject yield all that it promises, should it turn out on further trial that when the knot is applied on the antiseptic principle, we may calculate as securely as if it were absent on the occurrence of healing without any deep-seated suppuration, the deligation of main arteries in their continuity will be deprived of the two dangers that now attend it, viz., those of secondary hæmorrhage and an unhealthy state of the wound. Further, it seems not unlikely that the present objection to tying an artery in the immediate vicinity of a large branch may be done away with; and that even the innominate, which has lately been the subject of an ingenious experiment by one of the Dublin surgeons, on account of its well-known fatality under the ligature for secondary hæmorrhage, may cease to have this unhappy character when the tissues in the vicinity of the thread, instead of becoming softened through the influence of an irritating decomposing substance, are left at liberty to consolidate firmly near an unoffending though foreign body.

It would carry me far beyond the limited time which, by the rules of the Association, is alone at my disposal, were I to enter into the various applications of the antiseptic principle in the several special departments of surgery.

There is, however, one point more that I cannot but advert to, viz., the influence of this mode of treatment upon the general healthiness of an hospital. Previously to its introduction the two large wards in which most of my cases of accident and of operation are treated were among the unhealthiest in the whole surgical division of the Glasgow Royal Infirmary, in consequence apparently of those wards being unfavorably placed with reference to the supply of fresh air; and I have felt ashamed when recording the results of my practice, to have so often to allude to hospital gangrene or pyæmia. It was interesting, though melancholy, to observe that whenever all or nearly all the beds contained cases with open sores, these grievous complications were pretty sure to show themselves; so that I came to welcome simple fractures, though in themselves of little interest either for myself or the students, because their presence diminished the proportion of open sores among the patients. But since the antiseptic treatment has been brought into full operation, and wounds and abscesses no longer poison the atmosphere with putrid exhalations, my wards, though in other respects under precisely the same circumstances as before, have completely changed their character; so that during the last nine months not a single instance of pyæmia, hospital gangrene, or erysipelas has occurred in them.

As there appears to be no doubt regarding the cause of this change, the importance of the fact can hardly be exaggerated.

THE PHYSIOLOGICAL THEORY
OF FERMENTATION

BY
LOUIS PASTEUR

TRANSLATED BY
F. FAULKNER AND D. C. ROBB
AND REVISED

THE GERM THEORY AND
ITS APPLICATIONS TO MEDICINE
AND SURGERY

BY
MM. PASTEUR, JOURBERT, AND CHAMBERLAND
TRANSLATED BY
H. C. ERNST, M. D.
PROFESSOR OF BACTERIOLOGY IN THE HARVARD MEDICAL SCHOOL

ON THE EXTENSION OF THE
GERM THEORY TO THE ETIOLOGY
OF CERTAIN COMMON DISEASES

BY
LOUIS PASTEUR
TRANSLATED BY
H. C. ERNST, M. D.

INTRODUCTORY NOTE

LOUIS PASTEUR was born at Dôle, Jura, France, December 27, 1822, and died near Saint-Cloud, September 28, 1895. His interest in science, and especially in chemistry, developed early, and by the time he was twenty-six he was professor of the physical sciences at Dijon. The most important academic positions held by him later were those as professor of chemistry at Strasburg, 1849; dean of the Faculty of Sciences at Lille, 1854; science director of the École Normale Supérieure, Paris, 1857; professor of geology, physics, and chemistry at the École des Beaux Arts; professor of chemistry at the Sorbonne, 1867. After 1875 he carried on his researches at the Pasteur Institute. He was a member of the Institute, and received many honors from learned societies at home and abroad.

In respect of the number and importance, practical as well as scientific, of his discoveries, Pasteur has hardly a rival in the history of science. He may be regarded as the founder of modern stereo-chemistry; and his discovery that living organisms are the cause of fermentation is the basis of the whole modern germ-theory of disease and of the antiseptic method of treatment. His investigations of the diseases of beer and wine; of pébrine, a disease affecting silk-worms; of anthrax, and of fowl cholera, were of immense commercial importance and led to conclusions which have revolutionized physiology, pathology, and therapeutics. By his studies in the culture of bacteria of attenuated virulence he extended widely the practise of inoculation with a milder form of various diseases, with a view to producing immunity.

The following papers present some of the most important of his contributions, and exemplify his extraordinary powers of lucid exposition and argument.

TO

THE MEMORY OF MY FATHER

FORMERLY A SOLDIER UNDER THE FIRST EMPIRE
CHEVALIER OF THE LEGION OF HONOR

The longer I live, the better I understand the kindness of thy heart and the high quality of thy mind.

The efforts which I have devoted to these Studies, as well as those which preceded them, are the fruit of thy counsel and example.

Desiring to honor these filial remembrances, I dedicate this work to thy memory.

L. Pasteur.

AUTHOR'S PREFACE

OUR misfortunes inspired me with the idea of these researches. I undertook them immediately after the war of 1870, and have since continued them without interruption, with the determination of perfecting them, and thereby benefiting a branch of industry wherein we are undoubtedly surpassed by Germany.

I am convinced that I have found a precise, practical solution of the arduous problem which I proposed to myself—that of a process of manufacture, independent of season and locality, which should obviate the necessity of having recourse to the costly methods of cooling employed in existing processes, and at the same time secure the preservation of its products for any length of time.

These new studies are based on the same principles which guided me in my researches on wine, vinegar, and the silkworm disease—principles, the applications of which are practically unlimited. The etiology of contagious diseases may, perhaps, receive from them an unexpected light.

I need not hazard any prediction concerning the advantages likely to accrue to the brewing industry from the adoption of such a process of brewing as my study of the subject has enabled me to devise, and from an application of the novel facts upon which this process is founded. Time is the best appraiser of scientific work, and I am not unaware that an industrial discovery rarely produces all its fruit in the hands of its first inventor.

I began my researches at Clermont-Ferrand, in the laboratory, and with the help, of my friend M. Duclaux, professor of chemistry at the Faculty of Sciences of that town. I continued them in Paris, and afterwards at the great brewery of Tourtel Brothers, of Tantonville, which is admitted to be the first in France. I heartily thank these gentlemen for their extreme kindness. I owe also a public tribute of gratitude to M. Kuhn, a skillful brewer of Chamalières, near Clermont-Ferrand, as well as to M. Velten of Marseilles, and to MM. de Tassigny, of Reims, who have placed at my disposal their establishments and their products, with the most praiseworthy eagerness.

L. PASTEUR.

Paris, June 1, 1879.

THE PHYSIOLOGICAL THEORY OF FERMENTATION

§ I. On the Relations Existing Between Oxygen and Yeast

IT is characteristic of science to reduce incessantly the number of unexplained phenomena. It is observed, for instance, that fleshy fruits are not liable to fermentation so long as their epidermis remains uninjured. On the other hand, they ferment very readily when they are piled up in heaps more or less open, and immersed in their saccharine juice. The mass becomes heated and swells; carbonic acid gas is disengaged, and the sugar disappears and is replaced by alcohol. Now, as to the question of the origin of these spontaneous phenomena, so remarkable in character as well as usefulness for man's service, modern knowledge has taught us that fermentation is the consequence of a development of vegetable cells the germs of which do not exist in the saccharine juices within fruits; that many varieties of these cellular plants exist, each giving rise to its own particular fermentation. The principal products of these various fermentations, although resembling each other in their nature, differ in their relative proportions and in the accessory substances that accompany them, a fact which alone is sufficient to account for wide differences in the quality and commercial value of alcoholic beverages.

Now that the discovery of ferments and their living nature, and our knowledge of their origin, may have solved the mystery of the spontaneous appearance of fermentations in natural saccharine juices, we may ask whether we must still regard the reactions that occur in these fermentations as phenomena inexplicable by the ordinary laws of chemistry. We can readily see that fermentations occupy a special place in the series of chemical and biological phenomena. What gives to fermentations certain exceptional characters of which we are only now beginning to suspect the causes, is the mode of life in the minute plants designated under the generic name of *ferments,* a mode of life which is essentially different from that in other vegetables, and from which result phenomena equally exceptional throughout the whole range of the chemistry of living beings.

The least reflection will suffice to convince us that the alcoholic ferments must possess the faculty of vegetating and performing their functions out of contact with air. Let us consider, for instance, the method of vintage practised in the Jura. The bunches are laid at the foot of the vine in a large tub, and the grapes there stripped from them. When the grapes, some of which are uninjured, others bruised, and all moistened by the juice issuing from the latter, fill the tub—where they form what is called the *vintage*—they are conveyed in barrels to large vessels fixed in cellars of a considerable depth. These vessels are not filled to more than three-quarters of their capacity. Fermentation soon takes place in them, and the carbonic acid gas finds escape through the bunghole, the diameter of which, in the case of the largest vessels, is not more than ten or twelve centimetres (about four inches). The wine is not drawn off before the end of two or three months. In this way it seems highly probable that the yeast which produces the wine under such conditions must have developed, to a great extent at least, out of contact with oxygen. No doubt oxygen is not entirely absent from the first; nay, its limited presence is even a necessity to the manifestation of the phenomena which follow. The grapes are stripped from the bunch in contact with air, and the must which drops from the wounded fruit takes a little of this gas into solution. This small quantity of air so introduced into the must, at the commencement of operations, plays a most indispensable part, it being from the presence of this that the spores of ferments which are spread over the surface of the grapes and the woody part

THEORY OF FERMENTATION

of the bunches derive the power of starting their vital phenomena.[1] This air, however, especially when the grapes have been stripped from the bunches, is in such small proportion, and that which is in contact with the liquid mass is so promptly expelled by the carbonic acid gas, which is evolved as soon as a little yeast has formed, that it will readily be admitted that most of the yeast is produced apart from the influence of oxygen, whether free or in solution. We shall revert to this fact, which is of great importance. At present we are only concerned in pointing out that, from the mere knowledge of the practices of certain localities, we are induced to believe that the cells of yeast, after they have developed from their spores, continue to live and multiply without the intervention of oxygen, and that the alcoholic ferments have a mode of life which is probably quite exceptional, since it is not generally met with in other species, vegetable or animal.

Another equally exceptional characteristic of yeast and fermentation in general consists in the small proportion which the yeast that forms bears to the sugar that decomposes. In all other known beings the weight of nutritive matter assimilated corresponds with the weight of food used up, any difference that may exist being comparatively small. The life of yeast is entirely different. For a certain weight of yeast formed, we may have ten times, twenty times, a hundred times as much sugar, or even more decomposed, as we shall experimentally prove by-and-bye; that is to say, that whilst the proportion varies in a precise manner, according to conditions which we shall have occasion to specify, it is also greatly out of proportion to the weight of the yeast. We repeat, the life of no other being, under its normal physiological conditions, can show anything similar. The alcoholic ferments, therefore, present themselves to us as plants which possess at least two singular properties: they can live without air, that is without oxygen, and they can cause decomposition to an amount which,

[1] It has been remarked in practice that fermentation is facilitated by leaving the grapes on the bunches. The reason of this has not yet been discovered. Still we have no doubt that it may be attributed, principally, to the fact that the interstices between the grapes, and the spaces which the bunch leaves throughout, considerably increase the volume of air placed at the service of the germs of ferment.

though variable, yet, as estimated by weight of product formed, is out of all proportion to the weight of their own substance. These are facts of so great importance, and so intimately connected with the theory of fermentation, that it is indispensable to endeavour to establish them experimentally, with all the exactness of which they will admit.

The question before us is whether yeast is in reality an anaërobian[2] plant, and what quantities of sugar it may cause to ferment, under the various conditions under which we cause it to act.

The following experiments were undertaken to solve this double problem:—We took a double-necked flask, of three litres (five pints) capacity, one of the tubes being curved and forming an escape for the gas; the other one, on the right hand side (FIG. 1), being furnished with a glass tap. We filled this flask with pure yeast water, sweetened with 5 per cent. of sugar candy, the flask being so full that there was not the least trace of air remaining above the tap or in the escape tube; this artificial wort had, however, been itself aerated. The curved tube was plunged in a porcelain vessel full of mercury, resting on a firm support. In the small cylindrical funnel above the tap, the capacity of which was from 10 cc. to 15 cc. (about half a fluid ounce) we caused to ferment, at a temperature of 20° or 25° C. (about 75° F.), five or six cubic centimetres of the saccharine liquid, by means of a trace of yeast, which multiplied rapidly, causing fermentation, and forming a slight deposit of yeast at the bottom of the funnel above the tap. We then opened the tap, and some of the liquid in the funnel entered the flask, carrying with it the small deposit of yeast, which was sufficient to impregnate the saccharine liquid contained in the flask. In this manner it is possible to introduce as small a quantity of yeast as we wish, a quantity the weight of which, we may say, is hardly appreciable. The yeast sown multiplies rapidly and produces fermentation, the carbonic gas from which is expelled into the mercury. In less than twelve days all the sugar had disappeared, and the fermentation had finished. There was a sensible deposit of yeast adhering to the sides of the flask; collected and dried

---

[2] *Capable of living without free oxygen*—a term invented by Pasteur.—ED.

THEORY OF FERMENTATION

it weighed 2.25 grammes (34 grains). It is evident that in this experiment the total amount of yeast formed, if it required oxygen to enable it to live, could not have absorbed, at most, more than the volume which was originally held

FIG. 1

in solution in the saccharine liquid, when that was exposed to the air before being introduced into the flask.

Some exact experiments conducted by M. Raulin in our laboratory have established the fact that saccharine worts, like water, soon become saturated when shaken briskly with an excess of air, and also that they always take into solution a little less air than saturated pure water contains under the same conditions of temperature and pressure. At a temperature of 25° C. (77° F.), therefore, if we adopt the coefficient of the solubility of oxygen in water given in Bunsen's tables, we find that 1 litre (1¾ pints) of water saturated with air contains 5.5 cc. (0.3 cubic inch) of oxygen. The three litres of yeast-water in the flask, supposing it to have been saturated, contains less than 16.5 cc. (1 cubic inch) of oxygen, or, in weight, less than 23 milligrammes (0.35 grains). This was the maximum amount of oxygen, supposing the greatest possible quantity to have been absorbed, that was required by the yeast formed in the fermentation of 150 grammes (4.8 Troy ounces) of sugar. We shall better understand the significance of this result later on. Let us repeat the fore-

FIG. 2

going experiment, but under altered conditions. Let us fill, as before, our flask with sweetened yeast-water, but let this first be boiled, so as to expel all the air it contains. To effect this we arrange our apparatus as represented in the accompanying sketch. (FIG. 2.) We place our flask, A, on a tripod above a gas flame, and in place of the vessel of mercury substitute a porcelain dish, under which we can put a gas flame, and which contains some fermentable, saccharine liquid, similar to that with which the flask is filled. We boil the liquid in the flask and that in the basin simultaneously, and then let them cool down together, so that as the liquid in the flask cools some of the liquid is sucked from the basin into the flask. From a trial experiment which we

THEORY OF FERMENTATION

conducted, determining the quantity of oxygen that remained in solution in the liquid after cooling, according to M. Schützenberger's valuable method, by means of hydrosulphite of soda,[3] we found that the three litres in the flask, treated as we have described, contained less than one milligramme (0.015 grain) of oxygen. At the same time we conducted another experiment, by way of comparison (FIG. 3). We took a flask, B, of larger capacity than the former one, which we filled about half with the same volume as before of a saccharine liquid of identically the same composition. This liquid had been previously freed from alterative germs by boiling. In the funnel surmounting A, we put a few cubic centimetres of saccharine liquid in a state of fermentation, and when this small quantity of liquid was in full fermentation, and the yeast in it was young and vigorous, we opened the tap, closing it again immediately, so that a little of the liquid and yeast still remained in the funnel. By this means we caused the liquid in A to ferment. We also impregnated the liquid in B with some yeast taken from the funnel of A. We then replaced the porcelain dish in which the curved escape tube of A had been plunged, by a vessel filled with mercury. The following is a description of two of these comparative fermentations and the results they gave.

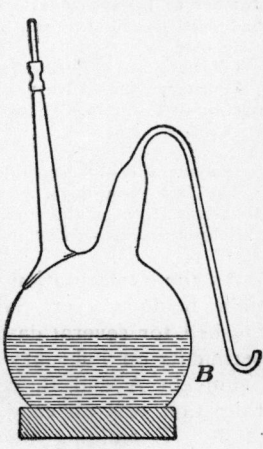

FIG. 3

The fermentable liquid was composed of yeast-water sweetened with 5 per cent. of sugar-candy; the ferment employed was *sacchormyces pastorianus*.

The impregnation took place on January 20th. The flasks were placed in an oven at 25° (77° F.).

Flask A, without air.

January 21st.—Fermentation commenced; a little frothy liquid issued from the escape tube and covered the mercury.

[3] $NaHSO_2$, now called *Sodium hyposulphite*.—D. C. R.

The following days, fermentation was active. Examining the yeast mixed with the froth that was expelled into the mercury by the evolution of carbonic acid gas, we find that it was very fine, young, and actively budding.

February 3rd.—Fermentation still continued, showing itself by a number of little bubbles rising from the bottom of the liquid, which had settled bright. The yeast was at the bottom in the form of a deposit.

February 7th.—Fermentation still continued, but very languidly.

February 9th.—A very languid fermentation still went on, discernible in little bubbles rising from the bottom of the flask.

Flask B, with air.

January 21st.—A sensible development of yeast.

The following days, fermentation was active, and there was an abundant froth on the surface of the liquid.

February 1st.—All symptoms of fermentation had ceased.

As the fermentation in A would have continued a long time, being so very languid, and as that in B had been finished for several days, we brought to a close our two experiments on February 9th. To do this we poured off the liquids in A and B, collecting the yeasts on tared filters. Filtration was an easy matter, more especially in the case of A. Examining the yeasts under the microscope, immediately after decantation, we found that both of them remained very pure. The yeast in A was in little clusters, the globules of which were collected together, and appeared by their well-defined borders to be ready for an easy revival in contact with air.

As might have been expected, the liquid in flask B did not contain the least trace of sugar; that in the flask A still contained some, as was evident from the non-completion of fermentation, but not more than 4.6 grammes (71 grains). Now, as each flask originally contained three litres of liquid holding in solution 5 per cent. of sugar, it follows that 150 grammes (2,310 grains) of sugar had fermented in the flask B, and 145.4 grammes (2,239.2 grains) in the flask A. The weights of yeast after drying at 100° C. (212° F.) were—

For the flask B, with air....1,970 grammes (30.4 grains).
For the flask A, without air..1,368 grammes[4].

[4] This appears to be a misprint for 1.638 grammes=25.3 grains.—D. C. R.

THEORY OF FERMENTATION

The proportions were 1 of yeast to 76 of fermented sugar in the first case, and 1 of yeast to 89 of fermented sugar in the second.

From these facts the following consequences may be deduced:

1. The fermentable liquid (flask B), which since it had been in contact with air, necessarily held air in solution, although not to the point of saturation, inasmuch as it had been once boiled to free it from all foreign germs, furnished a weight of yeast sensibly greater than that yielded by the liquid which contained no air at all (flask A) or, at least, which could only have contained an exceedingly minute quantity.

2. This same slightly aerated fermentable liquid fermented much more rapidly than the other. In eight or ten days it contained no more sugar; while the other, after twenty days, still contained an appreciable quantity.

Is this last fact to be explained by the greater quantity of yeast formed in B? By no means. At first, when the air has access to the liquid, much yeast is formed and little sugar disappears, as we shall prove immediately; nevertheless the yeast formed in contact with the air is more active than the other. Fermentation is correlative first to the development of the globules, and then to the continued life of those globules once formed. The more oxygen these last globules have at their disposal during their formation, the more vigorous, transparent, and turgescent, and, as a consequence of this last quality, the more active they are in decomposing sugar. We shall hereafter revert to these facts.

3. In the airless flask the proportion of yeast to sugar was $\frac{1}{89}$; it was only $\frac{1}{79}$ in the flask which had air at first.

The proportion that the weight of yeast bears to the weight of the sugar is, therefore, variable, and this variation depends, to a certain extent, upon the presence of air and the possibility of oxygen being absorbed by the yeast. We shall presently show that yeast possesses the power of absorbing that gas and emitting carbonic acid, like ordinary fungi, that even oxygen may be reckoned amongst the number of food-stuffs that may be assimilated by this plant, and that this fixation of oxygen in yeast, as well as the oxidations resulting from it, have the most marked effect on the life of yeast, on the multiplication of its cells, and on their activity as ferments acting upon sugar, whether immediately or afterwards, apart from supplies of oxygen or air.

In the preceding experiment, conducted without the presence of air, there is one circumstance particularly worthy of notice. This experiment succeeds, that is to say, the yeast sown in the medium deprived of oxygen develops, only when this yeast is in a state of great vigour. We have already explained the meaning of this last expression. But we wish now to call attention to a very evident fact in connection with this point. We impregnate a fermentable liquid; yeast develops and fermentation appears. This lasts for several days and then ceases. Let us suppose that, from the day when fermentation first appears in the production of a minute froth, which gradually increases until it whitens the surface of the liquid, we take, every twenty-four hours, or at longer intervals, a trace of the yeast deposited on the bottom of the vessel and use it for starting fresh fermentations. Conducting these fermentations all under precisely the same conditions of temperature, character and volume of liquid, let us continue this for a prolonged time, even after the original fermentation is finished. We shall have no difficulty in seeing that the first signs of action in each of our series of second fermentations appear always later and later in proportion to the length of time that has elapsed from the commencement of the original fermentation. In other words, the time necessary for the development of the germs and the production of that amount of yeast sufficient to cause the first appearance of fermentation varies with the state of the impregnating cells, and is longer in proportion as the cells are further removed from the period of their formation. It is essential, in experiments of this kind, that the quantities of yeast successively taken should be as nearly as possible equal in weight or volume, since, *ceteris paribus,* fermentations manifest themselves more quickly the larger the quantity of yeast employed in impregnation.

If we compare under the microscope the appearance and

character of the successive quantities of yeast taken, we shall see plainly that the structure of the cells undergoes a progressive change. The first sample which we take, quite at the beginning of the original fermentation, generally gives us cells rather larger than those later on, and possessing a remarkable tenderness. Their walls are exceedingly thin, the consistency and softness of their protoplasm is akin to fluidity, and their granular contents appear in the form of scarcely visible spots. The borders of the cells soon become more marked, a proof that their walls undergo a thickening; their protoplasm also becomes denser, and the granulations more distinct. Cells of the same organ, in the states of infancy and old age, should not differ more than the cells of which we are speaking, taken in their extreme states. The progressive changes in the cells, after they have acquired their normal form and volume, clearly demonstrate the existence of a chemical work of a remarkable intensity, during which their weight increases, although in volume they undergo no sensible change, a fact that we have often characterized as "the continued life of cells already formed." We may call this work a process of maturation on the part of the cells, almost the same that we see going on in the case of adult beings in general, which continue to live for a long time, even after they have become incapable of reproduction, and long after their volume has become permanently fixed.

This being so, it is evident, we repeat, that, to multiply in a fermentable medium, quite out of contact with oxygen, the cells of yeast must be extremely young, full of life and health, and still under the influence of the vital activity which they owe to the free oxygen which has served to form them, and which they have perhaps stored up for a time. When older, they reproduce themselves with much difficulty when deprived of air, and gradually become more languid; and if they do multiply, it is in strange and monstrous forms. A little older still, they remain absolutely inert in a medium deprived of free oxygen. This is not because they are dead; for in general they may be revived in a marvellous manner in the same liquid if it has been first aerated before they are sown. It would not surprise us to learn that at this point certain preconceived ideas suggest themselves to the mind of an attentive reader on the subject of the causes that may serve to account for such strange phenomena in the life of these beings which our ignorance hides under the expressions of *youth* and *age;* this, however, is a subject which we cannot pause to consider here.

At this point we must observe—for it is a matter of great importance—that in the operations of the brewer there is always a time when the yeasts are in this state of vigorous youth of which we have been speaking, acquired under the influence of free oxygen, since all the worts and the yeasts of commerce are necessarily manipulated in contact with air, and so impregnated more or less with oxygen. The yeast immediately seizes upon this gas and acquires a state of freshness and activity, which permits it to live afterwards out of contact with air, and to act as a ferment. Thus, in ordinary brewery practice, we find the yeast already formed in abundance even before the earliest external signs of fermentation have made their appearance. In this first phase of its existence, yeast lives chiefly like an ordinary fungus.

From the same circumstances it is clear that the brewer's fermentations may, speaking quite strictly, last for an indefinite time, in consequence of the unceasing supply of fresh wort, and from the fact, moreover, that the exterior air is constantly being introduced during the work, and that the air contained in the fresh worts keeps up the vital activity of the yeast, as the act of breathing keeps up the vigour and life of cells in all living beings. If the air could not renew itself in any way, the vital activity which the cells originally received, under its influence, would become more and more exhausted, and the fermentation eventually come to an end.

We may recount one of the results obtained in other experiments similar to the last, in which, however, we employed yeast which was still older than that used for our experiment with flask A (FIG. 2), and moreover took still greater precautions to prevent the presence of air. Instead of leaving the flask, as well as the dish, to cool slowly, after having expelled all air by boiling, we permitted the liquid in the dish to continue boiling whilst the flask was being cooled by artificial means; the end of the escape tube was then taken out of the still boiling dish and plunged into the mercury trough. In impregnating the liquid, instead of employing the contents of the small cylindrical funnel whilst still in a state of fermentation, we waited until this was finished. Under these conditions, fermentation was still going on in our flask, after a lapse of three months. We stopped it and found that 0.255 gramme (3.9 grains) of yeast had been formed, and that 45 grammes (693 grains) of sugar had fermented, the ratio between the weights of yeast and sugar being thus $\frac{0.255}{45} = \frac{1}{176}$. In this experiment the yeast developed with much difficulty, by reason of the conditions to which it had been subjected. In appearance the cells varied much, some were to be found large, elongated, and of tubular aspect, some seemed very old and were extremely granular, whilst others were more transparent. All of them might be considered abnormal cells.

In such experiments we encounter another difficulty. If the yeast sown in the non-aerated fermentable liquid is in the least degree impure, especially if we use sweetened yeast-water, we may be sure that alcoholic fermentation will soon cease, if, indeed, it ever commences, and that accessory fermentations will go on. The vibrios of butyric fermentation, for instance, will propagate with remarkable facility under these circumstances. Clearly then, the purity of the yeast at the moment of impregnation, and the purity of the liquid in the funnel, are conditions indispensable to success.

To secure the latter of these conditions, we close the funnel, as shown in FIG. 2, by means of a cork pierced with two holes, through one of which a short tube passes, to which a short length of india-rubber tubing provided with a glass stopper is attached; through the other hole a thin curved tube is passed. Thus fitted, the funnel can answer the same purposes as our double-necked flasks. A few cubic centimetres of sweetened yeast-water are put in it and boiled, so that the steam may destroy any germs adhering to the sides; and when cold the liquid is impregnated by means of a trace of pure yeast, introduced through the glass-stoppered tube. If these precautions are neglected, it is scarcely possible to secure a successful fermentation in our flasks, because the yeast sown is immediately held in check by a development of anaërobian vibrios. For greater security, we may add to the fermentable liquid, at the moment when it is prepared, a very small quantity of tartaric acid, which will prevent the development of butyric vibrios.

The variation of the ratio between the weight of the yeast and that of the sugar decomposed by it now claims special attention. Side by side with the experiments which we have just described, we conducted a third lot by means of the flask C (FIG. 4), holding 4.7 litres (8½ pints), and fitted up like the usual two-necked flasks, with the object of freeing the fermentable liquid from foreign germs, by boiling it to begin with, so that we might carry on our work under conditions of purity. The volume of yeast-water (containing 5 per cent. of sugar) was only 200 cc. (7 fl. oz.), and consequently, taking into account the capacity of the flask, it formed but a very thin layer at the bottom. On the day after impregnation the deposit of yeast was already considerable, and forty-eight hours afterwards the fermentation was completed. On the third day we collected the yeast after having analyzed the gas contained in the flask. This analysis was easily accomplished by placing the flask in a hot-water bath, whilst the end of the curved tube was plunged under a cylinder of mercury. The gas contained 41.4 per cent. of carbonic acid, and, after the absorption, the remaining air contained:—

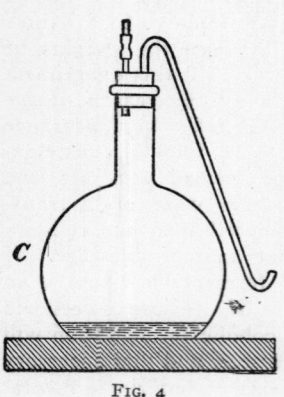

```
Oxygen .................................19.7
Nitrogen .........................  ......80.3
                                       ─────
                                       100.0
```

Taking into consideration the volume of this flask, this shows a minimum of 50 cc. (3.05 cub. in.) of oxygen to have been absorbed by the yeast. The liquid contained no more sugar, and the weight of the yeast, dried at a temperature of 100° C. (212° F.), was 0.44 grammes. The ratio between the weights of yeast and sugar is $\frac{0.44}{10} = \frac{1}{23.7}$ [5]. On this occasion, where we had increased the quantity of oxygen held in solution, so as to yield itself for assimilation at the beginning and during the earlier developments of the yeast, we found instead of the previous ratio of $\frac{1}{78}$ that of $\frac{1}{23}$.

The next experiment was to increase the proportion of oxygen to a still greater extent, by rendering the diffusion of gas a more easy matter than in a flask, the air in which is in a state of perfect quiescence. Such a state of matters hinders the supply of oxygen, inasmuch as the carbonic acid, as soon as it is liberated, at once forms an immovable layer on the surface of the liquid, and so separates off the oxygen. To effect the purpose of our present experiment, we used flat basins having glass bottoms and low sides,

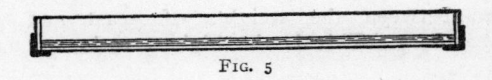

FIG. 5

also of glass, in which the depth of the liquid is not more than a few millimetres (less than $\frac{1}{4}$ inch (FIG. 5). The following is one of our experiments so conducted:—On April 16th, 1860, we sowed a trace of beer yeast ("high" yeast) in 200 cc. (7 fl. oz.) of a saccharine liquid containing 1.720 grammes (26.2 grains) of sugar-candy. From April 18th our yeast was in good condition and well developed. We collected it, after having added to the liquid a few drops of concentrated sulphuric acid, with the object of checking the fermentation to a great extent, and facilitating filtration. The sugar remaining in the filtered liquid, determined by Fehling's solution, showed that 1.04 grammes (16 grains) of sugar had disappeared. The weight of the yeast, dried at 100° C. (212° F.), was 0.127 gramme (2 grains), which gives us the ratio between the weight of

[5] 200 cc. of liquid were used, which, as containing 5 per cent., had in solution 10 grammes of sugar.—D. C. R.

the yeast and that of the fermented sugar $\frac{0.127}{1.04} = \frac{1}{8.1}$, which is considerably higher than the preceding ones.

We may still further increase this ratio by making our estimation as soon as possible after the impregnation, or the addition of the ferment. It will be readily understood why yeast, which is composed of cells that bud and subsequently detach themselves from one another, soon forms a deposit at the bottom of the vessels. In consequence of this habit of growth, the cells constantly covering each other prevents the lower layers from having access to the oxygen held in solution in the liquid, which is absorbed by the upper ones. Hence, these which are covered and deprived of this gas act on the sugar without deriving any vital benefit from the oxygen—a circumstance which must tend to diminish the ratio of which we are speaking. Once more repeating the preceding experiment, but stopping it as soon as we think that the weight of yeast formed may be determined by the balance (we find that this may be done twenty-four hours after impregnation with an inappreciable quantity of yeast), in this case the ratio between the weights of yeast and sugar is $\frac{0 \text{ gr. } 0.24 \text{ yeast}}{0 \text{ gr. } 0.98 \text{ sugar}} = \frac{1}{4}$. This is the highest ratio we have been able to obtain.

Under these conditions the fermentation of sugar is extremely languid: the ratio obtained is very nearly the same that ordinary fungoid growths would give. The carbonic acid evolved is principally formed by the decompositions which result from the assimilation of atmospheric oxygen. The yeast, therefore, lives and performs its functions after the manner of ordinary fungi: so far it is no longer a ferment, so to say; moreover, we might expect to find it to cease to be a ferment at all if we could only surround each cell separately with all the air that it required. This is what the preceding phenomena teach us; we shall have occasion to compare them later on with others which relate to the vital action exercised on yeast by the sugar of milk.

We may here be permitted to make a digression.

In his work on fermentations, which M. Schützenberger has recently published, the author criticises the deductions that we have drawn from the preceding experiments, and combats the explanation which we have given of the phenomena of fermentation.[6] It is an easy matter to show the weak point of M. Schützenberger's reasoning. We determined the power of the ferment by the relation of the weight of sugar decomposed to the weight of the yeast produced. M. Schützenberger asserts that in doing this we lay down a doubtful hypothesis, and he thinks that this power, which he terms *fermentative energy*, may be estimated more correctly by the quantity of sugar decomposed by the unit-weight of yeast in unit-time; moreover, since our experiments show that yeast is very vigorous when it has a sufficient supply of oxygen, and that, in such a case, it can decompose much sugar in a little time, M. Schützenberger concludes that it must then have great power as a ferment, even greater than when it performs its functions without the aid of air, since under this condition it decomposes sugar very slowly. In short, he is disposed to draw from our observations the very opposite conclusion to that which we arrived at.

M. Schützenberger has failed to notice that the power of a ferment is independent of the time during which it performs its functions. We placed a trace of yeast in one litre of saccharine wort; it propagated, and all the sugar was decomposed. Now, whether the chemical action involved in this decomposition of sugar had required for its completion one day, or one month, or one year, such a factor was of no more importance in this matter than the mechanical labour required to raise a ton of materials from the ground to the top of a house would be affected by the fact that it had taken twelve hours instead of one. The notion of time has nothing to do with the definition of work. M. Schützenberger has not perceived that in introducing the consideration of time into the definition of the power of a ferment, he must introduce at the same time, that of the vital activity of the cells which is independent of their character as a ferment. Apart from the consideration of the relation ex-

[6] International Science Series, vol. xx, pp. 179-182. London, 1876.— D. C. R.

isting between the weight of fermentable substance decomposed and that of ferment produced, there is no occasion to speak of fermentations or of ferments. The phenomena of fermentation and of ferments have been placed apart from others, precisely because, in certain chemical actions, that ratio has been out of proportion; but the time that these phenomena require for their accomplishment has nothing to do with either their existence proper, or with their power. The cells of a ferment may, under some circumstances, require eight days for revival and propagation, whilst, under other conditions, only a few hours are necessary; so that, if we introduce the notion of time into our estimate of their power of decomposition, we may be led to conclude that in the first case that power was entirely wanting, and that in the second case it was considerable, although all the time we are dealing with the same organism—the identical ferment.

M. Schützenberger is astonished that fermentation can take place in the presence of free oxygen, if, as we suppose, the decomposition of the sugar is the consequence of the nutrition of the yeast, at the expense of the combined oxygen, which yields itself to the ferment. At all events, he argues, fermentation ought to be slower in the presence of free oxygen. But why should it be slower? We have proved that in the presence of oxygen the vital activity of the cells increases, so that, as far as rapidity of action is concerned, its power cannot be diminished. It might, nevertheless, be weakened as a ferment, and this is precisely what happens. Free oxygen imparts to the yeast a vital activity, but at the same time impairs its power as yeast—*quâ* yeast, inasmuch as under this condition it approaches the state in which it can carry on its vital processes after the manner of an ordinary fungus; the mode of life, that is, in which the ratio between the weight of sugar decomposed and the weight of the new cells produced will be the same as holds generally among organisms which are not ferments. In short, varying our form of expression a little, we may conclude with perfect truth, from the sum total of observed facts, that the yeast which lives in the presence of oxygen and can assimilate

THEORY OF FERMENTATION

as much of that gas as is necessary to its perfect nutrition, ceases absolutely to be a ferment at all. Nevertheless, yeast formed under these conditions and subsequently brought into the presence of sugar, *out of the influence of air,* would decompose more *in a given time* than in any other of its states. The reason is that yeast which has formed in contact with air, having the maximum of free oxygen that it can assimilate is fresher and possessed of greater vital activity than that which has been formed without air or with an insufficiency of air. M. Schützenberger would associate this activity with the notion of time in estimating the power of the ferment; but he forgets to notice that yeast can only manifest this maximum of energy under a radical change of its life conditions; by having no more air at its disposal and breathing no more free oxygen. In other words, when its respiratory power becomes null, its fermentative power is at its greatest. M. Schützenberger asserts exactly the opposite (p. 151 of his work—Paris, 1875),[7] and so gratuitously places himself in opposition to facts.

In presence of abundant air supply, yeast vegetates with extraordinary activity. We see this in the weight of new yeast, comparatively large, that may be formed in the course of a few hours. The microscope still more clearly shows this activity in the rapidity of budding, and the fresh and active appearance of all the cells. FIG. 6 represents the yeast of our last experiment at the moment when we stopped the fermentation. Nothing has been taken from imagination, all the groups have been faithfully sketched as they were.[8]

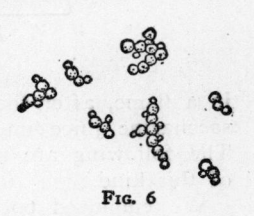

FIG. 6

In passing it is of interest to note how promptly the preceding results were turned to good account practically. In well-managed distilleries, the custom of aerating the wort and the juices to render them more adapted to fermentation, has been introduced. The molasses mixed with water, is permitted to run in thin threads through the

[7] Page 182, English edition.
[8] This figure is on a scale of 300 diameters, most of the figures in this work being of 400 diameters.

air at the moment when the yeast is added. Manufactories have been erected in which the manufacture of yeast is almost exclusively carried on. The saccharine worts, after the addition of yeast, are left to themselves, in contact with air, in shallow vats of large superficial area, realizing thus on an immense scale the conditions of the experiments which we undertook in 1861, and which we have already described in determining the rapid and easy multiplication of yeast in contact with air.

The next experiment was to determine the volume of oxygen absorbed by a known quantity of yeast, the yeast living in contact with air, and under such conditions that the absorption of air was comparatively easy and abundant.

With this object we repeated the experiment that we performed with the large-bottomed flask (FIG. 4), employin a vessel shaped like Fig. B (FIG. 7), which is, in point of fact, the flask A with its neck drawn out and closed

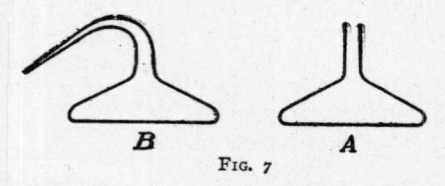

FIG. 7

in a flame, after the introduction of a thin layer of some saccharine juice impregnated with a trace of pure yeast. The following are the data and results of an experiment of this kind.

We employed 60 cc. (about 2 fluid ounces) of yeast-water, sweetened with two percent. of sugar and impregnated with a trace of yeast. After having subjected our vessel to a temperature of 25° C. (77° F.) in an oven for fifteen hours, the drawn-out point was brought under an inverted jar filled with mercury and the point broken off. A portion of the gas escaped and was collected in the jar. For 25 cc. of this gas we found, after absorption by potash 20.6, and after absorption by pyrogallic acid, 17.3. Taking into account the volume which remained free in the flask, which held 315 cc., there was a total absorption of 14.5 cc. (0.88 cub. in.) of oxygen.[9] The weight of the yeast, in a state of dryness, was 0.035 gramme.

It follows that in the production of 35 milligrammes (0.524 grain) of yeast there was an absorption of 14 or 15 cc. (about ⅞ cub. in.) of oxygen, even supposing that the yeast was formed entirely under the influence of that gas: this is equivalent to not less than 414 cc. for 1 gramme of yeast (or about 33 cubic inches for every 20 grains).[10]

Such is the large volume of oxygen necessary for the development of one gramme of yeast when the plant can assimilate this gas after the manner of an ordinary fungus.

Let us now return to the first experiment described in the paragraph on page 292 in which a flask of three litres capacity was filled with fermentable liquid, which, when caused to ferment, yielded 2.25 grammes of yeast, under circumstances where it could not obtain a greater supply of free oxygen than 16.5 cc. (about one cubic inch). According to what we have just stated, if this 2.25 grammes (34 grains) of yeast had not been able to live without oxygen, in other words, if the original cells had been unable to multiply otherwise than by absorbing free oxygen, the amount of that gas required could not have been less than 2.25×414 cc., that is, 931.5 cc. (56.85 cubic inches). The greater part of the 2.25 grammes, therefore, had evidently been produced as the growth of an anaërobian plant.

[9] It may be useful for the non-scientific reader to put it thus: that the 25 cc. which escaped, being a fair sample of the whole gas in the flask, and containing (1) 25—20.6=4.4 cc., absorbed by potash and therefore due to carbonic acid, and (2) 20.6—17.3=3.3 cc., absorbed by pyrogallate, and therefore due to oxygen, and the remaining 17.3 cc. being nitrogen, the whole gas in the flask, which has a capacity of 312 cc., will contain oxygen in the above proportion, and therefore its amount may be determined, provided we know the total gas in the flask before opening. On the other hand, we know that air normally contains, approximately, 1·5 its volume of oxygen, the rest being nitrogen, so that, by ascertaining the diminution of the proportion in the flask, we can find how many cubic centimetres have been absorbed by the yeast. The author, however, has not given all the data necessary for accurate calculation.—D. C. R.

[10] This number is probably too small; it is scarcely possible that the increase of weight in the yeast, even under the exceptional conditions of the experiment described, was not to some extent at least due to oxidation apart from free oxygen, inasmuch as some of the cells were covered by others. The increased weight of the yeast is always due to the action of two distinct modes of vital energy—activity, namely, in presence and activity in absence of air. We might endeavour to shorten the duration of the experiment still further, in which case we would still more assimilate the life of the yeast to that of ordinary moulds.

Ordinary fungi likewise require large quantities of oxygen for their development, as we may readily prove by cultivating any mould in a closed vessel full of air, and then taking the weight of plant formed and measuring the volume of oxygen absorbed. To do this, we take a flask of the shape shown in Fig. 8, capable of holding about 300 cc. (10½ fluid ounces), and containing a liquid adapted to the life of moulds. We boil this liquid, and seal the drawn-out point after the steam has expelled the air wholly or in part; we then open the flask in a garden or in a room. Should a fungus-spore enter the flask, as will invariably be the case in a certain number of flasks out of several used in the experiment, except under special circumstances, it will develop there and gradually absorb all the oxygen contained in the air of the flask. Measuring the volume of this air, and weighing, after drying, the amount of plant formed, we find that for a certain quantity of oxygen absorbed we have a certain weight of mycelium, or of mycelium together with its organs of fructification. In an experiment of this kind, in which the plant was weighed a year after its development, we found for 0.008 gramme (0.123 grain) of *mycelium,* dried at 100° C. (212° F.), an absorption that amounted to not less than 43 cc. (2.5 cubic inches) of oxygen at 25°. These numbers, however, must vary sensibly with the nature of the mould employed, and also with the greater or less activity of its development, because the phenomena is complicated by the presence of accessory oxidations, such as we find in the case of *mycoderma vini* and *aceti,* to which cause the large absorption of oxygen in our last experiment may doubtless be attributed.[11]

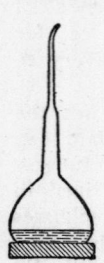

Fig. 8

[11] In these experiments, in which the moulds remain for a long time in contact with a saccharine wort out of contact with oxygen—the oxygen being promptly absorbed by the vital action of the plant (see our *Mémoire sur les Générations dites Spontanées,* p. 54, note)—there is no doubt that an appreciable quantity of alcohol is formed because the plant does not immediately lose its vital activity after the absorption of oxygen.

A 300-cc. (10-oz.) flask, containing 100 cc. of must, after the air in it had been expelled by boiling, was opened and immediately re-closed on August 15th, 1873. A fungoid growth—a unique one, of greenish-grey colour—developed from spontaneous impregnation, and decolorized the liquid, which originally was of a yellowish-brown. Some large crystals, sparkling like diamonds, of neutral tartrate of lime, were precipitated. About a year

THEORY OF FERMENTATION

The conclusions to be drawn from the whole of the preceding facts can scarcely admit of doubt. As for ourselves, we have no hesitation in finding them the foundation of the true theory of fermentation. In the experiments which we have described, fermentation by yeast, that is to say, by the type of ferments properly so called, is presented to us, in a word, as the direct consequence of the processes of nutrition, assimilation and life, when these are carried on without the agency of free oxygen. The heat required in the accomplishment of that work must necessarily have been borrowed from the decomposition of the fermentable matter, that is from the saccharine substance which, like other unstable substances, liberates heat in undergoing decomposition. Fermentation by means of yeast appears, therefore, to be essentially connected with the property possessed by this minute cellular plant of performing its respiratory functions, somehow or other, with oxygen existing combined in sugar. Its fermentative power—which power must not be confounded with the fermentative activity or the intensity of decomposition in a given time—varies considerably between two limits, fixed by the greatest and least possible access to free oxygen which the plant has in the process of nutrition. If we supply it with a sufficient quantity of free oxygen for the necessities of its life, nutrition, and respiratory combustions, in other words, if we cause it to live after the manner of a mould, properly so called, it ceases to be a ferment, that is, the ratio between the weight of the plant developed and that of the sugar decomposed, which forms its principal food, is similar in amount to that in the case of fungi.[12] On the other hand, if we deprive the yeast of air entirely, or cause it to develop in a saccharine medium deprived of free oxygen, it will multiply just as if air were present,

afterwards, long after the death of the plant, we examined this liquid. It contained 0.3 gramme (4.6 grains) of alcohol, and 0.053 gramme (0.8 grain) of vegetable matter, dried at 100° C. (212° F.). We ascertained that the spores of the fungus were dead at the moment when the flask was opened. When sown, they did did not develop in the least degree.

[12] We find in M. Raulin's note that "the minimum ratio between the weight of sugar and the weight of organized matter, that is, the weight of fungoid growth which it helps to form, may be expressed as $\frac{4.2}{1}=3.1$." JULES RAULIN, *Etudes chimiques sur la végétation. Recherches sur le développement d'une mucédinée dans un milieu artificiel*, p. 192, Paris, 1870. We have seen in the case of yeast that this ratio may be as low as $\frac{1}{4}$.

although with less activity, and under these circumstances its fermentative character will be most marked; under these circumstances, moreover, we shall find the greatest disproportion, all other conditions being the same, between the weight of yeast formed and the weight of sugar decomposed. Lastly, if free oxygen occurs in varying quantities, the ferment-power of the yeast may pass through all the degrees comprehended between the two extreme limits of which we have just spoken. It seems to us that we could not have a better proof of the direct relation that fermentation bears to life, carried on in the absence of free oxygen, or with a quantity of that gas insufficient for all the acts of nutrition and assimilation.

Another equally striking proof of the truth of this theory is the fact previously demonstrated that the ordinary moulds assume the character of a ferment when compelled to live without air, or with quantities of air too scant to permit of their organs having around them as much of that element as is necessary for their life as aërobian plants. Ferments, therefore, only possess in a higher degree a character which belongs to many common moulds, if not to all, and which they share, probably, more or less, with all living cells, namely the power of living either an aërobian or anaërobian life, according to the conditions under which they are placed.

It may be readily understood how, in their state of aërobian life, the alcoholic ferments have failed to attract attention. These ferments are only cultivated out of contract with air, at the bottom of liquids which soon become saturated with carbonic acid gas. Air is only present in the earlier developments of their germs, and without attracting the attention of the operator, whilst in their state of anaërobian growth their life and action are of prolonged duration. We must have recourse to special experimental apparatus to enable us to demonstrate the mode of life of alcoholic ferments under the influence of free oxygen; it is their state of existence apart from air, in the depths of liquids, that attracts all our attention. The results of their action are, however, marvellous, if we regard the products resulting from them, in the important industries of which they are the life and soul. In the case of ordinary moulds, the opposite holds good. What we want to use special experimental apparatus for with them, is to enable us to demonstrate the possibility of their continuing to live for a time out of contact with air, and all our attention, in their case, is attracted by the facility with which they develop under the influence of oxygen. Thus the decomposition of saccharine liquids, which is the consequence of the life of fungi without air, is scarcely perceptible, and so is of no practical importance. Their aërial life, on the other hand, in which they respire and accomplish their process of oxidation under the influence of free oxygen is a normal phenomenon, and one of prolonged duration which cannot fail to strike the least thoughtful of observers. We are convinced that a day will come when moulds will be utilised in certain industrial operations, on account of their power in destroying organic matter. The conversion of alcohol into vinegar in the process of acetification and the production of gallic acid by the action of fungi on wet gall nuts, are already connected with this kind of phenomena.[13] On this last subject, the important work of M. Van Tieghem (*Annales Scientifiques* de l'Ecole Normale, vol. vi.) may be consulted.

The possibility of living without oxygen, in the case of ordinary moulds, is connected with certain morphological modifications which are more marked in proportion as this faculty is itself more developed. These changes in the vegetative forms are scarcely perceptible, in the case of *penicillium* and *mycoderma vini*, but they are very evident in the case of *aspergillus*, consisting of a marked tendency on the part of the submerged mycelial filaments to increase in diameter, and to develop cross partitions at short intervals, so that they sometimes bear a resemblance to chains

[13] We shall show, some day, that the processes of oxidation due to growth of fungi cause, in certain decompositions, liberation of ammonia to a considerable extent, and that by regulating their action we might cause them to extract the nitrogen from a host of organic *débris*, as also, by checking the production of such organisms, we might considerably increase the proportion of nitrates in the artificial nitrogenous substances. By cultivating the various moulds on the surface of damp bread in a current of air we have obtained an abundance of ammonia, derived from the decomposition of the albuminoids effected by the fungoid life. The decomposition of asparagus and several other animal or vegetable substances has given similar results.

of conidia. In *mucor,* again, they are very marked, the inflated filaments which, closely interwoven, present chains of cells, which fall off and bud, gradually producing a mass of cells. If we consider the matter carefully, we shall see that yeast presents the same characteristics. * * * *

It is a great presumption in favor of the truth of theoretical ideas when the results of experiments undertaken on the strength of those ideas are confirmed by various facts more recently added to science, and when those ideas force themselves more and more on our minds, in spite of a *prima facie* improbability. This is exactly the character of those ideas which we have just expounded. We pronounced them in 1861, and not only have they remained unshaken since, but they have served to foreshadow new facts, so that it is much easier to defend them in the present day than it was to do so fifteen years ago. We first called attention to them in various notes, which we read before the Chemical Society of Paris, notably at its meetings of April 12th and June 28th, 1861, and in papers in the *Comtes rendus de l'Académie des Sciences.* It may be of some interest to quote here, in its entirety, our communication of June 28th, 1861, entitled, "Influences of Oxygen on the Development of Yeast and on Alcoholic Fermentation," which we extract from the *Bulletin de la Société Chimique de Paris:*—

"M. Pasteur gives the result of his researches on the fermentation of sugar and the development of yeast-cells, according as that fermentation takes place apart from the influence of free oxygen or in contact with that gas. His experiments, however, have nothing in common with those of Gay-Lussac, which were performed with the juice of grapes crushed under conditions where they would not be affected by air, and then brought into contact with oxygen.

"Yeast, when perfectly developed, is able to bud and grow in a saccharine and albuminous liquid, in the complete absence of oxygen or air. In this case but little yeast is formed, and a comparatively large quantity of sugar disappears—sixty or eighty parts for one of yeast formed. Under these conditions fermentation is very sluggish.

"If the experiment is made in contact with the air, and

with a great surface of liquid, fermentation is rapid. For the same quantity of sugar decomposed much more yeast is formed. The air with which the liquid is in contact is absorbed by the yeast. The yeast develops very actively, but its fermentative character tends to disappear under these conditions; we find, in fact, that for one part of yeast formed, not more than from four to ten parts of sugar are transformed. The fermentative character of this yeast nevertheless, continues, and produces even increased effects, if it is made to act on sugar apart from the influence of free oxygen.

"It seems, therefore, natural to admit that when yeast functions as a ferment by living apart from the influence of air, it derives oxygen from the sugar, and that this is the origin of its fermentative character.

"M. Pasteur explains the fact of the immense activity at the commencement of fermentations by the influence of the oxygen of the air held in solution in the liquids, at the time when the action commences. The author has found, moreover, that the yeast of beer sown in an albuminous liquid, such as yeast-water, still multiplies, even when there is not a trace of sugar in the liquid, provided always that atmospheric oxygen is present in large quantities. When deprived of air, under these conditions, yeast does not germinate at all. The same experiments may be repeated with albuminous liquid, mixed with a solution of non-fermentable sugar, such as ordinary crystallized milk-sugar. The results are precisely the same.

"Yeast formed thus in the absence of sugar does not change its nature; it is still capable of causing sugar to ferment, if brought to bear upon that substance apart from air. It must be remarked, however, that the development of yeast is effected with great difficulty when it has not a fermentable substance for its food. In short, the yeast of beer acts in exactly the same manner as an ordinary plant, and the analogy would be complete if ordinary plants had such an affinity for oxygen as permitted them to breathe by appropriating this element from unstable compounds, in which case, according to M. Pasteur, they would appear as ferments for those substances.

"M. Pasteur declares that he hopes to be able to realize this result, that is to say, to discover the conditions under which certain inferior plants may live apart from air in the presence of sugar, causing that substance to ferment as the yeast of beer would do."

This summary and the preconceived views that it set forth have lost nothing of their exactness; on the contrary, time has strengthened them. The surmises of the last two paragraphs have received valuable confirmation from recent observations made by Messrs. Lechartier and Bellamy, as well as by ourselves, an account of which we must put before our readers. It is necessary, however, before touching upon this curious feature in connection with fermentations to insist on the accuracy of a passage in the preceding summary; the statement, namely, that yeast could multiply in an albuminous liquid, in which it found a non-fermentable sugar, milk-sugar, for example. The following is an experiment on this point:—On August 15th, 1875, we sowed a trace of yeast in 150 cc. (rather more than 5 fluid ounces) of yeast-water, containing 2½ per cent. of milk-sugar. The solution was prepared in one of our double-necked flasks, with the necessary precautions to secure the absence of germs, and the yeast sown was itself perfectly pure. Three months afterwards, November 15th, 1875, we examined the liquid for alcohol; it contained only the smallest trace; as for the yeast (which had sensibly developed), collected and dried on a filter paper, it weighed 0.050 gramme (0.76 grain). In this case we have the yeast multiplying without giving rise to the least fermentation, like a fungoid growth, absorbing oxygen, and evolving carbonic acid, and there is no doubt that the cessation of its development in this experiment was due to the progressive deprivation of oxygen that occurred. As soon as the gaseous mixture in the flask consisted entirely of carbonic acid and nitrogen, the vitality of the yeast was dependent on, and in proportion to, the quantity of air which entered the flask in consequence of variations of temperature. The question now arose, was this yeast, which had developed wholly as an ordinary fungus, still capable of manifesting the character of a ferment? To settle this point we had taken the precaution on August 15th, 1875, of preparing another flask, exactly similar to the preceding one in every respect, and which gave results identical with those described. We decanted this November 15th, pouring some wort on the deposit of the plant, which remained in the flask. In less than five hours from the time we placed it in the oven, the plant started fermentation in the wort, as we could see by the bubbles of gas rising to form patches on the surface of the liquid. We may add that yeast in the medium which we have been discussing will not develop at all without air.

The importance of these results can escape no one; they prove clearly that the fermentative character is not an invariable phenomenon of yeast-life, they show that yeast is a plant which does not differ from ordinary plants, and which manifests its fermentative power solely in consequence of particular conditions under which it is compelled to live. It may carry on its life as a ferment or not, and after having lived without manifesting the slightest symptom of fermentative character, it is quite ready to manifest that character when brought under suitable conditions. The fermentative property, therefore, is not a power peculiar to cells of a special nature. It is not a permanent character of a particular structure, like, for instance, the property of acidity or alkalinity. It is a peculiarity dependent on external circumstances and on the nutritive conditions of the organism.

§ II. Fermentation in Saccharine Fruits Immersed in Carbonic Acid Gas

The theory which we have, step by step, evolved, on the subject of the cause of the chemical phenomena of fermentation, may claim a character of simplicity and generality that is well worthy of attention. Fermentation is no longer one of those isolated and mysterious phenomena which do not admit of explanation. It is the consequence of a peculiar vital process of nutrition which occurs under certain conditions, differing from those which characterize the life of all ordinary beings, animal or vegetable, but by which the latter may be affected, more or less, in a way which brings them, to some extent within the class of ferments, properly so called. We can even conceive that the fermentative character may belong to every organized form, to every animal or vegetable cell, on the sole condition that the chemico-vital acts of assimilation and excretion must be capable of taking place in that cell for a brief period, longer or shorter it may be, without necessity for recourse to supplies of atmospheric oxygen; in other words, the cell must be able to derive its needful heat from the decomposition of some body which yields a surplus of heat in the process.

As a consequence of these conclusions it should be an easy matter to show, in the majority of living beings, the manifestation of the phenomena of fermentation; for there are, probably, none in which all chemical action entirely disappears, upon the sudden cessation of life. One day, when we were expressing these views in our laboratory, in the presence of M. Dumas, who seemed inclined to admit their truth, we added: "We should like to make a wager that if we were to plunge a bunch of grapes into carbonic acid gas, there would be immediately produced alcohol and carbonic acid gas, in consequence of a renewed action starting in the interior cells of the grapes, in such a way that these cells would assume the functions of yeast cells. We will make the experiment, and when you come to-morrow—it was our good fortune to have M. Dumas working in our laboratory at that time—we will give you an account of the result." Our predictions were realized. We then endeavoured to find, in the presence of M. Dumas, who assisted us in our endeavour, cells of yeast in the grapes; but it was quite impossible to discover any.[1]

[1] To determine the absence of cells of ferment in fruits that have been immersed in carbonic acid gas, we must first of all carefully raise the pellicle of the fruit, taking care that the subjacent parenchyma does not touch the surface of the pellicle, since the organized corpuscles existing on the exterior of the fruit might introduce an error into our miscroscopical observations. Experiments on grapes have given us an explanation of a fact generally known, the cause of which, however, had hitherto escaped our knowledge. We all know that the taste and aroma of the vintage, that is, of the grapes stripped from the bunches and thrown into tubs, where they get soaked in the juice that issues from the wounded specimens, are very different from the taste and aroma of an uninjured bunch. Now grapes

THEORY OF FERMENTATION

Encouraged by this result, we undertoook fresh experiments on grapes, on a melon, on oranges, on plums, and on rhubarb leaves, gathered in the garden of the École Normale, and, in every case, our substance, when immersed in carbonic acid gas, gave rise to the production of alcohol and carbonic acid. We obtained the following surprising results from some *prunes de Monsieur*:[2]—On July 21, 1872, we placed twenty-four of these plums under a glass bell, which we immediately filled with carbonic acid gas. The plums had been gathered on the previous day. By the side of the bell we placed other twenty-four plums, which were left there uncovered. Eight days afterwards, in the course of which time there had been a considerable evolution of carbonic acid from the bell, we withdrew the plums and compared them with those which had been left exposed to the air. The difference was striking, almost incredible. Whilst the plums which had been surrounded with air (the experiments of Bérard have long since taught us that, under this latter condition, fruits absorb oxygen from the air and emit carbonic acid gas in almost equal volume) had become very soft and watery and sweet, the plums taken from under the jar had remained very firm and hard, the flesh was by no means watery, but they had lost much sugar. Lastly, when submitted to distillation, after crushing, they yielded 6.5 grammes (99.7 grains) of alcohol,

that have been immersed in an atmosphere of carbonic acid gas have exactly the flavour and smell of the vintage; the reason is that, in the vintage tub, the grapes are immediately surrounded by an atmosphere of carbonic acid gas, and undergo, in consequence, the fermentation peculiar to grapes that have been plunged in this gas. These facts deserve to be studied from a practical point of view. It would be interesting, for example, to learn what difference there would be in the quality of two wines, the grapes of which, in the one case, had been perfectly crushed, so as to cause as great a separation of the cells of the parenchyma as possible; in the other case, left, for the most part, whole, as in the case in the ordinary vintage. The first wine would be deprived of those fixed and fragrant principles produced by the fermentation of which we have just spoken, when the grapes are immersed in carbonic acid gas. By such a comparison as that which we suggest we should be able to form *à priori* judgment on the merits of the new system, which has not been carefully studied, although already widely adopted, of milled, cylindrical crushers, for pressing the vintage.

[2] We have sometimes found small quantities of alcohol in fruits and other vegetable organs, surrounded with ordinary air, but always in small proportion, and in a manner which suggested its accidental character. It is easy to understand how, in the thickness of certain fruits, certain parts of those fruits might be deprived of air, under which circumstances they would have been acting under conditions similar to those under which fruits act when wholly immersed in carbonic acid gas. Moreover, it would be useful to determine whether alcohol is not a normal product of vegetation.

more than 1 per cent. of the total weight of the plums. What better proof than these facts could we have of the existence of a considerable chemical action in the interior of fruit, an action which derives the heat necessary for its manifestation from the decomposition of the sugar present in the cells? Moreover, and this circumstance is especially worthy of our attention, in all these experiments we found that there was a liberation of heat, of which the fruits and other organs were the seat, as soon as they were plunged in the carbonic acid gas. This heat is so considerable that it may at times be detected by the hand, if the two sides of the bell, one of which is in contact with the objects, are touched alternately. It also makes itself evident in the formation of little drops on those parts of the bell which are less directly exposed to the influence of the heat resulting from the decomposition of the sugar of the cells.[3]

In short, fermentation is a very general phenomenon. It is life without air, or life without free oxygen, or, more generally still, it is the result of a chemical process accomplished on a fermentable substance capable of producing heat by its decomposition, in which process the entire heat used up is derived from a part of the heat that the decomposition of the fermentable substance sets free. The class of fermentations properly so called, is, however, restricted by the small number of substances capable of decomposing with the production of heat, and at the same time of serving for the nourishment of lower forms of life, when deprived of the presence and action of air. This, again, is a consequence of our theory, which is well worthy of notice.

[3] In these studies of plants living immersed in carbonic acid gas, we have come across a fact which corroborates those which we have already given in reference to the facility with which lactic and viscous ferments, and, generally speaking, those which we have termed the disease ferments of beer, develop when deprived of air, and which shows, consequently, how very marked their aërobian character is. If we immerse beet-roots or turnips in carbonic acid gas, we produce well-defined fermentations in those roots. Their whole surface readily permits the escape of the highly acid liquids, and they become filled with lactic, viscous, and other ferments. This shows us the great danger which may result from the use of pits, in which the beet-roots are preserved, when the air is not renewed, and that the original oxygen is expelled by the vital processes of fungi or other deoxidizing chemical actions. We have directed the attention of the manufacturers of beet-root sugar to this point.

The facts that we have just mentioned in reference to the formation of alcohol and carbonic acid in the substance of ripe fruits, under special conditions, and apart from the action of ferment, are already known to science. They were discovered in 1869 by M. Lechartier, formerly a pupil in the *Ecole Normale Supérieure,* and his coadjutor, M. Bellamy.[4] In 1821, in a very remarkable work, especially when we consider the period when it appeared, Bérard demonstrated several important propositions in connection with the maturation of fruits:

I. All fruits, even those that are still green, and likewise even those that are exposed to the sun, absorb oxygen and set free an almost equal volume of carbonic acid gas. This is a condition of their proper ripening.

II. Ripe fruits placed in a limited atmosphere, after having absorbed all the oxygen and set free an almost equal volume of carbonic acid, continue to emit that gas in notable quantity, even when no bruise is to be seen—" as though by a kind of fermentation," as Bérard actually observes—and lose their saccharine particles, a circumstance which causes the fruits to appear more acid, although the actual weight of their acid may undergo no augmentation whatever.

In this beautiful work, and in all subsequent ones of which the ripening of fruits has been the subject, two facts of great theoretical value have escaped the notice of the authors; these are the two facts which Messrs. Lechartier and Bellamy pointed out for the first time, namely, the production of alcohol and the absence of cells of ferments. It is worthy of remark that these two facts, as we have shown above, were actually fore-shadowed in the theory of fermentation that we advocated as far back as 1861, and we are happy to add that Messrs. Lechartier and Bellamy, who at first had prudently drawn no theoretical conclusions from their work, now entirely agree with the theory we have advanced.[5] Their mode of reasoning

---

[4] Lechartier and Bellamy, *Comptes rendus de l'Académie des Sciences,* vol. lxix., pp., 366 and 466, 1869.

[5] Those gentlemen express themselves thus: " In a note presented to the Academy in November, 1872, we published certain experiments which showed that carbonic acid and alcohol may be produced in fruits kept in a closed

is very different from that of the savants with whom we discussed the subject before the Academy, on the occasion when the communication which we addressed to the Academy in October, 1872, attracted attention once more to the remarkable observations of Messrs. Lechartier and Bellamy.[6] M. Fremy, in particular, was desirous of finding in these observations a confirmation of his views on the subject of *hemi-organism,* and a condemnation of ours, notwithstanding the fact that the preceding explanations, and, more particularly our Note of 1861, quoted word for word in the preceding section, furnish the most conclusive evidence in favor of those ideas which we advocate. Indeed, as far back as 1861 we pointed out very clearly that if we could find plants able to live when deprived of air, in the presence of sugar, they would bring about a fermentation of that substance, in the same manner that yeast does. Such is the case with the fungi already studied; such, too, is the case with the fruits employed in the experiments of Messrs. Lechartier and Bellamy, and in our own experiments, the results of which not only confirm those obtained by these gentlemen, but even extend them, in so far as we have shown that fruits, when surrounded with carbonic acid gas immediately produce alcohol. When surrounded with air, they live in their aërobian state and we have no fermentation; immersed immediately afterwards in carbonic acid gas, they now assume their anaërobian state, and at once begin to act upon the sugar in the manner of ferments, and emit heat. As for seeing in these facts anything like a confirmation of the theory of hemi-organism, imagined by M. Fremy, the idea of such a

vessel, out of contact with atmospheric oxygen, without our being able to discover alcoholic ferment in the interior of those fruits.

" M. Pasteur, as a logical deduction from the principle which he has established in connection with the theory of fermentation, considers that *the formation of alcohol may be attributed to the fact that the physical and chemical processes of life in the cells of fruit continue under new conditions, in a manner similar to those of the cells of ferment.* Experiments, continued during 1872, 1873, and 1874, on different fruits have furnished results all of which seem to us to harmonize with this proposition, and to establish it on a firm basis of proof."—*Comptes rendus,* t. lxxix., p. 949, 1874.

[6] PASTEUR, *Faites nouveaux pour servir à la connaissance de la théorie des fermentations proprement dites.* (*Comptes rendus de l'Académie des Sciences,* t. lxxv., p. 784.) See in the same volume the discussion that followed; also, PASTEUR, *Note sur la production de l'alcool par les fruits,* same volume, p. 1054, in which we recount the observations anterior to our own, made by Messrs. Lechartier and Bellamy in 1869.

thing is absurd. The following, for instance, is the theory of the fermentation of the vintage, according to M. Fremy.[7]

"To speak here of alcoholic fermentation alone,"[8] our author says, " I hold that in the production of wine it is the juice of the fruit itself that, in contact with air, produces grains of ferment, by the transformation of the albuminous matter; Pasteur, on the other hand, maintains that the fermentation is produced by germs existing outside of the grapes."

Now what bearing on this purely imaginary theory can the fact have, that a whole fruit, immersed in carbonic acid gas, immediately produces alcohol and carbonic acid? In the preceding passage which we have borrowed from M. Fremy, an indispensable condition of the transformation of the albuminous matter is the contact with air and the crushing of the grapes. Here, however, we are dealing with *uninjured fruits in contact with carbonic acid gas.* Our theory, on the other hand, which, we may repeat, we have advocated since 1861, maintains that all cells become fermentative when their vital action is protracted in the absence of air, which are precisely the conditions that hold in the experiments on fruits immersed in carbonic acid gas. The vital energy is not immediately suspended

[7] *Comptes rendus,* meeting of January 15th, 1872.
[8] As a matter of fact, M. Fremy applies his theory of hemi-organism, not only to the alcoholic fermentation of grape juice, but to all other fermentations. The following passage occurs in one of his notes (*Comptes rendus de l'Académie,* t. lxxv., p. 979, October 28th, 1872):
"Experiments on Germinated Barley.—The object of these was to show that when barley, left to itself in sweetened water, produces in succession alcoholic, lactic, butyric, and acetic fermentations, these modifications are brought about by ferments which are produced inside the grains themselves, and not by atmospheric germs. More than forty different experiments were devoted to this part of my work."
Need we add that this assertion is based on no substantial foundation? The cells belonging to the grains of barley, or their albuminous contents, never do produce cells of alcoholic ferment, or of lactic ferment, or butyric vibrios. Whenever those ferments appear, they may be traced to germs of those organisms, diffused throughout the interior of the grains, or adhering to the exterior surface, or existing in the water employed, or on the side of the vessels used. There are many ways of demonstrating this, of which the following is one: Since the results of our experiments have shown that sweetened water, phosphates, and chalk very readily give rise to lactic and butyric fermentations, what reason is there for supposing that if we substitute grains of barley for chalk, the lactic and butyric ferments will spring from those grains, in consequence of a transformation of their cells and albuminous substances? Surely there is no ground for maintaining that they are produced by hemi-organism, since a medium composed of sugar, or chalk, or phosphates of ammonia, potash, or magnesia contains no albuminous substances. This is an indirect but irresistible argument against the hemi-organism theory.

in their cells, and the latter are deprived of air. Consequently, fermentation must result. Moreover, we may add, if we destroy the fruit, or crush it before immersing it in the gas, it no longer produces alcohol or fermentation of any kind, a circumstance that may be attributed to the fact of the destruction of vital action in the crushed fruit. On the other hand, in what way ought this crushing to affect the hypothesis of hemi-organism? The crushed fruit ought to act quite as well, or even better than that which is uncrushed. In short, nothing can be more directly opposed to the theory of the mode of manifestation of that hidden force to which the name of hemi-organism has been given, than the discovery of the production of these phenomena of fermentation in fruits surrounded with carbonic acid gas; whilst the theory, which sees in fermentation a consequence of vital energy in absence of air, finds in these facts the strictest confirmation of an express prediction, which from the first formed an integral part of its statement.

We should not be justified in devoting further time to opinions which are not supported by any serious experiment. Abroad, as well as in France, the theory of the transformation of albuminous substances into organized ferments had been advocated long before it had been taken up by M. Fremy. It no longer commands the slightest credit, nor do any observers of note any longer give it the least attention; it might even be said that it has become a subject of ridicule.

An attempt has also been made to prove that we have contradicted ourselves, inasmuch as in 1860 we published our opinion that alcoholic fermentation can never occur without a simultaneous occurrence of organization, development, and multiplication of globules; or continued life, carried on from globules already formed.[9] Nothing, how-

---

[9] PASTEUR, *Mémoire sur la fermentation alcoolique*, 1860; *Annales de Chimie et de Physique*. The word globules is here used for cells. In our researches we have always endeavoured to prevent any confusion of ideas. We stated at the beginning of our Mémoir of 1860 that: " We apply the term alcoholic to that fermentation which sugar undergoes under the influence of the ferment known as *beer yeast*." This is, the fermentation which produces wine and all alcoholic beverages. This, too, is regarded as the type for a host of similar phenomena designated, by general usage, under the generic name of *fermentation,* and qualified by the name of one of the

THEORY OF FERMENTATION

ever, can be truer than that opinion, and at the present moment, after fifteen years of study devoted to the subject since the publication to which we have referred, we need no longer say, "we think," but instead, "we affirm," that it is correct. It is, as a matter of fact, to alcoholic fermentation, properly so called, that the charge to which we have referred relates—to that fermentation which yields, besides alcohol, carbonic acid, succinic acid, glycerine, volatile acids, and other products. This fermentation undoubtedly requires the presence of yeast-cells under the conditions that we have named. Those who have contradicted us have fallen into the error of supposing that the fermentation of fruits is an ordinary alcoholic fermentation, identical with that produced by beer yeast, and that, consequently, the cells of that yeast must, according to own theory, be always present. There is not the least authority for such a supposition. When we come to exact quantitative estimations—and these are to be found in the figures supplied by Messrs. Lechartier and Bellamy—it will be seen that the proportions of alcohol and carbonic acid gas produced in the fermentation of fruits differ widely from those that we find in alcoholic fermentations properly so called, as must necessarily be the case since in the former the ferment-action is effected by the cells of a fruit, but in the latter by cells of ordinary alcoholic ferment. Indeed we have a strong conviction that each fruit would be found to give rise to special action, the chemical equation of which would be different from that in the case of other fruits. As for the

essential products of the special phenomenon under observation. Bearing in mind this fact in reference to the nomenclature that we have adopted, it will be seen that the expression *alcoholic fermentation* cannot be applied to every phenomenon of fermentation in which alcohol is produced, inasmuch as there may be a number of phenomena having this character in common. If we had not at starting defined that particular one amongst the number of very distinct phenomena, which, to the exclusion of the others, should bear the name of alcoholic fermentation, we should inevitably have given rise to a confusion of language that would soon pass from words to ideas, and tend to introduce unnecessary complexity into researches which are already, in themselves, sufficiently complex to necessitate the adoption of scrupulous care to prevent their becoming still more involved. It seems to us that any further doubt as to the meaning of the words *alcoholic fermentation*, and the sense in which they are employed, is impossible, inasmuch as Lavoisier, Gay-Lussac, and Thénard have applied this term to the fermentation of sugar by means of beer yeast. It would be both dangerous and unprofitable to discard the example set by these illustrious masters, to whom we are indebted for our earliest knowledge of this subject.

circumstance that the cells of these fruits cause fermentation without multiplying, this comes under the kind of activity which we have already distinguished by the expression *continuous life in cells already formed*.

We will conclude this section with a few remarks on the subject of equations of fermentations, which have been suggested to us principally in attempts to explain the results derived from the fermentation of fruits immersed in carbonic acid gas.

Originally, when fermentations were put amongst the class of decompositions by contact-action, it seemed probable, and, in fact, was believed, that every fermentation has its own well-defined equation which never varied. In the present day, on the contrary, it must be borne in mind that the equation of a fermentation varies essentially with the conditions under which that fermentation is accomplished, and that a statement of this equation is a problem no less complicated than that in the case of the nutrition of a living being. To every fermentation may be assigned an equation in a general sort of way, an equation, however, which, in numerous points of detail, is liable to the thousand variations connected with the phenomena of life. Moreover, there will be as many distinct fermentations brought about by one ferment as there are fermentable substances capable of supplying the carbon element of the food of that same ferment, in the same way that the equation of the nutrition of an animal will vary with the nature of the food which it consumes. As regards fermentation producing alcohol, which may be effected by several different ferments, there will be as in the case of a given sugar, as many general equations as there are ferments, whether they be ferment-cells properly so called, or cells of the organs of living beings functioning as ferments. In the same way the equation of nutrition varies in the case of different animals nourished on the same food. And it is from the same reason that ordinary wort produces such a variety of beers when treated with the numerous alcoholic ferments which we have described. These remarks are applicable to all ferments alike; for instance, butyric ferment is capable of producing a host of distinct fermentations, in consequence of its ability to derive the carbonaceous part of its food from very different substances, from sugar, or lactic acid, or glycerine, or mannite, and many others.

When we say that every fermentation has its own peculiar ferment, it must be understood that we are speaking of the fermentation considered as a whole, including all the accessory products. We do not mean to imply that the ferment in question is not capable of acting on some other fermentable substance and giving rise to fermentation of a very different kind. Moreover, it is quite erroneous to suppose that the presence of a single one of the products of a fermentation implies the co-existence of a particular ferment. If, for example, we find alcohol among the products of a fermentation, or even alcohol and carbonic acid gas together, this does not prove that the ferment must be an alcoholic ferment, belonging to alcoholic fermentations, in the strict sense of the term. Nor, again, does the mere presence of lactic acid necessarily imply the presence of lactic ferment. As a matter of fact, different fermentations may give rise to one or even several identical products. We could not say with certainty, from a purely chemical point of view, that we were dealing, for example, with an alcoholic fermentation properly so called, and that the yeast of beer must be present in it, if we had not first determined the presence of all the numerous products of that particular fermentation under conditions similar to those under which the fermentation in question had occurred. In works on fermentation the reader will often find those confusions against which we are now attempting to guard him. It is precisely in consequence of not having had their attention drawn to such observations that some have imagined that the fermentation in fruits immersed in carbonic acid gas is in contradiction to the assertion which we originally made in our Memoir on alcoholic fermentation published in 1860, the exact words of which we may here repeat:—" The chemical phenomena of fermentation are related essentially to a vital activity, beginning and ending with the latter; we believe that alcoholic fermentation never occurs "—we were discussing the question of ordinary alcoholic fermentation produced by the yeast of beer—" without the simultaneous occurrence of organization, development, and multiplication of globules, or continued life, carried on by means of the globules already formed. The general results of the present Memoir seem to us to be in direct opposition to the opinions of MM. Liebig and Berzelius." These conclusions, we repeat, are as true now as they ever were, and are as applicable to the fermentation of fruits, of which nothing was known in 1860, as they are to the fermentation produced by the means of yeast. Only, in the case of fruits, it is the cells of the parenchyma that function as ferment, *by a continuation of their activity in carbonic acid gas,* whilst in the other case the ferment consists of cells of yeast.

There should be nothing very surprising in the fact that fermentation can originate in fruits and form alcohol without the presence of yeast, if the fermentation of fruits were not confounded completely with alcoholic fermentation yielding the same products and in the same proportions. It is through the misuse of words that the fermentation of fruits has been termed alcoholic, in a way which has misled many persons.[10] In this fermentation, neither alcohol nor carbonic acid gas exists in those proportions in which they are found in fermentation produced by yeast; and, although we may determine in it the presence of succinic acid, glycerine, and a small quantity of volatile acids[11] the relative proportions of these substances will be different from what they are in the case of alcoholic fermentation.

§ III. Reply to Certain Critical Observations of the German Naturalists, Oscar Brefeld and Moritz Traube.

The essential point of the theory of fermentation which we have been concerned in proving in the preceding para-

[10] See, for example, the communications of MM. Colin and Poggiale, and the discussion on them, in the *Bulletin de l'Académie de Médécine,* March 2d, 9th, and 30th, and February 16th and 23rd, 1875.

[11] We have elsewhere determined the formation of minute quantities of volatile acids in alcoholic fermentation. M. Béchamp, who studied these, recognized several belonging to the series of fatty acids, acetic acid, butyric acid, &c. "The presence of succinic acid is not accidental, but constant; if we put aside volatile acids that form in quantities which we may call infinitely small, we may say that succinic acid is the only normal acid of alcoholic fermentation."—Pasteur, *Comptes rendus de l'Académie,* t. xlvii., p. 224, 1858.

graphs may be briefly put in the statement that ferments properly so called constitute a class of beings possessing the faculty of living out of contact with free oxygen; or, more concisely still, we may say that fermentation is a result of life without air.

If our affirmation were inexact, if ferment cells did require for their growth or for their increase in number or weight, as all other vegetable cells do, the presence of oxygen, whether gaseous or held in solution in liquids, this new theory would lose all value, its very *raison d'être* would be gone, at least as far as the most important part of fermentations is concerned. This is precisely what M. Oscar Brefeld has endeavoured to prove in a Memoir read to the Physico-Medical Society of Wurzburg on July 26th, 1873, in which, although we have ample evidence of the great experimental skill of its author, he has nevertheless, in our opinion, arrived at conclusions entirely opposed to fact.

"From the experiments which I have just described," he says, "it follows, in the most indisputable manner, that *a ferment cannot increase without free oxygen*. Pasteur's supposition that a ferment, unlike all other living organisms, can live and increase at the expense of oxygen held in combination, is, consequently, altogether wanting in any solid basis of experimental proof. Moreover, since, according to the theory of Pasteur, it is precisely this faculty of living and increasing at the expense of the oxygen held in combination that constitutes the phenomenon of fermentation, it follows that the whole theory, commanding though it does such general assent, is shown to be untenable; it is simply inaccurate."

The experiments to which Dr. Brefeld alludes, consisted in keeping under continued study with the microscope, in a room specially prepared for the purpose, one or more cells of ferment in wort in an atmosphere of carbonic acid gas free from the least traces of free oxygen. We have, however, recognized the fact that the increase of a ferment out of contact with air is only possible in the case of a very young specimen; but our author employed brewer's yeast taken after fermentation, and to this fact we may attribute the non-success of his growths. Dr.

Brefeld, without knowing it, operated on yeast in one of the states in which it requires gaseous oxygen to enable it to germinate again. A perusal of what we have previously written on the subject of the revival of yeast according to its age will show how widely the time required for such revival may vary in different cases. What may be perfectly true of the state of a yeast to-day may not be so to-morrow, since yeast is continually undergoing modifications. We have already shown the energy and activity with which a ferment can vegetate in the presence of free oxygen, and we have pointed out the great extent to which a very small quantity of oxygen held in solution in fermenting liquids can operate at the beginning of fermentation. It is this oxygen that produces revival in the cells of the ferment and enables them to resume the faculty of germinating and continuing their life, and of multiplying when deprived of air.

In our opinion, a simple reflection should have guarded Dr. Brefeld against the interpretation which he has attached to his observations. If a cell of ferment cannot bud or increase without absorbing oxygen, either free or held in solution in the liquid, the ratio between the weight of the ferment formed during fermentation and that of oxygen used up must be constant. We had, however, clearly established, as far back as 1861, the fact that this ratio is extremely variable, a fact, moreover, which is placed beyond doubt by the experiments described in the preceding section. Though but small quantities of oxygen are absorbed, a considerable weight of ferment may be generated; whilst if the ferment has abundance of oxygen at its disposal, it will absorb much, and the weight of yeast formed will be still greater. The ratio between the weight of ferment formed and that of sugar decomposed may pass through all stages within certain very wide limits, the variations depending on the greater or less absorption of free oxygen. And in this fact, we believe, lies one of the most essential supports of the theory which we advocate. In denouncing the impossibility, as he considered it, of a ferment living without air or oxygen, and so acting in defiance of that law which governs all living beings, animal or vegetable, Dr. Brefeld

THEORY OF FERMENTATION 331

ought also to have borne in mind the fact which we have pointed out, that alcoholic yeast is not the only organized ferment which lives in an anaërobian state. It is really a small matter that one more ferment should be placed in a list of exceptions to the generality of living beings, for whom there is a rigid law in their vital economy which requires for continued life a continuous respiration, a continuous supply of free oxygen. Why, for instance, has Dr. Brefeld omitted the facts bearing on the life of the vibrios of butyric fermentation? Doubtless he thought we were equally mistaken in these: a few actual experiments would have put him right.

These remarks on the criticisms of Dr. Brefeld are also applicable to certain observations of M. Moritz Traube's, although, as regards the principal object of Dr. Brefeld's attack, we are indebted to M. Traube for our defence. This gentleman maintained the exactness of our results before the Chemical Society of Berlin, proving by fresh experiments that yeast is able to live and multiply without the intervention of oxygen. "My researches," he said, "confirm in an indisputable manner M. Pasteur's assertion that the multiplication of yeast can take place in media which contain no trace of free oxygen. . . . M. Brefeld's assertion to the contrary is erroneous." But immediately afterwards M. Traube adds: "Have we here a confirmation of Pasteur's theory? By no means. The results of my experiments demonstrate on the contrary that this theory has no true foundation." What were these results? Whilst proving that yeast could live without air, M. Traube, as we ourselves did, found that it had great difficulty in living under these conditions; indeed he never succeeded in obtaining more than the first stages of true fermentation. This was doubtless for the two following reasons: first, in consequence of the accidental production of secondary and diseased fermentations which frequently prevent the propagation of alcoholic ferment; and, secondly, in consequence of the original exhausted condition of the yeast employed. As long ago as 1861, we pointed out the slowness and difficulty of the vital action of yeast when deprived of air; and a little way back, in the preceding section, we have called attention to certain fermentations that cannot be completed under such conditions without going into the causes of these peculiarities. M. Traube expresses himself thus: "Pasteur's conclusion, that yeast in the absence of air is able to derive the oxygen necessary for its development from sugar, is erroneous; its increase is arrested even when the greater part of the sugar still remains undecomposed. *It is in a mixture of albuminous substances that yeast, when deprived of air, finds the materials for its development.*" This last assertion of M. Traube's is entirely disproved by those fermentation experiments in which, after suppressing the presence of albuminous substances, the action, nevertheless, went on in a purely inorganic medium, out of contact with air, a fact, of which we shall give irrefutable proofs.[1]

§ IV. FERMENTATION OF DEXTRO-TARTRATE OF LIME.[1]

TARTRATE of lime, in spite of its insolubility in water, is capable of complete fermentation in a mineral medium.

If we put some pure tartrate of lime, in the form of a granulated, crystalline powder, into pure water, together with some sulphate of ammonia and phosphates of potassium and magnesium, in very small proportions, a spon-

[1] Traube's conceptions are governed by a theory of fermentation entirely his own, a hypothetical one, as he admits, of which the following is a brief summary: "We have no reason to doubt," Traube says, "that the protoplasm of vegetable cells is itself, or contains within it, a chemical ferment which causes the alcoholic fermentation of sugar; its efficacy seems closely connected with the presence of the cell, inasmuch as, up to the present time, we have discovered no means of isolating it from the cells with success. In the presence of air this ferment oxidizes sugar by bringing oxygen to bear upon it; in the absence of air it decomposes the sugar by taking away oxygen from one group of atoms of the molecule of sugar and bringing it to act upon other atoms; on the one hand yielding a product of alcohol by reduction, on the other hand a product of carbonic acid gas by oxidation."

Traube supposes that this chemical ferment exists in yeast and in all sweet fruits, but only when the cells are intact, for he has proved for himself that thoroughly crushed fruits give rise to no fermentation whatever in carbonic acid gas. In this respect this imaginary chemical ferment would differ entirely from those which we call *soluble ferments,* since diastase, emulsine, &c., may be easily isolated.

For a full account of the views of Brefeld and Traube, and the discussion which they carried on on the subject of the results of our experiments, our readers may consult the *Journal of the Chemical Society of Berlin,* vii., p. 872. The numbers for September and December, 1874, in the same volume, contain the replies of the two authors.

[1] See PASTEUR, *Comptes rendus de l'Académie des Sciences,* t. lvi., p. 416.

taneous fermentation will take place in the deposit in the course of a few days, although no germs of ferment have been added. A living, organized ferment, of the vibrionic type, filiform, with tortuous motions, and often of immense length, forms spontaneously by the development of some germs derived in some way from the inevitable particles of dust floating in the air or resting on the surface of the vessels or material which we employ. The germs of the vibrios concerned in putrefaction are diffused around us on every side, and, in all probability, it is one or more of these germs that develop in the medium in question. In this way they effect the decomposition of the tartrate, from which they must necessarily obtain the carbon of their food without which they cannot exist, while the nitrogen is furnished by the ammonia of the ammoniacal salt, the mineral principles by the phosphate of potassium and magnesium, and the sulphur by the sulphate of ammonia. How strange to see organization, life, and motion originating under such conditions! Stranger still to think that this organization, life, and motion are effected without the participation of free oxygen. Once the germ gets a primary impulse on its living career by access of oxygen, it goes on reproducing indefinitely, absolutely without atmospheric air. Here then we have a fact which it is important to establish beyond the possibility of doubt, that we may prove that yeast is not the only organized ferment able to live and multiply when out of the influence of free oxygen.

Into a flask, like that represented in FIG. 9, of 2.5 litres (about four pints) in capacity, we put:

Pure, crystallized, neutral tartrate of lime....	100 grammes
Phosphate of ammonia......................	1 "
" magnesium...................	1 "
" potassium....................	0.5 "
Sulphate of ammonia........................	0.5 "

(1 gramme = 15.43 grains)

To this we added pure distilled water, so as entirely to fill the flask.

In order to expel all the air dissolved in the water and adhering to the solid substances, we first placed our flask in a bath of chloride of calcium in a large cylindrical white iron pot set over a flame. The exit tube of the flask was plunged in a test tube of Bohemian glass three-quarters full of distilled water, and also heated by a flame. We boiled the liquids in the flask and test-tube for a sufficient time to expel all the air contained in them. We

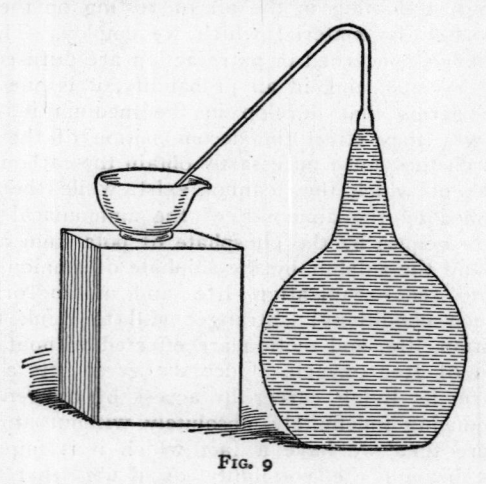

FIG. 9

then withdrew the heat from under the test-tube, and immediately afterwards covered the water which it contained with a layer of oil and then permitted the whole apparatus to cool down.

Next day we applied a finger to the open extremity of the exit-tube, which we then plunged in a vessel of mercury. In this particular experiment which we are describing, we permitted the flask to remain in this state for a fortnight. It might have remained there for a century without ever manifesting the least sign of fermentation, the fermentation of the tartrate being a consequence of life, and life after boiling no longer existed in the flask. When it was evident that the contents of the flask were perfectly inert, we impregnated them, rapidly, as follows: all the liquid contained in the exit-tube was removed by means

THEORY OF FERMENTATION 335

of a fine caoutchouc tube, and replaced by about 1 c. (about 17 minims) of liquid and deposit from another flask, similar to the one we have just described, but which had been fermenting spontaneously for twelve days; we lost no time in refilling completely the exit tube with water which had been first boiled and then cooled down in carbonic acid gas. This operation lasted only a few minutes. The exit-tube was again plunged under mercury. Subsequently the tube was not moved from under the mercury, and as it formed part of the flask, and there was neither cork nor india-rubber, any introduction of air was consequently impossible. The small quantity of air introduced during the impregnation was insignificant and it might even be shown that it injured rather than assisted the growth of the organisms, inasmuch as these consisted of adult individuals which had lived without air and might be liable to be damaged or even destroyed by it. Be this as it may, in a subsequent experiment we shall find the possibility removed of any aeration taking place in this way, however infinitesimal, so that no doubts may linger on this subject.

The following days the organisms multiplied, the deposit of tartrate gradually disappeared, and a sensible ferment action was manifest on the surface, and throughout the bulk of the liquid. The deposit seemed lifted up in places, and was covered with a layer of dark-grey colour, puffed up, and having an organic and gelatinous appearance. For several days, in spite of this action in the deposit, we detected no disengagement of gas, except when the flask was slightly shaken, in which case rather large bubbles adhering to the deposit rose, carrying with them some solid particles, which quickly fell back again, whilst the bubbles diminished in size as they rose, from being partially taken into solution, in consequence of the liquid not being saturated. The smallest bubbles had even time to dissolve completely before they could reach the surface of the liquid. In course of time the liquid was saturated, and the tartrate was gradually displaced by mammillated crusts, or clear, transparent crystals of carbonate of lime at the bottom and on the sides of the vessel.

The impregnation took place on February 10th, and on March 15th the liquid was nearly saturated. The bubbles then began to lodge in the bent part of the exit-tube, at the top of the flask. A glass measuring-tube containing mercury was now placed with its open end over the point of the exit-tube under the mercury in the trough, so that no bubble might escape. A steady evolution of gas went on from the 17th to the 18th, 17.4 cc. (1.06 cubic inches) having been collected. This was proved to be nearly absolutely pure carbonic acid, as indeed might have been suspected from the fact that the evolution did not begin before a distinct saturation of the liquid was observed.[2]

The liquid, which was turbid on the day after its impregnation, had, in spite of the liberation of gas, again become so transparent that we could read our handwriting through the body of the flask. Notwithstanding this, there was still a very active operation going on in the deposit, but it was confined to that spot. Indeed, the swarming vibrios were bound to remain there, the tartrate of lime being still more insoluble in water saturated with carbonate of lime than it is in pure water. A supply of carbonaceous food, at all events, was absolutely wanting in the bulk of the liquid. Every day we continued to collect and analyze the total amount of gas disengaged. To the very last it was composed of pure carbonic acid gas. Only during the first few days did the absorption by the concentrated potash leave a very minute residue. By April 26th all liberation of gas had ceased, the last bubbles having risen in the course of April 23rd. The flask had been all the time in the oven, at a temperature between 25° C. and 28° C. (77° F. and 83° F.). The total volume of gas collected was 2.135 litres (130.2 cubic inches). To obtain the whole volume of gas formed we had to add to this what was held in the liquid in the state of acid carbonate of lime. To determine this we poured a portion of the liquid from the flask into another flask of similar shape, but smaller, up to the gaugemark on the neck.[3] This

---

[2] Carbonic acid being considerably more soluble than other gases possible under the circumstances.—ED.

[3] We had to avoid filling the small flask completely, for fear of causing some of the liquid to pass on to the surface of the mercury in the meas-

smaller flask had been previously filled with carbonic acid. The carbonic acid of the fermented liquid was then expelled by means of heat, and collected over mercury. In this way we found a volume of 8.322 litres (508 cubic inches) of gas in solution, which, added to the 2.135 litres, gave a total of 10.457 litres (638.2 cubic inches) at 20° and 760 mm., which, calculated to 0°, C. and 760 mm. atmospheric pressure (32° F. and 30 inches) gave a weight of 19.700 grammes (302.2 grains) of carbonic acid.

Exactly half of the lime in the tartrate employed got used up in the soluble salts formed during fermentation; the other half was partly precipitated in the form of carbonate of lime, partly dissolved in the liquid by the carbonic acid. The soluble salts seemed to us to be a mixture or combination of 1 equivalent of metacetate of lime, with 2 equivalents of the acetate, for every 10 equivalents of carbonic acid produced, the whole corresponding to the fermentation of 3 equivalents of neutral tartrate of lime.[4] This point, however, is worthy of being studied with greater care: the present statement of the nature of the products formed is given with all reserve. For our point, indeed, the matter is of little importance, since the equation of the fermentation does not concern us.

After the completion of fermentation there was not a trace of tartrate of lime remaining at the bottom of the vessel: it had disappeared gradually as it got broken up into the different products of fermentation, and its place was taken by some crystallized carbonate of lime—the excess, namely, which had been unable to dissolve by the action of

uring tube. The liquid condensed by boiling forms pure water, the solvent affinity of which for carbonic acid, at the temperature we employ, is well known.

[4] The following is a curious consequence of these numbers and of the nature of the products of this fermentation. The carbonic acid liberated being quite pure, especially when the liquid has been boiled to expel all air from the flask, and capable of perfect solution, it follows that the volume of liquid being sufficient and the weight of tartrate suitably chosen—we may set aside tartrate of lime in an insoluble, crystalline powder, along with phosphates at the bottom of a closed vessel full of water, and find soon afterwards in their place carbonate of lime, and in the liquid soluble salts of lime, with a mass of organic matter at the bottom, without any liberation of gas or appearance of fermentation ever taking place, except as far as the vital action and transformation in the tartrate are concerned. It is easy to calculate that a vessel or flask of five litres (rather more than a gallon) would be large enough for the accomplishment of this remarkable and singularly quiet transformation, in the case of 50 grammes (767 grains) of tartrate of lime.

the carbonic acid. Associated, moreover, with this carbonate of lime there was a quantity of some kind of animal matter, which, under the microscope, appeared to be composed of masses of granules mixed with very fine filaments of varying lengths, studded with minute dots, and presenting all the characteristics of a nitrogenous organic substance.[5] That this was really the ferment is evident enough from all that we have already said. To convince ourselves more thoroughly of the fact, and at the same time to enable us to observe the mode of activity of the organism, we instituted the following supplementary observation. Side by side with the experiment just described, we conducted a similar one, which we intermitted after the fermentation was somewhat advanced, and about half of the tartrate dissolved. Breaking off with a file the exit-tube at the point where the neck began to narrow off, we took some of the deposit from the bottom by means of a long straight piece of tubing, in order to bring it under microscopical examination. We found it to consist of a host of long filaments of extreme tenuity, their diameter being about $\frac{1}{1000}$th of a millimetre (0.000039 in.); their length varied, in some cases being as much as $\frac{1}{50}$th of a millimetre (0.0019 in.). A crowd of these long vibrios were to be seen creeping slowly along, with a sinuous movement, showing three, four, or even five flexures. The filaments that were at rest had the same aspect as these last, with the exception that they appeared punctuate, as though composed of a series of granules arranged in irregular order. No doubt these were vibrios in which vital action had ceased, exhausted specimens which we may compare with the old granular ferment of beer, whilst those in motion may be compared with young and vigorous yeast. The absence of movement in the former seems to prove that this view is correct. Both kinds showed a tendency to form

FIG. 10

---

[5] We treated the whole deposit with dilute hydrochloric acid, which dissolved the carbonate of lime, and the insoluble phosphates of calcium and magnesium; afterwards filtering the liquid through a weighed filter paper. Dried at 100° C. (212° F.), the weight of the organic matter thus obtained was 0.54 gramme (8.3 grains), which was rather more than $\frac{1}{200}$th of the weight of fermentable matter.

clusters, the compactness of which impeded the movements of those which were in motion. Moreover, it was noticeable that the masses of these latter rested on tartrate not yet dissolved, whilst the granular clusters of the others rested directly on the glass, at the bottom of the flask, as if, having decomposed the tartrate, the only carbonaceous food at their disposal, they had then died on the spot where we captured them, from inability to escape, precisely in consequence of that state of entanglement which they combined to form, during the period of their active development. Besides these we observed vibrios of the same diameter, but of much smaller length, whirling round with great rapidity, and darting backwards and forwards; these were probably identical with the longer ones, and possessed greater freedom of movement, no doubt in consequence of their shortness. Not one of these vibrios could be found throughout the mass of the liquid.

We may remark that as there was a somewhat putrid odour from the deposit in which the vibrios swarmed, the action must have been one of reduction, and no doubt to this fact was due the greyish coloration of the deposit. We suppose that the substances employed, however pure, always contain some trace of iron, which becomes converted into the sulphide, the black colour of which would modify the originally white deposit of insoluble tartrate and phosphate.

But what is the nature of these vibrios? We have already said that we believe that they are nothing but the ordinary vibrios of putrefaction, reduced to a state of extreme tenuity by the special conditions of nutrition involved in the fermentable medium used; in a word, we think that the fermentation in question might be called putrefaction of tartrate of lime. It would be easy enough to determine this point by growing the vibrios of such fermentation in media adapted to the production of the ordinary forms of vibrio; but this is an experiment which we have not ourselves tried.

One word more on the subject of these curious beings. In a great many of them there appears to be something like a clear spot, a kind of bead, at one of their extremities. This is an illusion arising from the fact that the extremity of these vibrios is curved, hanging downwards, thus causing a greater refraction at that particular point, and leading us to think that the diameter is greater at that extremity. We may easily undeceive ourselves if we watch the movements of the vibrio, when we will readily recognize the bend, especially as it is brought into the vertical plane passing over the rest of the filament. In this way we will see the bright spot, *the head,* disappear, and then reappear.

The chief inference that it concerns us to draw from the preceding facts is one which cannot admit of doubt, and which we need not insist on any further—namely that vibrios, as met with in the fermentation of neutral tartrate of lime, are able to live and multiply when entirely deprived of air.

§ V.—Another Example of Life Without Air—Fermentation of Lactate of Lime

As ANOTHER example of life without air, accompanied by fermentation properly so called, we may lastly cite the fermentation of lactate of lime in a mineral medium.

In the experiment described in the last paragraph, it will be remembered that the ferment liquid and the germs employed in its impregnation came in contact with air, although only for a very brief time. Now, notwithstanding that we possess exact observations which prove that the diffusion of oxygen and nitrogen in a liquid absolutely deprived of air, so far from taking place rapidly, is, on the contrary, a very slow process indeed; yet we were anxious to guard the experiment that we are about to describe from the slightest possible trace of oxygen at the moment of impregnation.

We employed a liquid prepared as follows: Into from 9 to 10 litres (somewhat over 2 gallons) of pure water the following salts[1] were introduced successively, viz:

Pure lactate of lime.................... 225 grammes
Phosphate of ammonia.................... 0.75 "

[1] Should the solution of lactate of lime be turbid, it may be clarified by filtration, after previously adding a small quantity of phosphate of ammonia, which throws down phosphate of lime. It is only after this process of clarification and filtration that the phosphates of the formula are added. The solution soon becomes turbid if left in contact with air, in consequence of the spontaneous formation of bacteria.

Phosphate of potassium.................... 0.4 grammes
Sulphate of magnesium.................... 0.4   "
Sulphate of ammonia...................... 0.2   "
(1 gramme = 15.43 grains.)

On March 23rd, 1875, we filled a 6 litre (about 11 pints) flask, of the shape represented in Fig. 11, and placed it over a heater. Another flame was placed below a vessel containing the same liquid, into which the curved tube of the flask plunged. The liquids in the flask and in the basin

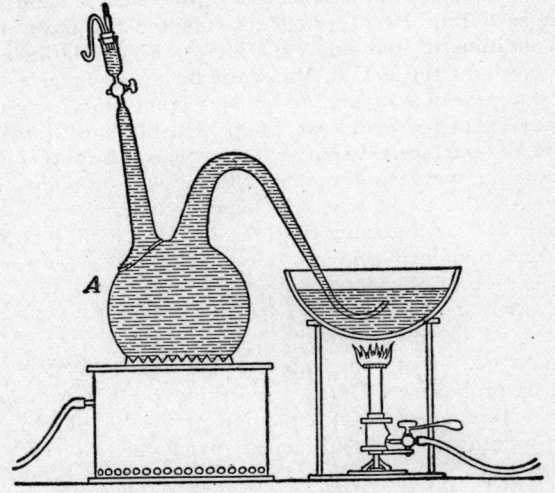

Fig. 11

were raised to boiling together, and kept in this condition for more than half-an-hour, so as to expel all the air held in solution. The liquid was several times forced out of the flask by the steam, and sucked back again; but the portion which re-entered the flask was always boiling. On the following day when the flask had cooled, we transferred the end of the delivery tube to a vessel full of mercury and placed the whole apparatus in an oven at a temperature varying between 25° C. and 30° C. (77° F. and 86° F.); then, after having refilled the small cylindrical tap-funnel with carbonic acid, we passed into it with all necessary precautions 10 cc. (0.35 fl. oz) of a liquid similar to that described, which had been already in active fermentation for several days out of contact with air and now swarmed with vibrios. We then turned the tap of the funnel, until only a small quantity of liquid was left, just enough to prevent the access of air. In this way the impregnation was accomplished without either the ferment-liquid or the ferment-germs having been brought in contact, even for the shortest space, with the external air. The fermentation, the occurrence of which at an earlier or later period depends for the most part on the condition of the impregnating germs, and the number introduced in the act, in this case began to manifest itself by the appearance of minute bubbles from March 29th. But not until April 9th did we observe bubbles of larger size rise to the surface. From that date onward they continued to come in increasing number, from certain points at the bottom of the flask, where a deposit of earthy phosphates existed; and at the same time the liquid, which for the first few days remained perfectly clear, began to grow turbid in consequence of the development of vibrios. It was on the same day that we first observed a deposit on the sides of carbonate of lime in crystals.

It is a matter of some interest to notice here that, in the mode of procedure adopted, everything combined to prevent the interference of air. A portion of the liquid expelled at the beginning of the experiment, partly because of the increased temperature in the oven and partly also by the force of the gas, as it began to be evolved from the fermentative action, reached the surface of the mercury, where, being the most suitable medium we know for the growth of bacteria, it speedily swarmed with these organisms.[2] In this way any

---

[2] The naturalist Cohn, of Breslau, who published an excellent work on bacteria in 1872, described, after Mayer, the composition of a liquid peculiarly adapted to the propagation of these organisms, which it would be well to compare for its utility in studies of this kind with our solution of lactate and phosphates. The following is Cohn's formula:

    Distilled water.................20 cc. (0.7 fl. oz.)
    Phosphate of potassium..........0.1 gramme (1.5 grains)
    Sulphate of magnesium...........0.1 " "
    Tribasic phosphate of lime......0.01 " (0.15 grain)
    Tartrate of ammonia.............0.2 " (3 grains)

This liquid, the author says, has a feeble acid reaction and forms a perfectly clear solution.

passage of air, if such a thing were possible, between the mercury and the sides of the delivery-tube was altogether prevented, since the bacteria would consume every trace of oxygen which might be dissolved in the liquid lying on the surface of the mercury. Hence it is impossible to imagine that the slightest trace of oxygen could have got into the liquid in the flask.

Before passing on we may remark that in this ready absorption of oxygen by bacteria we have a means of depriving fermentable liquids of every trace of that gas with a facility and success equal or even greater than by the preliminary method of boiling. Such a solution as we have described, if kept at summer heat, without any previous boiling, becomes turbid in the course of twenty-four hours from a *spontaneous* development of bacteria; and it is easy to prove that they absorb all the oxygen held in solution.[3] If we completely fill a flask of a few litres capacity (about a gallon) (FIG. 9) with the liquid described, taking care to have the delivery-tube also filled, and its opening plunged under mercury, and, forty-eight hours afterwards by means of a chloride of calcium bath, expel from the liquid on the surface of the mercury all the gas which it holds in solution, this gas, when analyzed, will be found to be composed of a mixture of nitrogen and carbonic acid gas, *without the least trace of oxygen.* Here, then, we have an excellent means of depriving the fermentable liquid of air; we simply have completely to fill a flask with the liquid, and place it in the oven, merely avoiding any addition of butyric vibrios, before the lapse of two or three days. We may wait even longer; and then, if the liquid does become impregnated spontaneously with vibrio germs, the liquid, which at first was turbid from the presence of bacteria, will become bright again, since the bacteria, when deprived of life, or, at least, of the power of moving, after they have exhausted all the oxygen in solution, will fall inert to the bottom of the vessel. On several occasions we have determined this interesting fact, which tends to prove that the butyric vibrios cannot be regarded as another form of bacteria, inasmuch as, on the

[3] On the rapid absorption of oxygen by bacteria, see also our *Mémoire* of 1872, *sur les Générations dites Spontanées,* especially the note on page 78.

hypothesis of an original relation between the two productions, butyric fermentation ought in every case to follow the growth of bacteria.

We may also call attention to another striking experiment, well suited to show the effect of differences in the composition of the medium upon the propagation of microscopic beings. The fermentation which we last described commenced on March 27th and continued until May 10th; that to which we are now to refer, however, was completed in four days, the liquid employed being similar in composition and quantity to that employed in the former experiment. On April 23, 1875, we filled a flask of the same shape as that represented in FIG. 11, and of similar capacity, viz., 6 litres, with a liquid composed as described at page 69. This liquid had been previously left to itself for five days in large open flasks, in consequence of which it had developed an abundant growth of bacteria. On the fifth day a few bubbles, rising from the bottom of the vessels, at long intervals, betokened the commencement of butyric fermentation, a fact, moreover, confirmed by the microscope, in the appearance of the vibrios of this fermentation in specimens of the liquid taken from the bottom of the vessels, the middle of its mass, and even in the layer on the surface that was swarming with bacteria. We transferred the liquid so prepared to the 6-litre flask arranged over the mercury. By evening a tolerably active fermentation had begun to manifest itself. On the 24th this fermentation was proceeding with astonishing rapidity, which continued during the 25th and 26th. During the evening of the 26th it slackened, and on the 27th all signs of fermentation had ceased. This was not, as might be supposed, a sudden stoppage due to some unknown cause; the fermentation was actually completed, for when we examined the fermented liquid on the 28th we could not find the smallest quantity of lactate of lime. If the needs of industry should ever require the production of large quantities of butyric acid, there would, beyond doubt, be found in the preceding fact valuable information in devising an easy method of preparing that product in abundance.[4]

[4] In what way are we to account for so great a difference between the two fermentations that we have just described? Probably it was owing to some modification effected in the medium by the previous life of the bac-

Before we go any further, let us devote some attention to the vibrios of the preceding fermentations.

On May 27th, 1862, we completely filled a flask capable of holding 2.780 litres (about five pints) with the solution of lactate and phosphates.[5] We refrained from impregnating it with any germs. The liquid became turbid from a development of bacteria and then underwent butyric fermentation. By June 9th the fermentation had become sufficiently active to enable us to collect in the course of twenty-four hours, over mercury, as in all our experiments, about 100 cc. (about 6 cubic inches) of gas. By June 11th, judging from the volume of gas liberated in the course of twenty-four hours, the activity of the fermentation had doubled. We examined a drop of the turbid liquid. Here are the notes accompanying the sketch (FIG. 12) as they stand in our note-book: "A swarm of vibrios, so active in their movements that the eye has great difficulty in following them. They may be seen in pairs throughout the field, apparently making efforts to separate from each other. The connection would seem to be by some invisible, gelatinous thread, which yields so far to their efforts that they succeed in breaking away from actual contact, but yet are, for a while, so far restrained that the movements of one have a visible effect on those of the other. By and by, however, we see a complete separation effected, and each moves on its separate way with an activity greater than it ever had before."

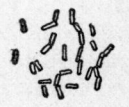

FIG. 12

One of the best methods that can be employed for the

teria, or to the special character of the vibrios used in impregnation. Or, again, it might have been due to the action of the air, which, under the conditions of our second experiment, was not absolutely eliminated, since we took no precaution against its introduction at the moment of filling our flask, and this would tend to facilitate the multiplication of anaërobian vibrios, just as, under similar conditions, would have been the case if we had been dealing with a fermentation by ordinary yeast.

[5] In this case the liquid was composed as follows: A saturated solution of lactate of lime, at a temperature of 25° C. (77° F.), was prepared, containing for every 100 cc. (3½ fl. oz.) 25.65 grammes (394 grains) of the lactate, $C_6H_5O_5CaO$ (*new notation*, $C_6H_{10}CaO_6$). This solution was rendered very clear by the addition of 1 gramme of phosphate of ammonia and subsequent filtration. For a volume of 8 litres (14 pints) of this clear saturated solution we used (1 gramme=15.43 grains):

>
> Phosphate of ammonia.....................2 grammes
> Phosphate of potassium....................1 "
> Phosphate of magnesium...................1 "
> Sulphate of ammonia......................0.5 "

microscopical examination of these vibrios, quite out of contact with air, is the following. After butyric fermentation has been going on for several days in a flask, (FIG. 13), we connect this flask by an india-rubber tube with one of the flattened bulbs previously described, which we then place on the stage of the microscope (FIG. 13). When we

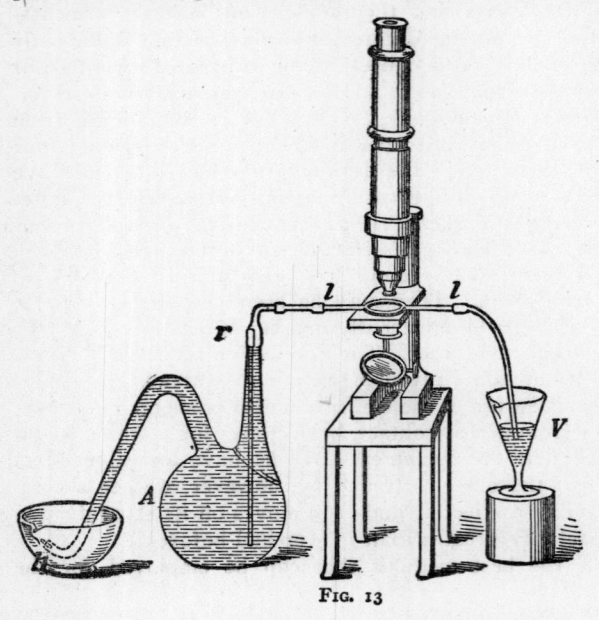

FIG. 13

wish to make an observation we close, under the mercury, at the point b, the end of the drawn-out and bent delivery-tube. The continued evolution of gas soon exerts such a pressure within the flask, that when we open the tap r, the liquid is driven into the bulb $l\,l$, until it becomes quite full and the liquid flows over into the glass V. In this manner we may bring the vibrios under observation without their coming into contact with the least trace of air, and with as much success as if the bulb, which takes the place of an object glass, had been plunged into the very

THEORY OF FERMENTATION

centre of the flask. The movements and fissiparous multiplication of the vibrios may thus be seen in all their beauty, and it is indeed a most interesting sight. The movements do not immediately cease when the temperature is suddenly lowered, even to a considerable extent, 15° C. (59° F.) for example; they are only slackened. Nevertheless, it is better to observe them at the temperatures most favourable to fermentation, even in the oven where the vessels employed in the experiment are kept at a temperature between 25° C. and 30° C. (77° F. and 86° F.).

We may now continue our account of the fermentation which we were studying when we made this last digression. On June 17th that fermentation produced three times as much gas as it did on June 11th, when the residue of hydrogen, after absorption by potash, was 72.6 per cent.; whilst on the 17th it was only 49.2 per cent. Let us again discuss the microscopic aspect of the turbid liquid at this stage. Appended is the sketch we made (FIG. 14) and our notes on it: "A most beautiful object: vibrios all in motion, advancing or undulating. They have grown considerably in bulk and length since the 11th; many of them are joined together in long sinuous chains, very mobile at the articulations, visibly less active and more wavering in proportion to the number that go to form the chain, of the length of the individuals." This description is applicable to the majority of the vibrios which occur in cylindrical rods and are homogeneous in aspect. There are others, of rare occurrence in chains, which have a clear corpuscle, that is to say, a portion more refractive than other parts of the segments, at one of their extremities. Sometimes the foremost segment has the corpuscle at one end, sometimes the other. The long segments of the commoner kind attain a length of from 10 to 30 and even 45 thousandths of a millimetre. Their diameter is from 1½ to 2, very rarely 3, thousandths of a millimetre.[6]

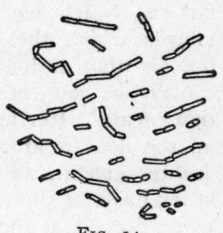

FIG. 14

---

[6] 1 millimetre=0.039 inch: hence the dimensions indicated will be— length, from 0.00039 to 0.00117, or even 0.00176 in.; diameter, from 0.000058 to 0.000078, rarely 0.000117 in.—D. C. R.

On June 28th, fermentation was quite finished; there was no longer any trace of gas, nor any lactate in solution. All the infusoria were lying motionless at the bottom of the flask. The liquid clarified by degrees, and in the course of a few days became quite bright. Here we may inquire, were these motionless infusoria, which from complete exhaustion of the lactate, the source of the carbonaceous part of their food, were now lying inert at the bottom of the fermenting vessel—were they dead beyond the power of revival?[7] The following experiment leads us to believe that they were not perfectly lifeless, and that they might behave in the same manner as the yeast of beer, which, after it has decomposed all the sugar in a fermentable liquid is ready to revive and multiply in a fresh saccharine medium. On April 22nd, 1875, we left in the oven at a temperature of 25° C. (77° F.) a fermentation of lactate of lime that had been completed. The delivery tube of the flask A, (FIG. 15), in which it had taken place, had never been withdrawn from under the mercury. We kept the liquid under observation daily, and saw it gradually become brighter; this went on for fifteen days. We then filled a similar flask, B, with the solution of lactate, which we boiled, not only to kill the germs of vibrios which the liquid might contain, but also to expel the air that it held in solution. When the flask, B, had cooled, we connected the two flasks, avoiding the introduction of air,[8] after having slightly shaken the flask, A, to stir up the deposit at the bottom. There was then a pressure due to carbonic acid at the end of the delivery tube of this latter flask, at the point *a,* so that on opening the taps *r* and *s,* the deposit at the bottom of flask A was driven over into flask B, which in consequence was impregnated with the deposit of a fermentation that had been completed fifteen days before. Two days after impregnation the flask B be-

[7] The carbonaceous supply, as we remarked, had failed them, and to this failure the absence of vital action, nutrition, and multiplication was attributable. The liquid, however, contained butyrate of lime, a salt possessing properties similar to those of the lactate. Why could not this salt equally well support the life of the vibrios? The explanation of the difficulty seems to us to lie simply in the fact that lactic acid produces heat by its decomposition, whilst butyric acid does not, and the vibrios seem to require heat during the chemical process of their nutrition.

[8] To do this it is sufficient, first, to fill the curved ends of the stopcocked tubes of the flasks, as well as the India-rubber tube *c c* which connects them, with boiling water that contains no air.

gan to show signs of fermentation. It follows that the deposit of vibrios of a completed butyric fermentation may

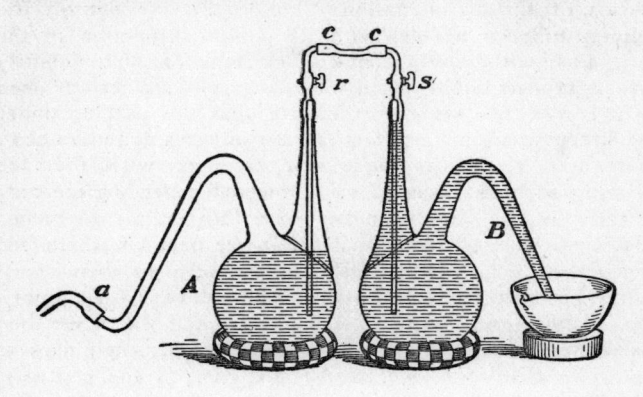

FIG. 15

be kept, at least for a certain time, without losing the power of causing fermentation. It furnishes a butyric ferment, capable of revival and action in a suitable fresh fermentable medium.

The reader who has attentively studied the facts which we have placed before him cannot, in our opinion, entertain the least doubt on the subject of the possible multiplication of the vibrios of a fermentation of lactate of lime out of contact with atmospheric oxygen. If fresh proofs of this important proposition were necessary, they might be found in the following observations, from which it may be inferred that atmospheric oxygen is capable of suddenly checking a fermentation produced by butyric vibrios, and rendering them absolutely motionless, so that it cannot be necessary to enable them to live. On May 7th, 1862, we placed in the oven a flask holding 2.580 litres (4½ pints), and filled with the solution of lactate of lime and phosphates, which we had impregnated on the 9th with two drops of a liquid in butyric fermentation. In the course of a few days fermentation declared itself: on the 18th it was active; on the 30th it was very active. On June 1st it yielded hourly 35 cc. (2.3 cubic inches) of gas, containing ten per cent. of hydrogen. On the 2nd we began the study of the action of air on the vibrios of this fermentation. To do this we cut off the delivery-tube on a level with its point of junction to the flask, then with a 50 cc. pipette we took out that quantity (1¾ fl. oz.) of liquid which was, of course, replaced at once by air. We then reversed the flask with the opening under the mercury, and shook it every ten minutes for more than an hour. Wishing to make sure, to begin with, that the oxygen had been absorbed we connected under the mercury the beak of the flask by means of a thin india-rubber tube filled with water, with a small flask, the neck of which had been drawn out and was filled with water; we then raised the large flask with the smaller kept above it. A Mohr's clip, which closed the india-rubber tube, and which we then opened, permitted the water contained in the small flask to pass into the large one, whilst the gas, on the contrary, passed upwards from the large flask into the small one. We analyzed the gas immediately, and found that, allowing for the carbonic acid and hydrogen, it did not contain more than 14.2 per cent. of oxygen, which corresponds to an absorption of 6.6 cc., or of 3.3 cc. (0.2 cubic inch) of oxygen for the 50 cc. (3.05 cubic inches) of air employed. Lastly, we again established connection by an india-rubber tube between the flasks, after having seen by microscopical examination that the movements of the vibrios were very languid. Fermentation had become less vigorous without having actually ceased, no doubt because some portions of the liquid had not been brought into contact with the atmospheric oxygen, in spite of the prolonged shaking that the flask had undergone after the introduction of the air. Whatever the cause might have been, the significance of the phenomenon is not doubtful. To assure ourselves further of the effect of air on the vibrios, we half filled two test tubes with the fermenting liquid taken from another fermentation which had also attained its maximum of intensity, into one of which we passed a current of air, into the other carbonic acid gas. In the course of half an hour, all the vibrios in the aerated tube were dead, or at least motionless, and fermentation had ceased. In the other tube, after three hours' exposure to the

THEORY OF FERMENTATION

effects of the carbonic acid gas, the vibrios were still very active, and fermentation was going on.

There is a most simple method of observing the deadly effect of atmospheric air upon vibrios. We have seen in the microscopical examination made by means of the apparatus represented in Fig. 13, how remarkable were the movements of the vibrios when absolutely deprived of air, and how easy it was to discern them. We will repeat this observation, and at the same time make a comparative study of the same liquid under the microscope in the ordinary way, that is to say, by placing a drop of the liquid on an object-glass, and covering it with a thin glass slip, a method which must necessarily bring the drop into contact with air, if only for a moment. It is surprising what a remarkable difference is observed immediately between the movements of the vibrios in the bulb and those under the glass. In the case of the latter, we generally see all movement at once cease near the edges of the glass, where the drop of liquid is in direct contact with the air; the movements continue for a longer or shorter time about the centre, in proportion as the air is more or less intercepted by the vibrios at the circumference of the liquid. It does not require much skill in experiments of this kind to enable one to see plainly that immediately after the glass has been placed on the drop, which has been affected all over by atmospheric air, the whole of the vibrios seem to languish and to manifest symptoms of illness—we can think of no better expression to explain what we see taking place—and that they gradually recover their activity about the centre, in proportion as they find themselves in a part of the medium that is less affected by the presence of oxygen.

Some of the most curious facts are to be found in connection with an observation, the correlative and inverse of the foregoing, on the ordinary aërobian bacteria. If we examine below the microscope a drop of liquid full of these organisms under a coverslip, we very soon observe a cessation of motion in all the bacteria which lie in the central portion of the liquid, where the oxygen rapidly disappears to supply the necessities of the bacteria existing there; whilst, on the other hand, near the edges of the cover-glass the movements are very active, in consequence of the constant supply of air. In spite of the speedy death of the bacteria beneath the centre of the glass, we see life prolonged there if by chance a bubble of air has been enclosed. All round this bubble a vast number of bacteria collect in a thick, moving circle, but as soon as all the oxygen of the bubble has been absorbed they fall apparently lifeless, and are scattered by the movement of the liquid.[9]

We may here be permitted to add, as a purely historical matter, that it was these two observations just described, made successively one day in 1861, on vibrios and bacteria, that first suggested to us the idea of the possibility of life without air, and caused us to think that the vibrios which we met so frequently in our lactic fermentations must be the true butyric ferment.

We may pause to consider an interesting question in reference to the two characters under which vibrios appear in butyric fermentations. What is the reason that some vibrios exhibit refractive corpuscles, generally of a lenticular form, such as we see in FIG. 14. We are strongly inclined to believe that these corpuscles have to do with a special mode of reproduction in the vibrios, common alike to the anaërobian forms which we are studying, and the ordinary aërobian forms in which also the corpuscles of which we are speaking may occur. The explanation of the phenomenon, from our point of view, would be that, after a certain number of fissiparous generations, and under the influence of variations in the composition of the medium, which is constantly changing through fermentation as well as through the active life of the vibrios themselves, cysts, which are simply the refractive corpuscles, form along them at different points. From these gemmules we have ultimately produced vibrios, ready to reproduce others by the process of transverse division for a certain time, to be themselves encysted, later on. Various observations incline us to believe that, in their ordi-

[9] We find this fact, which we published as long ago as 1863, confirmed in a work of H. Hoffman's, published in 1869 under the title of *Mémoire sur les bactéries*, which has appeared in French (*Annales des Sciences naturelles*, 5th series, vol. ix.). On this subject we may cite an observation that has not yet been published. Aërobian bacteria lose all power of movement when suddenly plunged into carbonic acid gas; they recover it, however, as if they had only been suffering from anæsthesia, as soon as they are brought into the air again.

THEORY OF FERMENTATION

nary form of minute, soft, exuberant rods, the vibrios perish when submitted to desiccation, but when they occur in corpuscular or encysted form they possess unusual powers of resistance and may be brought to the state of dry dust and be wafted about by winds. None of the matter which surrounds the corpuscle or cyst seems to take part in the preservation of the germ, when the cyst is formed, for it is all re-absorbed, gradually leaving the cyst bare. The cysts appear as masses of corpuscles, in which the most practiced eye cannot detect anything of an organic nature, or anything to remind one of the vibrios which produced them; nevertheless, these minute bodies are endowed with a latent vital action, and only await favourable conditions to develop long rods of vibrios. We are not, it is true, in a position to adduce any very forcible proofs in support of these opinions. They have been suggested to us by experiments, none of which, however, have been absolutely decisive in their favour. We may cite one of our observations on this subject.

In a fermentation of glycerine in a mineral medium—the glycerine was fermenting under the influence of butyric vibrios—after we had determined the, we may say, exclusive presence of lenticular vibrios, with refractive corpuscles, we observed the fermentation, which for some unknown reason had been very languid, suddenly become extremely active, but now through the influence of the ordinary vibrios. The gemmules with brilliant corpuscles had almost disappeared; we could see but very few, and those now consisted of the refractive bodies alone, the bulk of the vibrios accompanying them having undergone some process of re-absorption.

Another observation which still more closely accords with this hypothesis is given in our work on silk-worm disease (vol. 1, p. 256). We there demonstrated that, when we place in water some of the dust formed of desiccated vibrios, containing a host of these refractive corpuscles, in the course of a very few hours large vibrios appear, well-developed rods fully grown, in which the brilliant points are absent; whilst in the water no process of development from smaller vibrios is to be discerned, a fact which seems to show that the former had issued fully grown from the refractive corpuscles, just as we see *colpoda* issue with their adult aspect from the dust of their cysts. This observation, we may remark, furnishes one of the best proofs that can be adduced against the spontaneous generation of vibrios or bacteria, since it is probable that the same observation applies to bacteria. It is true that we cannot say of mere points of dust examined under the microscope, that one particular germ belongs to vibrio, another to bacterium; but how is it possible to doubt that the vibrios issue, as we see them, from an ovum of some kind, a cyst, or germ, of determinate character, when, after having placed some of those indeterminate motes of dust into clean water, we suddenly see, after an interval of not more than one or two hours, an adult vibrio crossing the field of the microscope, without our having been able to detect any intermediate state between its birth and adolescence?

It is a question whether differences in the aspect and nature of vibrios, which depend upon their more or less advanced age, or are occasioned by the influence of certain conditions on the medium in which they propagate, do not bring about corresponding changes in the course of the fermentation and the nature of its products. Judging at least from the variations in the proportions of hydrogen and carbonic acid gas produced in butyric fermentations, we are inclined to think that this must be the case; nay, more, we find that hydrogen is not even a constant product in these fermentations. We have met with butyric fermentations of lactate of lime which did not yield the minutest trace of hydrogen, or anything besides carbonic acid. FIG. 16 represents the vibrios which we observed in a fermentation of this kind. They present no special features. Butyl alcohol is, according to our observations, an ordinary product, although it varies and is by no means a necessary concomitant of these fermentations. It might be supposed, since butylic alcohol may be produced, and hydrogen be in deficit, that the proportion of the former of these products would attain its maximum when the latter assumed a minimum. This, however, is by no means the case; even in those few fermentations that we

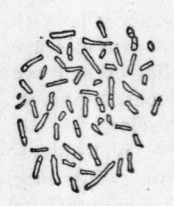

FIG. 16

have met with in which hydrogen was absent, there was no formation of butylic alcohol.

From a consideration of all the facts detailed in this section we can have no hesitation in concluding that, on the one hand, in cases of butyric fermentation, the vibrios which abound in them and constitute their ferment, live without air or free oxygen; and that, on the other hand, the presence of gaseous oxygen operates prejudicially against the movements and activity of those vibrios. But now does it follow that the presence of minute quantities of air brought into contact with a liquid undergoing butyric fermention would prevent the continuance of that fermentation or even exercise any check upon it? We have not made any direct experiments upon this subject; but we should not be surprised to find that, so far from hindering, air may, under such circumstances, facilitate the propagation of the vibrios and accelerate fermentation. This is exactly what happens in the case of yeast. But how could we reconcile this, supposing it were proved to be the case, with the fact just insisted on as to the danger of bringing the butyric vibrios into contact with air? It may be possible that *life without air* results from habit, whilst *death through air* may be brought about by a sudden change in the conditions of the existence of the vibrios. The following remarkable experiment is well-known: A bird is placed in a glass jar of one or two litres (60 to 120 cubic inches) in capacity which is then closed. After a time the creature shows every sign of intense uneasiness and asphyxia long before it dies; a similar bird of the same size is introduced into the jar; the death of the latter takes place instantaneously, whilst the life of the former may still be prolonged under these conditions for a considerable time, and there is no difficulty even in restoring the bird to perfect health by taking it out of the jar. It seems impossible to deny that we have here a case of the adaptation of an organism to the gradual contamination of the medium; and so it may likewise happen that the anaërobian vibrios of a butyric fermentation, which develop and multiply absolutely without free oxygen, perish immediately when suddenly taken out of their airless medium, and that the result might be different if they had been gradually brought under the action of air in small quantities at a time.

We are compelled here to admit that vibrios frequently abound in liquids exposed to the air, and that they appropriate the atmospheric oxygen, and could not withstand a sudden removal from its influence. Must we, then, believe that such vibrios are absolutely different from those of butyric fermentations? It would, perhaps, be more natural to admit that in the one case there is an adaptation to life with air, and in the other case an adaptation to life without air; each of the varieties perishing when suddenly transferred from its habitual condition to that of the other, whilst by a series of progressive changes one might be modified into the other.[10] We know that in the case of alcoholic ferments, although these can actually live without air, propagation is wonderfully assisted by the presence of minute quantities of air; and certain experiments which we have not yet published lead us to believe that, after having lived without air, they cannot be suddenly exposed with impunity to the influence of large quantities of oxygen.

We must not forget, however, that aërobian torulae and anaërobian ferments present an example of organisms apparently identical, in which, however, we have not yet been able to discover any ties of a common origin. Hence we are forced to regard them as a distinct species; and so it is possible that there may likewise be aërobian and anaërobian vibrios without any transformation of the one into the other.

The question has been raised whether vibrios, especially those which we have shown to be the ferment of butyric and many other fermentations, are in their nature, animal or vegetable. M. Ch. Robin attaches great importance to the solution of this question, of which he speaks as follows:[11] "The determination of the nature, whether animal or vegetable, of organisms, either as a whole or in respect to their anatomical parts, assimilative or reproductive, is a problem which has been capable of solution for a quarter of a century. The method has been brought to a state

---

[10] These doubts might be easily removed by putting the matter to the test of direct experiment.
[11] ROBIN, *Sur la nature des fermentations*, &c. (*Journal de l'Académie et de la Physiologie*, July and August, 1875, p. 386).

of remarkable precision, experimentally, as well as in its theoretical aspects, since those who devote their attention to the organic sciences consider it indispensable in every observation and experiment to determine accurately, before anything else, whether the object of their study is animal or vegetable in its nature, whether adult or otherwise. To neglect this is as serious an omission for such students as for chemists would be the neglecting to determine whether it is nitrogen or hydrogen, urea or stearine, that has been extracted from a tissue, or which it is whose combinations they are studying in this or that chemical operation. Now, scarcely any one of those who study fermentations, properly so-called, and putrefactions, ever pay any attention to the preceding data. . . . Among the observers to whom I allude, even M. Pasteur is to be found, who, even in his most recent communications, omits to state definitely what is the nature of many of the ferments which he has studied, with the exception, however, of those which belong to the cryptogamic group called *torulaceae*. Various passages in his work seem to show that he considers the cryptogamic organisms called *bacteria,* as well as those known as *vibrios,* as belonging to the animal kingdom (see *Bulletin de l'Académie de Médécine,* Paris, 1875, pp. 249, 251, especially 256, 266, 267, 289, and 290). These would be very different, at least physiologically, the former being anaërobian, that is to say, requiring no air to enable them to live, and being killed by oxygen, should it be dissolved in the liquid to any considerable extent."

We are unable to see the matter in the same light as our learned colleague does; to our thinking, we should be labouring under a great delusion were we to suppose " that it is quite as serious an omission not to determine the animal or vegetable nature of a ferment as it would be to confound nitrogen with hydrogen or urea with stearine." The importance of the solutions of disputed questions often depends on the point of view from which these are regarded. As far as the result of our labours is concerned, we devoted our attention to these two questions exclusively: 1. Is the ferment, in every fermentation properly so called, an organized being? 2. Can this organized being live without air? Now, what bearing can the question of the animal or vegetable nature of the ferment, of the organized being, have upon the investigation of these two problems? In studying butyric fermentation, for example, we endeavoured to establish these two fundamental points; 1. The *butyric ferment is a vibrio.* 2. *This vibrio may dispense with air in its life, and, as a matter of fact, does dispense with it in the act of producing butyric fermentation.* We did not consider it at all necessary to pronounce any opinion as to the animal or vegetable nature of this organism, and, even up to the present moment, the idea that vibrio is an animal and not a plant is in our minds, a matter of sentiment rather than of conviction.

M. Robin, however, would have no difficulty in determining the limits of the two kingdoms. According to him, " every variety of cellulose is, we may say, insoluble in ammonia, as also are the reproductive elements of plants, whether male or female. Whatever phase of evolution the elements which reproduce a new individual may have reached, treatment with this reagent, either cold or raised to boiling, leaves them absolutely intact under the eyes of the observer, except that their contents, from being partially dissolved, become more transparent. Every vegetable whether microscopic or not, every mycelium and every spore, thus preserves in its entirety its special characteristics of form, volume and structural arrangements; whilst in the case of microscopic animals, or the ova and microscopic embryos of different members of the animal kingdom, the very opposite is the case."

We should be glad to learn that the employment of a drop of ammonia would enable us to pronounce an opinion with this degree of confidence on the nature of the lowest microscopic beings; but is M. Robin absolutely correct in his assumptions? That gentleman himself remarks that spermatozoa, which belong to animal organisms, are insoluble in ammonia, the effect of which is merely to make them paler. If a difference of action in certain reagents, in ammonia, for example, were sufficient to determine the limits of the animal and vegetable kingdoms, might we not argue that there must be a very great and natural difference between moulds and bacteria, inasmuch as the presence of a small quantity of acid in the nutritive medium facilitates the growth and propagation of the former, whilst it is able to prevent the life of bacteria and vibrios? Although as is well known, movement is not an exclusive characteristic of animals, yet we have always been inclined to regard vibrios as animals, on account of the peculiar character of their movements. How greatly they differ in this respect from the diatomacae, for example! When the vibrio encounters an obstacle it turns, or after assuring itself by some visual effort or other that it cannot overcome it, it retraces its steps. The colpoda—undoubted infusoria—behave in an exactly similar manner. It is true one may argue that the zoospores of certain cryptogamia exhibit similar movements; but do not these zoospores possess as much of an animal nature as do the spermatozoa? As far as bacteria are concerned, when, as already remarked, we see them crowd round a bubble of air in a liquid to prolong their life, oxygen having failed them everywhere else, how can we avoid believing that they are animated by an instinct for life, of the same kind that we find in animals? M. Robin seems to us to be wrong in supposing that it is possible to draw any absolute line of separation between the animal and vegetable kingdoms. The settlement of this line however, we repeat again, no matter what it may be, has no serious bearing upon the questions that have been the subject of our researches.

In like manner the difficulty which M. Robin has raised in objecting to the employment of the word *germ,* when we cannot specify whether the nature of that germ is animal or vegetable, is in many respects an unnecessary one. In all the questions which we have discussed, whether we were speaking of fermentation or spontaneous generation, the word *germ* has been used in the sense of *origin of living organism.* If Liebig, for example, said of an albuminous substance that it gave birth to ferment, could we contradict him more plainly than by replying " No; ferment is an organized being, the germ of which is always present, and the albuminous substance merely serves by its occurrence to nourish the germ and its successive generations"?

In our Memoir of 1862, on so-called *spontaneous* generations, would it not have been an entire mistake to have attempted to assign specific names to the microscopic organisms which we met with in the course of our observations? Not only would we have met with extreme difficulty in the attempt, arising from the state of extreme confusion which even in the present day exists in the classification and nomenclature of these microscopic organisms, but we should have been forced to sacrifice clearness in our work besides; at all events, we should have wandered from our principal object, which was the determination of the presence or absence of life in general, and had nothing to do with the manifestation of a particular kind of life in this or that species, animal or vegetable. Thus we have systematically employed the vaguest nomenclature, such as mucors, torulae, bacteria, and vibrios. There was nothing arbitrary in our doing this, whereas there is much that is arbitrary in adopting a definite system of nomenclature, and applying it to organisms but imperfectly known, the differences or resemblances between which are only recognizable through certain characteristics, the true signification of which is obscure. Take, for example, the extensive array of widely different systems which have been invented during the last few years for the species of the genera bacterium and vibrio in the works of Cohn, H. Hoffmann, Hallier, and Billroth. The confusion which prevails here is very great, although we do not of course by any means place these different works on the same footing as regards their respective merits.

M. Robin is, however, right in recognizing the impossibility of maintaining in the present day, as he formerly did, "That fermentation is an exterior phenomenon, going on outside cryptogamic cells, a phenomenon of contact. It is probably," he adds, "an interior and molecular action at work in the innermost recesses of the substance of each cell." From the day when we first proved that it is possible for all organized ferments, properly so called, to spring up and multiply from their respective germs, sown, whether consciously or by accident, in a mineral medium free from organic and nitrogenous matters other than ammonia, in which medium the fermentable matter alone is adapted to provide the ferment with whatever carbon enters into its composition, from that time forward the theories of Liebig, as well of Berzelius, which M. Robin formerly defended, have had to give place to others more in harmony with facts. We trust that the day will come when M. Robin will likewise acknowledge that he has been in error on the subject of the doctrine of spontaneous generation, which he continues to affirm, without adducing any direct proofs in support of it, at the end of the article to which we have been here replying.

We have devoted the greater part of this chapter to the establishing with all possible exactness the extremely important physiological fact of life without air, and its correlation to the phenomena of fermentations properly so-called—that is to say, of those which are due to the presence of microscopic cellular organisms. This is the chief basis of the new theory that we propose for the explanation of these phenomena. The details into which we have entered were indispensable on account of the novelty of the subject no less than on account of the necessity we were under of combating the criticisms of the two German naturalists, Drs. Oscar Brefeld and Traube, whose works had cast some doubts on the correctness of the facts upon which we had based the preceding propositions. We have much pleasure in adding that at the very moment we were revising the proofs of this chapter, we received from M. Brefeld an essay, dated Berlin, January, 1876, in which, after describing his later experimental researches, he owns with praiseworthy frankness that Dr. Traube and he were both of them mistaken. Life without air is now a proposition which he accepts as perfectly demonstrated. He has witnessed it in the case of *mucor racemosus* and has also verified it in the case of yeast. "If," he says, "after the results of my previous researches, which I conducted with all possible exactness, I was inclined to consider Pasteur's assertion as inaccurate and to attack them, I have no hesitation now in recognizing them as true, and in proclaiming the service which Pasteur has rendered to science in being the first to indicate the exact relation of things in the phenomenon of fermentation." In his later researches, Dr. Brefeld has adopted the method which we have long employed for demonstrating the life and multiplication of butyric vibrios in the entire absence of air, as well as the method of conducting growths in mineral media associated with fermentable substance. We need not pause to consider certain other secondary criticisms of Dr. Brefeld. A perusal of the present work will, we trust, convince him that they are based on no surer foundation than were his former criticisms.

To bring one's self to believe in a truth that has just dawned upon one is the first step towards progress; to persuade others is the second. There is a third step, less useful perhaps, but highly gratifying nevertheless, which is, to convince one's opponents.

We therefore, have experienced great satisfaction in learning that we have won over to our ideas an observer of singular ability, on a subject which is of the utmost importance to the physiology of cells.

§ VI. REPLY TO THE CRITICAL OBSERVATIONS OF LIEBIG, PUBLISHED IN 1870.[1]

IN the Memoir which we published, in 1860, on alcoholic fermentation, and in several subsequent works, we were led to a different conclusion on the causes of this very remarkable phenomenon from that which Liebig had adopted. The opinions of Mitscherlich and Berzelius had ceased to be tenable in the presence of the new facts which we had brought to light. From that time we felt sure that the celebrated chemist of Munich had adopted our conclusions, from the fact that he remained silent on this question for a long time, although it had been until then the constant subject of his study, as is shown by all his works. Suddenly there appeared in the *Annales de Chimie et de Physique*

[1] LIEBIG, *Sur la fermentation et la source de la force musculaire* (*Annales de Chimie et de Physique*, 4th series, t. xxiii., p. 5, 1870).

a long essay, reproduced from a lecture delivered by him before the Academy of Bavaria in 1868 and 1869. In this Liebig again maintained, not, however, without certain modifications, the views which he had expressed in his former publications, and disputed the correctness of the principal facts enunciated in our Memoir of 1860, on which were based the arguments against his theory.

"I had admitted," he says, "that the resolution of fermentable matter into compounds of a simpler kind must be traced to some process of decomposition taking place in the ferment, and that the action of this same ferment on the fermentable matter must continue or cease according to the prolongation or cessation of the alteration produced in the ferment. The molecular change in the sugar, would, consequently, be brought about by the destruction or modification of one or more of the component parts of the ferment, and could only take place through the contact of the two substances. M. Pasteur regards fermentation in the following light: The chemical action of fermentation is essentially a phenomenon correlative with a vital action, beginning and ending with it. He believes that alcoholic fermentation can never occur without the simultaneous occurrence of organization, development, and multiplication of globules, or continuous life, carried on from globules already formed. But the idea that the decomposition of sugar during fermentation is due to the development of the cellules of the ferment, is in contradiction with the fact that the ferment is able to bring about the fermentation of a pure solution of sugar. The greater part of the ferment is composed of a substance that is rich in nitrogen and contains sulphur. It contains, moreover, an appreciable quantity of phosphates, hence it is difficult to conceive how, in the absence of these elements in a pure solution of sugar undergoing fermentation, the number of cells is capable of any increase."

Notwithstanding Liebig's belief to the contrary, the idea that the decomposition of sugar during fermentation is intimately connected with a development of the cellules of the ferment, or a prolongation of the life of cellules already formed, is in no way opposed to the fact that the ferment is capable of bringing about the fermentation of a pure solution of sugar. It is manifest to any one who has studied such fermentation with the microscope, even in those cases where the sweetened water has been absolutely pure, that ferment-cells do multiply, the reason being that the cells carry with them all the food-supplies necessary for the life of the ferment. They may be observed budding, at least many of them, and there can be no doubt that those which do not bud still continue to live; life has other ways of manifesting itself besides development and cell-proliferation.

If we refer to the figures on page 81 of our Memoir of 1860, Experiments D, E, F, H, I, we shall see that the weight of yeast, in the case of the fermentation of a pure solution of sugar, undergoes a considerable increase, even without taking into account the fact that the sugared water gains from the yeast certain soluble parts, since in the experiments just mentioned, the weights of solid yeast, washed and dried at 100° C. (212° F.), are much greater than those of the raw yeast employed, dried at the same temperature.

In these experiments we employed the following weights of yeast, expressed in grammes (1 gramme=15.43 grains):

(1) 2.313
(2) 2.626
(3) 1.198
(4) 0.699
(5) 0.326
(6) 0.476

which became, after fermentation, we repeat, without taking into account the matters which the sugared water gained from the yeast:

			grammes.		grains.
(1)	2.486	Increase	0.173	=	2.65
(2)	2.963	"	0.337	=	5.16
(3)	1.700	"	0.502	=	7.7
(4)	0.712	"	0.013	=	0.2
(5)	0.335	"	0.009	=	0.14
(6)	0.590	"	0.114	=	1.75

Have we not in this marked increase in weight a proof of life, or, to adopt an expression which may be preferred, a proof of a profound chemical work of nutrition and assimilation?

We may cite on this subject one of our earlier experiments, which is to be found in the *Comptes rendus de l'Académie* for the year 1857, and which clearly shows the great influence exerted on fermentation by the soluble portion that the sugared water takes up from the globules of ferment:

"We take two equal quantities of fresh yeast that have been washed very freely. One of these we cause to ferment in water containing nothing but sugar, and, after removing from the other all its soluble particles—by boiling it in an excess of water and then filtering it to separate the globules—we add to the filtered liquid as much sugar as was used in the first case along with a mere trace of fresh yeast insufficient, as far as its weight is concerned, to affect the results of our experiment. The globules which we have sown bud, the liquid becomes turbid, a deposit of yeast gradually forms, and, side by side with these appearances, the decomposition of the sugar is effected, and in the course of a few hours manifests itself clearly. These results are such as we might have anticipated. The following fact, however, is of importance. In effecting by these means the organization into globules of the soluble part of the yeast that we used in the second case, we find that a considerable quantity of sugar is decomposed. The following are the results of our experiment; 5 grammes of yeast caused the fermentation of 12.9 grammes of sugar in six days, at the end of which time it was exhausted. The soluble portion of a like quantity of 5 grammes of the same yeast caused the fermentation of 10 grammes of sugar in nine days, after which the yeast developed by the sowing was likewise exhausted."

How is it possible to maintain that, in the fermentation of water containing nothing but sugar, the soluble portion of the yeast does not act, either in the production of new globules or the perfection of old ones, when we see, in the preceding experiment, that after this nitrogenous and mineral portion has been removed by boiling, it immediately serves for the production of new globules, which, under the influence of the sowing of a mere trace of globules, causes the fermentation of so much sugar?[2]

In short, Liebig is not justified in saying that the solution of pure sugar, caused to ferment by means of yeast, contains none of the elements needed for the growth of yeast, neither nitrogen, sulphur nor phosphorus, and that, consequently, it should not be possible, by our theory, for the sugar to ferment. On the contrary, the solution does contain all these elements, as a consequence of the introduction and presence of the yeast.

Let us proceed without examination of Liebig's criticisms:

"To this," he goes on to say, "must be added the decomposing action which yeast exercises on a great number of substances, and which resembles that which sugar undergoes. I have shown that malate of lime ferments readily enough through the action of yeast, and that it splits up into three other calcareous salts, namely, the acetate, the carbonate and the succinate. If the action of yeast consists in its increase and multiplication, it is difficult to conceive this action in the case of malate of lime and other calcareous salts of vegetable acids."

This statement, with all due deference to the opinion of our illustrious critic, is by no means correct. Yeast has no action on malate of lime, or on other calcareous salts formed by vegetable acids. Liebig had previously, much to his own satisfaction, brought forward urea as being capable of transformation into carbonate of ammonia during alcoholic fermentation in contact with yeast. This has been proved to be erroneous. It is an error of the same kind that Liebig again brings forward here. In the fermentation of which

[2] It is important that we should here remark that, in the fermentation of pure solution of sugar by means of yeast, the oxygen originally dissolved in the water, as well as that appropriated by the globules of yeast in their contact with air, has a considerable effect on the activity of the fermentation. As a matter of fact, if we pass a strong current of carbonic acid through the sugared water and the water in which the yeast has been treated, the fermentation will be rendered extremely sluggish, and the few new cells of yeast which form will assume strange and abnormal aspects. Indeed this might have been expected, for we have seen that yeast, when somewhat old, is incapable of development or of causing fermentation even in a fermentable medium containing all the nutritive principles of yeast if the liquid has been deprived of air; much more should we expect this to be the case in pure sugared water, likewise deprived of air.

he speaks (that of malate of lime), certain spontaneous ferments are produced, the germs of which are associated with the yeast, and develop in the mixture of yeast and malate. The yeast merely serves as a source of food for these new ferments without taking any direct part in the fermentations of which we are speaking. Our researches leave no doubt on this point, as is evident from the observations on the fermentation of tartrate of lime previously given.

It is true that there are circumstances under which yeast brings about modifications in different substances. Doebereiner and Mitscherlich, more especially, have shown that yeast imparts to water a soluble material, which liquefies cane-sugar and produces inversion in it by causing it to take up the elements of water, just as diastase behaves to starch or emulsin to amygdalin.

M. Berthelot also has shown that this substance may be isolated by precipitating it with alcohol, in the same way as diastase is precipitated from its solutions.[8] These are

[8] DOEBEREINER, *Journal de Chimie de Schweigger*, vol. xii., p. 129, and *Journal de Pharmacie*, vol. i., p. 342.
MITSCHERLICH, *Monatsberichte d. Kön. Preuss. Akad. d. Wissen, zu Berlin*, and *Rapports annuels de Berzelius*, Paris, 1843, 3rd year. On the occasion of a communication on the inversion of cane-sugar by H. Rose, published in 1840, M. Mitscherlich observed: "The inversion of cane-sugar in alcoholic fermentation is not due to the globules of yeast, but to a soluble matter in the water with which they mix. The liquid obtained by straining off the ferment on a filter paper possesses the property of converting cane-sugar into uncrystallizable sugar."
BERTHELOT, *Comptes rendus de l'Académie*. Meeting of May 28th, 1860, M. Berthelot confirms the preceding experiment of Mitscherlich, and proves, moreover, that the soluble matter of which the author speaks may be precipitated with alcohol without losing its invertive power.
M. Béchamp has applied Mitscherlich's observation, concerning the soluble fermentative part of yeast, to fungoid growths, and has made the interesting discovery that fungoid growths, like yeast, yield to water a substance that inverts sugar. When the production of fungoid growths is prevented by means of an antiseptic, the inversion of sugar does not take place.
We may here say a few words respecting M. Béchamp's claim to priority of discovery. It is a well-known fact that we were the first to demonstrate that living ferments might be completely developed if their germs were placed in pure water together with sugar, ammonia, and phosphates. Relying on this established fact, that moulds are capable of development in sweetened water in which, according to M. Béchamp, they invert the sugar, our author asserts that he has proved that "living organized ferments may originate in media which contain no albuminous substances." (See *Comptes rendus*, vol. lxxv., p. 1519.) To be logical, M. Béchamp might say that he has proved that certain moulds originate in pure sweetened water without nitrogen or phosphates or other mineral elements, for such a deduction might very well be drawn from his work, in which we do not find the least expression of astonishment at the possibility of moulds developing in pure water containing nothing but sugar without other mineral or organic principles.
M. Béchamp's first note on the inversion of sugar was published in 1855. In it we find nothing relating to the influence of moulds. His second, in

remarkable facts, which are, however, at present but vaguely connected with the alcoholic fermentation of sugar by means of yeast. The researches in which we have proved the existence of special forms of living ferments in many fermentations, which one might have supposed to have been produced by simple contact action, had established beyond doubt the existence of profound differences between those fermentations, which we have distinguished as fermentations proper, and the phenomena connected with soluble substances. The more we advance, the more clearly we are able to detect these differences. M. Dumas has insisted on the fact that the ferments of fermentation proper multiply and reproduce themselves in the process whilst the others are destroyed.[4] Still more recently M. Müntz has shown that chloroform prevents fermentations proper, but does not interfere with the action of diastase (*Comptes rendus,* 1875) M. Bouchardat had already established the fact that hydrocyanic acid, salts of mercury, ether, alcohol, creosote, and the oils of turpentine, lemon, cloves, and mustard destroy or check alcoholic fermentations, whilst in no way interfering with the glucoside fermentations (*Annales de Chimie et de Physique,* 3rd series, t. xiv., 1845). We may add in praise of M. Bouchardat's sagacity, that that skilful observer has always considered these results as a proof that alcoholic fermentation is dependent on the life of the yeast-cell, and that a distinction should be made between the two orders of fermentation.

---

which that influence is noticed, was published in January, 1858, that is, subsequently to our work on lactic fermentation, which appeared in November, 1857. In that work we established for the first time that the lactic ferment is a living, organized being, that albuminous substances have no share in the production of fermentation, and that they only serve as the food of the ferment. M. Béchamp's note was even subsequent to our first work on alcoholic fermentation, which appeared on December 21st, 1857. It is since the appearance of these two works of ours that the preponderating influence of the life of microscopic organism in the phenomena of fermentation has been better understood. Immediately after their appearance M. Béchamp, who from 1855 had made no observation on the action of fungoid growths on sugar, although he had remarked their presence, modified his former conclusions. (*Comptes rendus,* January 4th, 1858.)

[4] "There are two classes of ferments; the first, of which the yeast of beer may be taken as the type, perpetuate and renew themselves if they can find in the liquid in which they produce fermentation food enough for their wants; the second, of which diastase is the type, always sacrifice themselves in the exercise of their activity." (DUMAS, *Comptes rendus de l'Académie,* t. lxxv., p. 277, 1872.)

M. Paul Bert, in his remarkable studies on the influence of barometric pressure on the phenomena of life, has recognized the fact that compressed oxygen is fatal to certain ferments, whilst under similar conditions it does not interfere with the action of those substances classed under the name of *soluble ferments,* such as diastase (the ferment which inverts cane sugar) emulsin and others. During their stay in compressed air, ferments proper ceased their activity, nor did they resume it, even after exposure to air at ordinary pressures, provided the access of germs was prevented.

We now come to Liebig's principal objection, with which he concludes his ingenious argument, and to which no less than eight or nine pages of the *Annales* are devoted.

Our author takes up the question of the possibility of causing yeast to grow in sweetened water, to which a salt of ammonia and some yeast-ash have been added—a fact which is evidently incompatible with his theory that a ferment is always an albuminous substance on its way to decomposition. In this case the albuminous substance does not exist; we have only the mineral substances which will serve to produce it. We know that Liebig regarded yeast, and, generally speaking, any ferment whatever, as being a nitrogenous, albuminous substance which, in the same way as emulsin, for example, possesses the power of bringing about certain chemical decompositions. He connected fermentation with the easy decomposition of that albuminous substance, and imagined that the phenomenon occurred in the following manner: "The albuminous substance on its way to decomposition possesses the power of communicating to certain other bodies that same state of mobility by which its own atoms are already affected; and through its contact with other bodies it imparts to them the power of decomposing or of entering into other combinations." Here Liebig failed to perceive that the ferment, in its capacity of a living organism, had anything to do with the fermentation.

This theory dates back as far as 1843. In 1846 Messrs. Boutron and Fremy, in a Memoir on lactic fermentation, published in the *Annales de Chimie et de Physique,* strained the conclusions deducible from it to a most unjustifiable extent. They asserted that one and the same nitrogenous substance might undergo various modifications in contact with air, so as to become successively alcoholic, lactic, butyric, and other ferments. There is nothing more convenient than purely hypothetical theories, theories which are not the necessary consequences of facts; when fresh facts which cannot be reconciled with the original hypothesis are discovered, new hypotheses can be tacked on to the old ones. This is exactly what Liebig and Fremy have done, each in his turn, under the pressure of our studies, commenced in 1857. In 1864 Fremy devised the theory of *hemi-organism*, which meant nothing more than that he gave up Liebig's theory of 1843, together with the additions which Boutron and he had made to it in 1846; in other words, he abandoned the idea of albuminous substances being ferments, to take up another idea, that albuminous substances in contact with air are peculiarly adapted to undergo organization into new beings— that is, the living ferments which we had discovered—and that the ferments of beer and of the grape have a common origin.

This theory of hemi-organism was word for word the antiquated opinion of Turpin. * * * The public, especially a certain section of the public did not go very deeply into an examination of the subject. It was the period when the doctrine of spontaneous generation was being discussed with much warmth. The new word hemi-organism, which was the only novelty in M. Fremy's theory, deceived people. It was thought that M. Fremy had really discovered the solution of the question of the day. It is true that it was rather difficult to understand the process by which an albuminous substance could become all at once a living and budding cell. This difficulty was solved by M. Fremy, who declared that it was the result of some power that was not yet understood, the power of "organic impulse."[*]

Liebig, who, as well as M. Fremy, was compelled to renounce his original opinions concerning the nature of ferments, devised the following obscure theory (Memoir by Liebig, 1870, already cited):

"There seems to be no doubt as to the part which the vegetable organism plays in the phenomenon of fermentation.

---

[*] Fremy, *Comptes rendus de l'Académie*, vol. lviii., p. 1065, 1864.

It is through it alone that an albuminous substance and sugar are enabled to unite and form this particular combination, this unstable form under which alone, as a component part of the mycoderm, they manifest an action on sugar. Should the mycoderm cease to grow, the bond which unites the constituent parts of the cellular contents is loosened, and it is through the motion produced therein that the cells of yeast bring about a disarrangement or separation of the elements of the sugar into molecules."

One might easily believe that the translator for the *Annales* has made some mistake, so great is the obscurity of this passage.

Whether we take this new form of the theory or the old one, neither can be reconciled at all with the development of yeast and fermentation in a saccharine mineral medium, for in the latter experiment fermentation is correlative to the life of the ferment and to its nutrition, a constant change going on between the ferment and its food-matters, since all the carbon assimilated by the ferment is derived from sugar, its nitrogen from ammonia and phosphorus from the phosphates in solution. And even all said, what purpose can be served by the gratuitous hypothesis of contact-action or communicated motion? The experiment of which we are speaking is thus a fundamental one; indeed, it is its possibility that constitutes the most effective point in the controversy. No doubt Liebig might say, "but it is the motion of life and of nutrition which constitutes your experiment, and this is the communicated motion that my theory requires." Curiously enough, Liebig does endeavour, as a matter of fact, to say this, but he does so timidly and incidentally: "From a chemical point of view, which point of view I would not willingly abandon, a *vital action* is a phenomenon of motion, and, in this double sense of *life* M. Pasteur's theory agrees with my own, and is not in contradiction with it (page 6)." This is true. Elsewhere Liebig says:

"It is possible that the only correlation between the physiological act and the phenomenon of fermentation is the production, in the living cell, of the substance which, by some special property analogous to that by which emulsin exerts a decomposing action on salicin and amygdalin, may bring about the decomposition of sugar into other organic molecules; the physiological act, in this view, would be necessary for the production of this substance, but would have nothing else to do with the fermentation (page 10)." To this, again, we have no objection to raise.

Liebig, however, does not dwell upon these considerations, which he merely notices in passing, because he is well aware that, as far as the defence of his theory is concerned, they would be mere evasions. If he had insisted on them, or based his opposition solely upon them, our answer would have been simply this: "If you do not admit with us that fermentation *is* correlated with the life and nutrition of the ferment, we agree upon the principal point. So agreeing, let us examine, if you will, the actual cause of fermentation; —this is a second question, quite distinct from the first. Science is built up of successive solutions given to questions of ever increasing subtlety, approaching nearer and nearer towards the very essence of phenomena. If we proceed to discuss together the question of how living, organized beings act in decomposing fermentable substances, we will be found to fall out once more on your hypothesis of communicated motion, since according to our ideas, the actual cause of fermentation is to be sought, in most cases, in the fact of life without air, which is the characteristic of many ferments."

Let us briefly see what Liebig thinks of the experiment in which fermentation is produced by the impregnation of a saccharine mineral medium, a result so greatly at variance with his mode of viewing the question.[6] After deep consideration he pronounces this experiment to be inexact, and the result ill-founded. Liebig, however, was not one to reject a fact without grave reasons for doing so, or with the sole object of evading a troublesome discussion. "I have repeated this experiment," he says, "a great number of times, with the greatest possible care, and have obtained the same results as M. Pasteur, excepting as regards the formation and increase of the ferment." It was, however, the formation and increase of the ferment that constituted the point of the experiment. Our discussion was, therefore, distinctly limited

[6] See our *Mémoire* of 1860 (*Annales de Chimie et de Physique*, vol. lviii., p. 61, and following, especially pp. 69 and 70, where the details of the experiment will be found).

to this: Liebig denied that the ferment was capable of development in a saccharine mineral medium, whilst we asserted that this development did actually take place, and was comparatively easy to prove. In 1871 we replied to M. Liebig before the Paris Academy of Sciences in a Note, in which we offered to prepare in a mineral medium, in the presence of a commission to be chosen for the purpose, as great a weight of ferment as Liebig could reasonably demand.[7] We were bolder than we should, perhaps, have been in 1860; the reason was that our knowledge of the subject had been strengthened by ten years of renewed research. Liebig did not accept our proposal, nor did he even reply to our Note. Up to the time of his death, which took place on April 18th, 1873, he wrote nothing more on the subject.[8]

When we published, in 1860, the details of the experiment in question, we pointed out at some length the difficulties of conducting it successfully, and the possible causes of failure. We called attention particularly to the fact that saccharine mineral media are much more suited for the nutrition of bacteria, lactic ferment, and other lowly forms, than they are to that of yeast, and in consequence readily become filled with various organisms from the spontaneous growth of germs derived from the particles of dust floating in the atmosphere. The reason why we do not observe the growth of alcoholic ferments, especially at the commencement of the experiments, is because of the unsuitableness of those media for the life of yeast. The latter may, nevertheless, form in them subsequent to this development of other organized forms, by reason of the modification produced in the original

[7] PASTEUR, *Comptes rendus de l'Académie des Sciences,* vol. lxxiii., p. 1419, 1871.
[8] In his *Mémoir* of 1870, Liebig made a remarkable admission: "My late friend Pelouze," he says, "had communicated to me nine years ago certain results of M. Pasteur's researches on fermentation. I told him that just then I was not disposed to alter my opinion on the cause of fermentation, and that if it were possible, by means of ammonia, to produce or multiply the yeast in fermenting liquors, industry would soon avail itself of the fact, and that I would wait to see if it did so; up to the present time, however, there had not been the least change in the manufacture of yeast." We do not know what M. Pelouze's reply was; but it is not difficult to conceive so sagacious an observer remarking to his illustrious friend that the possibility of deriving pecuniary advantage from the wide application of a new scientific fact had never been regarded as the criterion of the exactness of that fact. We could prove, moreover, by the undoubted testimony of very distinguished practical men, notably by that of M. Pezeyre, director of distilleries, that upon this point also Liebig was mistaken.

mineral medium by the albuminous matters that they introduce into it. It is interesting to peruse, in our Memoir of 1860, certain facts of the same kind relating to fermentation by means of albumens—that of the blood for example, from which, we may mention incidentally, we were led to infer the existence of several distinct albumens in the serum, a conclusion which, since then, has been confirmed by various observers, notably by M. Béchamp. Now, in his experiments on fermentation in sweetened water, with yeast-ash and a salt of ammonia, there is no doubt that Liebig had failed to avoid those difficulties which are entailed by the spontaneous growth of other organisms than yeast. Moreover, it is possible that, to have established the certainty of this result, Liebig should have had recourse to a closer microscopical observation than from certain passages in his Memoir he seems to have adopted. We have little doubt that his pupils could tell us that Liebig did not even employ that instrument without which any exact study of fermentation is not merely difficult but well-nigh impossible. We ourselves, for the reasons mentioned, did not obtain a simple alcoholic fermentation any more than Liebig did. In that particular experiment, the details of which we gave in our Memoir of 1860, we obtained lactic and alcoholic fermentation together; an appreciable quantity of lactic acid formed and arrested the propagation of the lactic and alcoholic ferments, so that more than half of the sugar remained in the liquid without fermenting. This, however, in no way detracted from the correctness of the conclusion which we deduced from the experiment, and from other similar ones; it might even be said that, from a general and philosophical point of view—which is the only one of interest here—the result was doubly satisfactory, inasmuch as we demonstrated that mineral media were adapted to the simultaneous development of several organized ferments instead of only one. The fortuitous association of different ferments could not invalidate the conclusion that all the nitrogen of the cells of the alcoholic and lactic ferments was derived from the nitrogen in the ammoniacal salts, and that all the carbon of those ferments was taken from the sugar, since, in the medium employed in our experiment, the sugar was the only substance that contained car-

THEORY OF FERMENTATION

bon. Liebig carefully abstained from noticing this fact, which would have been fatal to the very groundwork of his criticisms, and thought that he was keeping up the appearance of a grave contradiction by arguing that we had never obtained a simple alcoholic fermentation. It would be unprofitable to dwell longer upon the subject of the difficulties which the propagation of yeast in a saccharine mineral medium formerly presented. As a matter of fact, the progress of our studies has imparted to the question an aspect very different from that which it formerly wore; it was this circumstance which emboldened us to offer, in our reply to Liebig before the Academy of Sciences in 1871, to prepare, in a saccharine mineral medium, in the presence of a commission to be appointed by our opponent, any quantity of ferment that he might require, and to effect the fermentation of any weight of sugar whatsoever.

Our knowledge of the facts detailed in the preceding chapter concerning pure ferments, and their manipulation in the presence of pure air, enables us completely to disregard those causes of embarrassment that result from the fortuitous occurrence of the germs of organisms different in character from the ferments introduced by the air or from the sides of vessels, or even by the ferment itself.

Let us once more take one of our double-necked flasks, which we will suppose is capable of containing three or four litres (six to eight pints).

Let us put into it the following:

```
Pure distilled water.
Sugar candy ........................ 200 grammes
Bitartrate of potassium ............. 1.0     "
     "       ammonia................. 0.5     "
Sulphate af ammonia................. 1.5     "
Ash of yeast........................ 1.5     "
         (1 gramme = 15.43 grains)
```

Let us boil the mixture, to destroy all germs of organisms that may exist in the air or liquid or on the sides of the flask, and then permit it to cool, after having placed, by way of extra precaution, a small quantity of asbestos in the end of the fine curved tube. Let us next introduce a trace of ferment into the liquid, through the other neck, which, as we have described, is terminated by a small piece of india-rubber tube closed with a glass stopper.

Here are the details of such an experiment:—

On December 9th, 1873, we sowed some pure ferment—saccharomyces pastorianus. From December 11, that is, within so short a time as forty-eight hours after impregnation, we saw a multitude of extremely minute bubbles rising almost continuously from the bottom, indication that at this point the fermentation had commenced. On the following days, several patches of froth appeared on the surface of the liquid. We left the flask undisturbed in the oven, at a temperature of 25° C. (77° F.) On April 24, 1874, we tested some of the liquid, obtained by means of the straight tube, to see if it still contained any sugar. We found that it contained less than two grammes, so that 198 grammes (4.2 oz. Troy) had already disappeared. Some time afterwards the fermentation came to an end; we carried on the experiment, nevertheless, until April 18, 1875.

There was no development of any organism absolutely foreign to the ferment, which was itself abundant, a circumstance that, added to the persistent vitality of the ferment, in spite of the unsuitableness of the medium for its nutrition, permitted the perfect completion of fermentation. There was not the minutest quantity of sugar remaining. The total weight of ferment, after washing and drying at 100° C. (212° F.), was 2.563 grammes (39.5 grains).

In experiments of this kind, in which the ferment has to be weighed, it is better not to use any yeast-ash that cannot be dissolved completely, so as to be capable of easy separation from the ferment formed. Raulin's liquid[9] may be used in such cases with success.

All the alcoholic ferments are not capable to the same extent of development by means of phosphates, ammoniacal salts, and sugar. There are some whose development is arrested a longer or shorter time before the transformation of all the sugar. In a series of comparative experiments, 200 grammes of sugar-candy being used in each case, we

[9] M. Jules Raulin has published a well-known and remarkable work on the discovery of the mineral medium best adapted by its composition to the life of certain fungoid growths; he has given a formula for the com-

found that whilst saccharomyces pastorianus effected a complete fermentation of the sugar, the caseous ferment did not decompose more than two-thirds, and the ferment we have designated *new "high" ferment* not more than one-fifth: and keeping the flasks for a longer time in the oven had no effect in increasing the proportions of sugar fermented in these two last cases.

We conducted a great number of fermentations in mineral media, in consequence of a circumstance which it may be interesting to mention here. A person who was working in our laboratory asserted that the success of our experiments depended upon the impurity of the sugar-candy which we employed, and that if this sugar had been pure—much purer than was the ordinary, white, commercial sugar-candy, which up to that time we had always used—the ferment could not have multiplied. The persistent objections of our friend, and our desire to convince him, caused us to repeat all our previous experiments on the subject, using sugar of great purity, which had been specially prepared for us, with the utmost care, by a skilful confectioner, Seugnot. The result only confirmed our former conclusions. Even this did not satisfy our obstinate friend, who went to the trouble of preparing some pure sugar for himself, in little crystals, by repeated crystallizations of carefully selected commercial sugar-candy; he then repeated our experiments himself. This time his doubts were overcome. It even happened that the fermentations with the perfectly pure sugar instead of being slow were very active, when compared with those which we had conducted with the commercial sugar-candy.

position of such a medium. It is this that we call here "Raulin's liquid" for abbreviation.

Water	1,500
Sugar candy	70
Tartaric acid	4
Nitrate of ammonia	4
Phosphate of ammonia	0.6
Carbonate of potassium	0.6
Carbonate of magnesia	0.4
Sulphate of ammonia	0.25
Sulphate of zinc	0.07
Sulphate of iron	0.07
Silicate of potassium	0.07

—J. Raulin, Paris, Victor Masson, 1870, *Thèse pour le doctorat.*

We may here add a few words on the non-transformation of yeast into *penicillium glaucum*.

If at any time during fermentation we pour off the fermenting liquid, the deposit of yeast remaining in the vessel may continue there, in contact with air, without our ever being able to discover the least formation of *penicillium glaucum* in it. We may keep a current of pure air constantly passing through the flask; the experiment will give the same result. Nevertheless, this is a medium peculiarly adapted to the development of this mould, inasmuch as if we were to introduce merely a few spores of *penicillium* an abundant vegetation of that growth will afterwards appear on the deposit. The descriptions of Messrs. Turpin, Hoffmann, and Trécul have, therefore, been based on one of these illusions which we meet with so frequently in microscopical observations.

When we laid these facts before the Academy,[10] M. Trécul professed his inability to comprehend them:[11] "According to M. Pasteur," he said, "the yeast of beer is *anaërobian*, that is to say, it lives in a liquid deprived of free oxygen; and to become *mycoderma* or *penicillium* it is above all things necessary that it should be placed in air, since, without this, as the name signifies, an aërobian being cannot exist. To bring about the transformation of the yeast of beer into *mycoderma cerevisiae* or into *penicillium glaucum* we must accept the conditions under which these two forms are obtained. If M. Pasteur will persist in keeping his yeast in media which are incompatible with the desired modification, it is clear that the results which he obtains must always be negative."

Contrary to this perfectly gratuitous assertion of M. Trécul's we do not keep our yeast in media which are calculated to prevent its transformation into *penicillium*. As we have just seen, the principal aim and object of our experiment was to bring this minute plant into contact with air, and under conditions that would allow the *penicillium* to develop with perfect freedom. We conducted our experiments exactly as Turpin and Hoffmann conducted theirs,

---

[10] Pasteur, *Comptes rendus de l'Académie*, vol. lxxviii., pp. 213-216.
[11] Trécul, *Comptes rendus de l'Académie*, vol. lxxviii., pp. 217, 218.

and exactly as they stipulate that such experiments should be conducted—with the one sole difference, indispensable to the correctness of our observations, that we carefully guarded ourselves against those causes of error which they did not take the least trouble to avoid. It is possible to produce a ready entrance and escape of pure air in the case of the double-necked flasks which we have so often employed in the course of this work, without having recourse to the continuous passage of a current of air. Having made a file-mark on the thin curved neck at a distance of two or three centimetres (an inch) from the flask, we must cut round the neck at this point with a glazier's diamond, and then remove it, taking care to cover the opening immediately with a sheet of paper which has been passed through the flame, and which we must fasten with a thread round the part of the neck still left. In this manner we may increase or prolong the fructification of fungoid growths, or the life of the aërobian ferments in our flasks.

What we have said of *penicillium glaucum* will apply equally to *mycoderma cerevisiae*. Notwithstanding that Turpin and Trécul may assert to the contrary, yeast, in contact with air as it was under the conditions of the experiment just described, will not yield *mycoderma vini* or *mycoderma cerevisiae* any more than it will *penicillium*.

The experiments described in the preceding paragraphs on the increase of organized ferments in mineral media of the composition described, are of the greatest physiological interest. Amongst other results, they show that all the proteic matter of ferments may be produced by the vital activity of the cells, which, apart altogether from the influence of light or free oxygen (unless indeed, we are dealing with aërobian moulds which require free oxygen), have the power of developing a chemical activity between carbohydrates, ammoniacal salts, phosphates, and sulphates of potassium and magnesium. It may be admitted with truth that a similar effect obtains in the case of the higher plants, so that in the existing state of science we fail to conceive what serious reason can be urged against our considering this effect as general. It would be perfectly logical to extend the results of which we are speaking to all plants, and to believe that the proteic matter of vegetables, and perhaps of animals also, is formed exclusively by the activity of the cells operating upon the ammoniacal and other mineral salts of the sap or plasma of the blood, and the carbo-hydrates, the formation of which, in the case of the higher plants, requires only the concurrence of the chemical impulse of green light.

Viewed in this manner, the formation of the proteic substances, would be independent of the great act of reduction of carbonic acid gas under the influence of light. These substances would not be built up from the elements of water, ammonia, and carbonic acid gas, after the decomposition of this last; they would be formed where they are found in the cells themselves, by some process of union between the carbo-hydrates imported by the sap, and the phosphates of potassium and magnesium and salts of ammonia. Lastly, in vegetable growth, by means of a carbo-hydrate and a mineral medium, since the carbo-hydrate is capable of many variations, and it would be difficult to understand how it could be split up into its elements before serving to constitute the proteic substances, and even cellulose substances, as these are carbo-hydrates. We have commenced certain studies in this direction.

If solar radiation is indispensable to the decomposition of carbonic acid and the building up of the primary substances in the case of higher vegetable life, it is still possible that certain inferior organisms may do without it and nevertheless yield the most complex substances, fatty or carbo-hydrate, such as cellulose, various organic acids, and proteic matter; not, however, by borrowing their carbon from the carbonic acid which is saturated with oxygen, but from other matters still capable of acquiring oxygen, and so of yielding heat in the process, such as alcohol and acetic acid, for example, to cite merely carbon compounds most removed from organization. As these last compounds, and a host of others equally adapted to serve as the carbonaceous food of *mycoderms* and the mucedines, may be produced synthetically by means of carbon and the vapour of water, after the methods that science owes to Berthelot, it follows that, in the case of certain inferior beings, life would be possible even if it should be that the solar light was extinguished.[12]

[12] See on this subject the verbal observations which we addressed to the Academy of Sciences at its meetings of April 10th and 24th, 1876.

THE GERM THEORY
AND ITS APPLICATIONS TO MEDICINE AND SURGERY[1]

THE Sciences gain by mutual support. When, as the result of my first communications on the fermentations in 1857-1858, it appeared that the ferments, properly so-called, are living beings, that the germs of microscopic organisms abound in the surface of all objects, in the air and in water; that the theory of spontaneous generation is chimerical; that wines, beer, vinegar, the blood, urine and all the fluids of the body undergo none of their usual changes in pure air, both Medicine and Surgery received fresh stimulation. A French physician, Dr. Davaine, was fortunate in making the first application of these principles to Medicine, in 1863.

Our researches of last year, left the etiology of the putrid disease, or septicemia, in a much less advanced condition than that of anthrax. We had demonstrated the probability that septicemia depends upon the presence and growth of a microscopic body, but the absolute proof of this important conclusion was not reached. To demonstrate experimentally that a microscopic organism actually is the cause of a disease and the agent of contagion, I know no other way, in the present state of Science, than to subject the *microbe* (the new and happy term introduced by M. Sedillot) to the method of cultivation out of the body. It may be noted that in twelve successive cultures, each one of only ten cubic centimeters volume, the original drop will be diluted as if placed in a volume of fluid equal to the total volume

[1] Read before the French Academy of Sciences, April 29th, 1878. Published in *Comptes Rendus de l'Académie des Sciences*, lxxxvi., pp. 1037-43.

THE GERM THEORY

of the earth. It is just this form of test to which M. Joubert and I subjected the anthrax bacteridium.[2] Having cultivated it a great number of times in a sterile fluid, each culture being started with a minute drop from the preceding, we then demonstrated that the product of the last culture was capable of further development and of acting in the animal tissues by producing anthrax with all its symptoms. Such is—as we believe—the indisputable proof that *anthrax is a bacterial disease.*

Our researches concerning the septic vibrio had not so far been convincing, and it was to fill up this gap that we resumed our experiments. To this end, we attempted the cultivation of the septic vibrio from an animal dead of septicemia. It is worth noting that all of our first experiments failed, despite the variety of culture media we employed—urine, beer yeast water, meat water, etc. Our culture media were not sterile, but we found—most commonly—a microscopic organism showing no relationship to the septic vibrio, and presenting the form, common enough elsewhere, of chains of extremely minute spherical granules possessed of no virulence whatever.[3] This was an impurity, introduced, unknown to us, at the same time as the septic vibrio; and the germ undoubtedly passed from the intestines —always inflamed and distended in septicemic animals— into the abdominal fluids from which we took our original cultures of the septic vibrio. If this explanation of the contamination of our cultures was correct, we ought to find a pure culture of the septic vibrio in the heart's blood of an animal recently dead of septicemia. This was what happened, but a new difficulty presented itself; all our cultures remained sterile. Furthermore this sterility was accompanied by loss in the culture media of (the original) virulence.

It occurred to us that the septic vibrio might be an obligatory anaërobe and that the sterility of our inoculated culture fluids might be due to the destruction of the septic

---

[2] In making the translation, it seems wiser to adhere to Pasteur's nomenclature. *Bacillus anthracis* would be the term employed to-day.—Translator.
[3] It is quite possible that Pasteur was here dealing with certain septicemic streptococci that are now known to lose their virulence with extreme rapidity under artificial cultivation.—Translator.

vibrio by the atmospheric oxygen dissolved in the fluids. The Academy may remember that I have previously demonstrated facts of this nature in regard to the vibrio of butyric fermentation, which not only lives without air but is killed by the air.

It was necessary therefore to attempt to cultivate the septic vibrio either in a vacuum or in the presence of inert gases—such as carbonic acid.

Results justified our attempt; the septic vibrio grew easily in a complete vacuum, and no less easily in the presence of pure carbonic acid.

These results have a necessary corollary. If a fluid containing septic vibrios be exposed to pure air, the vibrios should be killed and all virulence should disappear. This is actually the case. If some drops of septic serum be spread horizontally in a tube and in a very thin layer, the fluid will become absolutely harmless in less than half a day, even if at first it was so virulent as to produce death upon the inoculation of the smallest portion of a drop.

Furthermore all the vibrios, which crowded the liquid as motile threads, are destroyed and disappear. After the action of the air, only fine amorphous granules can be found, unfit for culture as well as for the transmission of any disease whatever. It might be said that the air burned the vibrios.

If it is a terrifying thought that life is at the mercy of the multiplication of these minute bodies, it is a consoling hope that Science will not always remain powerless before such enemies, since for example at the very beginning of the study we find that simple exposure to air is sufficient at times to destroy them.

But, if oxygen destroys the vibrios, how can septicemia exist, since atmospheric air is present everywhere? How can such facts be brought in accord with the germ theory? How can blood, exposed to air, become septic through the dust the air contains?

All things are hidden, obscure and debatable if the cause of the phenomena be unknown, but everything is clear if this cause be known. What we have just said is true only of a septic fluid containing adult vibrios, in active

THE GERM THEORY

development by fission: conditions are different when the vibrios are transformed into their germs,[4] that is into the glistening corpuscles first described and figured in my studies on silk-worm disease, in dealing with worms dead of the disease called "flachérie." Only the adult vibrios disappear, burn up, and lose their virulence in contact with air: the germ corpuscles, under these conditions, remain always ready for new cultures, and for new inoculations.

All this however does not do away with the difficulty of understanding how septic germs can exist on the surface of objects, floating in the air and in water.

Where can these corpuscles originate? Nothing is easier than the production of these germs, in spite of the presence of air in contact with septic fluids.

If abdominal serous exudate containing septic vibrios actively growing by fission be exposed to the air, as we suggested above, but with the precaution of giving a substantial thickness to the layer, even if only one centimeter be used, this curious phenomenon will appear in a few hours. The oxygen is absorbed in the upper layers of the fluid—as is indicated by the change of color. Here the vibrios are dead and disappear. In the deeper layers, on the other hand, towards the bottom of this centimeter of septic fluid we suppose to be under observation, the vibrios continue to multiply by fission—protected from the action of oxygen by those that have perished above them: little by little they pass over to the condition of germ corpuscles with the gradual disappearance of the thread forms. So that instead of moving threads of varying length, sometimes greater than the field of the microscope, there is to be seen only a number of glittering points, lying free or surrounded by a scarcely perceptible amorphous mass.[5] Thus is formed, containing the latent germ life, no longer in danger from the destructive action of oxygen, thus, I

[4] By the terms "germ" and "germ corpuscles," Pasteur undoubtedly means "spores," but the change is not made, in accordance with note 2, above.—Translator.

[5] In our note of July 16th, 1877, it is stated that the septic vibrio is not destroyed by the oxygen of the air nor by oxygen at high tension, but that under these conditions it is transformed into germ-corpuscles. This is, however, an incorrect interpretation of facts. The vibrio is destroyed by oxygen, and it is only where it is in a thick layer that it is transformed to germ-corpuscles in the presence of oxygen and that its virulence is preserved.

repeat, is formed the septic dust, and we are able to understand what has before seemed so obscure; we can see how putrescible fluids can be inoculated by the dust of the air, and how it is that putrid diseases are permanent in the world.

The Academy will permit me, before leaving these interesting results, to refer to one of their main theoretical consequences. At the very beginning of these researches, for they reveal an entirely new field, what must be insistently demanded? The absolute proof that there actually exist transmissible, contagious, infectious diseases of which the cause lies essentially and solely in the presence of microscopic organisms. The proof that for at least some diseases, the conception of spontaneous virulence must be forever abandoned—as well as the idea of contagion and an infectious element suddenly originating in the bodies of men or animals and able to originate diseases which propagate themselves under identical forms: and all of those opinions fatal to medical progress, which have given rise to the gratuitous hypotheses of spontaneous generation, of albuminoid ferments, of hemiorganisms, of archebiosis, and many other conceptions without the least basis in observation. What is to be sought for in this instance is the proof that along with our vibrio there does not exist an independent virulence belonging to the surrounding fluids or solids, in short that the vibrio is not merely an epiphenomenon of the disease of which it is the obligatory accompaniment. What then do we see, in the results that I have just brought out? A septic fluid, taken at the moment that the vibrios are not yet changed into germs, loses its virulence completely upon simple exposure to the air, but preserves this virulence, although exposed to air on the simple condition of being in a thick layer for some hours. In the first case, the virulence once lost by exposure to air, the liquid is incapable of taking it on again upon cultivation: but, in the second case, it preserves its virulence and can propagate, even after exposure to air. It is impossible, then, to assert that there is a separate virulent substance, either fluid or solid, existing, apart from the adult vibrio or its germ. Nor can it be supposed that there is a virus which loses its virulence at the moment that the adult vibrio dies; for such a substance should also lose its virulence when the vibrios, changed to germs, are exposed to the air. Since the virulence persists under these conditions it can only be due to the germ corpuscles—the only thing present. There is only one possible hypothesis as to the existence of a virus in solution, and that is that such a substance, which was present in our experiment in nonfatal amounts, should be continuously furnished by the vibrio itself, during its growth in the body of the living animal. But it is of little importance since the hypothesis supposes the forming and necessary existence of the vibrio.[6]

I hasten to touch upon another series of observations which are even more deserving the attention of the surgeon than the preceding: I desire to speak of the effects of our microbe of pus when associated with the septic vibrio. There is nothing more easy to superpose—as it were—two distinct diseases and to produce what might be called a *septicemic purulent infection,* or a *purulent septicemia.* Whilst the microbe-producing pus, when acting alone, gives rise to a thick pus, white, or sometimes with a yellow or bluish tint, not putrid, diffused or enclosed by the so-called *pyogenic membrane,* not dangerous, especially if localized in cellular tissue, ready, if the expression may be used for rapid resorption; on the other hand the smallest abscess produced by this organism when associated with the septic vibrio takes on a thick gangrenous appearance, putrid, greenish and infiltrating the softened tissues. In this case the microbe of pus carried so to speak by the septic vibrio, accompanies it throughout the body: the highly-inflamed muscular tissues, full of serous fluid, showing also globules of pus here and there, are like a kneading of the two organisms.

By a similar procedure the effects of the anthrax bacteridium and the microbe of pus may be combined and the two diseases may be superposed, so as to obtain a purulent anthrax or an anthracoid purulent infection. Care must be taken not to exaggerate the predominance of the new mi-

[6] The regular limits, oblige me to omit a portion of my speech.

crobe over the bacteridium. If the microbe be associated
with the latter in sufficient amount it may crowd it out
completely—prevent it from growing in the body at all.
Anthrax does not appear, and the infection, entirely local,
becomes merely an abscess whose cure is easy. The microbe-producing pus and the septic vibrio (not)[7] being both
anaërobes, as we have demonstrated, it is evident that
the latter will not much disturb its neighbor. Nutrient
substances, fluid or solid, can scarcely be deficient in the tissues from such minute organisms. But the anthrax bacteridium is exclusively aërobic, and the proportion of oxygen
is far from being equally distributed throughout the tissues:
innumerable conditions can diminish or exhaust the supply
here and there, and since the microbe-producing pus is
also aërobic, it can be understood how, by using a quantity slightly greater than that of the bacteridium it might
easily deprive the latter of the oxygen necessary for it.
But the explanation of the fact is of little importance:
it is certain that under some conditions the microbe we
are speaking of entirely prevents the development of the
bacteridium.

Summarizing—it appears from the preceding facts that
it is possible to produce at will, purulent infections with no
elements of putrescence, putrescent purulent infections, anthracoid purulent infections, and finally combinations of
these types of lesions varying according to the proportions
of the mixtures of the specific organisms made to act on
the living tissues.

These are the principal facts I have to communicate to
the Academy in my name and in the names of my collabora-
tors, Messrs. Joubert and Chamberland. Some weeks ago
(Session of the 11th of March last) a member of the Section of Medicine and Surgery, M. Sedillot, after long medi-
tation on the lessons of a brilliant career, did not hesitate
to assert that the successes as well as the failures of Surgery find a rational explanation in the principles upon
which the germ theory is based, and that this theory would

---

[7] There is undoubtedly a mistake in the original. Pasteur could not have meant to say that both bacteria are anaërobes. The word "not" is introduced to correct the error.—Translator.

found a new Surgery—already begun by a celebrated English surgeon, Dr. Lister,[8] who was among the first to understand its fertility. With no professional authority, but with the conviction of a trained experimenter, I venture here to repeat the words of an eminent *confrère*.

[8] See Lord Lister's paper in the present volume.—Ed.

ON THE EXTENSION OF THE GERM THEORY TO THE ETIOLOGY OF CERTAIN COMMON DISEASES[1]

WHEN I began the studies now occupying my attention,[2] I was attempting to extend the germ theory to certain common diseases. I do not know when I can return to that work. Therefore in my desire to see it carried on by others, I take the liberty of presenting it to the public in its present condition.

I. Furuncles. In May, 1879, one of the workers in my laboratory had a number of furuncles, appearing at short intervals, sometimes on one part of the body and sometimes on another. Constantly impressed with the thought of the immense part played by microscopic organisms in Nature, I queried whether the pus in the furuncles might not contain one of these organisms whose presence, development, and chance transportation here and there in the tissues after entrance would produce a local inflammation, and pus formation, and might explain the recurrence of the illness during a longer or shorter time. It was easy enough to subject this thought to the test of experiment.

First observation.—On June second, a puncture was made at the base of the small cone of pus at the apex of a furuncle on the nape of the neck. The fluid obtained was at once sowed in the presence of pure air—of course with the precautions necessary to exclude any foreign germs, either at the moment of puncture, at the moment of sowing in the culture fluid, or during the stay in the oven, which was

[1] Read before the French Academy of Sciences, May 3, 1880. Published in *Comptes rendus de l'Académie des Sciences*, xc., pp. 1033-44.
[2] In 1880. Especially engaged in the study of chicken cholera and the attenuation of virulence.—Translator.

kept at the constant temperature of about 35° C. The next day, the culture fluid had become cloudy and contained a single organism, consisting of small spherical points arranged in pairs, sometimes in fours, but often in irregular masses. Two fluids were preferred in these experiments—chicken and yeast bouillon. According as one or the other was used, appearances varied a little. These should be described. With the yeast water, the pairs of minute granules are distributed throughout the liquid, which is uniformly clouded. But with the chicken bouillon, the granules are collected in little masses which line the walls and bottom of the flasks while the body of the fluid remains clear, unless it be shaken: in this case it becomes uniformly clouded by the breaking up of the small masses from the walls of the flasks.

Second observation.—On the tenth of June a new furuncle made its appearance on the right thigh of the same person. Pus could not yet be seen under the skin, but this was already thickened and red over a surface the size of a franc. The inflamed part was washed with alcohol, and dried with blotting paper passed through the flame of an alcohol lamp. A puncture at the thickened portion enabled us to secure a small amount of lymph mixed with blood, which was sowed at the same time as some blood taken from the finger of the hand. The following days, the blood from the finger remained absolutely sterile: but that obtained from the center of the forming furuncle gave an abundant growth of the same small organism as before.

Third observation.—The fourteenth of June, a new furuncle appeared on the neck of the same person. The same examination, the same result, that is to say the development of the microscopic organism previously described and complete sterility of the blood of the general circulation, taken this time at the base of the furuncle outside of the inflamed area.

At the time of making these observations I spoke of them to Dr. Maurice Reynaud, who was good enough to send me a patient who had had furuncles for more than three months. On June thirteenth I made cultures of the pus from a furuncle of this man. The next day there was a general cloudiness of the culture fluids, consisting entirely of the preceding parasite, and of this alone.

Fourth observation.—June fourteenth, the same individual showed me a newly forming furuncle in the left axilla: there was wide-spread thickening and redness of the skin, but no pus was yet apparent. An incision at the center of the thickening showed a small quantity of pus mixed with blood. Sowing, rapid growth for twenty-four hours and the appearance of the same organism. Blood from the arm at a distance from the furuncle remained completely sterile.

June 17, the examination of a fresh furuncle on the same individual gave the same result, the development of a pure culture of the same organism.

Fifth observation.—July twenty-first, Dr. Maurice Reynaud informed me that there was a woman at the Lariboisière hospital with multiple furuncles. As a matter of fact her back was covered with them, some in active suppuration, others in the ulcerating stage. I took pus from all of these furuncles that had not opened. After a few hours, this pus gave an abundant growth in cultures. The same organism, without admixture, was found. Blood from the inflamed base of the furuncle remained sterile.

In brief, it appears certain that every furuncle contains an aërobic microscopic parasite, to which is due the local inflammation and the pus formation that follows.

Culture fluids containing the minute organism inoculated under the skin of rabbits and guinea-pigs produce abscesses generally small in size and that promptly heal. As long as healing is not complete the pus of the abscesses contains the microscopic organism which produced them. It is therefore living and developing, but its propagation at a distance does not occur. These cultures of which I speak, when injected in small quantities in the jugular vein of guinea-pigs show that the minute organism does not grow in the blood. The day after the injection they cannot be recovered even in cultures. I seem to have observed as a general principle, that, provided the blood corpuscles are in good physiological condition it is difficult for aërobic parasites to develop in the blood. I have always thought that this is to be explained by a kind of struggle between the affinity of the blood corpuscles for oxygen and that belonging to the parasite in cultures. Whilst the blood corpuscles carry off, that is, take possession of all the oxygen, the life and development of the parasite become extremely difficult or impossible. It is therefore easily eliminated, digested, if one may use the phrase. I have seen these facts many times in anthrax and chicken-cholera, diseases both of which are due to the presence of an aerobic parasite.

Blood cultures from the general circulation being always sterile in these experiments, it would seem that under the conditions of the furuncular diathesis, the minute parasite does not exist in the blood. That it cannot be cultivated for the reason given, and that it is not abundant is evident; but, from the sterility of the cultures reported (five only) it should not be definitely concluded that the little parasite may not, at some time, be taken up by the blood and transplanted from a furuncle when it is developing to another part of the body, where it may be accidentally lodged, may develop and produce a new furuncle. I am convinced that if, in cases of furuncular diathesis, not merely a few drops but several grams of blood from the general circulation could be placed under cultivation frequent successful growths would be obtained.[3] In the many experiments I have made on the blood in chicken-cholera, I have frequently demonstrated that repeated cultures from droplets of blood do not show an even development even where taken from the same organ, the heart for example, and at the moment when the parasite begins its existence in the blood, which can easily be understood. Once even, it happened that only three out of ten chickens died after inoculation with infectious blood in which the parasite had just began to appear, the remaining seven showed no symptoms whatever. In fact, the microbe, at the moment of beginning its entrance into the blood may exist singly or in minute numbers in one droplet and not at all in its immediate neighbor. I believe therefore that it would be extremely instructive in furunculosis, to find a patient willing to submit to a number of punctures in dif-

---

[3] This prediction is fully carried out in the present day successful use of considerable amounts of blood in cultures and the resultant frequent demonstrations of bacteria present in the circulation in many infections.— Translator.

ferent parts of the body away from formed or forming furuncles, and thus secure many cultures, simultaneous or otherwise, of the blood of the general circulation. I am convinced that among them would be found growths of the micro-organism of furuncles.

II. On Osteomyelitis. Single observation. I have but one observation relating to this severe disease, and in this Dr. Lannelongue took the initiative. The monograph on osteomyelitis published by this learned practitioner is well known, with his suggestion of the possibility of a cure by trephining the bone and the use of antiseptic washes and dressings. On the fourteenth of February, at the request of Dr. Lannelongue I went to the Sainte-Eugènie hospital, where this skillful surgeon was to operate on a little girl of about twelve years of age. The right knee was much swollen, as well as the whole leg below the calf and a part of the thigh above the knee. There was no external opening. Under chloroform, Dr. Lannelongue made a long incision below the knee which let out a large amount of pus; the tibia was found denuded for a long distance. Three places in the bone were trephined. From each of these, quantities of pus flowed. Pus from inside and outside the bone was collected with all possible precautions and was carefully examined and cultivated later. The direct microscopic study of the pus, both internal and external, was of extreme interest. It was seen that both contained large numbers of the organism similar to that of furuncles, arranged in pairs, in fours and in packets, some with sharp clear contour, others only faintly visible and with very pale outlines. The external pus contained many pus corpuscles, the internal had none at all. It was like a fatty paste of the furuncular organism. Also, it may be noted, that growth of the small organism had begun in less than six hours after the cultures were started. Thus I saw, that it corresponded exactly with the organism of furuncles. The diameter of the individuals was found to be one one-thousandth of a millimeter. If I ventured to express myself so I might say that in this case at least the osteomyelitis was really a furuncle of the bone marrow.[*] It is undoubtedly easy to induce osteomyelitis artificially in living animals.

III. On puerperal fever.—First observation. On the twelfth of March, 1878, Dr. Hervieux was good enough to admit me to his service in the Maternity to visit a woman delivered some days before and seriously ill with puerperal fever. The lochia were extremely fetid. I found them full of micro-organisms of many kinds. A small amount of blood was obtained from a puncture on the index finger of the left hand, (the finger being first properly washed and dried with a *sterile* towel,) and then sowed in chicken bouillon. The culture remained sterile during the following days.

The thirteenth, more blood was taken from a puncture in the finger and this time growth occurred. As death took place on the sixteenth of March at six in the morning, it seems that the blood contained a microscopic parasite at least three days before.

The fifteenth of March, eighteen hours before death, blood from a needle-prick in the left foot was used. This culture also was fertile.

The first culture, of March thirteenth, contained only the organism of furuncles; the next one, that of the fifteenth, contained an organism resembling that of furunculosis, but which always differed enough to make it easy usually to distinguish it. In this way; whilst the parasite of furuncles is arranged in pairs, very rarely in chains of three or four elements, the new one, that of the culture of the fifteenth, occurs in long chains, the number of cells in each being indefinite. The chains are flexible and often appear as little tangled packets like tangled strings of pearls.

The autopsy was performed on the seventeenth at two o'clock. There was a large amount of pus in the peritoneum. It was sowed with all possible precautions. Blood from the basilic and femoral veins was also sowed. So also was pus from the mucous surface of the uterus, from the tubes, and finally that from a lymphatic in the uterine wall. These are the results of these cultures: in all there were the long chains of cells just spoken of above, and nowhere any mixture of other organisms, except in the culture from the peritoneal pus, which, in addition to the long

⁴ This has been demonstrated, as is well known.—Translator.

chains, also contained the small pyogenic vibrio which I describe under the name *organism of pus* in the Note I published with Messrs. Joubert and Chamberland on the thirtieth of April, 1878.[5]

Interpretation of the disease and of the death.—After confinement, the pus that always naturally forms in the injured parts of the uterus instead of remaining pure becomes contaminated with microscopic organisms from outside, notably the organism in long chains and the pyogenic vibrio. These organisms pass into the peritoneal cavity through the tubes or by other channels, and some of them into the blood, probably by the lymphatics. The resorption of the pus, always extremely easy and prompt when it is pure, becomes impossible through the presence of the parasites, whose entrance must be prevented by all possible means from the moment of confinement.

Second observation.—The fourteenth of March, a woman died of puerperal fever at the Lariboisière hospital; the abdomen was distended before death.

Pus was found in abundance by a peritoneal puncture and was sowed; so also was blood from a vein in the arm. The culture of pus yielded the long chains noted in the preceding observation and also the small pyogenic vibrio. The culture from the blood contained only the long chains.

Third observation.—The seventeenth of May, 1879, a woman, three days past confinement, was ill, as well as the child she was nursing. The lochia were full of the pyogenic vibrio and of the organism of furuncles, although there was but a small proportion of the latter. The milk and the lochia were sowed. The milk gave the organism in long chains of granules, and the lochia only the pus organism. The mother died, and there was no autopsy.

On May twenty-eighth, a rabbit was inoculated under the skin of the abdomen with five drops of the preceding culture of the pyogenic vibrio. The days following an enormous abscess formed which opened spontaneously on the fourth of June. An abundantly cheesy pus came from it. About the abscess there was extensive induration. On the eighth of June, the opening of the abscess was larger, the suppuration

[5] See preceding paper.

active. Near its border was another abscess, evidently joined with the first, for upon pressing it with the finger, pus flowed freely from the opening in the first abscess. During the whole of the month of June, the rabbit was sick and the abscesses suppurated, but less and less. In July they closed; the animal was well. There could only be felt some nodules under the skin of the abdomen.

What disturbances might not such an organism carry into the body of a parturient woman, after passing into the peritoneum, the lymphatics or the blood through the maternal placenta! Its presence is much more dangerous than that of the parasite arranged in chains. Furthermore, its development is always threatening, because, as said in the work already quoted (April, 1878) this organism can be easily recovered from many ordinary waters.

I may add that the organism in long chains, and that arranged in pairs are also extremely widespread, and that one of their habitats is the mucous surfaces of the genital tract.[6]

Apparently there is no puerperal parasite, properly speaking. I have not encountered true septicemia in my experiments: but it ought to be among the puerperal affections.

Fourth observation.—On June fourteenth, at the Lariboisière, a woman was very ill following a recent confinement: she was at the point of death: in fact she did die on the fourteenth at midnight. Some hours before death pus was taken from an abscess on the arm, and blood from a puncture in a finger. Both were sowed. On the next day (the fifteenth) the flask containing the pus from the abscess was filled with long chains of granules. The flask containing the blood was sterile. The autopsy was at ten o'clock on the morning of the sixteenth. Blood from a vein of the arm, pus from the uterine walls and that from a collection in the synovial sac of the knee were all placed in culture media. All showed growth, even the blood, and they all contained the long strings of granules. The peritoneum contained no pus.

[6] When, by the procedure I elsewhere described, urine is removed in a pure condition by the urethra from the bladder, if any chance growth occurs through some error of technic, it is the two organisms of which I have been speaking that are almost exclusively present.

Interpretation of the disease and of the death.—The injury of the uterus during confinement as usual furnished pus, which gave a lodging place for the germs of the long chains of granules. These, probably through the lymphatics, passed to the joints and to some other places, thus being the origin of the metastic abscesses which produced death.

Fifth observation.—On June seventeenth, M. Doléris, a well-known hospital interne, brought to me some blood, removed with the necessary precautions, from a child dead immediately after birth, whose mother, before confinement had had febrile symptoms with chills. This blood, upon cultivation, gave an abundance of the pyogenic vibrio. On the other hand, blood taken from the mother on the morning of the eighteenth (she had died at one o'clock that morning) showed no development whatever, on the nineteenth nor on following days. The autopsy on the mother took place on the nineteenth. It is certainly worthy of note that the uterus, peritoneum and intestines showed nothing special, but the liver was full of metastatic abscesses. At the exit of the hepatic vein from the liver there was pus, and its walls were ulcerated at this place. The pus from the liver abscesses was filled with the pyogenic vibrio. Even the liver tissues, at a distance from the visible abscesses, gave abundant cultures of the same organism.

Interpretation of the disease and of the death.—The pyogenic vibrio, found in the uterus, or which was perhaps already in the body of the mother, since she suffered from chills before confinement, produced metastatic abscesses in the liver and, carried to the blood of the child, there induced one of the forms of infection called purulent, which caused its death.

Sixth observation.—The eighteenth of June, 1879, M. Doléris informed me that a woman confined some days before at the Cochin Hospital, was very ill. On the twentieth of June, blood from a needle-prick in the finger was sowed; the culture was sterile. On July fifteenth, that is to say twenty-five days later, the blood was tried again. Still no growth. There was no organism distinctly recognizable in the lochia: the woman was nevertheless, they told me, dangerously ill and at the point of death. As a matter of fact, she did die on the eighteenth of July at nine in the morning: as may be seen, after a very long illness, for the first observations were made over a month before: the illness was also very painful, for the patient could make no movement without intense suffering.

An autopsy was made on the nineteenth at ten in the morning, and was of great interest. There was purulent pleurisy with a considerable pocket of pus, and purulent false membranes on the walls of the pleura. The liver was bleached, fatty, but of firm consistency, and with no apparent metastatic abscesses. The uterus, of small size, appeared healthy; but on the external surface whitish nodules filled with pus were found. *There was nothing in the peritoneum, which was not inflamed;* but there was much pus in the shoulder joints and the symphysis pubis.

The pus from the abscesses, upon cultivation, gave the long chains of granules—not only that of the pleura, but that from the shoulders and a lymphatic of the uterus as well. An interesting thing, but easily understood, was that the blood from a vein in the arm and taken three-quarters of an hour after death was entirely sterile. Nothing grew from the Fallopian tubes nor the broad ligaments.

Interpretation of the disease and of the death.—The pus found in the uterus after confinement became infected with germs of microscopic organisms which grew there, then passed into the uterine lymphatics, and from there went on to produce pus in the pleura and in the articulations.

Seventh observation.—On June eighteenth, M. Doléris informed me that a woman had been confined at the Cochin Hospital five days before and that fears were entertained as to the results of an operation that had been performed, it having been necessary to do an embryotomy. The lochia were sowed on the 18th; there was not the slightest trace of growth the next day nor the day after. Without the least knowledge of this woman since the eighteenth, on the twentieth I ventured to assert that she would get well. I sent to inquire about her. This is the text of the report: "*The woman is doing extremely well; she goes out tomorrow.*"

Interpretation of the facts.—The pus naturally formed on the surface of the injured parts did not become contaminated with organisms brought from without. *Natura medicatrix* carried it off, that is to say the vitality of the mucous surfaces prevented the development of foreign germs. The pus was easily resorbed, and recovery took place.

I beg the Academy to permit me, in closing, to submit certain definite views, which I am strongly inclined to consider as legitimate conclusions from the facts I have had the honor to communicate to it.

Under the expression *puerperal fever* are grouped very different diseases,[7] but all appearing to be the result of the growth of common organisms which by their presence infect the pus naturally formed on injured surfaces, which spread by one means or another, by the blood or the lymphatics, to one or another part of the body, and there induce morbid changes varying with the condition of the parts, the nature of the parasite, and the general constitution of the subject.

Whatever this constitution, does it not seem that by taking measures opposing the production of these common parasitic organisms recovery would usually occur, except perhaps when the body contains, before confinement, microscopic organisms, in contaminated internal or external abscesses, as was seen in one striking example (fifth observation). The antiseptic method I believe likely to be sovereign in the vast majority of cases. It seems to me that *immediately after confinement* the application of antiseptics should be begun. Carbolic acid can render great service, but there is another antiseptic, the use of which I am strongly inclined to advise, this is boric acid in concentrated solution, that is, four per cent. at the ordinary temperature. This acid, whose singular influence on cell life has been shown by M. Dumas, is so slightly acid that it is alkaline to certain test papers, as was long ago shown by M. Chevreul, besides this it has no odor like carbolic acid, which odor often disturbs the sick. Lastly, its lack of hurtful effects on mucous membranes, notably of the bladder, has been and is daily demon-

---

[7] Interesting as the starting point of the conception of diseases according to the etiological factor, not by groups of symptoms.—Translator.

strated in the hospitals of Paris. The following is the occasion upon which it was first used. The Academy may remember that I stated before it, and the fact has never been denied, that ammoniacal urine is always produced by a microscopic organism, entirely similar in many respects to the organism of furuncles. Later, in a joint investigation with M. Joubert, we found that a solution of boric acid was easily fatal to these organisms. After that, in 1877, I induced Dr. Guyon, in charge of the genito-urinary clinic at the Necker hospital, to try injections of a solution of boric acid in affections of the bladder. I am informed by this skilful practitioner that he has done so, and daily observes good results from it. He also tells me that he performs no operation of lithotrity without the use of similar injections. I recall these facts to show that a solution of boric acid is entirely harmless to an extremely delicate mucous membrane, that of the bladder, and that it is possible to fill the bladder with a warm solution of boric acid without even inconvenience.

To return to the confinement cases. Would it not be of great service to place a warm concentrated solution of boric acid, and compresses, at the bedside of each patient; which she could renew frequently after saturating with the solution, and this also after confinement. It would also be acting the part of prudence to place the compresses, before using, in a hot air oven at 150° C., more than enough to kill the germs of the common organisms.[8]

Was I justified in calling this communication *" On the extension of the germ theory to the etiology of certain common diseases?"* I have detailed the facts as they have appeared to me and I have mentioned interpretations of them: but I do not conceal from myself that, in medical territory, it is difficult to support one's self wholly on subjective foundations. I do not forget that Medicine and Veterinary practice are foreign to me. I desire judgment and criticism upon all my contributions. Little tolerant of frivolous or prejudiced contradiction, contemptuous of that ignorant criticism which doubts on principle, I welcome with open arms

[8] The adoption of precautions, similar to those here suggested, has resulted in the practically complete disappearance of puerperal fever.—Translator.

the militant attack which has a method in doubting and whose rule of conduct has the motto " More light."

It is a pleasure once more to acknowledge the helpfulness of the aid given me by Messrs. Chamberland and Roux during the studies I have just recorded. I wish also to acknowledge the great assistance of M. Doléris.

PREJUDICES WHICH HAVE RETARDED THE PROGRESS OF GEOLOGY

UNIFORMITY IN THE SERIES OF PAST CHANGES IN THE ANIMATE AND INANIMATE WORLD

BY
SIR CHARLES LYELL

INTRODUCTORY NOTE

Sir Charles Lyell *was born near Kirriemuir, Forfarshire, Scotland, on November 14, 1797. He graduated from Exeter College, Oxford, in 1819, and proceeded to the study of law. Although he practised for a short time, he was much hampered in this profession, as in all his work, by weak eyesight; and after the age of thirty he devoted himself chiefly to science.*

Lyell's father was a botanist of some distinction, and the son seems to have been interested in natural history from an early age. While still an undergraduate he made geological journeys in Scotland and on the Continent of Europe, and throughout his life he upheld by precept and example the importance of travel for the geologist.

The first edition of his "Principles of Geology" was published in 1830; and the phrase used in the sub-title, "an attempt to explain the former changes of the earth's surface, by reference to causes now in action," strikes the keynote of his whole work. All his life he continued to urge this method of explanation in opposition to the hypotheses, formerly much in vogue, which assumed frequent catastrophes to account for geologic changes. The chapters here printed give his own final statement of his views on this important issue.

Lyell's scientific work received wide recognition: he was more than once President of the Geological Society, in 1864 was President of the British Association, was knighted in 1848, and made a baronet in 1864. He possessed a broad general culture, and his home was a noted center of the intellectual life of London. He twice came to the United States to lecture, and created great interest. On his death, on February 22, 1875, he was buried in Westminster Abbey.

Persistent as were Lyell's efforts for the establishment of his main theory, he remained remarkably open-minded; and when the evolutionary hypothesis was put forward he became a warm supporter of it. Darwin in his autobiography thus sums up Lyell's achievement: "The science of geology is enormously indebted to Lyell—more so, as I believe, than to any other man who ever lived."

THE PROGRESS OF GEOLOGY[1]

I

PREPOSSESSIONS IN REGARD TO THE DURATION OF PAST TIME—PREJUDICES ARISING FROM OUR PECULIAR POSITION AS INHABITANTS OF THE LAND—OTHERS OCCASIONED BY OUR NOT SEEING SUBTERRANEAN CHANGES NOW IN PROGRESS—ALL THESE CAUSES COMBINE TO MAKE THE FORMER COURSE OF NATURE APPEAR DIFFERENT FROM THE PRESENT—OBJECTIONS TO THE DOCTRINE THAT CAUSES SIMILAR IN KIND AND ENERGY TO THOSE NOW ACTING, HAVE PRODUCED THE FORMER CHANGES OF THE EARTH'S SURFACE CONSIDERED

IF WE reflect on the history of the progress of geology * * * we perceive that there have been great fluctuations of opinion respecting the nature of the causes to which all former changes of the earth's surface are referable. The first observers conceived the monuments which the geologist endeavours to decipher to relate to an original state of the earth, or to a period when there were causes in activity, distinct, in a kind and degree, from those now constituting the economy of nature. These views were gradually modified, and some of them entirely abandoned, in proportion as observations were multiplied, and the signs of former mutations were skilfully interpreted. Many appearances, which had for a long time been regarded as indicating mysterious and extraordinary agency, were finally recognised as the necessary result of the laws now governing the material world; and the discovery of this unlooked-for conformity has at length induced some philosophers to infer, that, during the ages contemplated in geology, there has never been any interruption to the agency of the same uni-

---

[1] The text of the two following papers is taken from the 11th edition of Lyell's Principles of Geology, the last edition revised by the author.

form laws of change. The same assemblage of general causes, they conceive, may have been sufficient to produce, by their various combinations, the endless diversity of effects, of which the shell of the earth has preserved the memorials; and, consistently with these principles, the recurrence of analogous changes is expected by them in time to come.

Whether we coincide or not in this doctrine we must admit that the gradual progress of opinion concerning the succession of phenomena in very remote eras, resembles, in a singular manner, that which has accompanied the growing intelligence of every people, in regard to the economy of nature in their own times. In an early state of advancement, when a greater number of natural appearances are unintelligible, an eclipse, an earthquake, a flood, or the approach of a comet, with many other occurrences afterwards found to belong to the regular course of events, are regarded as prodigies. The same delusion prevails as to moral phenomena, and many of these are ascribed to the intervention of demons, ghosts, witches, and other immaterial and supernatural agents. By degrees, many of the enigmas of the moral and physical world are explained, and, instead of being due to extrinsic and irregular causes, they are found to depend on fixed and invariable laws. The philosopher at last becomes convinced of the undeviating uniformity of secondary causes; and, guided by his faith in this principle, he determines the probability of accounts transmitted to him of former occurrences, and often rejects the fabulous tales of former times, on the ground of their being irreconcilable with the experience of more enlightened ages.

Prepossessions in regard to the duration of past time.—As a belief in the want of conformity in the cause by which the earth's crust has been modified in ancient and modern periods was, for a long time, universally prevalent, and that, too, amongst men who were convinced that the order of nature had been uniform for the last several thousand years, every circumstance which could have influenced their minds and given an undue bias to their opinions deserves particular attention. Now the reader may easily satisfy himself, that, however undeviating the course of nature may have been from the earliest epochs, it was impossible for the first cultivators of geology to come to such a conclusion, so long as they were under a delusion as to the age of the world, and the date of the first creation of animate beings. However fantastical some theories of the sixteenth century may now appear to us,—however unworthy of men of great talent and sound judgment,—we may rest assured that, if the same misconception now prevailed in regard to the memorials of human transactions, it would give rise to a similar train of absurdities. Let us imagine, for example, that Champollion, and the French and Tuscan literati when engaged in exploring the antiquities of Egypt, had visited that country with a firm belief that the banks of the Nile were never peopled by the human race before the beginning of the nineteenth century, and that their faith in this dogma was as difficult to shake as the opinion of our ancestors, that the earth was never the abode of living beings until the creation of the present continents, and of the species now existing,—it is easy to perceive what extravagant systems they would frame, while under the influence of this delusion, to account for the monuments discovered in Egypt. The sight of the pyramids, obelisks, colossal statues, and ruined temples, would fill them with such astonishment, that for a time they would be as men spell-bound—wholly incapable of reasoning with sobriety. They might incline at first to refer the construction of such stupendous works to some superhuman powers of the primeval world. A system might be invented resembling that so gravely advanced by Manetho, who relates that a dynasty of gods originally ruled in Egypt, of whom Vulcan, the first monarch, reigned nine thousand years; after whom came Hercules and other demigods, who were at last succeeded by human kings.

When some fanciful speculations of this kind had amused their imaginations for a time, some vast repository of mummies would be discovered, and would immediately undeceive those antiquaries who enjoyed an opportunity of personally examining them; but the prejudices of others at a distance, who were not eye-witnesses of the whole phenomena, would not be so easily overcome. The concurrent report of many travellers would, indeed, render it necessary for them to accommodate ancient theories to some of the new facts, and much wit and ingenuity would be required to modify and defend their old positions. Each new invention would violate a greater number of known analogies; for if a theory be required to embrace some false principle, it becomes more visionary in proportion as facts are multiplied, as would be the case if geometers were now required to form an astronomical system on the assumption of the immobility of the earth.

Amongst other fanciful conjectures concerning the history of Egypt, we may suppose some of the following to be started. 'As the banks of the Nile have been so recently colonized for the first time, the curious substances called mummies could never in reality have belonged to men. They may have been generated by some *plastic virtue* residing in the interior of the earth, or they may be abortions of Nature produced by her incipient efforts in the work of creation. For if deformed beings are sometimes born even now, when the scheme of the universe is fully developed, many more may have been " sent before their time scarce half made up," when the planet itself was in the embryo state. But if these notions appear to derogate from the perfection of the Divine attributes, and if these mummies be in all their parts true representations of the human form, may we not refer them to the future rather than the past? May we not be looking into the womb of Nature, and not her grave? May not these images be like the shades of the unborn in Virgil's Elysium—the archetypes of men not yet called into existence?'

These speculations, if advocated by eloquent writers, would not fail to attract many zealous votaries, for they would relieve men from the painful necessity of renouncing preconceived opinions. Incredible as such scepticism may appear, it has been rivalled by many systems of the sixteenth and seventeenth centuries, and among others by that of the learned Falloppio, who, as we have seen (p. 33), regarded the tusks of fossil elephants as earthly concretions, and the pottery or fragments of vases in the Monte Testaceo, near Rome, as works of nature, and not of art. But when one generation had passed away, and another, not compromised to the support of antiquated dogmas, had succeeded, they would review the evidence afforded by mummies more impartially, and would no longer controvert the preliminary question, that human beings had lived in Egypt before the nineteenth century: so that when a hundred years perhaps had been lost, the industry and talents of the philosopher would be at last directed to the elucidation of points of real historical importance.

But the above arguments are aimed against one only of many prejudices with which the earlier geologists had to contend. Even when they conceded that the earth had been peopled with animate beings at an earlier period than was at first supposed, they had no conception that the quantity of time bore so great a proportion to the historical era as is now generally conceded. How fatal every error as to the quantity of time must prove to the introduction of rational views concerning the state of things in former ages, may be conceived by supposing the annals of the civil and military transactions of a great nation to be perused under the impression that they occurred in a period of one hundred instead of two thousand years. Such a portion of history would immediately assume the air of a romance; the events would seem devoid of credibility, and inconsistent with the present course of human affairs. A crowd of incidents would follow each other in thick succession. Armies and fleets would appear to be assembled only to be destroyed, and cities built merely to fall in ruins. There would be the most violent transitions from foreign or intestine war to periods of profound peace, and the works effected during the years of disorder or tranquillity would appear alike superhuman in magnitude.

He who should study the monuments of the natural world under the influence of a similar infatuation, must draw a no less exaggerated picture of the energy and violence of causes, and must experience the same insurmountable difficulty in reconciling the former and present state of nature. If we could behold in one view all the volcanic cones thrown up in Iceland, Italy, Sicily, and other parts of Europe, during the last five thousand years, and could see the lavas which have flowed during the same period; the dislocations, subsidences, and elevations caused during earthquakes; the lands added to various deltas, or devoured by the sea, together with the effects of devastation by floods, and imagine that all these events had happened in one year, we must form most exalted ideas of the activity of the agents, and the suddenness of the revolutions. If geologists, therefore, have misinterpreted the signs of a succession of events, so as to conclude that centuries were implied where the characters indicated thousands of years, and thousands of years where the language of Nature signified millions, they could not, if they reasoned logically from such false premises, come to any other conclusion than that the system of the natural world had undergone a complete revolution.

We should be warranted in ascribing the erection of the great pyramid to superhuman power, if we were convinced that it was raised in one day; and if we imagine, in the same manner, a continent or mountain-chain to have been elevated during an equally small fraction of the time which was really occupied in upheaving it, we might then be justified in inferring, that the subterranean movements were once far more energetic than in our own times. We know that during one earthquake the coast of Chili may be raised for a hundred miles to the average height of about three feet. A repetition of two thousand shocks, of equal violence, might produce a mountain-chain one hundred miles long, and six thousand feet high. Now, should one or two only of these convulsions happen in a century, it would be consistent with the order of events experienced by the Chilians from the earliest times: but if the whole of them were to occur in the next hundred years, the entire district must be depopulated, scarcely any animals or plants could survive, and the surface would be one confused heap of ruin and desolation.

One consequence of undervaluing greatly the quantity of past time, is the apparent coincidence which it occasions of events necessarily disconnected, or which are so unusual, that it would be inconsistent with all calculation of chances to suppose them to happen at one and the same time. When the unlooked-for association of such rare phenomena is witnessed in the present course of nature, it scarcely ever fails to excite a suspicion of the preternatural in those minds which are not firmly convinced of the uniform agency of

THE PROGRESS OF GEOLOGY

secondary causes;—as if the death of some individual in whose fate they are interested happens to be accompanied by the appearance of a luminous meteor, or a comet, or the shock of an earthquake. It would be only necessary to multiply such coincidences indefinitely, and the mind of every philosopher would be disturbed. Now it would be difficult to exaggerate the number of physical events, many of them most rare and unconnected in their nature, which were imagined by the Woodwardian hypothesis to have happened in the course of a few months: and numerous other examples might be found of popular geological theories, which require us to imagine that a long succession of events happened in a brief and almost momentary period.

Another liability to error, very nearly allied to the former, arises from the frequent contact of geological monuments referring to very distant periods of time. We often behold, at one glance, the effects of causes which have acted at times incalculably remote, and yet there may be no striking circumstances to mark the occurrence of a great chasm in the chronological series of Nature's archives. In the vast interval of time which may really have elapsed between the results of operations thus compared, the physical condition of the earth may, by slow and insensible modifications, have become entirely altered; one or more races of organic beings may have passed away, and yet have left behind, in the particular region under contemplation, no trace of their existence.

To a mind unconscious of these intermediate events, the passage from one state of things to another must appear so violent, that the idea of revolutions in the system inevitably suggests itself. The imagination is as much perplexed by the deception, as it might be if two distant points in space were suddenly brought into immediate proximity. Let us suppose, for a moment, that a philosopher should lie down to sleep in some arctic wilderness, and then be transferred by a power, such as we read of in tales of enchantment, to a valley in a tropical country, where, on awaking, he might find himself surrounded by birds of brilliant plumage, and all the luxuriance of animal and vegetable forms of which Nature is so prodigal in those regions. The most reasonable supposition, perhaps, which he could make, if by the necromancer's art he were placed in such a situation, would be, that he was dreaming; and if a geologist form theories under a similar delusion, we cannot expect him to preserve more consistency in his speculations, than in the train of ideas in an ordinary dream.

It may afford, perhaps, a more lively illustration of the principle here insisted upon, if I recall to the reader's recollection the legend of the Seven Sleepers. The scene of that popular fable was placed in the two centuries which elapsed between the reign of the emperor Decius and the death of Theodosius the younger. In that interval of time (between the years 249 and 450 of our era) the union of the Roman empire had been dissolved, and some of its fairest provinces overrun by the barbarians of the north. The seat of government had passed from Rome to Constantinople, and the throne from a pagan persecutor to a succession of Christian and orthodox princes. The genius of the empire had been humbled in the dust, and the altars of Diana and Hercules were on the point of being transferred to Catholic saints and martyrs. The legend relates, 'that when Decius was still persecuting the Christians, seven noble youths of Ephesus concealed themselves in a spacious cavern in the side of an adjacent mountain, where they were doomed to perish by the tyrant, who gave orders that the entrance should be firmly secured with a pile of huge stones. They immediately fell into a deep slumber, which was miraculously prolonged, without injuring the powers of life, during a period of 187 years. At the end of that time the slaves of Adolius, to whom the inheritance of the mountain had descended, removed the stones to supply materials for some rustic edifice: the light of the sun darted into the cavern, and the seven sleepers were permitted to awake. After a slumber, as they thought, of a few hours, they were pressed by the calls of hunger, and resolved that Jamblichus, one of their number, should secretly return to the city to purchase bread for the use of his companions. The youth could no longer recognise the once familiar aspect of his native country, and his surprise was increased by the appearance of a large cross triumphantly erected over the principal gate of

Ephesus. His singular dress and obsolete language confounded the baker, to whom he offered an ancient medal of Decius as the current coin of the empire; and Jamblichus, on the suspicion of a secret treasure, was dragged before the judge. Their mutual enquiries produced the amazing discovery, that two centuries were almost elapsed since Jamblichus and his friends had escaped from the rage of a pagan tyrant.'

This legend was received as authentic throughout the Christian world before the end of the sixth century, and was afterwards introduced by Mahomet as a divine revelation into the Koran, and from hence was adopted and adorned by all the nations from Bengal to Africa who professed the Mahometan faith. Some vestiges even of a similar tradition have been discovered in Scandinavia. 'This easy and universal belief,' observes the philosophical historian of the Decline and Fall, 'so expressive of the sense of mankind, may be ascribed to the genuine merit of the fable itself. We imperceptibly advance from youth to age, without observing the gradual, but incessant, change of human affairs; and even, in our larger experience of history, the imagination is accustomed, by a perpetual series of causes and effects, to unite the most distant revolutions. But if the interval between two memorable eras could be instantly annihilated; if it were possible, after a momentary slumber of two hundred years, to display the new world to the eyes of a spectator who still retained a lively and recent impression of the old, his surprise and his reflections would furnish the pleasing subject of a philosophical romance.'[2]

Prejudices arising from our peculiar position as inhabitants of the land.—The sources of prejudice hitherto considered may be deemed peculiar for the most part to the infancy of the science, but others are common to the first cultivators of geology and to ourselves, and are all singularly calculated to produce the same deception, and to strengthen our belief that the course of Nature in the earlier ages differed widely from that now established. Although these circumstances cannot be fully explained without assuming some things as proved, which it has been my object else-

[2] Gibbon, Decline and Fall, chap. xxxiii.

where to demonstrate,[2] it may be well to allude to them briefly in this place.

The first and greatest difficulty, then, consists in an habitual unconsciousness that our position as observers is essentially unfavourable, when we endeavour to estimate the nature and magnitude of the changes now in progress. In consequence of our inattention to this subject, we are liable to serious mistakes in contrasting the present with former states of the globe. As dwellers on the land, we inhabit about a fourth part of the surface; and that portion is almost exclusively a theatre of decay, and not of reproduction. We know, indeed, that new deposits are annually formed in seas and lakes, and that every year some new igneous rocks are produced in the bowels of the earth, but we cannot watch the progress of their formation, and as they are only present to our minds by the aid of reflection, it requires an effort both of the reason and the imagination to appreciate duly their importance. It is, therefore, not surprising that we estimate very imperfectly the result of operations thus unseen by us; and that, when analogous results of former epochs are presented to our inspection, we cannot immediately recognise the analogy. He who has observed the quarrying of stone from a rock, and has seen it shipped for some distant port, and then endeavours to conceive what kind of edifice will be raised by the materials, is in the same predicament as a geologist, who, while he is confined to the land, sees the decomposition of rocks, and the transportation of matter by rivers to the sea, and then endeavours to picture to himself the new strata which Nature is building beneath the waters.

Prejudices arising from our not seeing subterranean changes.—Nor is his position less unfavourable when, beholding a volcanic eruption, he tries to conceive what changes the column of lava has produced, in its passage upwards, on the intersected strata; or what form the melted matter may assume at great depths on cooling; or what may be the extent of the subterranean rivers and reservoirs of liquid matter far beneath the surface. It should, therefore, be remembered, that the task imposed on those who study the

[2] Elements of Geology, 6th edit., 1865; and Student's Elements, 1871.

earth's history requires no ordinary share of discretion; for we are precluded from collating the corresponding parts of the system of things as it exists now, and as it existed at former periods. If we were inhabitants of another element —if the great ocean were our domain, instead of the narrow limits of the land, our difficulties would be considerably lessened; while, on the other hand, there can be little doubt, although the reader may, perhaps, smile at the bare suggestion of such an idea, that an amphibious being, who should possess our faculties, would still more easily arrive at sound theoretical opinions in geology, since he might behold, on the one hand, the decomposition of rocks in the atmosphere, or the transportation of matter by running water; and, on the other, examine the deposition of sediment in the sea, and the imbedding of animal and vegetable remains in new strata. He might ascertain, by direct observation, the action of a mountain torrent, as well as of a marine current; might compare the products of volcanos poured out upon the land with those ejected beneath the waters; and might mark, on the one hand, the growth of the forest, and, on the other, that of the coral reef. Yet, even with these advantages, he would be liable to fall into the greatest errors, when endeavouring to reason on rocks of subterranean origin. He would seek in vain, within the sphere of his observation, for any direct analogy to the process of their formation, and would therefore be in danger of attributing them, wherever they are upraised to view, to some 'primeval state of nature.'

But if we may be allowed so far to indulge the imagination, as to suppose a being entirely confined to the nether world—some 'dusky melancholy sprite,' like Umbriel, who could 'flit on sooty pinions to the central earth,' but who was never permitted to 'sully the fair face of light,' and emerge into the regions of water and of air; and if this being should busy himself in investigating the structure of the globe, he might frame theories the exact converse of those usually adopted by human philosophers. He might infer that the stratified rocks, containing shells and other organic remains, were the oldest of created things, belonging to some original and nascent state of the planet.

'Of these masses,' he might say, 'whether they consist of loose incoherent sand, soft clay, or solid stone, none have been formed in modern times. Every year some of them are broken and shattered by earthquakes, or melted by volcanic fire; and when they cool down slowly from a state of fusion, they assume a new and more crystalline form, no longer exhibiting that stratified disposition and those curious impressions and fantastic markings, by which they were previously characterised. This process cannot have been carried on for an indefinite time, for in that case all the stratified rocks would long ere this have been fused and crystallised. It is therefore probable that the whole planet once consisted of these mysterious and curiously bedded formations at a time when the volcanic fire had not yet been brought into activity. Since that period there seems to have been a gradual development of heat; and this augmentation we may expect to continue till the whole globe shall be in a state of fluidity, or shall consist, in those parts which are not melted, of volcanic and crystalline rocks.'

Such might be the system of the Gnome at the very time that the followers of Leibnitz, reasoning on what they saw on the outer surface, might be teaching the opposite doctrine of gradual refrigeration, and averring that the earth had begun its career as a fiery comet, and might be destined hereafter to become a frozen mass. The tenets of the schools of the nether and of the upper world would be directly opposed to each other, for both would partake of the prejudices inevitably resulting from the continual contemplation of one class of phenomena to the exclusion of another. Man observes the annual decomposition of crystalline and igneous rocks, and may sometimes see their conversion into stratified deposits; but he cannot witness the reconversion of the sedimentary into the crystalline by subterranean heat. He is in the habit of regarding all the sedimentary rocks as more recent than the unstratified, for the same reason that we may suppose him to fall into the opposite error if he saw the origin of the igneous class only.

For more than two centuries the shelly strata of the

Subapennine hills afforded matter of speculation to the early geologists of Italy, and few of them had any suspicion that similar deposits were then forming in the neighbouring sea. Some imagined that the strata, so rich in organic remains, instead of being due to secondary agents, had been so created in the beginning of things by the fiat of the Almighty. Others, as we have seen, ascribed the imbedded fossil bodies to some plastic power which resided in the earth in the early ages of the world. In what manner were these dogmas at length exploded? The fossil relics were carefully compared with their living analogues, and all doubts as to their organic origin were eventually dispelled. So, also, in regard to the nature of the containing beds of mud, sand, and limestone: those parts of the bottom of the sea were examined where shells are now becoming annually entombed in new deposits. Donati explored the bed of the Adriatic, and found the closest resemblance between the strata there forming, and those which constituted hills above a thousand feet high in various parts of the Italian peninsula. He ascertained by dredging that living testacea were there grouped together in precisely the same manner as were their fossil analogues in the inland strata; and while some of the recent shells of the Adriatic were becoming incrusted with calcareous rock, he observed that others had been newly buried in sand and clay, precisely as fossil shells occur in the Subapennine hills.

In like manner, the volcanic rocks of the Vicentin had been studied in the beginning of the last century; but no geologist suspected, before the time of Arduino, that these were composed of ancient submarine lavas. During many years of controversy, the popular opinion inclined to a belief that basalt and rocks of the same class had been precipitated from a chaotic fluid, or an ocean which rose at successive periods over the continents, charged with the component elements of the rocks in question. Few will now dispute that it would have been difficult to invent a theory more distant from the truth; yet we must cease to wonder that it gained so many proselytes, when we remember that its claims to probability arose partly from the very circumstance of its confirming the assumed want of analogy between geological causes and those now in action. By what train of investigations were geologists induced at length to reject these views, and to assent to the igneous origin of the trappean formations? By an examination of volcanos now active, and by comparing their structure and the composition of their lavas with the ancient trap rocks.

The establishment, from time to time, of numerous points of identification, drew at length from geologists a reluctant admission, that there was more correspondence between the condition of the globe at remote eras and now, and more uniformity in the laws which have regulated the changes of its surface, than they at first imagined. If, in this state of the science, they still despaired of reconciling every class of geological phenomena to the operations of ordinary causes, even by straining analogy to the utmost limits of credibility, we might have expected, at least, that the balance of probability would now have been presumed to incline towards the close analogy of the ancient and modern causes. But, after repeated experience of the failure of attempts to speculate on geological monuments, as belonging to a distinct order of things, new sects continued to persevere in the principles adopted by their predecessors. They still began, as each new problem presented itself, whether relating to the animate or inanimate world, to assume an original and dissimilar order of nature; and when at length they approximated, or entirely came round to an opposite opinion, it was always with the feeling, that they were conceding what they had been justified *à priori* in deeming improbable. In a word, the same men who, as natural philosophers, would have been most incredulous respecting any extraordinary deviations from the known course of nature, if reported to have happened *in their own time,* were equally disposed, as geologists, to expect the proofs of such deviations at every period of the past. * * * *

UNIFORMITY OF CHANGE

II

SUPPOSED ALTERNATE PERIODS OF REPOSE AND DISORDER—OBSERVED FACTS IN WHICH THIS DOCTRINE HAS ORIGINATED—THESE MAY BE EXPLAINED BY SUPPOSING A UNIFORM AND UNINTERRUPTED SERIES OF CHANGES—THREE-FOLD CONSIDERATION OF THIS SUBJECT: FIRST, IN REFERENCE TO THE LAWS WHICH GOVERN THE FORMATION OF FOSSILIFEROUS STRATA, AND THE SHIFTING OF THE AREAS OF SEDIMENTARY DEPOSITION; SECONDLY, IN REFERENCE TO THE LIVING CREATION, EXTINCTION OF SPECIES, AND ORIGIN OF NEW ANIMALS AND PLANTS; THIRDLY, IN REFERENCE TO THE CHANGES PRODUCED IN THE EARTH'S CRUST BY THE CONTINUANCE OF SUBTERRANEAN MOVEMENTS IN CERTAIN AREAS, AND THEIR TRANSFERENCE AFTER LONG PERIODS TO NEW AREAS—ON THE COMBINED INFLUENCE OF ALL THESE MODES AND CAUSES OF CHANGE IN PRODUCING BREAKS AND CHASMS IN THE CHAIN OF RECORDS—CONCLUDING REMARKS ON THE IDENTITY OF THE ANCIENT AND PRESENT SYSTEM OF TERRESTRIAL CHANGES.

ORIGIN of the doctrine of alternate periods of repose and disorder.—It has been truly observed, that when we arrange the fossiliferous formations in chronological order, they constitute a broken and defective series of monuments: we pass without any intermediate gradations from systems of strata which are horizontal, to other systems which are highly inclined—from rocks of peculiar mineral composition to others which have a character wholly distinct —from one assemblage of organic remains to another, in which frequently nearly all the species, and a large part of the genera, are different. These violations of continuity are so common as to constitute in most regions the rule rather than the exception, and they have been considered by many geologists as conclusive in favour of sudden revolutions in the inanimate and animate world. We have already seen that according to the speculations of some writers, there have been in the past history of the planet alternate periods of tranquillity and convulsion, the former enduring for ages, and resembling the state of things now experienced by man; the other brief, transient, and paroxysmal, giving rise to new mountains, seas, and valleys, annihilating one set of organic beings, and ushering in the creation of another.

It will be the object of the present chapter to demonstrate that these theoretical views are not borne out by a fair interpretation of geological monuments. It is true that in the solid framework of the globe we have a chronological chain of natural records, many links of which are wanting: but a careful consideration of all the phenomena leads to the opinion that the series was originally defective—that it has been rendered still more so by time—that a great part of what remains is inaccessible to man, and even of that fraction which is accessible nine-tenths or more are to this day unexplored.

The readiest way, perhaps, of persuading the reader that we may dispense with great and sudden revolutions in the geological order of events is by showing him how a regular and uninterrupted series of changes in the animate and inanimate world must give rise to such breaks in the sequence, and such unconformability of stratified rocks, as are usually thought to imply convulsions and catastrophes. It is scarcely necessary to state that the order of events thus assumed to occur, for the sake of illustration, should be in harmony with all the conclusions legitimately drawn by geologists from the structure of the earth, and must be equally in accordance with the changes observed by man to be now going on in the living as well as in the inorganic creation. It may be necessary in the present state of science to supply some part of the assumed course of nature hypothetically; but if so, this must be done without any violation of probability, and always consistently with the analogy of what is known both of the past and present economy of our system. Although the discussion of so comprehensive a subject must carry the beginner far beyond his depth, it will also, it is hoped, stimulate his curiosity, and prepare him to read some elementary treatises on geology with advantage, and teach him the bearing on that science of the changes now in progress on the earth. At the same time it may enable him the better to understand the intimate connection between the Second and Third Books of this work, one of which is occupied with the changes of the inorganic, the latter with those of the organic creation.

In pursuance, then, of the plan above proposed, I will consider in this chapter, first, the laws which regulate the denudation of strata and the deposition of sediment; secondly, those which govern the fluctuation in the animate world; and thirdly, the mode in which subterranean movements affect the earth's crust.

Uniformity of change considered, first, in reference to denudation and sedimentary deposition.—First, in regard to the laws governing the deposition of new strata. If we survey the surface of the globe, we immediately perceive that it is divisible into areas of deposition and non-deposition; or, in other words, at any given time there are spaces which are the recipients, others which are not the recipients, of sedimentary matter. No new strata, for example, are thrown down on dry land, which remains the same from year to year; whereas, in many parts of the bottom of seas and lakes, mud, sand, and pebbles are annually spread out by rivers and currents. There are also great masses of limestone growing in some seas, chiefly composed of corals and shells, or, as in the depths of the Atlantic, of chalky mud made up of foraminifera and diatomaceæ.

As to the dry land, so far from being the receptacle of fresh accessions of matter, it is exposed almost everywhere to waste away. Forests may be as dense and lofty as those of Brazil, and may swarm with quadrupeds, birds, and insects, yet at the end of thousands of years one layer of black mould a few inches thick may be the sole representative of those myriads of trees, leaves, flowers, and fruits, those innumerable bones and skeletons of birds, quadrupeds, and reptiles, which tenanted the fertile region. Should this land be at length submerged, the waves of the sea may wash away in a few hours the scanty covering of mould, and it may merely impart a darker shade of colour to the next stratum of marl, sand, or other matter newly thrown down. So also at the bottom of the ocean where no sediment is accumulating, seaweed, zoophytes, fish, and even shells, may multiply for ages and decompose, leaving no vestige of their form or substance behind. Their decay, in water, although more slow, is as certain and eventually as complete as in the open air. Nor can they be perpetuated for indefinite periods in a fossil state, unless imbedded in some matrix which is impervious to water, or which at least does not allow a free percolation of that fluid, impregnated, as it usually is, with a slight quantity of carbonic or other acid. Such a free percolation may be prevented either by the mineral nature of the matrix itself, or by the superposition of an impermeable stratum; but if unimpeded, the fossil shell or bone will be dissolved and removed, particle after particle, and thus entirely effaced, unless petrifaction or the substitution of some mineral for the organic matter happen to take place.

That there has been land as well as sea at all former geological periods, we know from the fact that fossil trees and terrestrial plants are imbedded in rocks of every age, except those which are so ancient as to be very imperfectly known to us. Occasionally lacustrine and fluviatile shells, or the bones of amphibious or land reptiles, point to the same conclusion. The existence of dry land at all periods of the past implies, as before mentioned, the partial deposition of sediment, or its limitation to certain areas; and the next point to which I shall call the reader's attention is the shifting of these areas from one region to another.

First, then, variations in the site of sedimentary deposition are brought about independently of subterranean movements. There is always a slight change from year to year, or from century to century. The sediment of the Rhone, for example, thrown into the Lake of Geneva, is now conveyed to a spot a mile and a half distant from that where it accumulated in the tenth century, and six miles from the point where the

UNIFORMITY OF CHANGE

delta began originally to form. We may look forward to the period when this lake will be filled up, and then the distribution of the transported matter will be suddenly altered, for the mud and sand brought down from the Alps will thenceforth, instead of being deposited near Geneva, be carried nearly 200 miles southwards, where the Rhone enters the Mediterranean.

In the deltas of large rivers, such as those of the Ganges and Indus, the mud is first carried down for many centuries through one arm, and on this being stopped up it is discharged by another, and may then enter the sea at a point 50 or 100 miles distant from its first receptacle. The direction of marine currents is also liable to be changed by various accidents, as by the heaping up of new sandbanks, or the wearing away of cliffs and promontories.

But, secondly, all these causes of fluctuation in the sedimentary areas are entirely subordinate to those great upward or downward movements of land, which will presently be spoken of, as prevailing over large tracts of the globe. By such elevation or subsidence certain spaces are gradually submerged, or made gradually to emerge: in the one case sedimentary deposition may be suddenly renewed after having been suspended for one or more geological periods, in the other as suddenly made to cease after having continued for ages.

If deposition be renewed after a long interval, the new strata will usually differ greatly from the sedimentary rocks previously formed in the same place, and especially if the older rocks have suffered derangement, which implies a change in the physical geography of the district since the previous conveyance of sediment to the same spot. It may happen, however, that, even where the two groups, the superior and the inferior, are horizontal and conformable to each other, they may still differ entirely in mineral character, because, since the origin of the older formation, the geography of some distant country has been altered. In that country rocks before concealed may have become exposed by denudation; volcanos may have burst out and covered the surface with scoriæ and lava; or new lakes, intercepting the sediment previously conveyed from the upper country, may have been formed by subsidence; and other fluctuations may have occurred, by which the materials brought down from thence by rivers to the sea have acquired a distinct mineral character.

It is well known that the stream of the Mississippi is charged with sediment of a different colour from that of the Arkansas and Red Rivers, which are tinged with red mud, derived from rocks of porphyry and red gypseous clays in 'the far west.' The waters of the Uruguay, says Darwin, draining a granitic country, are clear and black, those of the Parana, red.[1] The mud with which the Indus is loaded, says Burnes, is of a clayey hue, that of the Chenab, on the other hand, is reddish, that of the Sutlej is more pale.[2] The same causes which make these several rivers, sometimes situated at no great distance the one from the other, to differ greatly in the character of their sediment, will make the waters draining the same country at different epochs, especially before and after great revolutions in physical geography, to be entirely dissimilar. It is scarcely necessary to add that marine currents will be affected in an analogous manner in consequence of the formation of new shoals, the emergence of new islands, the subsidence of others, the gradual waste of neighbouring coasts, the growth of new deltas, the increase of coral reefs, volcanic eruptions, and other changes.

Uniformity of change considered, secondly, in reference to the living creation.—Secondly, in regard to the vicissitudes of the living creation, all are agreed that the successive groups of sedimentary strata found in the earth's crust are not only dissimilar in mineral composition for reasons above alluded to, but are likewise distinguishable from each other by their organic remains. The general inference drawn from the study and comparison of the various groups, arranged in chronological order, is this: that at successive periods distinct tribes of animals and plants have inhabited the land and waters, and that the organic types of the newer formations are more analogous to species now existing than those of more ancient rocks. If we then turn to the present state of the animate creation, and enquire whether it has

[1] Darwin's Journal, p. 163, 2nd edit., p. 139.
[2] Journ. Roy. Geograph. Soc., vol. iii., p. 142.

now become fixed and stationary, we discover that, on the contrary, it is in a state of continual flux—that there are many causes in action which tend to the extinction of species, and which are conclusive against the doctrine of their unlimited durability.

There are also causes which give rise to new varieties and races in plants and animals, and new forms are continually supplanting others which had endured for ages. But natural history has been sucessfully cultivated for so short a period, that a few examples only of local, and perhaps but one or two of absolute, extirpation of species can as yet be proved, and these only where the interference of man has been conspicuous. It will nevertheless appear evident, from the facts and arguments detailed in the chapters which treat of the geographical distribution of species in the next volume, that man is not the only exterminating agent; and that, independently of his intervention, the annihilation of species is promoted by the multiplication and gradual diffusion of every animal or plant. It will also appear that every alteration in the physical geography and climate of the globe cannot fail to have the same tendency. If we proceed still farther, and enquire whether new species are substituted from time to time for those which die out, we find that the successive introduction of new forms appears to have been a constant part of the economy of the terrestrial system, and if we have no direct proof of the fact it is because the changes take place so slowly as not to come within the period of exact scientific observation. To enable the reader to appreciate the gradual manner in which a passage may have taken place from an extinct fauna to that now living, I shall say a few words on the fossils of successive Tertiary periods. When we trace the series of formations from the more ancient to the more modern, it is in these Tertiary deposits that we first meet with assemblages of organic remains having a near analogy to the fauna of certain parts of the globe in our own time. In the Eocene, or oldest subdivisions, some few of the testacea belong to existing species, although almost all of them, and apparently all the associated vertebrata, are now extinct. These Eocene strata are succeeded by a great number of more modern deposits, which depart gradually in the character of their fossils from the Eocene type, and approach more and more to that of the living creation. In the present state of science, it is chiefly by the aid of shells that we are enabled to arrive at these results, for of all classes the testacea are the most generally diffused in a fossil state, and may be called the medals principally employed by nature in recording the chronology of past events. In the Upper Miocene rocks (No. 5 of the table, p. 135) we begin to find a considerable number, although still a minority, of recent species, intermixed with some fossils common to the preceding, or Eocene, epoch. We then arrive at the Pliocene strata, in which species now contemporary with man begin to preponderate, and in the newest of which nine-tenths of the fossils agree with species still inhabiting the neighbouring sea. It is in the Post-Tertiary strata, where all the shells agree with species now living, that we have discovered the first or earliest known remains of man associated with the bones of quadrupeds, some of which are of extinct species.

In thus passing from the older to the newer members of the Tertiary system, we meet with many chasms, but none which separate entirely, by a broad line of demarcation, one state of the organic world from another. There are no signs of an abrupt termination of one fauna and flora, and the starting into life of new and wholly distinct forms. Although we are far from being able to demonstrate geologically an insensible transition from the Eocene to the Miocene, or even from the latter to the recent fauna, yet the more we enlarge and perfect our general survey, the more nearly do we approximate to such a continuous series, and the more gradually are we conducted from times when many of the genera and nearly all the species were extinct, to those in which scarcely a single species flourished which we do not know to exist at present. Dr. A. Philippi, indeed, after an elaborate comparison of the fossil tertiary shells of Sicily with those now living in the Mediterranean, announced, as the result of his examination, that there are strata in that island which attest a very gradual passage from a period when only thirteen in a hundred of the shells were like the species now living in the sea, to an era when the recent species had attained a proportion of ninety-five in a hundred.

There is, therefore, evidence, he says, in Sicily of this revolution in the animate world having been effected 'without the intervention of any convulsion or abrupt changes, certain species having from time to time died out, and others having been introduced, until at length the existing fauna was elaborated.'

In no part of Europe is the absence of all signs of man or his works, in strata of comparatively modern date, more striking than in Sicily. In the central parts of that island we observe a lofty table-land and hills, sometimes rising to the height of 3,000 feet, capped with a limestone, in which from 70 to 85 per cent. of the fossil testacea are specifically identical with those now inhabiting the Mediterranean. These calcareous and other argillaceous strata of the same age are intersected by deep valleys which appear to have been gradually formed by denudation, but have not varied materially in width or depth since Sicily was first colonised by the Greeks. The limestone, moreover, which is of so late a date in geological chronology, was quarried for building those ancient temples of Girgenti and Syracuse, of which the ruins carry us back to a remote era in human history. If we are lost in conjectures when speculating on the ages required to lift up these formations to the height of several thousand feet above the sea, and to excavate the valleys, how much more remote must be the era when the same rocks were gradually formed beneath the waters!

The intense cold of the Glacial period was spoken of in the tenth chapter. Although we have not yet succeeded in detecting proofs of the origin of man antecedently to that epoch, we have yet found evidence that most of the testacea, and not a few of the quadrupeds, which preceded, were of the same species as those which followed the extreme cold. To whatever local disturbances this cold may have given rise in the distribution of species, it seems to have done little in effecting their annihilation. We may conclude therefore, from a survey of the tertiary and modern strata, which constitute a more complete and unbroken series than rocks of older date, that the extinction and creation of species have been, and are, the result of a slow and gradual change in the organic world.

Uniformity of change considered, thirdly, in reference to subterranean movements.—Thirdly, to pass on to the last of the three topics before proposed for discussion, the reader will find, in the account given in the Second Book, Vol. II., of the earthquakes recorded in history, that certain countries have from time immemorial, been rudely shaken again and again; while others, comprising by far the largest part of the globe, have remained to all appearance motionless. In the regions of convulsion rocks have been rent asunder, the surface has been forced up into ridges, chasms have opened, or the ground throughout large spaces has been permanently lifted up above or let down below its former level. In the regions of tranquillity some areas have remained at rest, but others have been ascertained, by a comparison of measurements made at different periods, to have risen by an insensible motion, as in Sweden, or to have subsided very slowly, as in Greenland. That these same movements, whether ascending or descending, have continued for ages in the same direction has been established by historical or geological evidence. Thus we find on the opposite coasts of Sweden that brackish water deposits, like those now forming in the Baltic, occur on the eastern side, and upraised strata filled with purely marine shells, now proper to the ocean, on the western coast. Both of these have been lifted up to an elevation of several hundred feet above high-water mark. The rise within the historical period has not amounted to many yards, but the greater extent of antecedent upheaval is proved by the occurrence in inland spots, several hundred feet high, of deposits filled with fossil shells of species now living either in the ocean or the Baltic.

It must in general be more difficult to detect proofs of slow and gradual subsidence than of elevation, but the theory which accounts for the form of circular coral reefs and lagoon islands, and which will be explained in the concluding chapter of this work, will satisfy the reader that there are spaces on the globe, several thousand miles in circumference, throughout which the downward movement has predominated for ages, and yet the land has never, in a single instance, gone down suddenly for several hundred feet at once. Yet geology demonstrates that the persistency of subterranean movements in one direction has not been perpetual throughout all past time. There have been great oscillations of level, by which a surface of dry land has been submerged to a depth of several thousand feet, and then at a period long subsequent raised again and made to emerge. Nor have the regions now motionless been always at rest; and some of those which are at present the theatres of reiterated earthquakes have formerly enjoyed a long continuance of tranquillity. But, although disturbances have ceased after having long prevailed, or have recommenced after a suspension for ages, there has been no universal disruption of the earth's crust or desolation of the surface since times the most remote. The non-occurrence of such a general convulsion is proved by the perfect horizontality now retained by some of the most ancient fossiliferous strata throughout wide areas.

That the subterranean forces have visited different parts of the globe at successive periods is inferred chiefly from the unconformability of strata belonging to groups of different ages. Thus, for example, on the borders of Wales and Shropshire, we find the slaty beds of the ancient Silurian system inclined and vertical, while the beds of the overlying carboniferous shale and sandstone are horizontal. All are agreed that in such a case the older set of strata had suffered great disturbance before the deposition of the newer or carboniferous beds, and that these last have never since been violently fractured, nor have ever been bent into folds, whether by sudden or continuous lateral pressure. On the other hand, the more ancient or Silurian group suffered only a local derangement, and neither in Wales nor elsewhere are all the rocks of that age found to be curved or vertical.

In various parts of Europe, for example, and particularly near Lake Wener in the south of Sweden, and in many parts of Russia, the Silurian strata maintain the most perfect horizontality; and a similar observation may be made respecting limestones and shales of like antiquity in the great lake district of Canada and the United States. These older rocks are still as flat and horizontal as when first formed; yet, since their origin, not only have most of the actual mountain-chains been uplifted, but some of the very rocks of which those mountains are composed have been formed, some of them by igneous and others by aqueous action.

It would be easy to multiply instances of similar unconformability in formations of other ages; but a few more will suffice. The carboniferous rocks before alluded to as horizontal on the borders of Wales are vertical in the Mendip hills in Somersetshire, where the overlying beds of the New Red Sandstone are horizontal. Again, in the Wolds of Yorkshire the last-mentioned sandstone supports on its curved and inclined beds the horizontal Chalk. The Chalk again is vertical on the flanks of the Pyrenees, and the tertiary strata repose unconformably upon it.

As almost every country supplies illustrations of the same phenomena, they who advocate the doctrine of alternate periods of disorder and repose may appeal to the facts above described, as proving that every district has been by turns convulsed by earthquakes and then respited for ages from convulsions. But so it might with equal truth be affirmed that every part of Europe has been visited alternately by winter and summer, although it has always been winter and always summer in some part of the planet, and neither of these seasons has ever reigned simultaneously over the entire globe. They have been always shifting from place to place; but the vicissitudes which recur thus annually in a single spot are never allowed to interfere with the invariable uniformity of seasons throughout the whole planet.

So, in regard to subterranean movements, the theory of the perpetual uniformity of the force which they exert on the earth's crust is quite consistent with the admission of their alternate development and suspension for long and indefinite periods within limited geographical areas.

If, for reasons before stated, we assume a continual extinction of species and appearance of others on the globe, it will then follow that the fossils of strata formed at two distant periods on the same spot will differ even more certainly than the mineral composition of those strata. For rocks of the same kind have sometimes been reproduced in the same district after a long interval of time; whereas all the evidence derived from fossil remains is in favour of the opinion that species which have once died out have never been reproduced. The submergence, then, of land must be often attended by the commencement of a new class of sedimentary deposits, characterized by a new set of fossil animals and plants, while the reconversion of the bed of the sea into land may arrest at once and for an indefinite time the formation of geological monuments. Should the land again sink, strata will again be formed; but one or many entire revolutions in animal or vegetable life may have been completed in the interval.

As to the want of completeness in the fossiliferous series, which may be said to be almost universal, we have only to reflect on what has been already said of the laws governing sedimentary deposition, and those which give rise to fluctuations in the animate world, to be convinced that a very rare combination of circumstances can alone give rise to such a superposition and preservation of strata as will bear testimony to the gradual passage from one state of organic life to another. To produce such strata nothing less will be requisite than the fortunate coincidence of the following conditions: first, a never-failing supply of sediment in the same region throughout a period of vast duration; secondly, the fitness of the deposit in every part for the permanent preservation of imbedded fossils; and, thirdly, a gradual subsidence to prevent the sea or lake from being filled up and converted into land.

It will appear in the chapter on coral reefs, that, in certain parts of the Pacific and Indian Oceans, most of these conditions, if not all, are complied with, and the constant growth of coral, keeping pace with the sinking of the bottom of the sea, seems to have gone on so slowly, for such indefinite periods, that the signs of a gradual change in organic life might probably be detected in that quarter of the globe if we could explore its submarine geology. Instead of the growth of coralline limestone, let us suppose, in some other place, the continuous deposition of fluviatile mud and sand, such as the Ganges and Brahmapootra have poured for thousands of years into the Bay of Bengal. Part of this bay, although of considerable depth, might at length be filled up before an appreciable amount of change was effected in the fish, mollusca, and other inhabitants of the sea and neighbouring land. But if the bottom be lowered by sinking at the same rate that it is raised by fluviatile mud, the bay can never be turned into dry land. In that case one new layer of matter may be superimposed upon another for a thickness of many thousand feet, and the fossils of the inferior beds may differ greatly from those entombed in the uppermost, yet every intermediate gradation may be indicated in the passage from an older to a newer assemblage of species. Granting, however, that such an unbroken sequence of monuments may thus be elaborated in certain parts of the sea, and that the strata happen to be all of them well adapted to preserve the included fossils from decomposition, how many accidents must still concur before these submarine formations will be laid open to our investigation! The whole deposit must first be raised several thousand feet, in order to bring into view the very foundation; and during the process of exposure the superior beds must not be entirely swept away by denudation.

In the first place, the chances are nearly as three to one against the mere emergence of the mass above the waters, because nearly three-fourths of the globe are covered by the ocean. But if it be upheaved and made to constitute part of the dry land, it must also, before it can be available for our instruction, become part of that area already surveyed by geologists. In this small fraction of land already explored, and still very imperfectly known, we are required to find a set of strata deposited under peculiar conditions, and which, having been originally of limited extent, would have been probably much lessened by subsequent denudation.

Yet it is precisely because we do not encounter at every step the evidence of such gradations from one state of the organic world to another, that so many geologists have embraced the doctrine of great and sudden revolutions in the history of the animate world. Not content with simply availing themselves, for the convenience of classification, of those gaps and chasms which here and there interrupt the continuity of the chronological series, as at present known, they deduce, from the frequency of these breaks in the chain of records, an irregular mode of succession in the events themselves, both in the organic and inorganic world. But,

UNIFORMITY OF CHANGE

besides that some links of the chain which once existed are now entirely lost and others concealed from view, we have good reason to suspect that it was never complete originally.

It may undoubtedly be said that strata have been always forming somewhere, and therefore at every moment of past time Nature has added a page to her archives; but, in reference to this subject, it should be remembered that we can never hope to compile a consecutive history by gathering together monuments which were originally detached and scattered over the globe. For, as the species of organic beings contemporaneously inhabiting remote regions are distinct, the fossils of the first of several periods which may be preserved in any one country, as in America for example, will have no connection with those of a second period found in India, and will therefore no more enable us to trace the signs of a gradual change in the living creation, than a fragment of Chinese history will fill up a blank in the political annals of Europe.

The absence of any deposits of importance containing recent shells in Chili, or anywhere on the western coast of South America, naturally led Mr. Darwin to the conclusion that 'where the bed of the sea is either stationary or rising, circumstances are far less favourable than where the level is sinking to the accumulation of conchiferous strata of sufficient thickness and extension to resist the average vast amount of denudation.'[*] In like manner the beds of superficial sand, clay, and gravel, with recent shells, on the coasts of Norway and Sweden, where the land has risen in Post-tertiary times, are so thin and scanty as to incline us to admit a similar proposition. We may in fact assume that in all cases where the bottom of the sea has been undergoing continuous elevation, the total thickness of sedimentary matter accumulating at depths suited to the habitation of most of the species of shells can never be great, nor can the deposits be thickly covered by superincumbent matter, so as to be consolidated by pressure. When they are upheaved, therefore, the waves on the beach will bear down and disperse the loose materials; whereas, if the bed of the sea subsides slowly, a mass of strata, containing abundance of

[*] Darwin's S. America, pp. 136, 139.

such species as live at moderate depths, may be formed and may increase in thickness to any amount. It may also extend horizontally over a broad area, as the water gradually encroaches on the subsiding land.

Hence it will follow that great violations of continuity in the chronological series of fossiliferous rocks will always exist, and the imperfection of the record, though lessened, will never be removed by future discoveries. For not only will no deposits originate on the dry land, but those formed in the sea near land, which is undergoing constant upheaval, will usually be too slight in thickness to endure for ages.

In proportion as we become acquainted with larger geographical areas, many of the gaps, by which a chronological table, like that given at page 135, is rendered defective, will be removed. We were enabled by aid of the labours of Prof. Sedgwick and Sir Roderick Murchison, to intercalate, in 1838, the marine strata of the Devonian period, with their fossil shells, corals, and fish, between the Silurian and Carboniferous rocks. Previously the marine fauna of these last-mentioned formations wanted the connecting links which now render the passage from the one to the other much less abrupt. In like manner the Upper Miocene has no representative in England, but in France, Germany, and Switzerland it constitutes a most instructive link between the living creation and the middle of the great Tertiary period. Still we must expect, for reasons before stated, that chasms will for ever continue to occur, in some parts of our sedimentary series.

Concluding remarks on the consistency of the theory of gradual change with the existence of great breaks in the series.—To return to the general argument pursued in this chapter, it is assumed, for reasons above explained, that a slow change of species is in simultaneous operation everywhere throughout the habitable surface of sea and land; whereas the fossilisation of plants and animals is confined to those areas where new strata are produced. These areas, as we have seen, are always shifting their position, so that the fossilising process, by means of which the commemoration of the particular state of the organic world, at any given

UNIFORMITY OF CHANGE

time, is effected, may be said to move about, visiting and revisiting different tracts in succession.

To make still more clear the supposed working of this machinery, I shall compare it to a somewhat analogous case that might be imagined to occur in the history of human affairs. Let the mortality of the population of a large country represent the successive extinction of species, and the births of new individuals the introduction of new species. While these fluctuations are gradually taking place everywhere, suppose commissioners to be appointed to visit each province of the country in succession, taking an exact account of the number, names, and individual peculiarities of all the inhabitants, and leaving in each district a register containing a record of this information. If, after the completion of one census, another is immediately made on the same plan, and then another, there will at last be a series of statistical documents in each province. When those belonging to any one province are arranged in chronological order, the contents of such as stand next to each other will differ according to the length of the intervals of time between the taking of each census. If, for example, there are sixty provinces, and all the registers are made in a single year and renewed annually, the number of births and deaths will be so small, in proportion to the whole of the inhabitants, during the interval between the compiling of two consecutive documents, that the individuals described in such documents will be nearly identical; whereas, if the survey of each of the sixty provinces occupies all the commissioners for a whole year, so that they are unable to revisit the same place until the expiration of sixty years, there will then be an almost entire discordance between the persons enumerated in two consecutive registers in the same province. There are, undoubtedly, other causes, besides the mere quantity of time, which may augment or diminish the amount of discrepancy. Thus, at some periods a pestilential disease may have lessened the average duration of human life; or a variety of circumstances may have caused the births to be unusually numerous, and the population to multiply; or a province may be suddenly colonised by persons migrating from surrounding districts.

These exceptions may be compared to the accelerated rate of fluctuations in the fauna and flora of a particular region, in which the climate and physical geography may be undergoing an extraordinary degree of alteration.

But I must remind the reader that the case above proposed has no pretensions to be regarded as an exact parallel to the geological phenomena which I desire to illustrate; for the commissioners are supposed to visit the different provinces in rotation; whereas the commemorating processes by which organic remains become fossilised, although they are always shifting from one area to the other, are yet very irregular in their movements. They may abandon and revisit many spaces again and again, before they once approach another district; and, besides this source of irregularity, it may often happen that, while the depositing process is suspended, denudation may take place, which may be compared to the occasional destruction by fire or other causes of some of the statistical documents before mentioned. It is evident that where such accidents occur the want of continuity in the series may become indefinitely great, and that the monuments which follow next in succession will by no means be equidistant from each other in point of time.

If this train of reasoning be admitted, the occasional distinctness of the fossil remains, in formations immediately in contact, would be a necessary consequence of the existing laws of sedimentary deposition and subterranean movement, accompanied by a constant dying-out and renovation of species.

As all the conclusions above insisted on are directly opposed to opinions still popular, I shall add another comparison, in the hope of preventing any possible misapprehension of the argument. Suppose we had discovered two buried cities at the foot of Vesuvius, immediately superimposed upon each other, with a great mass of tuff and lava intervening, just as Portici and Resina, if now covered with ashes, would overlie Herculaneum. An antiquary might possibly be entitled to infer, from the inscriptions on public edifices, that the inhabitants of the inferior and older city were Greeks, and those of the modern towns Italians. But he would reason very hastily if he also concluded from these data, that there had been a sudden change from the Greek to the Italian language in Campania. But if he afterwards found *three* buried cities, one above the other, the intermediate one being Roman, while, as in the former example, the lowest was Greek and the uppermost Italian, he would then perceive the fallacy of his former opinion, and would begin to suspect that the catastrophes, by which the cities were inhumed might have no relation whatever to the fluctuations in the language of the inhabitants; and that, as the Roman tongue had evidently intervened between the Greek and Italian, so many other dialects may have been spoken in succession, and the passage from the Greek to the Italian may have been very gradual, some terms growing obsolete, while others were introduced from time to time.

If this antiquary could have shown that the volcanic paroxysms of Vesuvius were so governed as that cities should be buried one above the other, just as often as any variation occurred in the language of the inhabitants, then, indeed, the abrupt passage from a Greek to a Roman, and from a Roman to an Italian city, would afford proof of fluctuations no less sudden in the language of the people.

So, in Geology, if we could assume that it is part of the plan of Nature to preserve, in every region of the globe, an unbroken series of monuments to commemorate the vicissitudes of the organic creation, we might infer the sudden extirpation of species, and the simultaneous introduction of others, as often as two formations in contact are found to include dissimilar organic fossils. But we must shut our eyes to the whole economy of the existing causes, aqueous, igneous, and organic, if we fail to perceive *that such is not the plan of Nature.*

I shall now conclude the discussion of a question with which we have been occupied since the beginning of the fifth chapter—namely, whether there has been any interruption, from the remotest periods, of one uniform and continuous system of change in the animate and inanimate world. We were induced to enter into that enquiry by reflecting how much the progress of opinion in Geology had been influenced by the assumption that the analogy was slight in kind, and still more slight in degree, between the causes which produced the former revolutions of the globe, and those now in every-day operation. It appeared clear that the earlier geologists had not only a scanty acquaintance with existing changes, but were singularly unconscious of the amount of their ignorance. With the presumption naturally inspired by this unconsciousness, they had no hesitation in deciding at once that time could never enable the existing powers of nature to work out changes of great magnitude, still less such important revolutions as those which are brought to light by Geology. They therefore felt themselves at liberty to indulge their imaginations in guessing at what *might be,* rather than enquiring *what is;* in other words, they employed themselves in conjecturing what might have been the course of Nature at a remote period, rather than in the investigation of what was the course of Nature in their own times.

It appeared to them far more philosophical to speculate on the possibilities of the past, than patiently to explore the realities of the present; and having invented theories under the influence of such maxims, they were consistently unwilling to test their validity by the criterion of their accordance with the ordinary operations of Nature. On the contrary, the claims of each new hypothesis to credibility appeared enhanced by the great contrast, in kind or intensity, of the causes referred to and those now in operation.

Never was there a dogma more calculated to foster indolence, and to blunt the keen edge of curiosity, than this assumption of the discordance between the ancient and existing causes of change. It produced a state of mind unfavourable in the highest degree to the candid reception of the evidence of those minute but incessant alterations which every part of the earth's surface is undergoing, and by which the condition of its living inhabitants is continually made to vary. The student, instead of being encouraged with the hope of interpreting the enigmas presented to him in the earth's structure—instead of being prompted to undertake laborious enquiries into the natural history of the organic world, and the complicated effects of the igneous and aqueous causes now in operation—was taught to despond from the first. Geology, it was affirmed, could never rise to the rank

UNIFORMITY OF CHANGE

of an exact science; the greater number of phenomena must for ever remain inexplicable, or only be partially elucidated by ingenious conjectures. Even the mystery which invested the subject was said to constitute one of its principal charms, affording, as it did, full scope to the fancy to indulge in a boundless field of speculation.

The course directly opposed to this method of philosophising consists in an earnest and patient enquiry, how far geological appearances are reconcilable with the effect of changes now in progress, or which may be in progress in regions inaccessible to us, but of which the reality is attested by volcanos and subterranean movements. It also endeavours to estimate the aggregate result of ordinary operations multiplied by time, and cherishes a sanguine hope that the resources to be derived from observation and experiment, or from the study of Nature such as she now is, are very far from being exhausted. For this reason all theories are rejected which involve the assumption of sudden and violent catastrophes and revolutions of the whole earth, and its inhabitants—theories which are restrained by no reference to existing analogies, and in which a desire is manifested to cut, rather than patiently to untie, the Gordian knot.

We have now, at least, the advantage of knowing, from experience, that an opposite method has always put geologists on the road that leads to truth—suggesting views which, although imperfect at first, have been found capable of improvement, until at last adopted by universal consent; while the method of speculating on a former distinct state of things and causes has led invariably to a multitude of contradictory systems, which have been overthrown one after the other—have been found incapable of modification—and which have often required to be precisely reversed.

The remainder of this work will be devoted to an investigation of the changes now going on in the crust of the earth and its inhabitants. The importance which the student will attach to such researches will mainly depend on the degree of confidence which he feels in the principles above expounded. If he firmly believes in the resemblance or identity of the ancient and present system of terrestrial changes, he will regard every fact collected respecting the cause in diurnal action as affording him a key to the interpretation of some mystery in the past. Events which have occurred at the most distant periods in the animate and inanimate world will be acknowledged to throw light on each other, and the deficiency of our information respecting some of the most obscure parts of the present creation will be removed. For as, by studying the external configuration of the existing land and its inhabitants, we may restore in imagination the appearance of the ancient continents which have passed away, so may we obtain from the deposits of ancient seas and lakes an insight into the nature of the subaqueous processes now in operation, and of many forms of organic life which, though now existing, are veiled from sight. Rocks, also, produced by subterranean fire in former ages, at great depths in the bowels of the earth, present us, when upraised by gradual movements, and exposed to the light of heaven, with an image of those changes which the deep-seated volcano may now occasion in the nether regions. Thus, although we are mere sojourners on the surface of the planet, chained to a mere point in space, enduring but for a moment of time, the human mind is not only enabled to number worlds beyond the unassisted ken of mortal eye, but to trace the events of indefinite ages before the creation of our race, and is not even withheld from penetrating into the dark secrets of the ocean, or the interior of the solid globe; free, like the spirit which the poet described as animating the universe,

---------ire per omnes
Terrasque, tractusque maris, cœlumque profundum.[4]

[4] "To go through all lands, and the tracts of the ocean, and the boundless heaven."